GIUSEPPE GARIBALDI

GARIBALDI—PORTRAIT BY GEROLAMO INDUNO
By permission of The Museo del Risorgimento, Milan

GIUSEPPE GARIBALDI

A Biography

BY
DAVID LARG

With Maps and Illustrations

KENNIKAT PRESS
Port Washington, N. Y./London

GIUSEPPE GARIBALDI

First published in 1934
Reissued in 1970 by Kennikat Press
Library of Congress Catalog Card No. 73-112811
ISBN 0-8046-1078-9

Manufactured by Taylor Publishing Company   Dallas, Texas

CONTENTS

Author's Note	xi
Book One	1
Book Two	63
Book Three	173
Appendix A	322
Garibaldi's Memoirs and other Writings	
Appendix B	324
South America	
Appendix C	330
The Italian Risorgimento	
Appendix D	341
The Campaign of 1870	
Appendix E	344
Translation of a Letter from Garibaldi to Giuseppina Raimondi	
Appendix F	345
Garibaldi's Descendants	
Index	347

ILLUSTRATIONS

GARIBALDI. Portrait by Gerolamo Induno *Frontispiece*
By permission of the Museo del Risorgimento, Milan

GARIBALDI, ASTRIDE HIS FAVOURITE HORSE *to face p.* 176
From a signed photograph

GARIBALDI - - - - - - ,, 304
From a photograph

MAPS

PART OF S. AMERICA - - - - *to face p.* 32
ITALY IN GARIBALDI'S TIME - - - ,, 96
HOFSTETTER'S PLAN OF THE SIEGE OF ROME ,, 144

AUTHOR'S NOTE

IN SELECTING material suitable for the illustration of the biographical theme I have had to eliminate many events and personages of historical importance. Particularly in Book III the details of the fighting in Sicily are omitted and, in general, there is considerable compression which I am far from regarding myself as desirable. In part it is due to considerations of space. But to some extent also I was anxious that the story should emerge with sufficient simplicity. I did not wish to impose any arbitrary interpretation on the facts of Garibaldi's life. But it seemed to me that their poetic significance nowadays was of greater value than their relations to politics; and, considering the matter in this light, I formed the opinion that, while the siege of Rome may be taken as the high point or crisis of Garibaldi's life, the conquest of Sicily is less important (except from the historical point of view) than the tragedy of Aspromonte. I consider that from the point of view of poetical significance Garibaldi's life story is fully told when this episode has been given its full value as the supreme and final catastrophe. In the material sense the incident is insignificant. But for the biographer it shows that the sum of Garibaldi's action was to create a nation from which he excluded himself, as surely as the mason goes home who has built a house. I do not wish to dwell here on the importance or internal variety of this theme; nor have I sought anywhere to criticise the facts of Garibaldi's life except by the process of editing, in which inevitably the biographer expresses his own outlook and prejudices. I have been desirous to tell the story and to allow myself to be persuaded by it, as I hope the reader may be, to a wholesome admiration of Garibaldi in which the nature of the man reveals itself as greater than the consequences of his acts. I should add that while the portrait of Garibaldi shapes itself in the course of the book without undue prejudice, such minor portraits as occur take their lighting from the main character. Mazzini, for example, comes out rather as Garibaldi saw him than as he appears to his own biographers; and it would be a mistake to suppose that a just opinion of the former could be formed without correcting Garibaldi's contempt with his biographers' admiration. I am aware that this method is open to objection. But as the alternative was the introduction of irrelevant argument into the story I decided to adopt it. This is only one of many matters on which the technique of biography is at present undecided. Apart from this, the biography of a historical character presents a particular difficulty. The historian is most interested in the middle and end of the life where the external action of the character appears to become vastly important; and at this very time the biographer sees that his character is shrinking, repeating himself, imitating himself and sometimes caricaturing himself. The historian steps in when the biographer is finished, or nearly finished. Because of this divergence of view, I have drawn somewhat briefly the last years of Garibaldi, leaving the reader to seek elsewhere the details he requires for the purpose of historical information. As a background to the text of the three books I have, however, added appendices giving in very short outline some account of Argentine and Brazilian history, the Risorgimento and Garibaldi's campaign of 1870-1871. These the reader may use or neglect at his pleasure. They are not intended, I need hardly say, for those who seek specialised information.

Apart from my great debt to Garibaldi which I have no other means of acknowledging than by writing of him as I found him, I have had occasion to make frequent use of Professor Trevelyan's trilogy in which the history of the Italian Risorgimento and the tale of Italy's hero are woven into a noble tapestry. This great work combines the most accurate and comprehensive scholarship with a fine sense of poetry; and for the student and general reader remains the final authority on matters concerning Garibaldi. Since it appeared very little of importance has been written on the subject. The most important recent contribution has been from the pen of the late Mr. R. S. Garnett, who by translating into English the records of Dumas' cruise on the *Emma* has provided new information on the first Sicilian expedition. Mr. Garnett's translation of Dumas' edition of the *Memoirs* is also very useful.

Guerzoni's Italian biography of Garibaldi in two volumes is unlikely to find favour with English readers: it would require to be rewritten in order to be acceptable. But, with all its inequalities and defects, it is a repertory of information of permanent value. Italian scholars have provided all the bricks for a new edifice; and it is to be hoped that they will soon be put together in a definitive biography. There is a great deal of local erudition on the subject of Garibaldi, innumerable articles containing firsthand detail, as well as works such as Lœvinson's three volume study of the organisation and history of Garibaldi's Legion during the siege of Rome, which combine detail with a larger historical framework. But these have yet to be fitted together.

For much useful help in preparing the present volume I am indebted to Mr. and Mrs. Thomas Jack, who kindly read the manuscript, and to Miss Dora Yabsley, who has assisted me in so many ways that I have no space to enumerate them here. I have also the pleasant duty of acknowledging help in translation from the Italian from Mrs. Helen Lockhart. Signor Paul Arrigoni, of the Castello Sforzesco, Milan, provided a photograph of the oil-painting used as a frontispiece; and Mrs. Garnett and Messrs. Benn were good enough to allow me to quote from the English translation of Dumas' edition of Garibaldi's *Memoirs*.

DAVID LARG.

CROSS BANK, NITON, and
LONGBREDY RECTORY.

I

I

THE LIBERATION of Italy was to have begun that afternoon with an assault on the barracks of the gendarmes in the Piazza di Sarzana. Two hours passed without any assault. Then troops began to draw a cordon round the square where Garibaldi was waiting hopefully, pretending to read the *Gazzetta di Genova*. He withdrew to a fruitshop and, sitting in the back-shop, freely discussed the position with the friendly old lady who kept it. She advised him on no account to return to his ship, where Charles Albert's men would surely get him, but to wait till evening and make for the hills.

It was the evening of February 5, 1834, when he began the attempt, and it took him twenty days to reach Marseilles. He had to avoid the road; and that meant going over all the garden walls of all the villas that lay in direct line between the Piazza di Sarzana and the city boundary of Genoa. He came at last to the hills of Sestri and from there entered Nice. As he did not wish to frighten his parents, he went to his aunt's house in the Piazza Vittoria. She, too, was frightened enough and would not let him in at first, because he looked so little like her nephew Giuseppe and so much like a tramp. But he persuaded her and slept at her house and swam the Var next morning. His relief was great at finding himself in France. He told some customs' officers of his recent troubles, and to his great surprise they arrested him. He was at a loss to understand why, as he had always understood that France was the home of liberty. The distance from his window to the ground, however, was only fifteen feet, and nobody seemed to be about. The customs' officers were playing cards. He opened the window, cocked one leg over the sill, sat firmly athwart and swung the other leg over (this being the easiest way, he used to explain, with walls, fences, window ledges and such like) and jumped. He was making across country at a good speed when the customs' officers dropped their cards and clattered down the stairs after him.

He had a few crowns in his pocket and was aware of a familiar exhilaration. But he was hungry. Nearing Marseilles at last, he went into a village inn and found a young man and a young woman warming themselves by the fire in a room where the table was laid for supper. He ate and drank enormously (only water, however; he did not drink wine); after which he sat back to laugh inwardly at the joke he had played on the customs' officers. Over his dessert he remarked that it was nearly eighteen hours since he had had a bite, adding thoughtfully, that it was something just over that time since he had been jumping out of a first storey window at Draguignan, while the customs' officers, who had been stupid enough to arrest him in a free country, were playing cards and waiting for instructions from Paris. He was not boastful, but he mentioned the exploit with critical pleasure. It was of such things one talked in the evening. And his remarks caused a silence. The young host grew serious and said he fancied it might be his duty to arrest him, a proposition which, coming after a good meal and from such friendly people, struck the guest as having no reality at all.

'Not, at any rate,' he said politely, 'until I have finished dessert.' His smile, grave and sweet, was disarming; and he had by no means finished dessert. He was still eating when some twenty young men dropped in to drink and play cards. They were Frenchmen, sons of freedom; and, as if their irruption had provided a proper solution to the problem he was facing, Garibaldi stood up and began to sing in a fine tenor Béranger's *Dieu des bonnes gens*, pronouncing the French words in Italian fashion. The young men chimed in, clapped the sailorman on the back and shouted *Vive l'Italie!* while Garibaldi, with a sincerity which was not abated by his recent meal nor by the sight of his host's solemn face, replied with a sonorous *Vive la France!* He was broad-chested and spoke as he sang, musically, with a voice that played on the heart like the voice of a woman, though it was a level, manly voice. It was a voice that never expressed excitement. Emotion warmed it and made it more musical; but it contained the emotion firmly.

In the end the young men escorted the genial conspirator (who had told them all about the conspiracy) six miles along the road to Marseilles, and left him in the smallest hours of the morning. Garibaldi called himself Joseph Pane, selecting this name from a small wardrobe of patronymics with which he delighted to disguise himself. At first he lived very quietly. But he had been to Marseilles many times before and he knew the police did not trouble. It was there he had first met the chief conspirator, Giuseppe Mazzini, a yellow-skinned, clerkly young man with a high forehead. Garibaldi shared a room with a friend, Joseph Paris, and walked about the quais looking for a ship. He was familiar with the port and soon signed as second on *L'Union*, captain Gaza, bound for Odessa. Except that for the time being his home port was Marseilles and no longer Nice, where he had been born and brought up, and except that he must keep clear of Genoa, where they had a description of him as a deserter from the royal Piedmontese navy, he lived as he had always lived since boyhood, sailing up and down the Mediterranean, to and from Odessa, like that much-respected man, his father, the Padron Domenico, of whom it was said that he could make any port in the Mediterranean with his eyes shut.

The Garibaldis were Mediterranean people, and the name was a common name, found in many historical records. Paolo de Garibaldo of Chiavari, captain of the men-at-arms, is mentioned in a document relating to the year 1060 as having sought 'aid and authority to reduce the counts of Lavagna and other brigands to order, seeing that they oppressed the populace and confiscated the merchandise that came from Tunis'. A hundred years later a

Rubaldo Garibaldo was concerned in a riot. By the end of the middle ages the stock had increased and multiplied to such an extent that the singular form of the name, Garibaldo, is found replaced by the plural, Garibaldi; and it may be assumed from etymological considerations that the original ancestor was Germanic, a warrior probably who had elected to remain in the fertile plains of northern Italy rather than recross the mountains to his home. Quick in war his name proclaimed him. And quick in war his descendants seem to have been. Individually they were men of mark. But in characteristic Germanic fashion they tended to scatter, forming rather a tribe than a family, of which at one and the same time one member might be a duke and another a citizen. For example, in 1060, while Paolo de Garibaldo was a mere captain of the men-at-arms in Genoa, another Garibaldi (or Garibaldo) was Duke of Turin. At the end of the twelfth century they were numerous rather than powerful; and this characteristic remained. Perhaps they were naturally democratic, as some Italian scholars maintain. At all events, whether by instinct, intention or chance, they did not constitute a compact, noble family, as it seems they might well have been, but became ordinary, fighting commoners, interested in municipal and local affairs. In 1507, Bartolomeo Garibaldi of Genoa engaged somewhat vigorously in a dispute against the nobility, and was banished with his son to the town of Chiavari. There appears to be no proof of continuity. But this Bartolomeo Garibaldi is held to have been the ancestor of the Garibaldis of Nice.[1]

There is a gap of two hundred years before we pass with some certainty from the general history of the Garibaldi tribe to what may be safely assumed to be the particular history of the family as certified by records of birth, baptism, marriage and death. A Stefano Domenico Garibaldi was born in Chiavari in 1708 and married Angiola Maria Gandolfii, by whom he had a son, Angelo Maria.

[1] Jessie White Mario, *Supplement to the Autobiography of Giuseppe Garibaldi*, p. 2 f.

This son married in 1765 and had three sons and two daughters, with whom about 1770 or 1780 he removed to Nice, where the men of the family were sailors or shipbuilders, a profession which seems to have been adopted by the Garibaldi family ever since they were first known in Chiavari. Domenico Garibaldi, one of the three sons of Angelo Maria, reached man's estate about the time of the French Revolution. In the midst of it he took to wife Rosa Maria Nicoletta Raimondi, whose son, although they little suspected it, was to bring fame and many a heartache to both of them. But it was thought for many years that the certificate of this most important marriage had been lost or destroyed in the turmoil of the Revolution; if, indeed, it had ever been made out. And it was after Brignardello had declared finally that the search was hopeless that Jessie White Mario, an English lady of singular tenacity of character, discovered the missing document in the archives of the church of St. Martin at Nice. The parish priest had had to conceal his profession during the Terror, as well as to forego the usual entries in the church register: but being a man of habit and conscience, who knew that the affairs of the Church are those of life itself, whereas politics are the expression of the changing opinions of men, he kept his records in small copy-books, from which, at last, the vital reference was extracted:

February, 1794.
To-day, 1st. of February, 1794, I, Father Vittore Massa, have celebrated matrimony between Domenico Garibaldi, son of Angelo of Chiavari, in the western Riviera of Genoa, with Rosa Raimondi, daughter of Giuseppe of Loano, both inhabitants, for many years past, of this parish. By letter of the citizen vicar, G^{te} de Garideli, dated the 29th. of this last month of January, 1794, the three usual proclamations of the banns, day and place, are dispensed with.

Witnesses: Giuseppe Raimondi, Andrea Falchi.

It was a fruitful but not an inconsiderate marriage. Domenico was twenty-eight and his bride eighteen.[1] For

---
[1] The birth certificate of Rosa Raimondi is conserved in the register of the parish church of Loano:
1776 die vigesima octava januari: Ego Sebastianus Rocca præpositus hujus

ten years, either for reasons of personal prudence or because of the unsettled political conditions that followed the Terror, there were no children. The first came in 1804, Angelo. Three years later, after a due interval, Giuseppe Garibaldi was methodically born. If dates have any significance at such a distance of time, they would seem to suggest that he was born because his parents wished for another child and judged that they could afford one, their embrace being a mingling of natural affection and strong common sense. On the afternoon of the day of his birth, July 4, the child was carried in the arms of the midwife, dame Catherine Bandello, to the town hall of Nice, where the latter declared the names of the parents in the presence of grandfather Angelo Garibaldi (described as a merchant) and of a sister of mercy. These two signed their names as witnesses, but the midwife did not sign, as she could not write. A fortnight later the child was baptized as Giuseppe Maria, the name Giuseppe being evidently selected as a compliment to the godfather, Giuseppe Garibaldi, also a merchant and presumably a brother of Domenico. The second name of the child placed it in the sacred keeping of the Holy Virgin; and in this way its interests, both material and spiritual, were properly safeguarded. The child was blessed by Pio Papacin, rector of the parish of St. Martin and brought back to its mother.[1]

Two other boys, Michael and Felix, were born. Then came a girl, Teresa, who lived merrily amongst her four elder brothers until an accident happened, and she received burns from which she died. Angelo and Michael, the eldest and the youngest, both followed the sea; and Angelo soon found himself on the other side of the Atlantic, trad-

---

Parrochialis Ecclesiæ Sancti Joannis Baptistæ præsentis loci Lodani, babtizavi infantem natam ex Josepho Raimondi quondam Mathei, de Cogoleto, incola Lodani, et Magdalena . . . Conjugibus cui impositum est nomen Rosa Maria Nicoleta—patrini fuerunt R. Nicolaus Borro, quondam Benedicti de Petra, et Angela Conti Joannis Baptistæ, de Alessio, incola Lodani. Cf. Ximenes, *Epistolario*, i. p. 17 *n*.

[1] Jessie White Mario, *op. cit.* p. 5 f.; Guerzoni, *Garibaldi*, i. p. 5 f.

ing in New York. Felix remained in Nice, and got himself a reputation as a man who had an eye for pretty women. But he had also an eye for business, and was probably the most prosperous of the family. Their mother was beautiful and pious and taught them all to pray, though they seem to have taken this as a sign rather of her goodness than as a duty laid on themselves; nor does she appear to have hoped that anything better would come of it than that perhaps their male rudeness might be tempered by a more gentle spirit. She thought for some little time that Giuseppe might become a priest; or, if not a priest, a lawyer, for of all her children he had the sweetest voice and a gentleness of disposition not unlike her own. He was willing to learn and showed a quick talent for writing with the pen. He made shapely and firm letters, with good upstrokes and downstrokes; but he was better at making letters than at reading them. He learned under two priests and then under a layman, Signor Arena, who discovered that with the calligraphy went a bent for mathematics. Signora Rosa was not so pleased at this. When he began to study logarithms she knew he wanted, like his father, to go to sea. He was very independent in an affable way, making up his mind and doing what he chose to do. He learned to play draughts, but said that chess was too much bother: the result, he considered, was not in proportion to the effort expended, as, with so much thinking, one ought at least to become a great general. His education was, in a sense, a failure because he took what he wanted and left the rest, refusing to be coaxed in the direction of the learned professions. Many times when he ought to have been at his lessons it was found he had taken a gun and gone rabbiting, or else he was trawling oysters in a borrowed boat. Sometimes he went alone, sometimes in company. 'It was no use', said one of his playmates, 'to try and *make* him join any of our schemes for mischief': Peppino would join if he felt inclined, and if he did not he would go off with a book and read under an olive tree. He himself remembered three events in his boyhood very clearly.

Once, as a child, he caught a cricket and carried it into the house in his fist, only to find that he had broken its leg. He shut himself up in a room alone and cried for several hours. On another occasion he went hunting with a cousin and came on an old woman who had fallen head first into a deep ditch where the hemp was soaked. He was eight years old then: but he did not go home until he had pulled her out and saved her life. Lastly, he remembered running away from home. It seemed to him one day that it would be a good thing to go to Genoa and try his luck there. With some companions he put provisions in a boat, took fishing tackle in case the provisions ran out, hoisted a sail and made good way to as far as Monaco, where they were overhauled by a 'corsair', and fetched back in shame to Nice. This incident must have convinced his father and mother that, in spite of his mellow voice, he was neither priest nor lawyer. Domenico spoke to Capitano Pesante of the brigantine *Costanza*, and Giuseppe, trembling slightly with joy, took his kit aboard for a voyage to Odessa. He thought the *Costanza* with her slink masting, her broad, smooth deck and her high prow, the most beautiful ship he had ever seen. He watched with admiration the cat-footed sailors of San Remo swaying to the roll of her and, with a thrill of pride, tuned in his young pipe to the chanties they sang. The prow of the *Costanza* reminded him vaguely of the breast of a woman. *Pettoruto*, she was, this ship; high-bosomed. He envied Captain Pesante for being master of her and forgot the tears he had seen in the eyes of the Signora Rosa as she gave him his bundle.

 On his return Domenico took his son aboard his own *tartana*, the *Santa Reparata*, for a voyage to Rome; and after a few voyages his apprenticeship advanced rapidly. He was a good seaman, who took pride in coiling a rope to look as tight as a woven basket. When he swabbed the decks they gleamed with a special whiteness. And, although he was son of the boss, he made no ill-blood and claimed no privileges. He did not understand at first why his mother had wept. But as he was coming back on the

Enea, captain Gervino, from Cagliari and they were reaching Cape Noli, the *libeccio* (south-west wind) blew up a heavy sea and swamped a Catalan felucca just ahead of them. She was on their weather bow and they could do nothing for her. They saw her turn over and a few men clambering on her upper side for a second before they were washed under. They heard afterwards that nine of the crew who were drowned belonged to the same family.[1]

II

Up to the date of his adventure on the Piazza di Sarzana he had had about eleven years sailing up and down the Mediterranean. He used to say later that a boy who was meant for the sea should begin to get his sea-legs when he was eight years old. He was not in favour, in his old age, of the new-fangled notions by virtue of which a lad went to Paris until he was twenty and, when he was too old to learn the business, came with his logarithms to be sick on his first ship. At the same time his own career, even as a tramp sailor of the Mediterranean, was more ambitious than that of his father. For several years he went to the Levant and elsewhere with ships belonging to the Casa Gioan. He remembered also a trip to Gibraltar and the Canaries on *Coromandel*, captain Giuseppe Galleano; after which he returned to the Levant on the brigantine *Cortese*, captain Carlo Semeria. And this voyage proved memorable, or at any rate more noteworthy than the others (of which he remembered nothing at all) because when the *Cortese* sailed from Constantinople he was for the first time in his life left behind sick and took a long while to get better. His money was exhausted. But, to his own surprise, he found himself calling in a matter-of-fact way on an Italian doctor of medicine, Signor Diego (the same, possibly, who had attended him), and obtaining a recommendation as tutor to the three boys of the widow Timoni.

[1] *Memorie*, p. 22 ff.; Jessie White Mario, *op. cit.* p. 11.

Without much success, he attempted to remember the little Latin he had learned; and with some curiosity he tried to learn Greek. But he was not good at languages. He did some more useful reading on his own account; for he was determined to be a captain and, little as he liked study, he never shirked the means to an end, when he had made up his mind what the means must be. They were algebra, astronomy, geography and commercial law. Domenico had done without them. But his father belonged to the old generation of captains. Another was already on the way. Thanks to his scholarship and to his reputation as a sailor, Giuseppe left Constantinople on the brigantine *Nostra Signora delle Grazie* for Maone and Gibraltar (February 1832) as master. She was the first ship to be placed in his charge. Perhaps for that reason he has nothing to say about her; his few words of praise are kept in the *Memorie* for the shapely timbers of the *Costanza*. When he attempted long after to recollect these eleven years, there passed before his eyes a stately procession of ships, their names clearly lettered, their figure-heads hewn in his memory; while obediently his memory also brought back to him the names of the captains and sometimes the names of the firms they traded for. Beyond that all was blank, except that at Smyrna he fished a Nice lad, one of his own contemporaries, Claudio Terese, out of the water.[1] This was probably his second rescue; for he was a strong swimmer on whom these affairs fell as a duty. It became difficult to remember later how many people he had pulled out of the water at one time or another. The total, he thought, might be sixteen.

His book learning, small as it was, sufficed to distinguish the younger Captain Garibaldi from the elder. The Padron Domenico was a conservative. It may have been that this conservatism was inherent in his character; for there is no record that Garibaldi's father ever jumped into

---

[1] Dumas (*Memoirs of Garibaldi*, ed. Garnett, p. 37) and Elpis Melena (*Denkwürdigkeiten*, i. p. 13) both affirm that Garibaldi was attacked by pirates three times.

the water to save anyone; whereas it was one of Giuseppe's most pronounced characteristics that he had, with his other abilities, a talent for ingenious loafing which made him at an early age a natural vortex of circumstance, so that whatever events were forward in his vicinity propelled themselves gently towards him and were sucked into the whirl of his casual activity. Peppino always seemed to be hanging about when things were happening; as possibly he was also hanging about when nothing was happening. There was always a certain generous leisure in his mind which made him think that what occurred outside was more likely to be important and interesting than what might, at the same moment, be going on inside his own mind. The Padron Domenico, if he had ever held such a view, had given it up. He had seen so many things in his time, that his eyes closed naturally at the proper moment. He had the impression that the events of the world were beyond him. And that it was better so. There was excuse for him in the fact that he was getting on in years and that somehow the events which he had forgotten or tried to forget appeared to be attempting to repeat themselves. He himself had thanked God when Napoleon Bonaparte had put an end to the Revolution. He wanted no more revolutions. And when he was told that the *tartane* were again carrying queer goods and occasionally queer people, he made up his mind to ask no questions and to know nothing. It was not the business of the captain of a caboteur to know that the olives might be shot for Sicily or the *articles de Paris* (from Marseilles for Genoa) a bundle of inflammatory newsprint from the headquarters of the *Giovine Italia*. On these matters there was a natural difference of opinion between Domenico and his son which did not come to open expression: but which was there. Every time Domenico came home after a voyage to find the Signora Rosa praying and taking her basket to market as usual, he thanked God that it was so: but Giuseppe, while he preserved his tenderness for his mother, was inclined to think (an opinion with which his recent knowledge of logarithms may have had something to do) that her prayers were an anachronism.

He had heard at Constantinople of the war between Russia and the Porte; and of the gallant fight of the Greeks against the tyranny of the Turks. Then at Taganrog in 1833 he encountered a real conspirator, Cuneo of Genoa,[1] an Italian who had been engaged in a recent attempt to thrust new ideas on Charles Albert, King of Savoy and Piedmont. On July 4, 1832, a trunk of substantial appearance addressed to Messrs. Rini Brothers of Genoa had been opened by the customs officers there, and was found to conceal, underneath a double bottom, sheets of printed instructions for the agents of the *Giovine Italia* in the length and breadth of Italy. There were thirteen letters from Giuseppe Mazzini, head of the organisation, to various people in Palermo and Naples, as well as propagandist literature. The find was brought to the notice of Charles Albert, and copies of the relevant documents were sent to Metternich in Vienna, as well as to the chancelleries of the reactionary duchies, grand-duchies, Papal States and political sundries that constituted the heterogeneous fabric of Italy; and, of course, to the kingdom of Naples and Sicily. All of which powers proceeded with stealth to put the addressees and others implicated under lock and key. In particular in Savoy and Piedmont, whence the young conspirators hoped that the *risorgimento* would begin, it was repressed with extraordinary ferocity. Cuneo told Garibaldi how Jacopo Ruffini, who had been Mazzini's right-hand man, had killed himself in prison for fear that the torture awaiting him would cause him to reveal the names of his accomplices.[2]

Up to this time young Garibaldi had not shown any interest in politics. Until the events of 1832–33,[3] he had seen no reason to suppose that theories of government

---

[1] Giovanni Battista Cuneo di Oneglia. He died in 1875.
[2] *Memorie*, p. 26 ff.; Jessie White Mario, *op. cit.* p. 28 ff.
[3] See Appendix C.

might be the prelude to strange adventures in which exhilaration and reflection combined. There was proof enough, indeed, that the government under which his father and mother had lived was not more intolerable than most governments. Within his own recollection Nice had been governed from Paris; and it was now governed from Turin as part of Piedmont. If the matter had been left to him he would probably not have noticed when the one government left off and the other began. But now Garibaldi was filled with righteous anger. He considered Cuneo with pleasure. He got up and embraced him after his story; and soon he had a name for him. *Il Credente*, he called him, with a smile. Cuneo was a man who *believed*, the first *man* he had met who believed. Of the violence of men Garibaldi had had experience; but rather of the drunken and purposeless violence of sailors in port, or the rebellious violence of the brutish able-bodied seamen who preferred seaboard to jail or a lunatic asylum. Faith such as Cuneo's he had only met in women, in the Signora Rosa and the nuns she brought about the house.

He went to Marseilles as soon as his ship had discharged her cargo and found the man he had been told he would find, Giuseppe Mazzini, whose pamphlets he had read. Mazzini formulated the articles of the creed. 'Sire', he had written to Charles Albert himself, 'have you never cast a glance, one of those eagle glances which reveal a world, on this Italy, beautified with nature's smile, crowned with twenty centuries of sublime memories, the home of genius, endowed with infinite means, requiring only unity, surrounded by such natural defences as a strong will and a few brave breasts would ensure, to protect her from the foreigner's insult? Have you never said to yourself, "This Italy is created for great destinies"? Have you never contemplated this people who inhabit it, splendid despite the shadow of servitude which hangs over their heads; great by the instinct of life, by the light of intellect, by the energy of passions—passions blind and ferocious, it may be, since the times are against the development of nobler ones—but who are, nevertheless, the elements from which nations are created; great indeed, since misfortune has neither crushed them nor deprived them of hope? Has the thought never dawned on you to evolve, as God from chaos, a new world from those dispersed elements; to reunite the dissevered members, and exclaim, "Italy is happy, and all my own! Like God, I can become the creator of twenty millions of men, whose cry shall be, 'God in heaven, and Charles Albert on the earth'"?'

Garibaldi did not know that the arch-conspirator had carefully thought out this address in which the Almighty entered into close co-operation with the King of Piedmont for the unification of Italy. Mazzini calculated that Charles Albert would not be displeased to have the matter put to him in this way; and he had been disappointed at the poor result of his manœuvres. Garibaldi was concerned chiefly with his own new functions as a conspirator. He wanted something to do, and asked Mazzini what use could be made of a merchant captain with eleven years' experience of the sea. Mazzini told him to enrol as an A.B. in the navy of the King of Piedmont; instructions and money would be sent to him and his name would be, for the purposes of the *Giovine Italia*, Joseph Borel. The watchword was *ora e sempre*, now and always.

This interview took place in the autumn of 1833. Shortly after, in December, Garibaldi had ceased to be a merchant captain and was employed as a pilot on board the Piedmontese ship-of-war *Eurydice*, on whose register he figured as a 'sailor of the third-class levy, height five feet six and a half inches; hair and eyebrows reddish, chestnut-coloured eyes, spacious forehead, aquiline nose, medium mouth, rounded chin, healthy colour, no special marks.' His nose was not aquiline, nor were his eyes chestnut-coloured; but the remainder of the description was accurate. Apparently he did not wear a beard. He carried out his instructions faithfully. They were to gain influence with the men on his ship and interest them in the cause of the *Giovine Italia*; and on the occasions when he went ashore to seek to extend this influence among other naval ratings and the troops of the garrison. He never discovered to what extent he had been successful in his propaganda, which continued quietly until the morning of February 3, 1834. On that day, which happened to be the day before that fixed by Mazzini for the outbreak of the revolution in Genoa, an order came that Giuseppe Garibaldi was to be embarked on the admiral's flagship *Desgeneys*. He found himself thus, on the day of the event, cut off from the comrades who were pledged to follow; and he suspected that something had gone wrong.

He is reported as having 'deserted' from the *Desgeneys* on February 4. Probably he dropped overboard and swam ashore, to find that the city of Genoa was enjoying an unusual calm. Of the band of insurgents who were to have made their way down from Savoy there was no sign; nor had the mutineers, as arranged, seized the arsenal on the Piazza di Sarzana. He lounged hopefully, hoping he had misheard a voice which said audibly in his neighbourhood: *Tutto è scoperto*. The *Gazzetta di Genova* which he had bought contained a paragraph announcing that a body of undisciplined insurgents had made a brief appearance in Savoy and had disappeared again, presumably into Switzerland. As the royal troops began to draw a cordon round the square he judged that it was time for himself to disappear. He was wary as well as courageous; and the fruit-shop, having a back as well as a front, offered a convenient shelter. When he emerged that night he had left behind his sailor's uniform and was wearing a suit of old clothes belonging to the husband of the old lady who had given the conspirator such good advice.[1]

The months wore on. Pippo, as Mazzini was called, was as busy as ever with his pamphlets: but he signified that there was nothing to be done, and Garibaldi found himself a mate instead of a captain, and in a state of virtual

[1] Jessie White Mario, *op. cit.* p. 37; Dumas (Garnett), *Memoirs of Garibaldi*, p. 44 f.

unemployment. A boy fell into the harbour, and by a malediction it was Sunday and Garibaldi was wearing his best suit. But the boy's mother was grateful and wet the rescuer's cheek with her tears; that, and the fact that he had had to dive three times to find the boy, made the event interesting. Then, coming home in a Turkish brig from the port of Goulette, he heard that the cholera was at Marseilles and presented himself at the hospital with a stretcher. They took him on as an assistant for a few weeks until the epidemic came to an end; after which there was nothing for it but to sign on again for another jog along the Mediterranean. About the beginning of July he was once more back in port and was reading the *Peuple souverain*, the organ of the democrats in Marseilles, when a name caught his eye, his own name—Garibaldi, Giuseppe Maria, followed by his age, twenty-six years. He was reading the sentence of the divisional court-martial which on June 14 had considered the case of nine conspirators, six of whom were under arrest and three, including himself, still at large, but to be sought for diligently by all loyal subjects of His Majesty Charles Albert, as bandits of the first category. *Di primo catalogo*, the document said. Garibaldi, with two others, was found guilty of distributing sums of money among the men of the Royal Corps of Artillery and otherwise inciting His Majesty's loyal troops and naval ratings to revolt. The council, having heard the relation of the offences and invoked the assistance of God, condemned Garibaldi to be 'ignominiously executed'.[1] More precisely the sentence meant that Charles Albert not only refused the collaboration of Mazzini and the *Giovine Italia* in looking after the affairs of his kingdom, but proposed in rage and contempt to treat the conspirators as common criminals. Garibaldi knew that if he were caught he would be put against a wall and shot in the back. Such was the procedure, and the threat of it fanned the flame of patriotism in his bosom. He began to feel as a personal

[1] Guerzoni, i. p. 1. The *Peuple souverain* copied the sentence from the *Gazzetta Piemontese* of June 17, 1834.

matter the belief which he saw in the eyes of Cuneo and
Mazzini; until now he had subscribed to it in a somewhat
vague way, like a country boy putting down his money at
the door of a theatre. That he himself was an actor in the
drama was proved by the newspaper, which he read and
re-read. Never before had he seen his name in print. It was
a momentous occasion which gave him as direct a thrill of
pleasure as he had ever had. To the end of his life he never
forgot his gratitude to the printed word, and would turn to
the newspapers after a battle to see what they had to
say of it, and if the account was good, he would cry out
with pleasure. He studied his own history in this way and
knew that he had become famous when, spelling his
way through its columns, he discovered his name in *The
Times*.

Meantime, however, there was nothing to keep him in
the Mediterranean; the cholera had abated and the affairs
of Italy were in abeyance; and there was at least one good
reason why he should go away. He had some qualms lest
he might be leaving a possible revolution behind: but,
finding the *Nautonnier*, captain Beauregard, about to sail
for Rio de Janeiro, he signed as second and, still obeying
the curious poetic inspiration which commanded him to
thread the insignificant events of life in some sort of
dream, making them decisive and graceful like the
strokes of his handwriting, he was borne away from the
old world towards the new. His friends said he was a poet;
and, thinking they might be right, he tried to compose
poems.

When he had nothing to do he looked at the water.
He could spend hours in this way. The world, land
and water (but especially water), was extraordinarily
interesting.[1]

[1] *Memoirs* (Dumas), p. 49. The *Nautonnier* left probably in late September
1836. She arrived at Cape Frio on October 15, 1836 (Ximenes, i. p. 1).

III

GARIBALDI liked the look of Rio harbour. It was a 'hidden water', as the Indians called it; hidden from the ocean by a curtain of granite rocks, and when these were passed you came on a bay calm as a lake, dotted with islands, with the city on the western shore lying under the shelter of the sharp Pao de Acucar. From a distance Rio looked like a poet's dream, with white houses nestling against tropical green. Everywhere there were ships. Rio was big enough to hold all the navies of the world. And the land sloped down to a white beach on which small waves broke quietly.

The port enjoyed in 1836 a variety of smells. The white beaches that looked so pleasant to the eye when viewed from a distance by men who had not seen land for many days were littered with decaying fruit and offal of all kinds. There were (it appeared) no police in Rio. And the mulattos who rowed out with fruit to the incoming ships and failed to sell their load, dumped it as often as not on the beach as they landed, and left it there to rot in the mist and the sun. The sea washed it about among the huge wooden piles of the landing stage, threw it up on the beach and sucked it back again. The prevailing smell came from the abundance of this vegetable material in all the stages preceding and following putrefaction. But there was also another smell, that of the sardinhas and pork sold from the stalls that lined the way to the customs, where the chief officer sat amid a staff of a dozen clerks and preserved great dignity by means of silk stockings, court hose and elegant ruffles at the wrist, while about him surged an international medley of adventurers, Dutch, German, English, Italian and French. It was a scene that would have been exhilarating but for the smell and the heat, a heat of which steam seemed to be the principal element. As one threaded one's way from the mud of the quayside through the single narrow street that led to the town, houses rose comfortably on either side, four storeys high, with not a pane of glass in any of them. As in the past centuries (four at any rate), a hand would appear and cautiously lift an end of the latticed jalousies and, curiosity being satisfied, as cautiously drop it again. Costume was diverse. It varied from nothing at all in the case of the chattering negro porters to elaborate suits that might have graced, and probably did at one time grace, the court of that illustrious and pervading monarch, Louis XIV. The whole of the civilised population seemed to have taken its cue from the gentleman who presided at the customs. It seemed to be prepared for a *bal masqué* or a dinner party in the best eighteenth century style. Everywhere were black coats, satin breeches, silk stockings and gold or silver buckles; the more important merchants added to this equipment gold-headed canes which they wagged at each other importantly, and large gold seals suspended padlockwise on broad strips of ribbon across their stomachs. It was evident from the conversation of these gentlemen that they held a watching brief over the material interests of the port of Rio, and that their duty compelled them to spend long hours sitting at the doors of their shops talking with polite animation, gently waving dramatic cigars (whose smoke in their hands described curves, parabolas and asymtotes of infinite art), while occasionally they bent their heads with an air of exceptional concentration and took a sip of maté.

It was difficult for a stranger to distinguish between the various layers of importance and respectability. Very few of the black-coated gentlemen were more than clerks from the stores; and among them a careful eye might pick a lawyer taking an hour off from his office. For various reasons there were many lawyers in Rio. And, recalling the vast plains that lay beyond the city and explained its prosperity, an estanciero, distinguishable by his poncho and the assiduity of the black men around him, would be sitting disconsolately, full of the knowledge that the money he had just obtained for his bullocks would be taken from him again by his agents in a courteous game of cards. Here in Rio, as in Nice, there was a liveliness of discourse suggesting that the dull routine of business was livened with politics; and whether it was the little finger of God, the long arm of coincidence or merely the natural operation of the laws governing the caprice of human behaviour, the black men gave each other the day's prices and went on to talk vigorously about 'civil liberty', the 'freedom of the Press', the 'privileges of the constitution' in a way that was bound to make an Italian exile feel at home. An intelligent observer would soon have learned, in fact, that on September 20, 1836, the citizens of Porto Alegre had revolted against the imperial president, José Aranjo Ribeira, and had nominated a president of their own, Bento Gonçales de Silva; an act which was held to offer a parallel to the French Revolution, on which model it was exactly based. But the observer would also have noted that the politics of the country were like its coastline. From a distance they showed the crags of liberty and high principle: and near at hand they steamed with plenteous corruption. For which reason, perhaps, the self-proclaimed republic of Rio Grande had not begun too auspiciously, having little but its principles to offer in exchange for public support. After a brief campaign the imperial government of Rio de Janeiro had put its hand on Bento Gonçales de Silva (and on his Italian secretary, Livio Zambeccari), and locked them up outside the city in the fortress of Santa Cruz.[1] It was this hazard, and more particularly this association of high principles with misfortune, which were to attract Garibaldi and cause him to change his plans.

Cuneo had gone to Montevideo and begun a newspaper there for the Italian colony. And Garibaldi had picked up a compatriot, Luigi Rossetti of Genoa, with whom he entered into a temporary business partnership. There are two letters dating from this period of Garibaldi's life, both of them addressed to Cuneo and both characteristically brief; they contain a hint of what he was doing and thinking; and, moreover, they are the earliest letters extant. For it would seem that during all the previous eleven odd years when he

[1] See Appendix B.

was many times absent from home for long intervals, he either wrote to his parents not at all or they did not preserve his letters.

BROTHER,
 This is only to announce to you our arrival on the 15th and to tell you that the daughter of our Caulker is beautiful, ma bella, sai, with a beauty such as your romantic imagination often leads you to picture, and I am moved to the depths of my heart. I assure you if she were not so unapproachable (*selvatica*), I would get together our disused instruments (*vorrei organizzare i tanto dimenicati strumenti*). But for the moment we shall do nothing. Money, money is what we need most, for we can find beauties in Italy just as well. But here we have to hang about doing nothing day after day, and the thought of it worries me. Patience, brother!!
Capo Frio, October 17, 1836.

With the letter was enclosed a receipt for a sum of money lent to Garibaldi by Cuneo's cousin and an enquiry concerning prices in Rio. At Capo Frio, millet, said Garibaldi, was fetching a thousand reis the alquere, a detail which shows that he had already begun on the coasting trade: but his main interest was in the 'caulker's daughter', a phrase which conveyed to Cuneo that Garibaldi had been looking out for some ship on which, if the 'romantic imagination' of Cuneo were to be believed, an expedition would shortly set forth from South America for the coast of Italy. Two months later this pleasant dream was fading, and the conspirator found himself a tramp sailor again, handicapped by his ignorance of the coast and his inability to grasp the fact that all the merchants in the trade were rascals:

Our trips (he wrote in his second letter) were lucky enough, but they did not bring much money because we put faith in people whom we thought to be friends and who turned out to be scoundrels. Our lack of acquaintance of the places we touched at had a good deal to do with it. One must learn in order to know, that is certain.
 The company seems to have a monopoly, as they are shipping on their own account 240 alquari of millet and 100 of flour which we shall sell at Campos or Macae where we shall take sugar and spirits.

Concerning myself I can only tell you that I am not happy, that I am tortured by the idea that I can do nothing to advance our own affairs, that I have need of storm rather than calm and that I am ready for extreme measures.
Write to P. (i.e. Pippo or Mazzini) and tell him to send us a recipe and we will have it made up, dear brother. It is not the first time I importune you; do not be angry. I am tired, per Dio, of leading a life so useless to our land, tired of being a merchant sailor. Be assured we are destined for greater things; we are out of our element, and I long to plunge into it again.

Capo Frio, 27th December, 1836.[1]

It needed no prophet to foretell what would happen. Trading, Garibaldi warned Cuneo, 'muddled his brain'; and the 'recipe' expected from Mazzini which Garibaldi hoped to make up in the new world and deliver personally in the old, was not forthcoming. A note received by Cuneo warned him some time in 1837 that he need not expect to hear from his friend for some time; nor could the latter give explanations by letter. 'All I can tell you', wrote Garibaldi, 'is that I am setting out upon a new path, guided ever by our principles, with that goal in view which you first put before me. I trust to you to set our work in its true light. You know me and can answer for me as for yourself.'[2]

No doubt Cuneo drew his own conclusions and prepared, in his capacity as newspaper editor, to give Garibaldi a good Press, suspecting that the explanation of the mysterious note lay in the identity of Garibaldi's principles with those professed by the new republic of Rio Grande which was still maintaining itself with a desperate impertinence against the army of the royal house of Portugal. It had been less fortunate than its neighbour, Buenos Ayres, which had simply sent a junta of leading citizens to surround the Spanish viceroy and oblige him to sign the statute of the republic in the name of His Majesty Ferdinand VII, a bloodless operation which was completed later by the deportation of the viceroy to the Canary Isles. Rio Grande, with the same ambitions, was confronted by the opposing might of Brazil, and had to fight for the demo-

---

[1] Cf. Ximenes, i. pp. 1-3.   [2] Jessie White Mario, *op. cit.* p. 42.

cratic privileges which Buenos Ayres had obtained for nothing.

Garibaldi became acquainted with Secretary Zambeccari, and he accepted letters of marque to cruise on behalf of the new republic of Rio Grande against Brazil.[1]

The *Jornal do commercio* of Rio de Janeiro, under the heading *Movimento marittimo*, announced the departure on May 7, 1837, of the *Mazzini*, described as a *lancia* of twenty tons, captain Cipriano Alves, crew five men, cargo meat. There was one passenger, an Italian Luigi Rossetti. The *Mazzini* had been lying at anchor opposite the fish market until the morning of May 7, when she picked up the anchor, hoisted a small sail and slid off in the direction of the Marica islands, in the mouth of the roads. There were two facts about her of which the port authorities were unaware. One was that the captain was not Cipriano Alves but Giuseppe Garibaldi who, for reasons best known to himself, chose to conceal his identity until the vessel was clear of port. The other fact was that the cargo of meat cured with manioc was a dummy cargo. There was just enough meat to feed the crew of ten men for a short period. Underneath the meat was a small but select store of arms and ammunition. The *Mazzini* headed for the largest of the islands, and there Garibaldi stepped ashore, climbed to the highest point and uttered a cry of joy. He was commander of the Rio Grande navy and master of the seas. He liked being on an eminence, whether it was a horse, a ship, or a crag of rock. At that moment he was tempted to compare himself to an eagle or a seagull.

He was in this frame of mind when he sighted from his eminence a schooner bearing the flag of Brazil. He leaped down to oar the *Mazzini* off the beach, and bore straight down on the stranger, calling on her to surrender in the name of the Republic of Rio Grande. The schooner made no show of resistance. She was just out from the island of Grande on the other side of the roads, and was bound for

[1] See Appendix B.

Europe with a cargo of coffee. She had aboard one passenger, a Portuguese gentleman who disappeared below and came up again with the price of his ransom in his hands, a boxful of diamonds. Garibaldi explained to him that he had better keep his diamonds for a proper pirate. The operation had taken place very quickly and without fuss, so that the shore batteries noticed nothing amiss until it was observed that the *Mazzini* sank lower in the water and presently disappeared. Garibaldi had scuttled her and taken over the schooner as the flagship of the Rio Grande navy. Off Santa Catharina Garibaldi ordered the yawl to be lowered and all the crew and passengers of the captured ship to be put ashore. Five negroes elected to stay with Garibaldi, while the remainder took their astonishing tale to Rio de Janeiro. The *Jornal do commercio* reported in its columns of June 14 that a schooner emerging from the port of Rio had been assaulted and captured by another vessel which had just left the same port. The pirate had then sunk his own ship, disembarked his new passengers after six days' voyage within sight of Itapocoroy, and proceeded towards Maldonato. The same paper gave further news on June 30. According to a letter received from Montevideo, the 'pirate who has caused himself to be so much spoken of lately' had cast anchor at Maldonato, where he exhibited papers of authority signed by Major Lima; he flew the flag of the 'so-called republic of Piratiny'. His ship was undoubtedly the schooner *Luisa* which he had lately captured at the mouth of the Rio.

Conversations took place between the representative of Brazil and the representative of the Oriental Republic with a view (as the papers put it) to detaining the pirate; and orders were given to the brigantine *Imperial Pedro* to make all sail and put an end to the nuisance. It was arranged that Oribe, the president of the Oriental Republic, should endeavour to prolong Garibaldi's stay at Maldonato as long as might be possible, introducing his crew to the pleasures of the port and flattering the pirate by diplomatic attentions until the *Imperial Pedro* should arrive and catch the mouse in the trap. Garibaldi was pleased that his official position should be so politely recognised and, while the *Luisa* lingered in the harbour of Maldonato and the crew took their ease ashore, he sent Luigi Rossetti to sell the coffee which had been found in her hold in Montevideo.[1]

IV

THE old viceregents of Spain and Portugal acted according to one consistent belief, that as little money as possible should be sent home to Europe in the form of taxes, as little as possible be spent on the upkeep of their small armies, as little as possible be given to such educational institutions as the university of Cordova, which produced lawyers and priests but no doctors; and finally that as much as possible should stick in the pockets of viceregents. So satisfied were they with what they could obtain by petty bribery and corruption that they remained largely indifferent to the incredible wealth that flowed down the broad waterways to the cities of the coast. They did nothing to stop these cities from growing; and they cordially agreed with the citizens that the wealth of the country should flow into the cities but no further: it must not be packed on British or Dutch or French ships and be taken away altogether. There was really no quarrel between the old viceregents and the cities, except that the cities were natural republics, and when they were strong enough they annexed the backlands and called themselves by their proper name. The viceroys were replaced by a president, the viceregal court by a senate, the cabildo superseded by a justice of the peace, and the council of state by a provincial assembly. When these changes had been made everything was exactly as before, except that there were more officials, and therefore the system of bribery and corruption had to be extended to cover the needs of presidents, senators, judges and clerks, who were now so numerous that it might fairly

[1] *Memorie*, p. 31 ff.; Dumas, p. 51 ff.

be contended that the purposes of democracy were in some measure being fulfilled.

The old institutions had lasted since the XVIIth century; and they had the advantage over the new of being simple. The science of modern politics was plain and noble on paper; but, like the pleadings of the creole lawyers (whose numbers also had increased formidably), it proved to be capable of infinite complexity and to lead to curious effects; so that while the declaration of the rights of man was the merest commonplace in any shopkeeper's daily conversation and much appreciated as a preamble to business deals, it did not follow that one republic should forego the privilege or habit of making war on another; for example, the republic of Buenos Ayres might with propriety arrange with the sister republic known as the Oriental to crush the aspirations of the republic of Rio Grande. The possible permutations and combinations of political bodies showed the diversity of perfect chance; a fact which was made plain to Garibaldi after he had been eight days at the port of Maldonato. The negotiations with the coffee merchant were suspiciously prolonged. The merchant had agreed to take the goods but did not hand over the money; and in a moment of good humour the agent of the Oriental Republic explained that the merchant, like himself, was acting under the highest instructions and would in due course, if all went well, get his coffee for nothing. In a few hours Garibaldi had rounded up his tipsy crew, made all shipshape on the *Luisa*, and called with a couple of pistols in his belt on the merchant, whom he found puffing a cigar and enjoying the moonlight at the door of his house.

'My money', he said, pressing the barrel of a pistol against the merchant's chest.

At the third reiteration the merchant counted out two thousand patacons, and at eleven o'clock the *Luisa* was out of port and heading up the Plata River. The night had turned dark and Garibaldi sailed carefully by compass: yet, in the morning the ship was three miles out of her course, riding for the rocks of Piedras Negras; an unheard-of thing in Garibaldi's experience. He did not understand until his eye fell on the cabin beside the binnacle; the compass needle was pointing straight at this cabin into which, in the hurry of departure, all the weapons on board had been thrown in expectation of the arrival of the *Imperial Pedro*. At Jesus Maria provisions gave out and, as there was no boat (the *Luisa*'s yawl had been given to the Portuguese gentleman and the late crew so that they could put themselves ashore), a raft had to be made from a table and some barrels before Garibaldi, with one man, could pole his way across the shallows inshore. He found himself on flat country that looked as if it had just been created, a vast prairie of green spotted with flowers, where there was no sign that man existed at all. The land belonged to the herds of animals that roamed freely about, deer, ostriches, gazelles, cattle, antelopes and horses, horses of the Oriental plains that stood quivering on stretched legs and neighed and bounded off into the high grass. Whoever was master of them was master of the cattle; and, by implication and in all reality, master of the cities and of South America. There was an inevitable logic in the sequence of facts which Garibaldi was quick to understand.

In the emptiness he found a lonely estancia where a woman refused to sell him a bullock until her husband, the capataz, returned; although, with a charming South American courtesy not unlike that practised in the port of Maldonato, she recited Dante, Petrarch and Tasso to her guest lest the time should seem long. For her sake Garibaldi agreed it would be well if he learned Spanish; in order, as she said, that he might become familiar with the poetry of Quintana. But these considerations were brought to an end by the arrival of the capataz, who fixed his price and dragged the bullock on a lasso to the beach, where it was killed, bled, skinned, cut up and, not without some ado, loaded on to the raft. The *Luisa* had lost three days, thanks to this excursion, and, as she was hoisting sail at last, a couple of lanciónes appeared from the direction of Montevideo; no sooner were they alongside than their decks swarmed with men who opened fire point-blank while, from one of them which had thrown irons, attackers swarmed aboard the *Luisa* swinging cutlasses. As Garibaldi sprang to take the place of the dead helmsman a ball struck him in the neck and he fell unconscious. When he opened his eyes again, it was to find that the lanciónes had been driven off (they had not been prepared for real fighting, thinking that the usual procedure of shout and gesticulation would suffice), and the survivors of Rio Grande's navy were looking respectfully down on what they took to be the dead body of their admiral.

At Santa Fé on the Paraná a young doctor removed the bullet, which had passed miraculously between spine and pharynx. Garibaldi had a high fever and difficulty in swallowing. But when the ball was out he mended quickly.

The doctor who attended Garibaldi was the private physician of Don Pasquale Echaguë, governor of the province of Entre Rios; a lucky circumstance, for there was a notable shortage of doctors in the country, and an abundance of mulatto quacks who pulled teeth and let blood for a consideration. The governor had left his physician to attend to Garibaldi and had ridden up country, after explaining that the schooner would be confiscated, but that an allowance of a crown a day would be made to Garibaldi in exchange for it. The confiscation seemed to indicate that the province of Entre Rios was not on good terms with the republic of Rio Grande, while the payment of money in a country where nobody ever had any (a bullock would have been another matter) was a gesture of exceptional friendliness. Garibaldi thought he was beginning to understand how the South American mind worked and argued the case within himself. He was held a prisoner and yet allowed, as soon as he was able, to ride on the pampas; on the understanding, however, that he would not ride away; and following the apparent reasoning of his captors, he concluded that, while they were obliged to hold him as a matter of courtesy to the greater powers (and no doubt the governor was absent on business that concerned him), it was no less incumbent on him to acknowledge the kindness shown to him by relieving the government of Entre Rios of the necessity of paying him a crown a day. Instead of taking his usual exercise Garibaldi did a stretch of fifty-four miles in the direction of the left bank of the Paraná, where he hoped to find a ship for Buenos Ayres or Montevideo. He stopped in sight of Ibiqui and rested. But he had evidently misunderstood the South American mind. A band of horsemen overtook him as he was about to remount, tied his hands behind his back and his feet to the saddle girth and rode him back through the mosquito swamps to Gualeguy. By the time they got there his face and hands were flayed and, in this condition, he was brought before Leonardo Millan, the deputy-governor, to whom he refused to disclose the identity of his accomplices in his escape. Leonardo Millan struck him across the face with his whip and ordered him to be taken to the cells; a cord was run round his wrists and he was strung over a beam so that his feet hung off the ground. Presently Leonardo entered to question him again, and was imprudent enough to come near the prisoner who, in a manner he had learned on the quayside at Nice, collected some spittle and projected it in the deputy-governor's face. At the end of two hours he was cut down more dead than alive, to lie for a couple of months in the prison of Bajada; after which, the governor having returned, a message came 'desiring him to be informed' that he might leave the province. Captain Ventura, an Italian, conveyed Garibaldi on his brigantine as far as the mouth of the Iguassu river; whence the latter reached Montevideo by way of the Paraná. The Italians in Montevideo were, for the most part, shopkeepers; and if Garibaldi's talents had lain towards commerce, he had opportunity to abandon his roving life. But at the end of a month Luigi Rossetti arrived from Rio Grande and they set off together to join the president of the republic, Bento Gonçales. They took eight horses between them, changing the saddle from one to the other every half-dozen leagues, and so came to Piratinim in a short time.

Garibaldi was learning the great lesson that South America had to teach him. He had brought with him from the old world the dexterity and weather-wisdom of the Mediterranean sailor. But he had yet to discover what a man could do with a horse; and what he could do with a poncho, that simple and manifold garment which might be, according to its owner's taste and circumstances, stitched with the worth of many thousands of bullocks or be a rag of threadbare blanket. The poncho was the mark of a free man. With it a man might go anywhere, sleep anywhere, and be the real owner of as much country as a squad of good horses would take him over. The poncho kept you cool in hot weather by flapping about you; and it kept you warm in cold. It kept off the rain. It kept off the sun. During the siesta it could be hung on a pair of sticks to serve as an awning; in some parts of the country it was good enough for a tent. If you could sit a horse all day and not be tired, you had the freedom of South America, war or no war: and if, in addition, you could put a lasso round the forefeet of an ox at full gallop there was no need ever to go hungry. There was a freemasonry between people who lived thus; and by virtue of it Garibaldi found that his real friend was the gaucho, swart under his straw hat, elegantly bearing a carving-knife and a brace of chased pistols in his belt, and holding up his formidable slacks by a broad red sash. At the end of the day it was a pleasure to unhitch the recado and lie down under the stars. In some places in the republic of Rio Grande it could be done quite comfortably; in the mountain region, for example, which had a climate like that of Nice, albeit there was small resemblance otherwise. The pine trees of Rio Grande rose two hundred feet, and six men hand to hand could scarcely reach round the bottom of some of them. Reeds grew to eighty feet. In likely places the first settlers had hacked a clearing, and so the cities of the interior, like Lima and Lages, had grown up gradually.

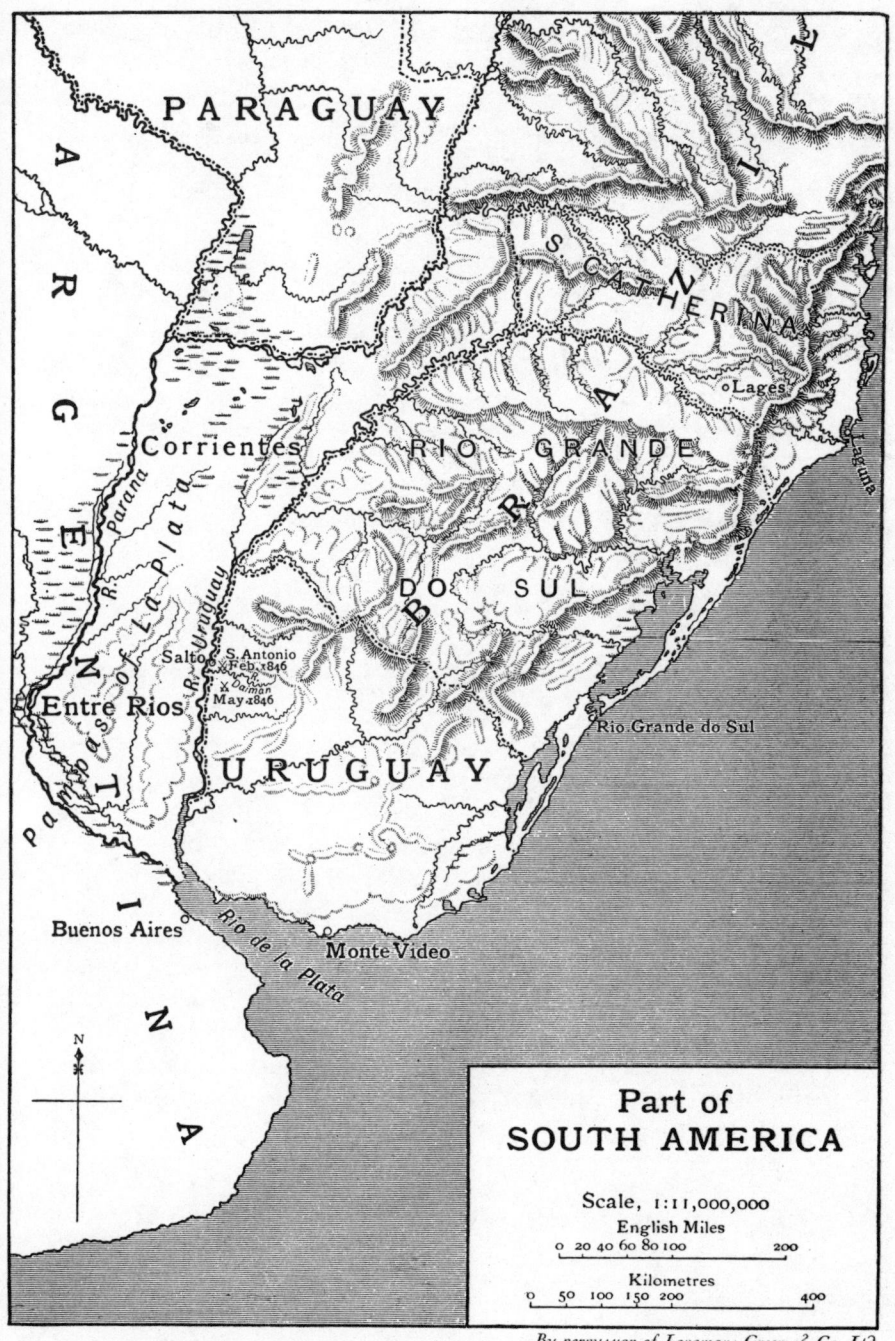

Bento Gonçales turned out to be a man like a child. He was very pleased to meet the commander of his navy, even without the navy. Over roast meat and water they talked as if they had known each other all their lives. Bento Gonçales looked sixty off a horse, twenty-five on, and in reality was about fifty. He had no luck and no cunning, was worshipped by all the gauchos of Rio and could not win anything so complicated as a battle.

V

THE making of a fresh navy took some time. Garibaldi was awarded full command, with the rank of *capitano tenente*; and, with an American, John Griggs, and a mulatto blacksmith, built a couple of sloops, finding wood in one direction and iron in another. The sloops took the water like ducks, and occasionally shot out from the shallows to incommode the thirty war-vessels and one steamship of the Imperial navy. The ships of the Imperial navy could not pursue them in the shallows: Garibaldi's flotilla had only to run aground on their flat bottoms, the crews jumped on horseback, wheeled into the reeds that grew along the bank and scattered on a long front, when they let off muskets at odd points to give an impression of great numbers. On one particularly successful morning they caught a rich cargo off Camaquam, shared out the booty and, with the proceeds, bought uniforms for the crews. When Garibaldi felt in need of music or civilised conversation, he called at the estancias of Doña Anna or Doña Antonia, the sisters of Bento Gonçales.

Most of the estancias were deserted because of the war; and although they still contained an abundance of house shelter and animals of all sorts, beef on the hoof and remounts in any desired quantity, as well as sweet potatoes, wheat and oranges, there were no women about, a lack which the estancias of Doña Anna and Doña Antonia supplied. These had accommodated themselves to a state of warfare. The first, at Arroyo Grande, was hidden from the water by a little wood, and the second by a thick grove of orange trees: and whenever the signal was given that the men might go in one direction or the other there was great joy. The men were a mixed lot from half the nations in the world and had no excess of continence or natural virtue. In the back premises of the estancias they found love to their liking: and Garibaldi himself enjoyed the privileges of the front door and the company of ladies, for which he had the same liking as a traveller may have for the solace of a pleasant arbour in the heat of the sun or for the warmth of an inn fire on a winter night. He considered women with a vague gratitude, finding that they increased in him that feeling of happiness engendered in him when he contemplated the created world and found in it a flowering of beauty in excess of the strict needs of man. In this respect he was never free from a feeling of wonder, so permanent that it constituted a kind of religion, a possible pantheism defining itself slowly underneath the lessons of the Signora Rosa. He was never quite sure why he enjoyed these visits so enormously or remembered them so well; perhaps it was because he was twenty-six, perhaps he was beginning to understand life in South America as it required to be understood, a settler's life, maybe, and a rough one; but with a tertulia at the centre of it for conversation and music; or perhaps his peculiar needs found an intimate satisfaction, a temporary and blissful solution. In no other country could one spend the morning chasing enemy craft on one or other of the five fingers of the lagoon of Rio Grande, the afternoon whooping after a herd of bullocks or breaking in a mare for the following week's riding, and the evening looking into the dark eyes of a woman who had been longing for many days for company and wished from her heart to make the visit so pleasant that even a gaucho crossed with a corsair would be certain to remember it. Doña Anna was no longer young but she was lively. She made a frame for the picture. And in the centre of the picture were three young girls, daughters of Doctor

Paolo Ferreira of Pelotas, each of them seemingly more beautiful than the other two when one happened to be with that one. In Garibaldi's eyes the most adorable of the three dark Graces was called Manoela; she was engaged to a son of Bento Gonçales, and this fact brought his affectior for her into line with the lost causes he favoured. He loved Manoela irreparably and respectfully and prayed for those sudden squalls, common on the Camaquam, that drove the ships off the water towards the estancias.

News came that Colonel Juan Pietro de Abrecu, the most cunning soldier on the Imperialist side, was prowling within two or three leagues of the estancia of La Barra with the intention of catching the pirate whose exploits were making navigation on the Camaquam so uncertain. He was said to have about seventy horsemen and eighty infantry, most of them Germans or Austrians; for it was noticeable that Germans and Austrians seemed to obey some natural instinct that made them the servants of despotism whereas Poles, Irish, English and true-blue Americans (like John Griggs) always found themselves allocated by the Almighty to defend the forlorn hopes of the world. Garibaldi reckoned that his own sixty men would be more than enough to deal with the emergency. But the notorious colonel charged the estancia one afternoon when he had just had his midday meal and was sipping maté in front of the curing-shed in which the meat was salted. Of all the ducks (as the amphibious sailors of the Rio Grande navy liked to call themselves) there remained only the cook who was skimming broth in a cauldron in the yard. The others were on the beach working or fishing in quiet corners.

The guns were ready loaded on a rack in the shed. The cook reloaded while Garibaldi, having banged and bolted the door, let off six guns in rapid succession into the solid bulk of the enemy, getting a man every time, because it was impossible to miss. The colonel drew off to a hundred paces and volleyed at the shed, thinking apparently that there were sixty men in it. About thirteen of Garibaldi's followers, hearing the firing, rushed up from the beach and took part in the defence, hacking loopholes with their bayonets in the walls of the shed. The colonel's men hopelessly outnumbered Garibaldi's, but they were in the open and Garibaldi's under cover. It was about three in the afternoon that a shot smashed the colonel's arm; whereupon he collected his wounded and withdrew, leaving fifteen dead. As a fight it was one of the hottest in which Garibaldi had up to then engaged. Three of his men were wounded beyond recovery; and, as there was no doctor within miles, they elected to be finished off by their best friends, who performed the last office with a musket or pistol. Sad, tired, bloody and triumphant, the survivors dragged across to Doña Antonia's estancia.[1]

The occasion was celebrated by a fête. And Garibaldi learned that Manoela had gone white when she heard of his peril.

The Lagoon dos Patos, or lagoon of the ducks, in which Garibaldi's little fleet conducted its operations was shaped like a sausage; it lay squeezed between the hinterland of the Rio Grande pampas and a fork of land that severed it from the Atlantic, forming a very convenient field of manœuvre for the shallow-draught vessels that Garibaldi had designed to skid about its surface. At the end of a long chase they would run aground on a sandbank, the crew jumped into the water, hoisted their ship on their shoulders and staggered over the sandbank out of reach of the enemy's guns. The lagoon, however, had one disadvantage; it was landlocked or nearly so. At its southerly extremity it terminated in a narrow neck of water leading into the Atlantic. Here the Imperialists took the pleasures of the town of Rio Grande do Sul, which sat on the channel like a cork in a bottle, and waited until Garibaldi would attempt to make the open sea. He would not have done so, being well pleased to be near the estancias, but for an order from General Canabarra, who said that Garibaldi ought to

[1] See Appendix B for Garibaldi's official report of this action. It took place on April 17, 1839.

be off the coast of Santa Catharina 'making a demonstration', while he came down on the province of that name from the mountains. The nature of the demonstration to be made by a couple of ships on a coast-line of a thousand miles was problematical; but Garibaldi was fascinated by the absurdity of Canabarra's proposal. It was impossible, and for that reason it interested him; and, on examination, it proved, like most undertakings described as impossible, only very difficult. He was surprised how easy it was to forget Manoela when he thought of it. Her face, and the earthly paradise of which she was the centre, faded; and in their place he saw the vision of a fresh adventure.

They slipped quietly away from the neighbourhood of the estancias and cast anchor at the northern end of the lagoon. Garibaldi's plan was to treat the fifty-four miles of land separating the northern end of the lagoon from Lake Tramandaï (which connected with the sea) as a sandbank. They were to pick up their ships, carry them fifty-four miles and topple them into the ravine that led into the lake; in this way they would, God willing, emerge into the Atlantic by the shallow head of water through which Lake Tramandaï spilled into the sea. In practice the picking up required thought. A clever shipwright named Abreu was engaged to make eight enormous wheels. On these was built a superstructure strong enough to take any weight. The waggons were then dragged to the ravine, the *Rio Pardo* and the *Seival* heaved on the waggons and a team of two oxen began to take the strain. The waggons trembled and the navy was trundled off 'just like a bale of ordinary goods'. Under the amazed eyes of the inhabitants the cortège proceeded to the lake, where the ships swam off the waggons into the water. Three days after the arrival they were ready for the sea. They cleared the rough shallows by eight in the evening, and were standing out to sea, the *Rio Pardo* somewhat top-heavy and overloaded, with a twelve-pounder aft and a great number of heavy chests, as well as a more than adequate crew of thirty, commanded by Garibaldi. John Griggs, the American, followed on the *Seival*. At three o'clock in the following afternoon, when Garibaldi was at the top of the foremast looking out, a breaker caught the *Rio Pardo* and sent her right over. He was hurled a clean thirty feet into the sea, and from there saw his ship with her masts slopping in the water, while the waves washed over the deck. But for the masts she would have sunk like a stone. Seeing Luigi Carniglia, a compatriot, clinging to the poop and unable to make any attempt to swim because of his heavy greatcoat, he swam to him and was slitting the collar of it with a jack-knife when a tremendous breaker smashed the *Rio Pardo* to pieces and threw them all back into the sea. Garibaldi swam round and round in the hope of helping some of the crew ashore. He could hear cries in the gathering darkness, and once caught sight of another compatriot, Edoardo Mutru, clinging to a fragment of the hatch. When the survivors collected about him on the shore near the mouth of the Asonugua, sixteen of the thirty were missing, and among the sixteen every man of the six Italians who had accompanied him. And among those who came safely ashore were youngsters who had lately been helped over a ten-foot stream. The drowned Italians could all swim like fish.[1]

Garibaldi sat down on the beach and held his head between his hands. He found tears on his fingers; for he loved his countrymen, and his friendship with Mutru went back to 1834, when the same court-martial had sentenced them both to death. A chattering voice moaned: We are cold! His own hands were numb, but he seized the nearest man and, pulling him to his feet, started to run.

About four miles inland, on the right bank of the Asonugua, they came to an estancia, where they were warmed and fed; and within a few days of the disaster the survivors rode on borrowed horses into the townlet of Santa Catharina on the lagoon of the same name and took possession. They found a small but useful fleet of three ships; while,

[1] *Memorie*, p. 69. Dumas, p. 80 ff.

to their delight, a consignment of munitions arrived a few days later escorted by a body of soldiers. The soldiers were Imperialists and had been sent to hold Santa Catharina: but they made off hurriedly when they found the town occupied and left the munitions behind. General Canabarra had got to Giuliana, the most important town on the lagoon of Santa Catharina, where he proclaimed the republic and nominated as its first president a patriarchal priest who smilingly accepted the honour. Canabarra was a rough diamond, inclined to metaphor and with some inkling of classical mythology. He announced to a deputation of notables that the republic would rise like a hydra from the waters of the lagoon and devour the old empire.

In a detached and melancholy frame of mind Garibaldi was standing on the deck of the *Itaparika*, one of the captured schooners, and scanning the coast through a telescope; for it was a habit of his when he was on ship to look at the land (and when no land was there, to look down into the water or far away over the sea), as it was also his habit to look from the land out to sea; and when he did so, he did not like to be disturbed. There was a remote expression in his eye, an expression which could not be said to be restless, but which those who knew him interpreted to mean that some thought was turning about in him and would presently be released in the form of action. Since the drowning of the Italians he had been very silent. Now suddenly, after gazing intently at the shoulder of land called La Barra, he jumped into a boat and rowed ashore. He was proceeding, it seemed, towards an estancia visible on the promontory. A fluttering of white might indicate that some women or girls were working in front of the estancia. He went straight for the promontory and strode up the beach to the door. Inside (as he himself records) there was a dark-haired young woman with large almond-shaped eyes. Her mouth was generous and made to snap. She had a head of the same shape as Manoela's, and she looked as if she belonged to the same race; for she had the same kind of beauty, a beauty bringing to him so imminent a remembrance that he walked up to her like a man seeing something he thought to have left behind. 'Maiden', he said, 'thou shalt be mine.'[1] He had not enough knowledge of Portuguese to make a long speech; and, moreover, since he had left Manoela he had looked closely at death and was aware of urgency. An Indian soothsayer had predicted that she would love a fair man, who would come from over the seas, and that she would marry him and be happy, endure great hardship and battle by his side and die a queen. She told him that her name was Anita.

They made a good pair. He was built like a Scandinavian pirate, broad across the shoulders and not over tall. He was a heavy-boned man at thirty-six, with nothing quick or excitable about his movements. His arms and legs moved with a slow rhythm, and he had a sway in walking that betokened the sailor. He looked sometimes like a lion and sometimes like the pictures of Jesus Christ. There was a curious contrast between the sweetness of his eyes and the structure of his face, at which no man could look attentively and fail to see how the set of his cheekbones and the slope of his temples recalled some great animal of prey. His nose declared good intentions. It ran impartially down the middle of his face, a feature so perfect in its straightness that it might have belonged to a statue. His nose, and the forehead which took on an academical spread above the eyebrows, distinguished him from the gauchos of the pampas and showed him under his tan as a man of Europe. The fact that he had some vanity would scarcely have struck a casual observer. He did not stop to look much at himself; but he imagined himself a good deal and enjoyed, and was tormented by, a mystical persuasion. His conception of himself, as of life, was romantic; he lived poised in a dream in which adventure served the purpose of saintliness. Withal the connexion between these two appeared to him natural; and, if he had formulated the matter in an axiom (which he was not likely to do) he would

---

[1] 'La salutai finalmente, e le dissi: "tu devi esser mia".' *Memorie*, p. 78. The version in Dumas is not quite the same.

have said that all courageous men are good or that courage is the beginning of holiness. As a romantic he took to the sombrero, which he now wore constantly; and the saint in him experienced pleasure in combing his silken blond hair so that it fell 'Nazarene fashion' (*alla nazarena*) on his nape. He had a peculiarity worth noting. When he was angry the blue of his eye turned the colour of ink, like a sea with a cloud over it. That was the danger signal.[1]

The Brazilian poet Araujo Figueiredo cites the report of an old inhabitant of Laguna who said that Anita (as Garibaldi writes her name) or Annita (as the South Americans prefer it) was tall, fat, and had longish and prominent breasts. The same inhabitant declared that her father was Bento Ribeiro, a native of San Paolo, and her mother Maria Bento Ribeiro e Antunes, of Tubarâo. According to the same authority Anita was already married to Manuel José Duarte, a fisherman of La Barra, a piece of information which has recently been confirmed by the researches of a granddaughter of Garibaldi. It is now established beyond question that Anita, at the time of her meeting with Garibaldi, had already been for four years the wife of Manuel Duarte de Aguiar. The date of her marriage with the latter is given as 1835; and it is known that she joined Garibaldi on the *Rio Pardo* some time between August and October 1839, without fee or ceremony. The predictions of the soothsayer weighed more heavily with her than the admonitions of the Church. She was smiling and youthful, Garibaldi's granddaughter was told in Laguna; and, on the occasion of her marriage with Manuel Duarte her shoe had fallen off her foot as she came out of church. This incident, taken in conjunction with the words of the soothsayer, convinced her of the nature of her true duty.[2]

[1] Cf. Bartolomeo Mitre. *Ricordi dell' assedio di Montevideo*. (Italian translation from the Spanish.) Cit. Curàtulo, *Anita Garibaldi*, p. 76 ff. Cf. also Appendix B.

[2] 'Who was Anita? Of the family of Antunes on her mother's side, Ribeiro da Silva on her father's;—of direct Portuguese descent. . . . In a group of small houses in the part of the town which is called Morrinhos, from the name of a small mountain near by, and situated on the bank of the river, Anita spent

'I had come upon a forbidden treasure, but treasure of great value! If any fault had been committed, the fault was mine alone. And fault there was! ... Yes! ... two hearts were united with an immense love, and the life of an innocent one was broken.'[1]

Thus Garibaldi in his memoirs. Long before scholars knew of the existence of Manuel Duarte, Garibaldi wrote the confession of his guilt and left the commentators to make what they could of it. He wanted Anita for himself and, with a pang of remorse drowned in his 'immense love', enjoyed the dark woman on the *Rio Pardo*.[2]

VI

THE part of the soothsayer's prediction which concerned battle and hardship was soon verified. Garibaldi put into the friendly port of Imbituba and was there executing repairs when three Imperialist ships appeared in the bay, where they tacked methodically back and fore and poured shot into the defenceless *Rio Pardo*. Anita refused to go ashore. She only dropped her smoking carbine once in order to take up a sabre with which she disappeared below

the years of her childhood. Afterwards married to a young man of the neighbouring town of Laguna, she set up house with her husband on the Morro de la Barra.

'The anchoring of the republican ship almost underneath her windows and the presence of the Rio Grande sailors had brought an ususual note into her monotonous life. The appearance of the young Italian, already notable through his personality and reputation, in the company of her husband and on the threshold of her house, changed suddenly the aspect and the orientation of her life. . . . In Laguna everyone talks about her. Her smiling youthfulness is remembered, and her virile spirit; also her first marriage and the incident of the shoe that fell from her foot as she went out of the church.' Cf. *Garibaldi en America*, by Anita Garibaldi, Buenos Ayres, 1930, and the same author's *Anita Garibaldi*, Buenos Ayres, 1931. Some interesting new facts will be found also in Gino Doria's preface to the 1932 edition of Bandi's *Anita Garibaldi*.

[1] The text of the statement varies, but it is given as follows in the latest (official) version of the *Memorie* (1932). 'Io avevo incontrato un proibito tesoro, ma pure un tesoro di gran prezzo!!! Se vi fu colpa, io l'ebbi intiera! E . . . vi fu colpa! Si! . . . si rannodavano due cuori con amore immenso, e s'infrangeva l'esistenza d'un innocente!' (p. 79).

[2] The *Itaparika* was renamed *Rio Pardo*, after the lost ship.

and reappeared, driving on the point of it three sailors who had lost stomach for warfare. When he had seen her sweating, bloody and dishevelled, Garibaldi realised that she did not resemble Manoela. But he did not love her less. She came to him after her day's killing, panting like a good hound, loving and jealous and ready to snap if he did not caress her.

But the luck had turned. The inhabitants of Santa Catharina had given thought to the metaphor of the hydra and awaited its issue from the lake with trepidation: but, instead, Canabarra was driven down from the mountains and in danger of falling into the lake himself. Garibaldi arrived in time to see his discomfited army debouching from the hills with the Imperialists hot behind them; and as the republican ships stood by to cover the passage across the neck of water, twenty Imperialist vessels suddenly appeared and battered them with grape-shot. John Griggs the American, as fine a sailor as ever sailed a ship, was cut in two by case-shot on board the *Cassapara*. Garibaldi did not find him till the end of the day, when the order was given to fire the flotilla and make for land. He carried out this order on the *Rio Pardo* and boarded the *Cassapara* to put a match to her, when he saw the trunk of John Griggs bolt upright on the deck, squarely facing the enemy. His face was grimy with battle and he was stone dead. In the midst of the carnage Anita made twenty journeys in an open boat, standing up while the oarsmen crouched as low as they could over their oars. She brought the remaining munitions ashore.

This defeat was followed by others. And Garibaldi found himself wandering on land with forty men. The rest of the army had gone home, partly because, being republican and vowed to the principles of liberty and equality, it was seasonal and tended to disperse at harvest time; and partly because defeat acted on it like a blight on potatoes. It was not very long before Bento Gonçales and his secretary were on their way to Rio Janeiro, where they were once again confined to the fortress of Santa Cruz. At the battle of Coritybanos (after a successful action at Vittoria in the mountains), Anita, who was pregnant, was captured and taken to the tent of the enemy commander, whom she so much astonished by fluent abuse that he let her go. She rode through the forest to Vaccaria, and at San Simón, an estancia at the north end of the Lagoon dos Patos, she gave birth to a boy.[1] In the course of her ride she had fallen from her horse and the child bore a scar from it on the side of his head. They called him Menotti; and when they rode together Garibaldi tied his son in a bundle on his back. The father was perfectly happy, asking for nothing better than to continue as the unpaid servant of a theoretical republic; he had a shirt to his back, a carbine, a horse between his knees and the black-haired, faithful woman at his side. But, for her sake and for the child's, Garibaldi decided that he must make a move to the city, and obtained the permission of the late president to disband himself and attend to his private affairs.

He rounded up nine hundred head of cattle, his pay for six years of war, and started for Montevideo. By the time he had driven them across the Rio Negro and counted them, that number was reduced to five hundred, of which half were foundered and likely to die on the way. The alternative was to kill; but he could not cut up and salt five hundred head himself, and the capataz whom he was forced to employ as assistant understood his business so well that Garibaldi was left to pursue his journey with a meagre sum of one hundred crowns, out of which he had to provide house-room, kitchen utensils, odds and ends of furniture and clothes for Anita and the children. All being provided, he had no money left; once again he had to earn his living, and in a city which for the time being was quite peaceful and seemed to contain nothing but lawyers and pompous little storekeepers swaggering about in black breeches. He had no particular affection for any kind of city; and his affection for Montevideo was seriously impaired when he began to hawk Italian paste and Rouen textiles from shop

[1] September 16, 1840.

to shop. As a commercial traveller he had only one gift. He could talk. But his merchandise did not inspire him. He frequented mostly the shops of his Italian compatriots and talked about the coming revolution in Italy. Mazzini, he heard, was in London and had published in his newspaper, *L'Apostolato*, a glowing account of Garibaldi's exploits in South America.[1] The days passed. And at the end of them Garibaldi returned to his lodging and dandled Menotti, the son born to them in the mountains of Rio Grande.[2] Anita, in her new surroundings, discovering the limitations of the magical power of her husband, developed a shrewish tongue, of which, although he did not confess it, the hero, especially when he had had a bad day, went in some fear. But Anita had not changed. She was as generous and shrill as ever, and watched her husband with the same dog-like eye. He was very handsome now; while such beauty as she had had was changed to a relative handsomeness, the moral virtues shining through a robust and coarsened frame. She did not spare him her suspicions. But they were needless. He was thinking of other things.

Unlike many Italians in Montevideo, he had no thought of settling in South America. He was just as he had come, six years before; no richer and no poorer. And so firm and natural was his love of Italy that it seemed no more remote to him now that he had a wife and children than when he stood, a young bachelor, on the Piazza di Sarzana. Perhaps the secret knowledge of her own unimportance, and of the relative unimportance of the children she had given to Garibaldi, was a more powerful cause of jealousy than any sign that he preferred other women. Anita, from her own experience, knew that no woman would ever get him; and she could see that, though women admired him, he did not respond. He was very calm and in no way distressed at being poor. When a certain vivacity became noticeable, she thought perhaps he had read the Italian newspapers.

[1] Jessie White Mario, *op. cit.* p. 43.

[2] Rosita, a daughter, was born on November 30, 1843. A second girl, Teresa, was born on Feb. 22, 1845. On Feb. 24, 1847, a son, Ricciotti, was added to the family. (Curàtulo, *Anita Garibaldi*, p. 89.)

It generally was so. But there was little in them. With his aptitude for making the most of events, however, he was taking an interest in the refugees who were dumping their bundles in Montevideo and the territory of the Oriental Republic. They came from Buenos Ayres, where the republic had been taken over by a tyrant named Rosas, who, perceiving the flaw of democracy, had placed himself between the opposing parties and finally driven them out. Rosas ruled by terror, gunning his opponents in daily batches and collecting their corpses from the gutters each morning. He was experiencing the exhilaration of power; and he ordered the president of the Oriental Republic, Oribe, to drive out all refugees who came from the territory of Buenos Ayres. Oribe attempted to obey, but was himself driven out by the indignant citizens of Montevideo, and replaced by Rivera. After which events, to Garibaldi's delight, the city of Montevideo had the prospect of being at war, whether it liked it or not, with the greatest tyrant in South America. The Montevideans were flattered. They heard without excitement that their expelled president was taking the trouble to advance on the city with an army; and the shrewd ones thought that, according to the law of averages in the matter of presidential revolutions, a few firearms would be let off in the square and business in wine and small goods would be exceptionally brisk for perhaps a week. In any case they did not propose to do their own fighting. They were the promoters. The fighting, if there was any, would have to be done by such poor chacareros as Rivera could lay hands on.

As was inevitable, Garibaldi was approached. It was proposed that, in view of his late exploits, he should take charge of some part of Montevideo's navy. He had difficulty in carrying his point with Anita. But in the end it was settled that they would go to church and get married in Christian fashion, so that, if the worst came to the worst, she would be a respectable widow. After that he could do as he liked. There was now no obstacle to their marriage, for Manuel Duarte, they heard, was dead.

The war was on. And the first step taken on the side of the Montevideans was to scrap their small fleet of ships on the ground that they were too costly to keep up. It seemed to Garibaldi an odd way to prepare to meet an enemy. The Montevideans had heard of battles at sea, but evidently did not believe in them; to them, as to most South Americans, war meant the meeting of armies on land. Garibaldi's own orders were mysterious. He was given three ships saved from the salvage heap, the *Constitución*, which was to be his own ship, the *Procida* and the brigantine *Pereira*. With this flotilla of three he was instructed to sail, not against Admiral Brown, the commander of the Buenos Ayres navy, but up the Paraná river to Corrientes, a province that had been on the point of declaring for the Oriental Republic for a long time and needed encouragement. It was a trip of six hundred miles; and either the suggestion that it should be made came from a fool or there was something (some by-product of the South American mind) behind it. To run three ships for any part of that immense distance on a river held on both sides by the enemy was asking for trouble; and asking for it for nothing. It might even be that Garibaldi was not intended to come back alive, and that these arrangements were made to get him killed at the first opportunity. The order came from Vidal, who had succeeded Rivera as president. He was the man responsible for the breaking up of the fleet. Perhaps Vidal had been paving the way for a capitulation to Rosas when the popular clamour thrust the blond pirate upon him; if he was resolved to get rid of Garibaldi at the first opportunity, he was taking the right way. These considerations did not escape Garibaldi; nor the corollary (also included in the South American scheme of calculation), that if he declined the undertaking it would be said he was afraid. But he decided he would go. Before he went he took Anita to a Roman Catholic church. He was not sure he was a Roman Catholic; and Anita's religion was also vague. But a Roman Catholic church was the only place where a ceremony of marriage was legal.

He equipped himself with two witnesses. But having no money he took none; and he was astonished when, as a preliminary to the ceremony, the vicar of the church of San Francisco held out a white palm and asked for his fee. No fee, no marriage, he explained; for the hard times pressed also on the Church, which seized such opportunities as it could to find the coin which, since the war, had become so scarce in Montevideo. Of late, the old system of barter which had prevailed before English and Dutch merchants introduced the use of money, had come back again, and it was common to hear women and girls in the streets shouting that they would exchange sausages for bread, salt for flour, beef for white linen or (more often) white linen for beef. The vicar was firm; and Anita told Garibaldi he must give the man of God his watch, a silver one made for a large pocket, and somewhat damaged by sea-water. It was his one possession, apart from the clothes he stood in and Anita's kitchen utensils, which would not have been acceptable. He had a seaman's respect for an instrument that combined so neatly science and beauty, as well as some affection for it as his one worldly possession. But he gave it up and the ceremony proceeded. Anita returned to their lodging with her marriage-lines, specifying that she, Doña Ana Maria de Jesus, legitimate daughter of Don Benito Riveiro de Silva and Doña Maria Antonia de Jesus, was now the legitimate wife of Don José Garibaldi, a natural of Italy. The date on the certificate was March 26, 1842.[1]

---

[1] A copy of this marriage certificate is reproduced in Jessie Mario White, *op. cit.* p. 46 f. It is as follows: 'On March 26, 1842, Don Zenon Aspiazu, curate of this parish of San Francisco de Asis in Montevideo, authorized the ecclesiastical marriage verbally contracted between Don José Garibaldi, native of Italy, legitimate son of Don Domingo Garibaldi and Doña Rosa Raimundi, with Doña Ana Maria de Jesus, native of Laguna in Brazil, legitimate daughter of Don Benito Riveiro de Silva and of Doña Maria Antonia de Jesus, the bride and bridegroom both present. The superintendent and vicar-general, having fulfilled all the conditions prescribed by law, allowed the second and third proclamations of the banns to be dispensed with. The couple did not receive the nuptial benediction, because the marriage took place during the season (*i.e.* Lent), when the Church does not accord it.

'The witnesses were Don Paolo Semedei and Doña Feliciana Garcia Villagran.

'This document I for truth's sake sign, Lorenzo A. Fernandez.'

He prepared his ships quietly and dropped down the estuary at the beginning of July.

VII

AT Martin Garzia there is an island of that name well in the neck of the estuary at a point where the navigable channel is narrowed by long sandbanks. The flotilla had to pass right under the guns of the fort. An Italian officer, Pocarobba, had his head knocked off by a cannon-ball, and eight or ten men were wounded. It was not a bright start.

All around Martin Garzia are shallows; and presently, before they had gone another three miles, Garibaldi's ship, the *Constitución*, which was the biggest of the three, ran aground. There was nothing for it but to put the heavy guns on the *Procida*: and this task was being finished when round the corner of the island came seven ships of war, the squadron of Admiral Brown. As if this interesting development had been advertised in advance, the shores were lined with spectators who cheered to the echo. Of Garibaldi's fleet (if it can be dignified by such a name), two ships could not fire, the *Constitución* because her guns were on the *Procida*, and the *Procida* because her own guns were masked by the lumber on her deck. The *Pereira* had come alongside, and her crew had been helping to shift the guns from the *Constitución*. They had to get back in a hurry and man their guns. Garibaldi had only one advantage: the enemy ships were big and could not come inshore. He hugged the island and ordered the *Procida* to clear a space for firing.

Admiral Brown had been fighting in these waters for many years, ever since he had come out from England as a young man. He was grey-haired, worn in the ways of his Argentine employers but still young enough to revel in a fight; and he was bearing down now, ready to let off his first broadside, when the prow of his flagship shivered gently and he found himself stationary, fast on a sandbank.

Like Garibaldi, he could do only one thing, transfer his guns. While he was doing so and the remaining ships of his squadron were standing by to help, the *Constitución* lifted her nose and came afloat. In a short time Garibaldi had reshipped his guns and was ready to fight or run: but it was not much use running with such an enemy behind, so he did not attempt it. The enemy flagship refloated shortly after the *Constitución*, and the ships of both fleets were manœuvring for position when the haze which had been lurking in the swamps rose after the sundown and covered the estuary. A thick mist hid the shore, where the disappointed spectators broke up disconsolately and went home. There was a chance to run and Garibaldi took it. His three small vessels passed through the squadron of Admiral Brown and slipped off up the Paraná. At dawn Admiral Brown made all sail after him, and, coming to the fork of the estuary, took to the right up the Uruguay: the Paraná was a difficult stream to navigate, and he was quite sure Garibaldi would avoid it.

However, at San Nicola, Garibaldi found an unwilling pilot and stood over him with drawn sabre while he directed a course. As far as Boyada they had a peaceful journey and even picked up a few small craft as prizes: but Boyada was a garrisoned town. Scarcely had Garibaldi come within sight when a rapid fire saluted him. Luckily he had the wind well behind and could crowd on sail and keep as far as possible out of range until he got away. At Las Conchas he sent a party ashore to obtain provisions and had taken them safely aboard and weighed anchor before the Boyada garrison got wind of his halt. They sent a few shots after him and that was all. Worse was waiting for him a little higher up, where the river narrowed still further and twisted between sandbanks like a lazy snake, uncoiling its rings below Cerrito, where a thumping cannonade of forty guns tore up the water beside his ships. He answered gun for gun as near as he could. And, courage being generally the last thing that the troops of the Argentine Federation possessed, he scared them sufficiently to get past. A few traders had come up under his bows on the far side to shelter from the fire: they were added to the small flotilla of prizes and accompanied Garibaldi upstream. But not far. It soon became plain that even his light ships would never make Corrientes. At Nueva Cava the shallows extended right across the channel, and only a dribble of water flowed round the sandbanks. He could either make for the shore or fight it out there. Brown, he knew, could not be far behind. Garibaldi decided he would stay and see it through; and, commending his soul to his patron saint, the great god Chance, he ran out the small ships on both sides so that they formed a gangway to the land. On this gangway he hoisted his guns and abided the coming of Brown. The *Constitución* lay in midstream in the deeper water, anchored against the heavy current that swept down the channel. The *Pereira* took up her position between the *Constitución* and the *Procida*. Garibaldi hoped that by these dispositions he would be master of the left bank of the river and by means of his gangway be able to send men ashore to harass the enemy's flank.

It was the evening of August 14, 1842, when Brown hove in sight and, seeing what was in front of him, cast anchor out of gunshot. Garibaldi made no move. The night passed peacefully. But with the first rays of the morning sun the guns opened on both sides and battered at the opposing targets the whole day long, until darkness fell again. The odds were seven to three on the wrong side: and at night when Garibaldi looked over his ships he found that the *Procida* had an enormous gash, and was settling gradually in the water. Her companion ships were scarcely in better case. The commander of the *Pereira* was killed. Still, Garibaldi thought he might do a little more on the morrow. They spent the night breaking up anchor chains to make shot, pumping water to keep themselves afloat, and biting old cartridge ends to make new. They had completely run out of ammunition. Nor was this the most bitter blow. That came from an unexpected quarter. About midday on the 16th a squadron of light boats appeared on the river from the direction of Corrientes. They were, in fact, the Corrientes fleet come to the rescue of Garibaldi. But no sooner had their commander Villegas seen that a fight was going on than he turned about and made off with all speed. *Gradasso se mai ne fu*, said Garibaldi, spitting in the water. It was a weary dawn. The decks were covered with wounded: and those who were not hit lay dog-tired, like men who would never rise again. Garibaldi told the bugler to sound the reveille. The survivors struggled to their feet and listened while he talked softly to them, like a father.

The eighteen cannons of the *Constitución* were for the most part disabled and the remainder spat bits of anchor chain viciously but without much effect. Brown saw he could deploy and he did so, opening out a murderous fire on the broken wrecks before him. Under this fire Garibaldi had the wounded transported to land by the gangway, along with the remaining stores and rifles. When this was done he set a charge of powder in the hulks that were all that was left of his little navy, ordered his men ashore, put a match to the fuses himself, and as the splinters were blasted into the air, waded, swam, and staggered to land.

The plan to destroy Garibaldi (if such a plan existed and he had not suffered merely from the civilian omniscience common in republics) almost succeeded. But not quite. It was a full month later when he reappeared in Montevideo. He had lost his little navy. But he had picked up an army; for, passing in the vicinity of Arroyo Grande just after the Orientals had been badly defeated, he gathered the stragglers together and marched them back to Montevideo.

Having achieved the victory of Arroyo Grande, Oribe encamped at Cerrito, outside Montevideo, and waited for his friends inside the walls to open the gates. In the normal process of a South American presidential war this event should have logically followed the victory. But the gates were not opened. Instead Vidal was deposed and replaced by Joaquin Souarez, who was reputed to be ready to face a siege. An engineer was set to fortify the walls; and Garibaldi put up a proclamation in Italian inviting his fellow-countrymen who valued their honour and their skins to form a legion of defence. The French inhabitants did not wish to see the defence of the city conducted by Italians, so they also formed a legion. And the Spanish inhabitants, remembering that they, after all, were the original colonists of the country, enlisted a doubtful contingent of adventurers to carry the Spanish flag. The zeal required for the defence poured in a pure stream from the Italian colony, inspired by the fiery spirit of Garibaldi; and, for the time being, this zeal penetrated the life of the city and had astonishing results. Suddenly, the financial corruption which was as natural to the city as the stones out of which it was built, came to an end. Anzani, another Italian exile and a friend of Garibaldi's, had taken control of the administration and swiftly brought malpractices to an end. Anzani was well informed and had less trust in human nature than Garibaldi; he was not astonished to learn that there was as much irritation as gratitude in Montevideo in the hearts of those who saw their time-honoured methods of settling disputes interfered with in arbitrary fashion. Garibaldi was naturally heroic. But this was not the case of the citizens of Montevideo; they enjoyed the convivial concomitants of war and had an artistic appreciation of Garibaldi's speeches, but in the main they considered that his heroism was in the nature of a nuisance. A proposal which Oribe put forward for the silent assassination of Garibaldi and Anzani received some support. But Anzani heard of it and the project came to nothing.

The Montevideans, thanks to Garibaldi's activities, were in some embarrassment. For they alone had supplied no soldiers for the defence; indeed they saw themselves in the unpleasant position of being defended by foreign immigrants whom they hated and whom they accused of taking away overseas the wealth which belonged to them as South Americans. In this dilemma they remembered that there were in the city a large number of negro slaves;

for, although it had been one of the principles of the French Revolution that every man, whatever his colour, should be a free man; and although this principle had been adopted along with the others when South America began her crusade for freedom, the practice of slavery continued. Slavers, specially fitted for the cargo, sailed regularly from the ports of the eastern coast, laid in a cargo of blacks in Africa, and brought them to Rio or Montevideo or Buenos Ayres to be drafted to all parts of the continent. They were well treated in the cities, where they lived as domestics, and were probably much better off than in their native country; but up country in the estancias they would occasionally fall into the hands of cruel masters who flogged as a matter of course, and expressed their grave displeasure by special punishments such as castration and the rubbing of pepper in the vagina of female slaves. Reports of these abuses reached the Earl of Aberdeen, who dispatched two new steamships to catch the slavers and bring them to a so-called international court at Sierra Leone; and the Earl of Aberdeen was gratified, therefore, to receive, along with other South American papers, a copy of the new decree by which the Oriental Republic granted liberty to all slaves on its territory. The first article of the decree (dated December 12, 1842) announced that from the time of the promulgation of the resolution there would no longer be any slaves on the territory of the Oriental Republic. But the second article went on to say that the government of the republic would 'appoint' the able-bodied men who had been slaves to the service of arms for such time as it should consider necessary. And a third article said that those ex-slaves who were not able-bodied or were women, would stay in their situations 'as wards in the service of their masters'. In this way the shopkeepers of Montevideo acquired by one stroke a reputation for humanity and a corps of some five thousand able-bodied negro soldiers. They were amenable to discipline, had plenty spirit and enjoyed the holiday.

The Italian legion, under Garibaldi, performed many

deeds of heroism and held Oribe at bay; so that, in March 1843, the spirit of the defence being still unbroken, the Oriental general Pachecho held a review and publicly praised these soldiers and their leader. The following month the legion's flag was blessed, an extraordinary black flag in the centre of which smouldered a volcano. It represented Italy with a fire of revolution burning in her heart; for Garibaldi impressed on his soldiers that the cause of freedom was everywhere the same and that in South America they were being hardened for the battle which was still to be fought in their own country. None the less the result which the unromantic business men of Montevideo had foreseen had come about: Oribe could not enter Montevideo, but he sat with his army at Cerrito, cutting the city off from its supplies, while the Imperial fleet in the bay paralysed the shipping trade of the port. Garibaldi offered to end the siege by kidnapping Rosas (an offer which for some unexplained reason was declined); he also escorted many ships into harbour under the nose of the Imperial warships, and he made the Federalist troops run like rabbits before his bayonets. But he could not alter the fact that Montevideo was under blockade; at the end of 1843 this state of affairs still continued, and President Rosas, reviewing the recent circumstances, told the Gentlemen Representatives that 'never fading laurels' and 'deathless renown' had fallen to the lot of the Federalist arms, while the 'sanguinary Unitarians' had everywhere been trampled underfoot. The remainder of his speech was a series of thumping lies, and this was also: but it was a fact that he and Oribe had put a ring round Montevideo and awaited the outcome with tranquillity.

We are not concerned here with the history of this blockade nor with the negotiations which, some years later, brought it to an end. The reader may learn from the British State Papers that the condition of blockade affected the interests of our shipping; and the Earl of Aberdeen dispatched an envoy to treat with President Rosas, who, after maintaining for some time that he was not at war with

Montevideo at all (surely, he said, the representative of Her Britannic Majesty must be confounding him with General Oribe, an ex-president of the Oriental Republic who sought to regain power), agreed finally to desist from the blockade when it had been raised by British and French warships. Before the end of hostilities the tables were turned and the whole of the coastline of the Argentine Federation was declared by England and France to be under blockade. Released from the defence of the city, Garibaldi took the Italian legion out to look for the army of Oribe and defeated it in a great and memorable fight at the Salto San Antonio. His fame had reached Europe, and the French admiral Lainé, commander of one of the blockading fleets, paid a call to offer his congratulations on the victory. He found Garibaldi's house in the Calle del Portone and, having pushed the door open, fell over a chair. The house was in darkness. Presently the admiral heard Garibaldi's voice telling Anita to light up.

'How wilt thou that I should', screamed Anita, 'when there is not a penny to buy a candle?'

Lainé reported this state of affairs to the Oriental minister of war who sent a hundred patacons in a bag. Garibaldi kept enough to buy a pound of candles and distributed the rest among the widows of his soldiers. They were not disliked in Montevideo because, poor as they were, they paid for what they had. Their uniform was a red woollen shirt, with which went gaucho trousers and a broad-brimmed hat; an outfit which was in part the natural costume of a horseman and in part the outcome of a bargain between the Oriental government and the firm which supplied red shirts to the employees of the slaughterhouse at Ensenada, near Buenos Ayres. The blockade had left the firm with a heavy stock of red shirts and no prospect of getting rid of them until the end of the war; consequently they were available for the legion at a very cheap price. But the men took a pride in their conspicuous uniform, which, although it made them a target for enemy bullets, soon inspired a special terror in the soldiers of the

Argentine Federation. *El diavolo*, as Garibaldi was called, made frequent raids right up to Cerrito and drove off cattle under the enemy's fire; and, having accomplished a raid in the morning, he would embark picked troops at nightfall on a fast schooner and, sailing up the river under cover of dark, would suddenly fall on Sta. Lucia or Colonia. On his return to Montevideo an Italian band would play the legion to the plaza, where it would dismiss to billets.

Garibaldi had now learned all that South America had to teach him. He sat his horse 'like a centaur'. Captain Ingram, who was with the English squadron, noted this characteristic, as well as the strength of his frame. 'He wore his hair and beard long', writes Ingram. 'They were then of a dark brown colour, with a reddish tint in the latter. His countenance was remarkable for its serenity, and the lips pressed close together denoted a strong will, whilst his eyes were steadfast and piercing in their gaze. In stature he was of medium height, and was altogether the beau-ideal of a chief of irregular troops. His scarlet tunic fitted loosely to the body, and round its collar were tied the two ends of a gaudy handkerchief, which lay unfolded on the back of the uniform. His cavalry sword-belt confined the dress to the waist, and in his saddle-holsters were a pair of pistols. On his head was the same description of black felt hat and feather as worn by all his corps.'[1]

Garibaldi's joy in the victory was marred by the death of his elder daughter, Rosita. The news was brought to him at the Salto San Antonio in a laconic message from General Pachecho y Obes: 'Your daughter Rosita is dead', said the message: 'this you ought to know'. And soon after Anita begged to be allowed to come and join him. 'A man is proud of his work,' wrote Garibaldi; 'he would like it to be better than that of another. And woman, *poverina*, who suffers so much in the performance of her work, has she no right to think that she has given birth to a good and

[1] Winnington-Ingram, *Hearts of Oak*, p. 92 f. Bartolomeo Mitre, however, says Garibaldi himself did not wear the red shirt at this time.

beautiful being in the boy or girl she brings forth to the light? My poor Anita thought so, at any rate, and were I to recount all the qualities she found in our Rosita it would seem incredible—Rosita was the most beautiful, the sweetest of little girls. She died between four and five years old. Her intelligence was most precocious. She faded away in her mother's arms, as the light of the first-born of nature fades away in the infinite—gradually, gently, affectionately. She died without complaining, begging her mother not to grieve, telling her that they would meet again soon. A world of gracious things was in that child. Perhaps I shall pass for a visionary, but so sincere, so true, so bearing the impress of her spirit seemed to me the last words of the child to her mother, as my Anita told them to me when she arrived at Salto—where I summoned her, really fearing that her mind would give way—that I answered my broken-hearted wife, "Yes, yes, we shall see our Rosita again; the soul is immortal,—and this life of littlenesses is but an episode of immortality, a divine spark, part of the infinite flame that animates the universe".'[1]

It was shortly after this painful event that Garibaldi began to form definite plans for a return to Italy. He wished his remaining children to be near the Signora Rosa at Nice, where he felt no harm could come to them; and while he formed this project it brought to his mind the scheme which he had been discussing with the emissaries of Mazzini for so many years, a scheme which began to have some reality now that there existed in Montevideo a corps of trained Italians ready to fight on the soil of Italy. Not until 1847, however, was Garibaldi's mind made up; and then it was noticed by his friend Cuneo that his face, which of late had worn an expression of bitterness, now seemed like the face of a man looking forward to some great pleasantness. Garibaldi had heard of the accession of the new liberal Pope, Pius IX; and he saw at last, or thought he saw, how the salvation of Italy could be effected; by an alliance between this new Pope, the 'political Messiah', and

---
[1] Jessie White Mario, *op. cit.* p. 66 f.

the body of trained soldiers he had formed in South America. The Pope would proclaim with his spiritual authority the idea of freedom, and Garibaldi with his soldiers would carry it into effect. With the help of Anzani he wrote to the apostolic nuncio in Montevideo and set forth his offer. 'If His Holiness', said the letter, 'has now a use for hands that are accustomed to war, we need not say that we offer them to one who is doing so much for Church and country. We shall esteem ourselves fortunate if, with our companions on whose behalf we also speak, we may help in the redemptive work of Pius IX, and we shall not think it too dear a price to pay for the privilege with all our blood.' The letter was written on October 12, 1847; and the following month the Papal nuncio replied, saying he had dispatched it to Rome; 'If the ocean dividing the two hemispheres', said the nuncio, 'should prevent such magnanimous offers from being accepted, their merit cannot be diminished, nor the satisfaction of receiving them lessened. May all those enrolled under your orders remain ever worthy of the name that they have honoured, and of the blood which runs in their veins!'

From other sources Garibaldi heard that a rising led by himself would, at any rate, have some chance of popular support in Italy. Enthusiastic letters arrived in Montevideo saying that his name was in everyone's mouth and that a portrait of him 'à la gaucho' was carried in the breast pocket of half the young men of Piedmont. There were poems in his honour:

In ogni seno palpiti—Il cor di Garibaldi.

His right arm was famous, the arm that smote tyrants, the arm from which flashed the bright steel of deliverance, the weapon of vengeance and of joy. With *his* right arm let us fight, the young men were singing:

Col braccio pugnerem d'un Garibaldi.

Garibaldi put Anita and the children on a sailing ship bound for Genoa in December 1847; and he hoped to follow them almost immediately. But the Oriental Republic was not anxious to lose him and gently put obstacles in the way of his departure. At last, in the spring of 1848, they could hold him no longer. There was news from Italy that the revolution was ablaze everywhere, and Garibaldi feared that by the time he got there with his legion all would be over. With eighty-five men he embarked on the *Speranza* and set sail.[1] Seeing that his departure was inevitable, the Oriental Republic presented at the last moment two cannon and eight hundred muskets; but the equipment of the expedition was lamentable. Some of the legionaries had no clothes at all, having subscribed their last stitch for the purchase of the little brigantine which was to transport them. They kept below in rough weather and were to be seen, when it was fine, promenading the deck in a blanket.

Garibaldi was thoughtful. He sat a good deal on the *Speranza's* bowsprit, harpooning dolphins.

[1] April 15, 1848. Cf. Guerzoni, i. p. 205. The body of Rosita was disinterred from the Montevideo cemetery and brought on the *Speranza* in a lead coffin to Nice.

REFERENCES

Garibaldi's *Memorie* (1932 edition); also other editions of his memoirs, in particular Elpis Melena, *Denkwürdigkeiten* (Hamburg, 1861), and Dumas, *Mémoires de Garibaldi* (Paris, 1862). I have used also an English translation of Dumas, by R. S. Garnett, published by Benn, 1931. To these should be added Cuneo's short *Biografia di Giuseppe Garibaldi* (Genoa, no date), which is a primary source for the South American period.

The following contain useful additional information:

Guerzoni, *Garibaldi*, vol. i. (Florence, 1882); Jessie White Mario, *Supplement to the Autobiography of Giuseppe Garibaldi* (London, 1889); Bandi, *Anita Garibaldi*, containing a preface by Gino Doria (Florence, 1932); Winnington-Ingram, *Hearts of Oak* (London, 1889); and *State Papers* for the period 1843-1849.

In addition to the general histories of the South American republics, the travel books of the Robertson brothers give many interesting glimpses of the country; viz.

Robertson, J. P. and W. P., *Letters on Paraguay* (1838, 3 vols.); *Letters on South America* (1843, 3 vols.).

Cf. also

Sarmiento, *Life in the Argentine Republic*, New York, 1868 (American edition): Fletcher and Kidder, *Brazil and the Brazilians*, 9th edition, 1879 (London): Dawson. *South American Republics*, New York, 1904. Mulhall, *Rio Grande do Sul* London, 1873.

See Appendix B.

Trevelyan refers to the South American period in the opening chapters of *Garibaldi and the Defence of the Roman Republic*.

Ximenes, *Epistolario di Giuseppe Garibaldi*, is a collection of Garibaldi's letters, mostly gathered from such published sources as existed at the date of publication.

Also

Garibaldi, A., *Garibaldi in South America*, Buenos Ayres, 1931; and by the same author, *Anita Garibaldi*, Buenos Ayres, 1932.

Curàtulo, *Anita Garibaldi*, Milan, 1932.

II

VIII

IT WAS on June 2, 1846, that Pope Gregory XVI asked: 'Am I to appear before God without having taken the bread of life?', and on the evening of the same day his body lay embalmed on a bed fringed with gold in the chapel of Sextus IV. All his life he had loved the study of canon law, and towards the end of it, becoming suspicious and ill-tempered, he vowed a special hatred to radicals, railways and suspension bridges. Now, with his death, arose the question whether his successor would also hate these things.

On June 14 the cardinals heard mass at St. Peter's and listened to a sermon in which they were admonished to choose wisely this successor. The five cardinal bishops, thirty-two cardinal priests and seven cardinal deacons took oath to conform to the apostolical bulls concerning the matter in hand before they retired to the cells which had been prepared for them. The clock of the Quirinal struck eleven, a signal that all strangers must withdraw to allow the doors to be locked. They were closed inside and out with proper ceremony, while in all the churches of the city of Rome the collect *pro eligendo summo Pontifice* was recited at every mass. On the door of each cell were the armorial bearings of its distinguished occupant. The following morning the Masters of Ceremonies tapped on the doors, pronouncing the customary words, 'Ad Capellam, domini!' whereupon, robed in violet serge, the cardinals proceeded to the chapel and received communion before drawing lots to settle who should be the scrutators or counters of the votes. This was done by drawing from a bag in which were balls marked with the several names of all the members of the Conclave. The scrutators then took up their position in front of the little table before the high altar and began their duties.

In spite of the place and the character of the ceremony, the atmosphere was not religious; there were conservative cardinals and progressive cardinals, and their future, as well as that of the world, depended on the result of the election. Among the former was old Ludovico Micara, general of the Capuchins, whose face was like that of a dead man and whose eyes burned like coals. His carriage had been stopped as he went to the Conclave by a crowd of fervent supporters, and he had put out his head and said: 'With me for Pope you'll have bread in plenty—and the gallows!' Also, among the progressives, was the plump young Bishop of Imola, a prelate of fifty-four on whose carriage a white pigeon had perched as he drove towards Rome. Thirty years before he had been a nervous and romantic young man and an admirer of the first Napoleon. Petrucelli della Gattina records of him that he could then empty a bottle at a draught; he played billiards and tennis and spent long hours colouring the bowls of his pipes. At this time his costume was half civil, half military. He wore a grey frock coat with black cuffs and a collar, a red foraging cap, pantaloons with stripes down the seams, large shirt collars turned down over his shoulders and a red cravat flying in the wind. To these were added some final items of adornment, spurs, a flower in his buttonhole and always a cigar between his lips. Developing a tendency towards epilepsy, he had given up his military ambitions and entered the Church, where his promotion had been swift; he had family influence, a kindly disposition, good manners, an excellent pulpit voice; and, although his liberalism had not disappeared, it was not ebullient. It was known, however, that in private conversation he had confessed that he could not understand why gas, railway trains, suspension bridges and such like should be the enemies of theology. The case seemed to him to be better put by Gioberti, who, in his recent *Primato morale e civile degli Italiani*, declared that the Italians were the greatest people in the world. That being so, an intelligent Pope might orchestrate the clamouring voices of Italy and blend them into a harmony which, spreading with the authority of religion throughout the world, would begin a new era of peace and enlightenment.

The Vatican tailor had prepared as usual three sets of vestments, a large, a small and a medium: for, however the opinions of Popes might vary, their bodies were either large, small or medium. But the problem for the cardinals was whether their votes would bring to the Papal throne a safe Pope or a Pope *with ideas*. The Bishop of Imola was suspect: Austria had heard that he was progressive and sent a messenger to say that he must not be elected. But the messenger arrived too late. On June 15 there were two ballots, one in the morning and the other in the evening; at the first, fifteen votes went to Lambruschini, thirteen to the Bishop of Imola, and five to an outsider. In the evening there was some shuffling: Lambruschini had thirteen and the Bishop of Imola seventeen. At a third ballot on the 16th, the Bishop of Imola rose to twenty-seven votes and Lambruschini dropped to eleven. The conservative cardinals retired to their cells looking thoughtful; and when the 'Ad Capellam, domini!' brought them forth again a heavy gloom was visible on their faces. The scrutators for the evening were Vannicelli, Fieschi and the Bishop of Imola himself. He read out his own name time after time, speaking it in a faint voice that could scarcely be heard in the chapel. At the twenty-eighth repetition he said he could not go on: but his supporters told him to take his time and have no fear. He paused and began again. When he came to the thirty-fourth vote he fell forward in a faint.

The same night he wrote to his brothers to pray for him, saying he was Pope Pius IX; and at the foot of his letter he gave them, with some trembling, the apostolic benediction. There followed many ceremonies, of which the most splendid was the procession to the Vatican Church for the coronation. The Master of the Ceremonies, followed by the Swiss guards carrying their halberds, led the way; and in long and solemn sequence there came the procurators of the colleges, the procurators-general of the religious orders, the choristers and artists of the Papal chapel, the apostolical sub-deacon bearing the cross with the image of Christ turned towards the new Pope, the acolytes with the seven gilt chandeliers, the ushers of the Red Rod, the penitentiaries of St. Peter, the mitred abbots and Commanders of the Holy Ghost, the archbishop, patriarchs, deans, the Roman senators in their robes of gold, the Governor of Rome in white ermine, the secret chamberlains, the farrier major, the dean of the Sediarii and the Sediarii in red cimars carrying the Sedia beside which walked eight referendaries in lawn sleeves holding up the poles of the canopy. Under it sat Pius IX, rubicund and dignified, beaming with pleasure. For three nights following the coronation the whole of Rome was illuminated and the populace stood in the summer darkness watching the girandola, a new firework, shooting into the air, breaking into luminous curves and sputtering out behind St. Angelo.

The crowds before the Vatican grew larger and larger each night, surging below the windows with a fearsome noise like that of the sea. But Pius IX appeared on the balcony with unfailing patience and extended his fingers. To mark that a new era had begun he sanctioned the construction of a railway line from Rome to Bologna, released the prisoners who had been kept by Gregory in the secret dungeons of the Appennines, granted freedom of speech and of the Press; and (this with a pang of misgiving) abandoned the Papal privilege of omniscience in favour of an advisory council.

The *Speranza* had just cleared the Straits of Gibraltar and was entering the Mediterranean when a ship was sighted flying a flag which looked like a French tricolour but which was not; through the glasses the blue did not seem to be blue. And on closer inspection it turned out that the flag was the red, white and green of Italy. The legionaries on deck set up a tremendous shout. Garibaldi, who was on the bridge, hailed the stranger through a megaphone and asked what was the news: 'Milan has risen', was the answer. 'The Austrians are flying. The revolution is all over Italy. Viva la libertà!' In a twinkling the Montevidean flag was hauled down from the masthead of the *Speranza* and half a bedsheet, crossed with a red shirt and patched with green facings torn from the legionaries' uniforms, was run up. A few fiddles and mouth-organs struck up and a dance began. They called at Alicante to buy oranges and a goat for Anzani who was at his last gasp with tuberculosis of the lungs; and there the vice-consul confirmed the news, adding that Charles Albert had granted a constitution and was at war with Austria; and that the new Pope was a good Italian. On June 21, 1848, the *Speranza* came in sight of Nice. Garibaldi believed all the good news he had heard: but, being an old soldier who never took an unnecessary risk, he hauled down the patchwork tricolour which would have put him in the power of Piedmont, and the *Speranza* entered port under the colours of the Republic of Montevideo.

A few days before, a reporter of the *Echo des Alpes maritimes* had picked up the information from a Sardinian vessel just returned from Montevideo that 'general' Garibaldi was on his way from South America with the Italian Legion and would shortly arrive. 'This means', the newspaper announced, 'that we shall not be long in seeing the valorous general and in congratulating him.' As the *Speranza* cast anchor, it seemed that the whole town was on the quayside, swarming about the Signora Rosa, with whom were Anita and the three children. He had scarcely a minute to embrace them before he was surrounded by patriots who wanted him to make a speech. On the 26th the hall of the York Hotel was decorated with flags and flowers, and Garibaldi sat down with a select gathering of citizens to a banquet offered by the town of Nice to himself and his valiant legionaries. The newspaper report said that, after the speeches and felicitations, the general spoke in French with a certain facility, although it was fifteen years since he had left Nice. 'You know', he said to the republican gathering, 'whether I have been in the past the friend of kings. But since Charles Albert has become the defender of the people's cause I think it is my duty to offer him my collaboration, and that of my friends.' He added a word of warning to the recruits who were flocking enthusiastically to join the Legion. 'Do not think you are going to have a carnival', he said. 'You will have to suffer hunger and thirst, sleep on the bare ground under the open sky and endure all kinds of peril and hardship. The Legion never retreats. I do not intend that the Legion shall ever retreat.'

Anita told him how she had been welcomed at Genoa by the Montevidean consul and a crowd of three thousand people (more than three thousand, she thought), who had assembled under her windows and shouted: 'Viva Garibaldi! Viva la famiglia del nostro Garibaldi!' A tricolour was thrust into her hand and a patriot begged her to give it to her husband as soon as he set foot on Lombard soil. And she had clutched the banner in her right hand and cried to the crowd: 'Viva l'Italia e gl'Italiani!': after which it had politely dispersed to allow her to rest. She told him of this and of her visits to the theatre of Genoa; she had received many invitations. Also a sword of honour had been designed by the artist Francesco Vagnetti and a picture of it was to be seen in the *Mondo illustrato* of Turin; the sword would be presented to Garibaldi as soon as an opportunity occurred. An account of the exploits of the Italian Legion had been printed as early as 1846, and was circulating as *Documenti intorno a Garibaldi e la legione Italiana a Montevideo*. Garibaldi listened to these accounts of his fame. But there was no time to be lost. After seven days at Nice he marched with one hundred and fifty legionaries to Genoa, carrying the twin flags of Italy and Savoy; and when the men were safely bestowed in barracks at San Leonardo, he hastened to find the dying Anzani.

Anzani lay in the palace of the Marchese Gavotto, in a room once occupied by the painter Gallino. His one thought was for Italy. In a whisper he told Garibaldi he must go to Charles Albert and offer him the Legion. And to Medici, who visited him after Garibaldi had gone, he said: 'Do not be hard on Garibaldi. He is a man who has been blessed with such good fortune from heaven that it is well to rely on him and follow him. The future of Italy is with him. It is foreordained'.

The king's armies had been lying some weeks at Roverbella; and during these weeks it became apparent that, for the time being at any rate, the fate of the new movement of Italy was held in the hands of Charles Albert rather than in those of the new Pope. The behaviour of the diplomats proved this; they had lately been in Rome, and now, like seagulls gathering behind a plough, they had come north to the camp of the king. Pius IX was reported to be hesitating, saying at one time that the *brutti musi* (*i.e.* the Austrians) must be sent back over the mountains, and again that on no account must the general of the Papal army become involved in any kind of fighting; for the Pope was the father of all men, even of Austrians. And Charles Albert, hearing of the changing moods of the head of the Church, alternated himself between enthusiasm and deep despair. Abercromby, acting on instructions from London, whispered in his ear that he who sows the wind may reap the whirlwind. The hard-bitten Savoyard courtiers sneered at Gioberti, who, fat and vulgar, with bright rat's eyes twinkling behind an ominous pair of spectacles, expounded chapters of his *Primato d'Italia* in a laryngitical croak. Surrounded by so many counsellors, Charles Albert prayed to God for enlightenment. In the course of a meeting he would be seen to move silently to the door of his private chapel, where he fell on his knees before the altar, remaining in this position for hours, while courtiers and diplomats peered at the strange spectacle through the keyhole. It was said that he flogged himself and wore a hair shirt next his skin; and certainly he grew more gaunt every day. On public occasions he spoke courageously. 'L'Italia', he declared in a memorable sentence, 'farà da se.' Italy would act alone! He said it boldly: but he knew that Italy would not be allowed to act alone, and that whatever she did would be jealously watched by the rest of Europe. He had granted a constitutional government which, in astonishment at its own existence and as if to prove its reality, began to pass one or two timid measures: but he sought advice only from God and from a nun, Sister Maria Theresa, who saw visions and informed him of them. In a tight corner he closed his eyes and asked guidance from her spirit. He was not without moments of wistful lucidity: 'little Piedmont', he saw, was in a dilemma. It could do nothing against the might of Europe if Europe did not choose to approve the campaign for freedom: and it was not likely to do much against the hordes of Austria. In the circumstances, after long meditation and self-torture, he reached the conclusion that it was his duty to preserve a calm front and, at the first opportunity, find death and release in battle. He had two answers for visitors. If they were of the kind who made long speeches like Gioberti, he said he was a constitutional sovereign and could do nothing without the assent of parliament. If they were young heroes eager to drink the blood of Austrians, he sent them to the recruiting office or the Minister of War at Turin.

Either on the 3rd or 4th of July, 1848, he received Garibaldi, having apparently forgotten that his visitor was a bandit of the first category. There is no reliable account of what took place, since they were alone: but Vecchi (*La Italia, Storia di due anni*) attributes to Garibaldi the following speech:

Sire, I have fought on foreign soil for the liberty of an hospitable country, and God was favourable to our arms, making famous the name of the Italian legionaries. With a few of my followers I have come in time to take part in this honourable enterprise. There beats in my breast a heart that truly loves Italy and begs as a boon to be allowed to co-operate in whatever may be to her advantage and honour.

It is possible Garibaldi did say something of this kind, winding up with the offer of the right arm which he had wished to place at the service of the Pope. But the result was that he was gently told to see the Minister of War at Turin; and, having sat for a few hours in the latter's waiting room, and confessed that he had no military training (as distinct from military experience), he listened with indignation while General Ricci suggested to him that there were lagoons at Venice where his peculiar methods and tradition might be of service.

Some days after this event Medici encountered Garibaldi walking under the arcades of Turin.

'These people', said Garibaldi, with a wave of his arm, 'are not fit to be served by hearts like ours.'

The King of Savoy had declined his services, perhaps because he was reputed to be a republican. And the Pope had returned no reply to his letter. There remained Milan, where a five-day old republic was being feverishly organised while, at any moment, the expelled Austrians might return.

The same night Garibaldi and Medici set off for Milan.

IX

WHILE Garibaldi had been preparing the expedition at Montevideo, Milan had had its five glorious and historic days. To the consternation of the well-meaning liberals, who, up to that time, had considered themselves as advanced revolutionaries, the population had taken advantage of the spring disorders in Vienna to plant one thousand five hundred and twenty-three barricades across the streets. They grew up overnight like mushrooms, observed and counted by Radetzky, the Austrian military governor, who reported the extraordinary vegetation to Vienna, and added that the Milanesi, formerly peaceful and well-behaved, had suddenly gone mad universally; young and old, rich and poor, male and female, they had united in a decision to get rid of the Austrians.

The barricades were curiously compounded of benches from the Scala Theatre, grand pianos, kitchen tables, mattresses, carriage wheels and masonry from the Palazzo d'Adda. They were manned by men, women and children; and, as the people had no weapons, the patrician families Uboldi and Poldi-Pozzoli opened their private collections and equipped the crowd with priceless firearms dating from the Middle Ages, and with damascened swords worth a king's ransom. Field-Marshal Radetzky said in his official report that the 'very foundations of the city' were torn up. He held on until March 22, parleying with the members of the civic council. Then he gave it up, making an inglorious exit from the city in a carriage camouflaged as a hay-waggon; remembering, no doubt, with some bitterness the report in which he had affirmed not many days before that he had the situation well in hand. He had his decorations in his pocket and a sum of four lire.

However, it was now midsummer; and nothing had been done since Radetzky's departure. Peasants came to gape at the barricades and watch the illuminations, of which there was no end. They broke out afresh on the slightest pretext. There were special illuminations to celebrate Garibaldi's arrival; and, of course, banquets and a parade of the legionaries. But Garibaldi was shocked: he told the crowd from the balcony of the *Bella Venezia* that it was not a time for shouting. Of fervour there was plenty. Mazzini had seen to that. He had been in the city since May, and his newspaper kept up a high tone of democratic enthusiasm. He welcomed Garibaldi and commended him to the heroes of the barricades. But these heroes were not anxious to stand in the summer sun and be drilled mercilessly by Medici, who had been put in command of a battalion of volunteers called the Anzani battalion. The civic authorities were gracious. They gave Garibaldi the rank of general, and they indicated he could do what he liked, but on his own responsibility and with his own resources. A man in spectacles at the Ministry of War sneered circumspectly at Garibaldi. 'A sabreur', he said. 'Do not waste money on him.'

Garibaldi undertook to supply weapons, but insisted that he must have uniforms. There were no uniforms, he was told, except those that had been left behind by the Austrian troops, Austrian, Hungarian and Croatian uniforms which the indignant patricians of Milan refused to touch; they preferred to parade in their dress coats and velvet jackets. But Garibaldi did not want to have his soldiers shot as spies; he looked through the stores and decided that something could be made from the uniforms of the Austrian ritters, a blouse of white linen, which, roughly adapted, was served out to the volunteers. They accepted it with mixed feelings in which, fortunately, laughter predominated; for they looked, as Medici said, like a regiment of cooks. The Committee of Milan ordered this strange force to proceed to Bergamo; and no sooner had it got there than another order arrived, recalling it urgently to Milan. The end of the five months' rejoicing was at hand.

Charles Albert in his camp at Roverbella had dallied too long. Fate had given him two military chances. The first was given him early in the campaign by the flight of Radetzky, whom he could have cut off from the northern mountains; the second still remained open after the first had been neglected. He could still block the passes by which reinforcements were likely to arrive from Austria. But he did neither; waiting until Radetzky had assembled forces twice as great as his own before he matched himself finally against him. With an overwhelmingly superior force Radetzky drove Charles Albert across the Mincio River and back on Milan. When Garibaldi arrived at Monza he learned that the city had capitulated and that the Austrians were once more in possession.

Garibaldi's men were tired and hungry after their long forced march; and the spectacle of half the population of

Milan drifting out of the city like frightened sheep was too much for them. When a muster was held at Como, Medici found that out of the five thousand there were eight hundred remaining; four thousand odd, the bulk of the force, had crossed the mountains to Switzerland. Garibaldi published a peremptory notice that Charles Albert was a traitor to his country, a bitter and emphatic piece of rhetoric which the circumstances of the moment amply excused; then he took up a position in advance of Como, at the cross-roads of La Camerlata. He placed his cannon and dispatched messengers to the other generals commanding troops in Upper Lombardy, to Griffini, Durando, Manara and Apice, advising them of his whereabouts and exhorting them to hold on to their positions. In the square of San Fermo he harangued his handful of men. There were, he said, many advantages in guerila warfare. The enemy took all the risks and the attackers the opportunities. All that was needed was courage and confidence. In the morning, however, half his eight hundred men had disappeared, and there was no answer from the other patriot generals with whom he had sought to establish contact. Sorrowfully, with the last handful of men, Garibaldi began to retreat.

At Castelletto on the Ticino he stopped, choking with rage; his blue eye was sombre with despair. Looking towards Medici, he said:

'Take a good horse and a stick and scour the country for those deserters.'

Medici rounded up three hundred between Castelletto and Lugano, so that the muster was brought to near seven hundred and fifty men. With this reinforcement Garibaldi went back to the lake and seized two steamers and some smaller craft at Arona; on these the small army embarked and, sailing by night, reached Luino at dawn next day. There was an inn at Luino on the outskirts of the village called La Beccaccia.

'I will sleep for two hours', Garibaldi said to Medici. 'Keep an eye on the road.'

They did not know where the Austrians were, or if there

were any at all in the neighbourhood; but the probability was that the enemy lay beyond Luino, in which case they would come on La Beccaccia first and find Garibaldi's troops resting in a field separated from the inn by a small stream. The men's rifles were stacked beside the bridge. The two hours were not up before Medici's scouts came rushing back:

'The Austrians!'

'Bene', said Garibaldi, springing from bed. He had gone to bed with a temperature, and was now in the height of fever.

He took a rapid glance at the country from the window.

'Form the men in two columns', he ordered. 'Hold the road with one and keep the other ready to protect the flank.'

The Austrians, about twelve hundred strong, were occupying the inn and bridge head when four hundred Garibaldians flung themselves on them with the bayonet. The Austrians poured a devastating fire through the windows of the inn while Medici's men scaled the wall and rushed at them in a desperate charge. About fifty yards from the scene of action Garibaldi sat on his horse. When the moment had come he launched the flanking column. The Austrians turned and fled, throwing away rifles, cartridges, haversacks; Medici, who was sent in pursuit, reported that they did not stop till they reached Varese. A hundred of their number lay dead or wounded on the floors of the inn, and the victors had on their hands eighty sheepish and astonished prisoners.

The chief had tasted Austrian blood and liked the taste of it. He looked sinister, unbending somewhat when the main body of his troops occupied Varese amid the cheers of the population. They ascended the slope of Buimo di Sopra, from which position they dominated the town and were secure from attack in the rear. A dubious-looking peasant who was found prowling round the encampment was brought before Garibaldi. The man spoke a dialect that was not native to the country.

'Austriaco', said Garibaldi briefly. 'Take him away and shoot him.'

Charles Albert had thrown himself headlong at belching batteries and never a shot had touched him; and in the same way Garibaldi had sat his horse at La Beccaccia while the air was thick with bullets and he, too, had come out unscathed. But whereas the melancholy king sought for death, Garibaldi faced it with the cold courage of a man who knew he would not die. In his desperation there was an element of lucid calculation. Three columns of ·Austrians were moving against him, one heading for Como, another for Varese, a third for Luino, making a three-pronged fork on one spit or other of which he was sure to be caught if Radetzky's plans held good. Garibaldi knew he could not save Italy (and his rage against Charles Albert was only the bitter echo of the hope he had put in him): but there was time, he thought, for a last blow before he and Medici disappeared into Switzerland. Medici seized three villages, Catzone, Ligurno and Rodero, which, together, formed a strategic triangle. Behind them rose the grim bulk of San Maffeo which presented one front to Italy and the other to Switzerland. When Medici had dealt his blow he had only to curl up and roll into neutral territory.

He divided his men into three bodies and manned a village with each; but just after daybreak the Austrians began firing from Rodero, from which one section of Medici's men had decamped in the night, preferring to roll down the San Maffeo in darkness and safety with a whole skin. Medici's position was turned; he had to whistle his garrison back from Catzone and scramble up the rock face of San Maffeo. They counted their cartridges and found twenty apiece. With these they retorted carefully to the Austrian fire, awakening the morning echoes of the mountains and scaring the Swiss villagers out of their beds. A few bold spirits from the Swiss side came panting along with rifles, eager to pot the Austrians; and with these reinforcements they looked down into the valley and saw the Austrian cannon puffing noisily but ineffectively at them.

The amateurs were good marksmen and picked off their targets to their own satisfaction. At the end of a not unpleasing day San Maffeo was intact and the cartridges exhausted; dusk was crowning the hills. The Swiss amateurs led the forlorn hope down the hill by a rough path known only to the natives and showed them a convenient spot in a wood where they could bury their carbines until better times.

Garibaldi, Medici imagined, was either lost or captured. But, once again, he encountered the man of fate lying in bed at Lugano.

As Medici looked at him he remembered the words of Anzani.

'I have had a walk', said Garibaldi wearily. 'A long walk.'

He had been walking, he said, for sixteen hours. While Medici had been holding San Maffeo he had advanced on Luino with five hundred men, only to find that the Austrians had got there before him. Not only that, but they had cut him off from Switzerland; and he could only find a rock and sell his life dearly. He chose Morazzone. The Austrians drew a cordon right round and began an attack which lasted till nightfall, when the fire on both sides cooled down and the Austrians, having disposed their sentries, prepared to rest. In the midst of the darkness Garibaldi's five hundred burst suddenly on them, charging down the hillside. They drove right through the Austrian lines and reached open country. There Garibaldi told his men to break up and meet him in Switzerland.

In the retreat from Milan Garibaldi had been joined by Mazzini, in whom defeat had produced a strange exaltation. He trudged through the dust, carrying a banner, until he stumbled and fell down in a faint. And his company suggested reflections to Garibaldi, not all of which were pleasant. He admired the small man's courage: but of the admiration he had once had for Pippo, the dark conspirator of Marseilles, nothing was left. If liberty were to be had by scattering pamphlets and writing books, Italy would have been saved already, for the country was full of clever men, sincere and fanatical patriots who had yet to learn that their country would not be free until they could shut their mouths and shoot straight. And his cheerful compatriots of the lower orders who had flagged Milan and applauded below his balcony, expert reasoners all of them in small matters, had lived so long under a régime of tyranny that they ranked the hazards of politics with the vagaries of the sun, moon and stars. Cynical and superstitious alternately, courageous and cowardly, they had a lesson to learn, too, the same lesson as their garrulous leaders, that of discipline, patience and courage.

X

THERE were many centres of revolution in Italy, so many that an agitator would apparently have no difficulty in choosing a field of activity: but in each of these centres the position was the same, made of the same ingredients and handled by the same kind of people. These minor conflagrations dotting the map of Italy resembled a glow of scattered forest fires faintly illuminating a general darkness. Thus it seemed to Garibaldi as he recuperated in Switzerland. But on action of some kind he was determined. He asked Medici whether he still had his men with him; and, being reassured on this point, he made a careful circle through French territory and passed through Nice to Genoa. Once more he was on Italian ground; and no sooner had he got there than a delegate from Sicily informed him that a French ship was waiting in the harbour, ready to take him and such men as he could find, to help the revolution in Sicily. With seventy-two followers, chiefly followers who had taken part in the recent fighting, and some recruits enlisted in Switzerland, he embarked: but he remembered what Anita had told him about his popularity in Tuscany, and insisted that the *Pharamond* should call at the port of Leghorn. It entered the harbour at eight o'clock on the morning of October 25, 1848.

Garibaldi was still undecided what he should do. He was steady only in his fixed resolve to place his arm at the disposal of whosoever should be willing and able to save Italy; and it seemed from the commotion of the port of Leghorn that at any rate some interesting developments were possible there. The Grand Duke had left for Florence with Montanelli and other liberal ministers and was on the point of forming a new ministry under the constitution which, like many other European rulers, he had just granted. The ministers imagined that their responsibilities would end with this innovation; for Tuscany enjoyed a pleasant climate, was peacefully disposed and had not much cause to complain of the behaviour of the Grand Duke. In common with other States, Tuscany had felt the spring winds of the 'forty-eight'; but they wafted mildly over a contented people who merely asked of their Grand Duke not to withhold from them a sample of the new constitutions which were being handed out; and as he had done this promptly he had every reason to hope that all would be well. The deliberations of the ministers at Florence were, however, interrupted by a telegram from Leghorn which said: 'General Garibaldi aboard steamship *Pharamond* from Genoa has come into harbour. It appears he is bound for Sicily. Orders have been given to receive him with honours befitting such an illustrious Italian'. A guard of honour composed of a detachment of the municipal guard and members of the town's volunteers had lined the approaches to the quay, while in a twinkling the Via Grande and the piazza were hung with flags. The enthusiasm of the crowd swept Garibaldi from the harbour into the city, and there it was represented to him that it would be a pity to go to Sicily when good work could be done nearer home. The two governors who had been left in charge of the city were obliged to bow to the storm; they asked Garibaldi if he would stay and received the reply that he would, if the new Tuscan ministry expressly invited him and agreed to his conditions. The sequel to these events is contained in a series of telegrams now preserved in the archives of Florence and published by the Italian scholar Giovanni Sforza:

Leghorn. October 25. 11 a.m. Garibaldi, although meaning to go to Sicily, would not be disinclined to offer services Tuscan government. Say what you think of this. He would leave at four afternoon if there is no advice to contrary.

Leghorn. October 25. 12.30 p.m. Must have urgent reply to first wire concerning presence here of General Garibaldi.

Florence. October 25. 3 p.m. Ministry not constituted here yet. Cannot promise anything positive about Garibaldi. If possible, ask him delay departure.

The next telegram said that Menichetti, one of the two governors of Leghorn, had taken the train for Florence and urgently wished to speak to Montanelli. The remaining governor, Isolani, was evidently still not satisfied. Thirteen minutes later the wire was buzzing with a fresh message:

The people of Leghorn wishes Garibaldi to remain in service of Tuscany, whatever the conditions. Have succeeded in delaying departure of ship until seven. Must have definite reply at once. The population is out of hand.

Seven o'clock came and there was no answer. Garibaldi was angry. The next telegram came from himself:

Do I take command of Tuscan forces against Bourbon? Yes or no. Garibaldi.

At six minutes past eight Montanelli wired to Isolani:

Confirm what I wrote, that if Garibaldi can postpone departure I will give decision as soon as ministry constituted. At the moment have no authority.

At twenty-three minutes past he repeated the message in different words to Garibaldi:

Must know what forces we have before I reply. As ministry is not constituted cannot give answer.

A little later came the last communication for that day, this time from Menichetti to his co-governor:

9.35 p.m. Have explained everything to Montanelli and he gave me the reply previously sent to Garibaldi, that he cannot take any steps until ministry is constituted.

Meantime, the *Pharamond* had sailed; and for better or for worse, Garibaldi remained behind on Tuscan soil. He was assured by Isolani that the decision of the ministry would be favourable and that a strong column could be formed in Leghorn and in the grand-duchy with which he could march southwards towards Sicily, taking Naples on his way. It was an alluring project and not an impossible one. For obviously the revolt of Italy was weakest in the north where at any moment the last embers might be stamped out by the heel of Austria. On the other hand, the Bourbon referred to in Garibaldi's telegram, Ferdinand of Sicily, held his power insecurely. He was detested by his subjects, who might, with some encouragement, begin a *levée en masse* that had at least a chance of being successful and spreading northward. The die was cast. The seventy odd legionaries were disembarked and billeted in the city while Garibaldi himself sought accommodation in the house of the patriot Carlo Notary. Early on the following day the battle of telegrams was resumed:

Garibaldi has postponed departure for Sicily and awaits government's instructions. Yesterday evening his men landed and have taken quarters in city. I have given orders for rations to be issued.

A similar message reached Florence from Notary, to whom Montanelli replied impatiently:

Have already replied to Garibaldi. Leave us in peace. Am busy with programme of new government which, although brief, needs meditation.

Montanelli was a good-natured man; no sooner had he sent this telegram, in which the stress of the times was too visibly manifested, than he suffered a pang of conscience. Once more the Florence post office was put in action with a wire which followed after an interval of only sixteen minutes on the heels of its predecessor:

Greatly esteem the courageous Italian and you did well to entertain him. But the decrees have not come yet because of usual formalities and we cannot take any decision.

That was all for two days. Nothing could be done under the new constitutional ministry until the Grand Duke had countersigned the nominations. When, however, the signatures had been appended and the new ministry announced in the *Gazzetta di Firenze* of October 27, there was still no sign that it was in a hurry to acquire Garibaldi's services. His arrival had merely provided the new ministers with responsibilities which they were not anxious to shoulder; and which, on the other hand, they could not safely disregard. For if they paid no attention to Garibaldi they might find him marching on Florence from Leghorn with the dregs of that turbulent seaport at his heels; and if they took the opposite line he might, by their own action, acquire an inconvenient importance. Garibaldi's only claim to their notice (after they had unwillingly recognised his value as a 'great Italian') was that he could make trouble; no one could tell how much.

Notary's report came on the 30th and indicated that Garibaldi could make a good deal of trouble if he chose to:

Yesterday evening (29th), on pretext of arrival of deputation from Elba, unpleasant disturbance; troops broke barracks to fraternise; some windows broken. This was all the material damage, but the moral damage is greater. Was at theatre with Garibaldi and so could not prevent demonstration. Great ovation to Garibaldi. As soon as you can, think please about him. Say if you want him there.

The ministers still did not know. D'Ayala, the Minister of War, had already six generals and said he had no use for a seventh. Montanelli, not wishing to hurt Garibaldi's feelings, sent a secret messenger to Leghorn to convey this fact by word of mouth. But Garibaldi had already had some taste of military officialdom; and now with the population of a city clamouring at his heels he was not inclined to mince his words. *Comincia a brontolarsi*, Notary telegraphed; *he is beginning to grumble*. Garibaldi had a grievance. He had broken something like a promise to the Sicilian delegate in order to offer his sword to Tuscany. At a critical moment when every day counted they had kept him waiting idly the better part of a week; and they seemed no nearer to making up their minds.

The telegraph was busy in other parts of Italy. In the north enthusiastic newspaper editors were finding it useful for magnifying small events and making them into large ones. General Pepe had made a sortie from Venice which was described as a signal victory in which the Austrians had lost four hundred prisoners and four cannons. The journalistic imagination running riot, the editors said that the whole of Lombardy and La Valtellina were up in arms and Italian troops marching on Treviso. Notary himself had a letter from Lugano saying that the insurrection in Valtellina was 'well developed'. Also a number of columns were marching on Bergamo. There was other news which the letter described as official. The conclusion was that the patriots of Tuscany should create a diversion by an attack on Modena, in which case the letter writer and his friends undertook to be in Milan by the following Saturday or Sunday. As if to point the moral of the tale, a Turin newspaper, the *Concordia*, informed its readers that Garibaldi had already left Leghorn 'precipitately' to take the lead. 'His name alone', said the article, 'is enough to scatter confusion amongst Haynau's bullies; what will happen now he appears in person, supported by the inhabitants?'

There was no reason to suppose that these rumours were not true; and Garibaldi was very ready to believe any news in which there was a glimmer of hope. Having found that the popular enthusiasm in Leghorn was held in check by timid officialdom, he turned to the next bidder, who happened to be Castellani, a Venetian delegate on business in Leghorn. Castellani put the case of Venice and found a ready hearing. In a very short time Garibaldi decided to add what recruits he could in Tuscany and obtain whatever help might be wrung from the timorous government; then he would march north to Venice and if honour fell to their arms place it to the credit of the more enterprising republic of the Adriatic. These matters were hotly discussed and again the telegraph communicated the results.

Notary, in great indignation, advised the minister Guerrazzi that Castellani was likely to steal Garibaldi:

> Arrival of Castellani postpones Garibaldi's visit to Florence. This evening you will see he will be stolen from us. Shall we be criticised or no?

The government was willing to take the risk; and it showed in its reply an unusual explicitness and alacrity.

November 1st. Concede all that Garibaldi requires.

The government was delighted, being evidently of opinion that the sooner Garibaldi marched away the better. In due course it received a note of the latter's demands:

Permission to enrol men for Garibaldi's column.
300 greatcoats.
300 pairs of shoes.
250 rifles with bayonets and strap.
20 swords with belts for officers.
Such assistance as minister deems proper to facilitate march to Bologna.
3 horses and saddles.
3 waggons for transport of munitions and baggage.
One guide.
1000 packets cartridges.
Facilities to be given for recruits from Genoa to link up with column on way to Bologna.

Finally Garibaldi said that he was willing to attach this column to the Tuscan army if the ministry wished. But no such request was made by the ministry. The government of Tuscany was ready to supply weapons, clothes, rations; all on condition that Garibaldi went as far away with them as possible. Their only anxiety now was that Garibaldi proposed to pass through Florence, where they feared his arrival would provoke the same excitement as in Leghorn. In this they were quite right; but it could not be prevented. On November 3, Garibaldi and his men entrained for Florence about ninety strong. In spite of all the *vivas* only a handful of volunteers came forward, and his total force was still under one hundred men.

The usual crowd was at the Leopolda railway station, as well as the usual bands and flags. Garibaldi made a short speech and allowed himself to be escorted to the Piazza S. Maria Novella, where he was installed in the Casa de Gregori. He appeared on the balcony and made another speech, beginning: *Immensa è la gratitudine che io sento per voi, o Toscani.* . . . He had not forgotten the sword which Tuscany had presented to him.

He was particularly welcomed by the Circolo del Popolo, a democratic and revolutionary club whose activities were being anxiously watched by the new government. The Circolo was not in favour of constitutional government by a duke; it wanted a thorough overhaul after the fashion of the French Revolution. And by a stroke of coincidence it found to its hand a group of figure-heads of whom Garibaldi was certainly the most romantic. He was closely followed as a hero of popular appeal by the two brothers Romeo, fresh from the insurrection they had organised in Calabria, and by another intriguing personage, no less than Carlo Luciano Bonaparte, Prince of Canino, who had been fomenting trouble in Rome. In addition there was the dubious figure of Carlo Pigli, ex-professor and doctor of medicine, who was reputed to handle ideas and money with equal dexterity, and who found his way to the hearts of the lower class Italians by standing on platforms and bawling like a lunatic. Pigli was at once made president of the Circolo and ordained a mass meeting to celebrate the arrival of Garibaldi. Usually the club meetings were held in the Teatro Leopoldo; but it was rightly assumed that it would not be big enough. The meeting was transferred to the Teatro Goldoni and was packed to the doors.

Carlo Pigli was in good form. At eight o'clock on the evening of November 5 he ushered his distinguished company on to the stage and began a harangue in which his habitual violence was displayed:

Look behind, and what do you see? Everywhere gallows, pyres, the axe of the executioner, and the poisoned cup. Ebbene! these instruments of death are the glorious cradle of the true life of the people. They are the throne of the people's majesty and of its irresistible power.

Men may die, but the *ideal* does not die. Become gigantic, it rules the world. When the axe strikes off the head of a just man, his thought rises from his blood and becomes an immortal ray of that limpid sun which will one day illumine the triumph of humanity.

After a good deal more in this style the orator came to Garibaldi:

From the remote land of America came the news that a valorous Italian exile, unable to fight for his own country, was fighting for the liberty of distant brothers. But when at last Italy shook the accursed yoke we heard that he had crossed the seas and set foot on the Italian shore, causing the earth to tremble under the feet of the barbaric invader. The heroes of Piedmont had been constrained to take shelter in a treaty with a king: but his treaty was with the people which has sworn to conquer; I do not say to conquer or die, because it is kings who die, and not peoples.

And this valorous man, this hero, he is here in your presence. Honour, O citizens, the brave Garibaldi.

Garibaldi rose to his feet amid thunderous applause. He spoke as a soldier who had become entoiled in the wiles of administrators and could understand nothing of them except their fatal consequences in time of war. The deliverance of Italy was a matter of time. It could be accomplished in a day or a week by swift and decisive action; but if Italy chose to fight like Austria, assembling laboriously the parts of a clumsy military machine, Italy was lost:

I am of opinion, he said, that the Tuscan ministry should not merely be pushed; it should be compelled and driven; I say compelled because the obstacles that surround it do not allow it to act according to its conscience. Therefore, if the people is aware of the need for prompt action, I repeat, it must not be content to push, it must compel the ministry, if it believes this to be in the interests of Italy; if you are convinced that something must be done urgently, let us say in a day instead of in a month. I insist on the need for prompt action because I believe it indispensable in the present position of Italy, because it seems to me that any delay, any dilatoriness on our side is a crime, because I think that what you propose to do in six months should be done in six days.

Compel morally, I mean, by making demonstrations. When it is clear they are needed and when the ministry is hesitating to take a decision you should rouse the people. Propose whatever is for the good of the people, and you will find these men disposed to do what the people wishes. The time for illusion is past. I do not flatter; and as I do not flatter princes I do not flatter the people, because I esteem and venerate the people. Italy to-day, it seems to me, can choose one of two ways with her rulers. She can overthrow them or drag them with her. There is no middle course. It is the one way or the other.

The positive advantage that the Tuscan people has to-day over the other peoples of Italy is that it can take its prince with it in its progress and set him on the way of Italy's salvation.

These words, as well as those of Pigli and of Carlo Luciano Bonaparte, were reported in *Il Popolano*, the newspaper of the Circolo del Popolo, where they were read by the Grand Duke and by the ministers engaged in the task of organising the new ministry. The Grand Duke heard without pleasure that he was to be either overthrown or dragged along; and the moderate liberals who composed the ministry were not pleased to hear that they were to be compelled or driven. Garibaldi himself called on Montanelli, whom he found to be, as he was led to expect, loyal, frank, modest, and a fervent patriot whose energy was neutralised by the timidity of his colleagues. As a result of the speeches at the Teatro Goldoni, Garibaldi found himself dropped by the Minister of War, and had to borrow from friends in order to feed his men. Whether or not D'Ayala issued the stores and equipment which had been requested from Leghorn is not clear. But in a letter dated November 8, Garibaldi asked as an 'ordinary kindness' that he might receive a *feuille de route* for one hundred and fifty men, with whom he proposed to start the next day for Calfaggiolo; also he would be 'most grateful' for fifty rifles.

D'Ayala was sulking. Believing that the best thing to be done was to pass the adventurer and his rabble out of Tuscany, he issued the needful permit; and in private he communicated to the authorities on the frontier that the way was to be made plain; that and no more. Guerrazzi, another minister, was more explicit. 'They are', he wrote, 'a swarm of grasshoppers. Let us consider them as one of the plagues of Egypt, and let us do our utmost to induce them to get away quickly and contaminate as few places as possible.'[1]

XI

MAZZINI had been living in the fogs of London when he, too (somewhat earlier than Garibaldi), had heard of the election of Pio Nono. In Mazzini the appetites of humanity dwindled to nothing. They were represented by a wisp of blue smoke that came from the cheap cigars he incessantly smoked. He was a small tidy man who gave the impression of being almost bodiless; and it was strange to find that he held obstinate and secure convictions. He gave advice to the wives of ministers and high officials in London and pursued by way of the post-office his dream of a restored Italy; seeing Italy not as a sunny country where the dust whitened the leaves of the olive trees but as a palace of glass where politics would one day make heaven. He enraged Carlyle and mystified the G.P.O., which had been warned that he was a conspirator. For many nights after the accession of Pius IX, he sat biting his pen and smoking cigars over a sheet of paper on which he had written the words:

TO THE FRIENDS OF ITALY

It was a confidential document, intended, not for the ordinary members of the secret societies, but for the leaders only; and it was drawn up methodically under seven headings:

I. PRINCES

In great countries regeneration must be attained by means of the people; in your country by means of the princes. It is absolutely

[1] Cf. Giovanni Sforza, *Garibaldi in Toscano nel 1848*, Rome, 1897.

necessary to commit them to the enterprise. To do so is easy. *The Pope will advance on the path of reform from principles and from necessity.* The King of Piedmont from the hope of obtaining the crown of Italy. The Grand Duke of Tuscany from inclination and imitation. The King of Naples because of being forced. And the smaller princes will have enough to think of besides the repressing of reform. . . .

II. Nobles

The assistance of the nobles is indispensable as an instalment towards reform in a feudal society. If you have only the people misgivings will arise at the first step, and all will be lost. If the movement be led by some of the nobles these will serve as guarantors of the people. Italy is still in the condition in which France was before the Revolution. It has need of its Mirabeaux, its Layfayettes, and many others. *A great noble may be held in check by his material interests; but he can be taken by his vanity. Few of them will be willing to go on to the end. The essential point is that the goal of the great revolution should be unknown to them.* They should never be allowed to see farther than the first step taken.

A third heading dealt with the clergy, which was to be handled gently, with the same tact as the princes and nobles, so that it should serve ends it did not understand and make up its mind about them when they had come to be realities. Suppose, for example, to put these instructions into practice, suppose 'a king gives a more liberal law': 'Applaud it, demanding at the same time that which logically ought to follow it. A minister indicates his views of progress—hold him up as a model. A great noble shows he does not care for his privileges—put yourselves under his direction. If he wants to stop short you will always be in time to leave him. . . .' Further: 'All personal discontents, all illusions, all irritated ambitions may be made to serve the cause of progress if others know how to give them a good direction.' Lastly, assemble crowds. 'Take advantage of the smallest concession to make an opportunity for bringing together masses of people, if only in attestation of gratitude. Festivals, songs, agglomerations of people, numerous relationships established between men of every shade of opinion, suffice to cause the generation of ideas, to give the people the sentiment of its strength, and to render it exigent.' 'Profound and learned discussions are neither needful nor opportune. There are generating words that contain all in themselves, and which ought to be repeated frequently to the people: Liberty! Rights of Man! Progress! Equality! Fraternity! This is what the people will comprehend, especially when to these words you oppose the words, Despotism! Privilege! Tyranny! Slavery! The difficult thing is not the convincing of people but the getting of them together. The day in which the people shall be assembled together will be the first of a new era.... Associate! associate! associate!'

'When a large number of associates', concluded this encyclical, 'receiving the word to spread certain ideas, and to make public opinion consist of them, shall be able to make a concerted movement, they will find the old edifice riddled and honeycombed in all its parts, and ready to fall as by a miracle.... They will see themselves stricken with wonder to behold kings, princes, the rich, the priests, who formed the old social edifice, flying before the sole power of opinion. Courage, then, and perseverance.'

Pio Nono noticed that the crowds came night after night; they brought orchestras with them which took up their position beneath his windows and fiddled while a fat man, whom he discovered to be Ciceruacchio, the wine dealer, moved about inciting the multitude to further demonstrations. At last the Pope gave them his blessing and told them he was distressed to see his children wasting so much of their time and money under his balconies; and as this did not produce any effect he forbade them to assemble near the Vatican any longer. But he heard that they continued to assemble elsewhere, and that they had a new cry. 'Viva Pio Nono *solo*!', they shouted, with emphasis on the last word. And they added: 'Morte ai preti!' ('death to the priests!')

This was an aspect of progress which Pius IX had not

contemplated and which inspired in him the sudden realisation that, after all, his predecessor Gregory might have had his reasons for distrusting the new ideas. Pius IX found small sympathy among his cardinals, who blamed him for all the troubles that had come to them in the past months, and he was glad at last to confide the government to a strong man, Pellegrino Rossi, who at once issued a firm proclamation. 'Pius IX', he published, 'is not led by particular interests or ambitious views. He seeks nothing, he desires nothing but the happiness of Italy and the regular development of those institutions which he has given to his people. But at the same time he will never lose sight of what he owes to the dignity of the Holy See and to the glory of Rome. Any proposal whatever that is incompatible with this sacred duty will be vainly offered to the Sovereign of Rome and the Head of the Church. The Pontificate is the only living greatness which remains to Italy. . . .' The announcement appeared in the *Vatican Gazette*, and was followed by a still more explicit statement which said that the Pope had nothing in common with the party which 'openly stirred up the passions and inexperience of a portion of the people' and sought to 'hurry the entire fabric of society into dissolution and anarchy'. The government was watching the fomenters of disorder and was 'resolved to do its duty'.

On the morning of November 15 a letter came to Pellegrino Rossi warning him there was a plot against him. The same post brought another warning from a lady who said she had 'strong presentiments of evil'. A kind missive from an old Polish general informed the Papal minister that the threats which were being made against him were not mere wind. A priest came in haste to say that he knew a scheme was afoot to assassinate Rossi on the day of the opening of parliament. And, sure enough, on that day there were unusual crowds in the vicinity of the Chamber on the Piazza della Cancelleria. A detachment of the Civic Guard had taken up its position there, but not near enough to cover the entrance to the palace, which was surrounded by a rabble of lazzaroni and unemployed cab-drivers. Among them were some villainous-looking ex-soldiers in tattered uniforms decorated with nondescript collections of medals. At half-past one the carriage drew up. The prefect of police had jumped off the step after a vain attempt to persuade Rossi to go home. Rossi took his time, traversing the intervening distance at a walk which was neither brisker nor slower than usual. He paid no attention to the shouts, but when he was on the steps someone pushed hard against his left side and he turned his head in that direction. A knife flashed for a second in the sun and Rossi fell into the arms of General Righetti, who, with his servant, helped to carry the minister upstairs to the rooms of Cardinal Gazzoli. The carotid artery had been severed, and in a few moments Rossi was dead. The same night the cardinals took refuge in the Quirinal, while outside the mob shouted: 'Hurrah for the second Brutus!'

Sadly the Pope endeavoured to understand the meaning of these things and to express his will in an address to his people. 'We granted before we were asked', he wrote, 'all that appeared to us to be useful and good. We granted, as soon as it was asked, of that which many desired, all that appeared to us possible and right.' And he concluded, 'If it is wished to subject us to violence at the cost of crime, we shall bitterly deplore the shame to which the wickedness of a few exposes a good and generous population; but we are ready with humility of heart to suffer anything rather than bend our will to that to which we cannot and ought not to consent. On the contrary, with a firm voice, we fulfil the obligation of the ministry which God has entrusted to us, to preach justice to all men in the midst of the drunkenness of terror of the passions. We remember that above all peoples and above all princes there is the judgment of the Most High God....' He had not long finished writing when Galletti, whom he had begged to form a ministry, returned to say that the crowd insisted he should appear. He replied that he would not appear and would grant nothing under compulsion; and he maintained this attitude while a cannon was set up before the main door of the Quirinal. The side door in the Via Quirinale was already in flames.

Monsignore Palma, an expert in Latin letters, who dealt with the Latin correspondence of the Pope, was sitting at a window when a ball entered his temple and he pitched to the floor. The Civic Guard and the Carabinieri were outside, but facing the wrong way, towards the palace instead of towards the mob; and when an officer was asked if he could assure the defence, he said the gates could not be held, and inevitably the defenders would be driven up the staircase, where the attackers would pass over their dead bodies into the apartments of the Pope. A message was brought at this point from the leader of the insurgents, who said that the cannon would open fire in a quarter of an hour if the Pope had not signified by that time that the people were henceforth free to elect their own ministers. Pius IX turned to the diplomatic representatives who were present and said to them: 'From now on I am under constraint. All that I do is null and void'. He sat down and wrote the concession, which was taken to the ringleaders outside. In a short time the crowd dispersed and went home.

About five o'clock on the evening of November 24, Pius IX threw off his robes and dressed himself in the habit of a priest. He put on a very broad-brimmed hat and tied round his neck the sacred locket which had been worn by Pius VI when he was carried off from Rome to France. A winding stair led down to the Courtyard of the Swiss, where he stepped into a carriage which, shortly after, passed through the gate leading to the Appian Way. The carriage was changed several times and, at six o'clock next morning, His Holiness crossed the southern frontier of his territory into the kingdom of Naples.

The news of the flight of the Pope was received with mixed feelings by the nations of Europe; and the citizens of Rome were puzzled to find that, as a result of their demonstrations, the Holy Father, dispenser of blessings, was gone.

XII

One of the last acts of Pellegrino Rossi as chief minister of Pius IX had been to write the following letter to General Zucchi at Bologna:

EXCELLENCY,
    The Tuscan government has requested the Pontifical Government to allow the passage of 350 men under the leadership of Signor Garibaldi, who is proceeding with them to Venice. The Government of His Holiness begs Your Excellency to take steps to see that the passage be effected speedily and without disturbance. I do not know which route should be preferred. Your Excellency should confer on this matter with the Signor Prolegate and write to His Ex. the Cardinal Legate of Forli and to the Prolegate of Ravenna. With sentiments of high esteem, I am your most obedient servant,
ROSSI.
Rome, November 6, 1848.

Garibaldi and his Legion were, in fact, at Filigare, on the frontier, awaiting permission to cross the Papal territory, while four hundred Swiss guards, dispatched in haste from Bologna, blocked the road. 'Yesterday', said a Bolognese newspaper, 'at four in the afternoon 400 Swiss, commanded by a major left here for the Tuscan frontier, marching in the direction of Pianoro. This move has aroused some conjectures which are not flattering to our Minister; all agree, however, that the movement of troops has been occasioned by the expected arrival of General Garibaldi with some of his legionaries.' The *Alba*, a Florence newspaper, was more explicit: 'A traveller from Bologna', it wrote, 'brings the news that the Pontifical Government has refused permission for Garibaldi's troops to enter Papal territory, and has sent a force of 400 dragoons and Swiss to enforce this order. The announcement of this measure was not well received in Bologna, where the orders affixed to barracks were torn down and destroyed by the populace.'

General Zucchi found himself in a dilemma similar to

MAP OF ITALY IN GARIBALDI'S TIME

that of the government of Tuscany: but Rossi's instructions freed him from responsibility. He conferred rapidly with the local authorities and sent for Garibaldi, with whom he arranged that the latter's men should march to Ravenna, where they could embark for Venice. All arms, it was stipulated, were to be left at the frontier and restored to the expedition at the seaport. These conditions Garibaldi accepted, but he was unable to prevent the excited populace of Bologna from unharnessing the horses from his carriage and dragging it triumphantly through the streets under the eyes of the embarrassed Papal representative. In spite of the popular fervour, Garibaldi kept his word exactly and delivered the authorities of his presence on November 10, in the morning.[1] However, he did not hurry; in fact he showed such a pronounced inclination to linger by the wayside that General Latour was dispatched with a contingent of Swiss to keep him moving. The condition of the Papal States was such that anything might happen; and a timely insurrection initiated by the people might have the effect of changing the government and delivering Garibaldi from his promise of neutrality. But no insurrection took place and, after a most leisurely march, he reached Ravenna.

There an amusing situation developed. Garibaldi showed no anxiety to embark. Latour stormed at him; and the populace, faithful to their hero, made it abundantly plain that if Latour took steps against Garibaldi they would take steps against Latour. The civic authorities had democratic leanings and solved the difficulty by offering banquets of honour to both Latour and Garibaldi, an attention which did nothing to make the situation easier. But the tension was not to last long; for presently the news came through that Rossi had been assassinated in Rome, and Latour, guessing that his services would be needed elsewhere, retired to Bologna after he had extracted a promise from Garibaldi that he would not 'disturb the peace'. Soon after, while Garibaldi was in the midst of the

[1] Giovanni Sforza, *op. cit.*

reflections suggested by the constant changes in the political situation, the telegraph reported that the Pope had fled from Rome, where a revolutionary committee had taken control; and with the arrival of this final piece of news the authorities at Bologna began to look on Garibaldi with great respect. Now it was not they but the council of the city of Ravenna which suggested urgently that Garibaldi and his troops should move on; the council had just had to face a bill of 70,769 scudi for the upkeep of the men, and its patriotism was seriously impaired. With much humility and sincerity they implored Garibaldi to remove himself; and he, who had been deaf to other pleadings, was sensitive to the practical argument and prepared to move.[1]

The Ravenna burghers were abject: but they raised an issue which was of great importance. Troops on the march were entitled to three days' upkeep at the expense of the communes through which they were passing; but only on the assumption that they were regular government troops. There was no provision for the peculiar case of Garibaldi's Legion, which at the moment owned no master, and, unless it became attached to one authority or another, was likely to become a plague and a terror to the countryside. Italy, Garibaldi realised, was not South America; it was a civilised country passing through an abnormal crisis, not a prairie in which civilisation, with its inconveniences, was occasional and local. The position of the Legion must be regularised; and, indeed, it was not the fault of Garibaldi that it was not so already, for, since his arrival in Italy, he had done nothing but offer his services to people of all categories, only to find them discreetly rejected. The choice now lay between Venice and Rome. But in reality there was no choice, since Rome was the potential capital and the heart of Italy. He sent a letter to the provisional committee and received a reply saying that he would be graded as lieutenant-colonel and have the right to enrol a strictly determined number of men. The rank was not flat-

[1] Lœvinson, *Garibaldi e la sua legione nello stato romano*, i. p. 22 ff.

tering to one who had been called a general, but that did not matter to Garibaldi; only when he was again warned off from the outskirts of the Eternal City and sent with his four hundred legionaries to prowl uselessly in the neighbourhoods of Macerata and Rieti, did he realise that even here he was suspect. Mazzini, by some trick of his inscrutable wizardry, had translated himself to Rome with his dreams; while Garibaldi, the soldier, was banished to the hills under pretext that the priests were doing their best to provoke a rising amongst the peasants in favour of the Pope.

The priests appealed to the greed of the peasants and succeeded in conveying the impression that the garibaldini were a rabble of adventurers battening on the small wealth of humble, hard-working Italians; and, after an interval, the commune of Macerata begged to be relieved of the presence of the troopers. But now Garibaldi had the republican government of Rome behind him and stood firm. He moved about watchfully, accompanied by the tall negro servant Aguyar who had been with him in Montevideo, and by a little dog called Guerrillo that ran absent-mindedly between the horses' legs. His orderly officer was Nino Bixio, a soldier of irascible temper, whose name was destined to become famous. Garibaldi had been baffled for so long that he had reached a point when he felt it necessary to speak his mind; and accordingly, when the new government ordered democratic elections to be held throughout the area under its control, he determined that he should be elected to parliament. At eleven o'clock on the Sunday morning of January 21, 1849, the whole of the Legion marched up to the polling booth of Macerata with their voting papers ready signed.[1] There were sixteen vacancies; and in spite of Garibaldi's forceful procedure, his name was thirteenth only on the list of those elected. It was not a brilliant popular triumph, nor even a legal one, for, according to the terms of the new provisional constitution, neither Garibaldi nor his legionaries had any right, as paid servants of the government, to figure in the election. But

[1] Lœvinson, *op. cit.* p. 97.

Garibaldi was not in a mood for quibbling; and, with some triumph, he came to Rome to speak his mind at the opening session of the new Chamber.

The Minister of the Interior rose to read a long inaugural speech, after which the assembly began to examine in detail the powers which the constitution conferred on it. But Garibaldi's patience gave way. Standing up, he shouted: 'Let us drop formalities! Let us here and now proclaim the Republic, the sole government worthy of Rome!'

He had mistaken the occasion. The new deputies asked for nothing better than a grave and lengthy debate on the technique of democratic government. Gioberti, who had been elected, saw an opportunity for incorporating some chapters of his book in the fabric of the constitution. Garibaldi's unseemly interruption was disregarded and he returned in disgust to resume soldiering at Rieti.

The spring came, one of the driest that Rome had known for years; and with it came a succession of disasters. On March 22, Charles Albert was finally defeated at the battle of Novara: on March 27, Venice sent out its last defiance to Haynau, the Austrian commander: on March 28, Genoa broke into a last desperate revolt: on April 6, the Catanian insurrection was crushed: on April 12, the Grand Duke was restored to full power in Tuscany; and on April 21, a French expedition set sail from Marseilles for the purpose of restoring the Pope to his throne.[1]

How these events affected Garibaldi is seen in the following letter addressed to Anita:

Subiaco, 19 April, 1849.

MOST BELOVED CONSORT,
I write to tell you that I am well and that I am ordered with the column to Anagni, which we shall probably reach to-morrow, and where I cannot say how long we may stay. I shall receive in Anagni the rifles and the rest of the clothing for the men. I shall not be easy till I have heard from you that you have got safely to Nice. Write me

[1] Guerzoni, i. p. 259.

at once; I need to have news of you, dearest Anita—tell me what is the impression made by the events in Genoa and Tuscany. O strong and generous woman, with what scorn you must look on this hermaphroditic generation of Italians, on these my countrymen whom I have praised so often to you and who were so unworthy of my praise. It is true. Treason has paralysed every courageous endeavour: and we are dishonoured and the name of Italy made a laughing stock among all nations. I am grieved to belong to a family in which there are so many cowards; but do not believe that I am disheartened, or that I doubt of my country's destiny. I cherish more hope now than ever. An individual may be dishonoured with impunity, but not a nation. The traitors are known. The heart of Italy still beats, and if it is not wholly sound, it is yet capable of cutting out those parts that are diseased. The reaction, by slander and calumny, has succeeded in terrifying the people: but the people will not forgive the slander and calumny. It will arise from its stupor and destroy the instruments of its dishonour.

Write, please, I repeat; I need news of you and of my mother and the children: do not worry about me, I am stronger than ever, and with my one thousand two hundred armed men I feel invincible. Rome has become a place of grandeur. Men of heart gather round her and God will help us. Present my salutations to Augusto, to the Galli, Gustarini, Court and all friends. I love you dearly! and I beg you not to worry. A kiss for me to the children, and to my mother whom I commend to you.

Addio, thy

GARIBALDI.

XIII

AT last the rain came. It began to fall on the morning of April 21, and it fell all day. The twenty-first was the natal day of Rome, and the Republic had arranged to celebrate the occasion with feasts and illuminations at least equal in splendour to those that Rome had enjoyed under the Popes. The populace was superstitious, and thought the omens were against the new rulers.

But on the following day the sun blazed out and the postponed celebrations took place. General Avezzana, the Minister of War, reviewed ten thousand troops and twenty pieces of artillery in the piazza before St. Peter's. In the evening the Colosseum was filled with an immense crowd. Somewhere in the dark a band played. One national hymn followed another. Then a light began to invade the arena while the people clapped. It spread until the whole amphitheatre was illumined with the three colours of the Republic. The basement was red, the next two storeys green, and the top was white.

Mazzini sat closeted for more than an hour that day with a French envoy who explained to him that the new Republic needed protection, and could have it from France on certain terms. A little later, the French envoy having gone, a scholarly-looking Englishman appeared from the anteroom where he had been waiting for more than an hour. Mazzini's interview with the Frenchman had been a duel of wits; and it was with relief that the Italian greeted Arthur Hugh Clough, whose mild and humorous countenance concealed nothing but the most benevolent curiosity about the Republic. They agreed that *The Times* had been publishing ridiculous articles, probably inspired from Vienna; and Mazzini begged Clough to tell his English friends that the Italians were in earnest; they were neither mountebanks nor children. Mazzini had not lived in England for nothing. Out of the well-stocked larder of his mind he selected the items which he thought suitable for London. The Republic, he said, was essentially 'respectable'. Socialism, or indeed any social changes, were 'undreamt of'. The rumour that Church lands were to be divided among the peasants was not true: only a surplus would be thus divided after the interests of the institutions to which they belonged had been adequately considered. Money, he regretted, was scarce; but this was the case in all revolutions.

There were, said Mazzini proudly, about 22,000 troops under arms, and the Republic meant to increase the number to 50,000. Not, of course, that such a force could hope to repel the army of a European nation; but it would be able to give some account of itself. Above all, concluded

Mazzini, emerging from the cloud of diplomacy and showing a glint of fire, there would be no restoration of the temporal power of the Pope. A spiritual leader he remained: but the left and right of the Assembly were firm in their agreement that if the Pope were restored to the enjoyment of his temporal power there would be no end to the régime of distrust, conspiracy and assassination.

Mazzini talked for half an hour. He had much to do, but his love of civil conversation was unabated. Clough had expected to find a flaming fanatic and was pleased to discover a man of the world. 'He is a less fanatical, fixed-idea sort of man than I had expected', he wrote to his friend Palgrave.[1] 'He appeared shifty and practical enough. He seemed in excellent spirits, and generally confident and at ease. He asked me if I had seen anything of the pillaging which the English papers were acquainted with: he said that any of the English residents would bear witness to the perfect tranquillity, even greater than before, which prevailed in the city (and certainly I see nothing to the contrary).'

Thousands of pilgrims, said Clough, were kissing the toe of St. Peter 'as fast as they could have done in the best days'.

The day after Clough's visit, however, a squadron of five ships, carrying ten thousand men, anchored in the bay of Civita Vecchia, a matter of forty miles from Rome. The French envoy had hinted that such an expedition might appear, and he suggested that it should be welcomed in a friendly manner; but the expedition was equipped with sixteen field and six siege guns, an armament intended, it was explained, to prevent bloodshed. General Oudinot, the French general in command, sent a member of his staff, Colonel Leblanc, to interview Mazzini. France, Leblanc said, had decided to put Italy's affairs in order, by which was meant, among other things, and first and foremost, the restoration without haggling or conditions of the Pope.

[1] *Prose Remains*, p. 147 f.

Mazzini blew cigar smoke thoughtfully, 'And if we do not wish to have the Pope restored?' he enquired.

'He will', answered Leblanc, 'be restored all the same.'

Mazzini was convinced that Rome would fall, however it was defended. His function, as he conceived it, was to snatch a few moments of time and in them build a temporary edifice of beautiful proportions. It might last a week or a year: not longer. But while it lasted it would have the perfection of a dream, on the memory of which he could live. His smile betrayed a slight weariness, the weariness of a Christian at war with the realities of the world, at war with the Chamber, with the imperfect citizens of Rome as well as with the Pope. He knew that the world as he wanted it was not likely ever to be a real world; but he was glad that in his lifetime the chance had come to show what a Christian republic should be. He was glad, too, that the transient republic was in Rome, established in the city where the grandeur of Italy had left traces in the stones. To Clough, the English poet, the ruins of Rome were overrated masonry, but to Mazzini they meant that in the past Italians had given such an example to the world as he thought to give now.

The cafés were full. Sallow youths clanked sabres and took off their drinks with a martial air. Garibaldi's legionaries entered the city on April 27; they had shaggy beards, unkempt hair, and wore conical hats with black feathers. Garibaldi rode a white horse. Many in Rome saw him for the first time, and the cosmopolitan colony of artists noted with astonishment that he did not look like an Italian. With his broad forehead and blond hair he looked Germanic. There was nothing ferocious about him; he had the modest appearance of a man who fought in a good cause. And there was something else. There was a touch of the Christ in him as there was in Mazzini. In Mazzini it was the Christ awaiting crucifixion, and in Garibaldi it was a Christ who would lead his followers to a chosen land.

A Dutch artist named Koelman happened to enter the

piazza before the convent of San Silvestro just at the moment when Garibaldi's troops were parading in the square. A few nuns were scurrying out of the convent, lifting their heavy skirts and elbowing their way into the carriages which had been hastily summoned to drive them and their belongings away; and while this was going on Garibaldi stood grimly watching. Outside the gates of Rome he had halted his men only the day before to tell them that they must behave in an orderly way, so that the slanders of the clericals should be rebutted; but no one had informed the unfortunate nuns of the convent of San Silvestro that the town-major proposed to billet the garibaldini there. When the latter arrived the nuns had just been warned and were packing. Garibaldi had had to endure many slights in the past weeks and he fancied this was another; he ordered his men in, nuns or no nuns.[1] As the nuns filed out, the garabaldini filed in. They did not wear ugly shakos and an abundance of braid like the other defenders of Rome, but loose blue tunics and black belts in which was stuck a short dagger. Some of them carried muskets and others spears.

The convent gate was wide open. Koelman asked a sentry if it was permitted to go inside. 'Sicuro', said the latter without troubling to rise from the carved seat on which he had disposed himself; but there was little to see inside, where the troops had strawed the floors and were throwing themselves down to rest. They paid no attention to Garibaldi when he came in, nor did the sentry move from his place on the seat, although Garibaldi, by a recent edict, had been promoted to the rank of general. Koelman politely removed his hat and asked an officer if the garibaldini were always so little respectful; at which the officer smiled. They were more respectful on the battlefield, he said. Garibaldi, meantime, stood talking to an aide-de-camp while his blue eye ranged quietly over the hall. Koelman wondered at the power of the eyes and decided that their expression was one of frankness. The face of the hero was not beautiful, being burned a bright red by the sun and marked with freckles.

[1] Lœvinson, i. p. 159.

The nose was broad at the root and this, with the long chestnut hair that hung on his neck, gave him a leonine appearance. He had a short beard and a heavy moustache.

There was no suggestion of the general about him. He carried his own cartridge-bag at his left side and wore, instead of the blue shirt of his men, a red shirt he had brought from South America.[1]

The Republic of Rome was now in being, so far as that could be accomplished by the promulgation of edicts; and with the help of Avezzana, a business man who had been made Minister of War, it was prepared to deal with any enemy who unduly interfered with it. But, being a Republic, it liked to see its soldiers inside the walls, where their presence increased the confidence of the citizens; and for this reason, although obviously Rome could only be defended from the outside by forces playing on the flank of the attacker, it neglected to dispatch any portion of the garrison outside, consenting only as a measure of evident military necessity to manning certain strong points beyond the walls and to covering the approaches to the northern and western gates. On the morning of April 28, after a review of the troops by Avezzana, the garibaldini were transferred to billets in the Trastevere quarter, and Garibaldi took up his position in the villas on the high ground outside the Porta San Pancrazio. On the night of the 29th-30th, he sent out a patrol which brought back a prisoner. This was the first act of war. Then, on the morning of April 30, there was a furious clanging of bells from the Montecitorio and the Campidoglio. A sentry posted on the northern wall of St. Peter's had seen a French column moving on Rome along the road from Civita Vecchia.

The French were in good spirits. They had been sent to occupy Rome and did not anticipate any difficulty. As they drew near to the city they heard the bells and concluded that the Romans had already begun to rejoice at the coming of their deliverers. The French force was about eight

---

[1] Koelman, J. P., *In Rome*, 1869, quoted by Trevelyan, *Defence*, p. 116 ff.

thousand strong, under generals Molière and Levaillant. At the end of the column trailed a couple of field pieces.

Oudinot hoped that the column would walk in. But he was prepared for some resistance and had formulated his plan of attack. The column, at a certain distance from Rome, was to divide. One section was to advance on the Angelica gate, the other on the Cavaleggieri gate: and this dual movement having puzzled the defenders, the French would make good their entry and assemble in the Piazza of Saint Peter. It was a plan that implied a great contempt for the enemy; or a belief that when the troops of the Republic got within hailing distance they would be welcomed as brothers. The bells had stopped ringing, but the bands of some of the newly formed Roman regiments had struck up the Marseillaise, and kept up the music all day.

The Chasseurs de Vincennes went left towards the Angelica gate. They were experienced troops, trained to take advantage of natural cover; and their experience was soon needed. A hail of grapeshot rained down on them, compelling them to lie down and reply with musket fire. But it seemed that the whole population of Rome was manning the walls. In the centre Garibaldi was watching the progress of the fight from the Pamfili gardens and judged that a charge against the main column of the enemy might settle the fate of the day. The amateurs on the walls, seeing beneath them a surging rush of men whom they took to be the enemy, fired on their friends: but, after a halt, Garibaldi resumed his attack and drove the French before him at the point of the bayonet. They retired on the main column, and a consultation took place among the French staff. A Captain Faby, who said he knew a road which led right up to the Vatican gardens to a point where they could storm the Angelica gate, was entrusted with a detachment of men which got as far as the Consular road. There the glinting of the sun on the bayonets betrayed the detachment to the defenders on the walls, and the rain of grapeshot began again more murderously than before. Captain Faby was wounded by a bullet. The detachment, caught between convergent fire from three sides, ran to ground in wayside cottages. A similar fate befell a detachment under Colonel Picard, which held on to some high ground for a few hours and found itself at last boxed in a villa and besieged on all sides. Colonel Picard surrendered with three hundred men.

The attack on Rome had failed. After ten hours' fighting the French had lost thirteen hundred men, killed, wounded or prisoners, against a hundred casualties on the side of the Romans.[1] Garibaldi held all the high ground and was in a position to cut off the retreat of the French survivors towards Civita Vecchia. He sent a message to Avezzana asking for fresh troops, with which he promised to prevent the French ever reaching their ships. But Mazzini intervened, declaring that if a crushing defeat were inflicted on France that country would become the mortal enemy of the Roman Republic. The argument had no military validity; and small validity of any kind. But it prevailed; and Oudinot was allowed to retire to Civita Vecchia to concoct dispatches in which he minimised his losses and ascribed his defeat to the treachery of the Italians. 'Quel Mazzini', said Garibaldi many years later, when a friend spoke to him about the unsatisfactory conclusion of the day's fighting, 'che ha sempre avuto la smania di fare il Generale e non ne capiva.'[2] It was a defect of republics which he had noticed before, and was to notice again.

'Perhaps it will amuse you hereafter', wrote Arthur Hugh Clough to his sister, 'to have a letter commenced while the guns are firing, and I suppose men falling dead and wounded. Such is the case on the other side of the Tiber, while I peacefully write in my distant chamber with only the sound in my ears. I went up to the Pincian hill and saw the smoke and heard the occasional big cannon and the sharp succession of skirmishers' volleys—bang, bang, bang,—away beyond St. Peter's. They say the French have settled down in three positions, and do not mean to enter

---

[1] French accounts put the losses of the attackers at about nine hundred.
[2] Guerzoni, i. p. 272.

till the Neapolitans arrive. And the affair of to-day is probably only with their advanced guard: the Romans profess to have carried off four cannon and fifty prisoners, but who knows?'

The Romans did not know what to do with their three hundred odd prisoners. They showed them the sights of Rome, presented them (at Mazzini's instigation) with cigars, and after a day or two sent them back to their friends at Civita Vecchia. Some French officers who had lost their swords were presented with swords from the Republic's armoury. The wounded, French and Roman, were devotedly nursed by Roman ladies under the direction of the Princess Belgioso.

XIV

A GREAT composure had come to Pius IX since he had endured the worst disaster that can befall a Pope; his mind, which had formerly been full of hope and indecision, was now as placid as the surface of a lake over which the storm has passed. With a detachment which surprised the eager French ambassador he listened to an account of the expedition which had set out to restore him to Rome; and which, said the ambassador, would accomplish this object in spite of temporary set-backs. Pius IX seemed to remember only one thing concerning France; which was that it was a republic, a democratic country; and between such a country and the Papal throne there could be, he said, no alliance. These dreams were past; no, he repeated, he would give France no guarantee of any kind in exchange for her services. Even if they were successful he promised nothing.

He had discovered, in the interval, that a defeated Pope was more precious than rubies. Whereas in Rome he had been buffeted between his cardinals and bullied by ominous Austrian diplomats, at Gaeta, where he was now the guest of Ferdinand of Sicily, he was besieged by flattery and inundated with offers of service. Without any invitation or prayer on his part a Spanish squadron had begun to sail up the Mediterranean; the Austrians were descending on the Legations from the north; and, as the ambassador assured him, the French were preparing to retrieve their first defeat under the walls of Rome. Last but not least, his host, Ferdinand of Sicily, nicknamed Bomba because of the bombs with which he had quelled the insurrection in his own kingdom, was marching north to the southern fringe of the Roman provinces. Bomba was a Bourbon, charming in personal manner, adventurous and cynical in his conversation, clever, humorous and unsentimental. He had things to say about liberals which Pius enjoyed hearing; and he treated the Pontiff with a respectful decorum that was in itself a pleasure. Of all his possible deliverers Pius preferred Bomba and hoped he would succeed. He liked Bomba, Bomba was in a military sense as likely a knight as any; and his reactionary mentality, after the Pope's recent experiences, was singularly comforting.

Hearing of the French defeat, Bomba was advancing with twenty thousand men, thirty-six field guns, a respectable force of cavalry, and the prestige that came from a recent easy victory over his own subjects in Sicily and Calabria. By the beginning of May he had occupied Velletri, Albano and Frascati, and his advanced posts cantered insolently within a few miles of the southern walls of Rome.

On May 4 Garibaldi was dispatched to meet him; and on that day the legionaries paraded about two thousand five hundred strong in the Piazza del Popolo; they were reinforced by a battalion of bersaglieri under Manara, two companies of the National Guard and young men from the citizen classes enrolled as members of the University Legion or the Customs battalion. Hoffstetter, a German Swiss who had been trying to find employment in the Roman armies, was allocated to the staff. He was modest, painstaking and useful, having had some military experience that was to prove of service, and he kept a diary also, a fact which is of still greater importance, for this diary is one of the sources from which the tale of the Roman

Republic, as well as of its defender Garibaldi, is derived. He had a few days to spare before Garibaldi's expedition left Rome, and he spent them as a sightseer, taking stock of the Eternal City. At night there were only a few patches of darkness where houses had been left empty by absconding nobles. The rest was illuminated. The joy of the Romans, Hoffstetter noted, was not unseemly. There had only been one unpleasant case. A priest had been caught red-handed firing a revolver at the Roman troops on April 30. A military tribunal had condemned him to death; but on one of the Tiber bridges he was torn from the escort, beaten to death and thrown into the river.

The parade took place at six o'clock, and punctually at that hour Garibaldi rode on to the square. He sat his horse as if he had been born on it, and wore a felt hat with a narrow brim adorned with an ostrich feather. A reddish beard covered the lower part of his face, and from under the hat appeared clusters of brown hair. A short white cloak fluttered loosely over a red shirt. Immediately behind Garibaldi was Aguyar, the negro, in a long black cloak. About eight o'clock in the failing light the troops formed into column and marched off the square.

No one knew where they were going. They turned right after passing through the Porta del Popolo and bore round in a long curve until they struck the Via Pranestina, which leads in the direction of Palestrina. Every now and then the column halted in an open space and awaited the reports of officers who were sent out in several directions to reconnoitre. The march continued thus throughout the night, ending at a mountain's foot about an hour's distance from Tivoli. They had covered twenty-four miles instead of the eighteen which separate Tivoli from Rome: but they had led the spies to believe that the expedition was intended against the French, whereas it now lay ready to attack the flank of Bomba's army.

Aguyar unsaddled Garibaldi's horse and made a rough tent by throwing the general's cloak over his sword and sheath propped crosswise on a lance. The general scribbled some notes, threw his horse blanket on the ground, lay down on it and was asleep in a moment. Hoffstetter considered the prostrate form in astonishment. There were other details which surprised but did not displease him. The horses were not tethered, but let loose to browse at will; and when they were wanted again their proprietors went after them with lassos, a system which did not seem to provide for the case of a surprise attack by the enemy. On the other hand, although no sentries were posted, the officers set off in various directions and appeared to reconnoitre the surrounding country very thoroughly. A herd of sheep had been driven in and slaughtered with knife and bayonet. The apportioning of the rough lumps of carcase was a delicate matter which took a long time, after which the camp lay down to sleep, gorged and happy. There was no bread nor any sign that the column was likely to be provided for except by such means as it had adopted.

At five o'clock on the same day the camp broke up and the column moved to Hadrian's Villa, where officers and men were accommodated in the shelter of the famous ruins and in the cellars and underground galleries. From the heights of Tivoli Hoffstetter could see the dome of St. Peter's. He bought rum, sugar and lemons in a shop in Tivoli to regale his new friends: but, returning in the darkness, he found them all fast asleep.

The ground in the neighbourhood of Tivoli appeared as a vast unbroken sea of green: but it was cut by narrow gorges, through one of which, on the following day, the column moved towards the high road of Palestrina. In spite of its appearance, the country was wild and uncultivated, with never a house to be seen. The column encamped at midday in a valley where there was shade and water. At half-past five the march was resumed, this time uphill. It was one in the morning before they came out on the Palestrina road; but the men were not unduly tired. Garibaldi, not knowing what might be in store, had ordered frequent halts.

While the officers, following their custom, set off on reconnaissances, the troops were marched into the town of Palestrina and ordered to occupy quarters in the monasteries. There was other accommodation in plenty, but Garibaldi preferred not to use it; they were making war, he said, against *all* the enemies of the Republic, and his procedure indicated that he meant to make war on the monks by the same kind of indirect means which they used themselves. Hoffstetter's section was sent to the monastery of Sant' Antonio, where the monks at first refused to open the gates, and were persuaded only by the threat that the gates would be broken down. Once in possession, the troops fetched the mattresses out of the cells and made the monks bring wine, cheese and cigars. At the Augustine convent Manara's detachment knocked for an hour. Then they sent for sappers, who removed the doors. The monks thereupon packed their goods and left, much to the satisfaction of the new inmates, who investigated the contents of the cells and promenaded the corridors in long white robes and Dominican hats. At roll-call every man of Manara's troop appeared with an enormous wax candle in his hand. The private correspondence of the monks occasioned a great deal of frivolous comment. In this way, not altogether without some intention on his own part, Garibaldi strengthened the report which declared him an enemy of religion; his repugnance in dealing with monks and priests was so spontaneous that he did not stop to consider whether such actions furthered the cause of the Republic or of Italy. Least of all did he ask himself how they would affect his own career or his own reputation. The monks represented in his view obscurantism and tyranny; and they called for an obedience that as a free natural leader he was bound to dislike. They were men of another faith; almost, he thought, of another God.

The enemy was known to be in the neighbourhood of Valmontone about five hundred strong, while the main Neapolitan army lay across the Rome-Naples coast road, protected on their left flank by the sea. Valmontone itself was a natural stronghold from which it would have been difficult to dislodge anyone who had a mind to resist; and it was plain to Garibaldi that if he did hazard such an attack the defenders would hold on until the main force came up to their assistance. Instead, therefore, of concealing his presence, he sent parties of men to canter somewhat obviously in the open around Valmontone. Also the garibaldini marched ostentatiously out of Palestrina, to the relief of the monks, and equally ostentatiously marched in again to their disgust. These movements were intended to puzzle the observers at Valmontone, and no doubt they served their purpose. The troops, somewhat puzzled themselves, made the most of the monks' wine and enjoyed the caprices of their cunning leader.

Garibaldi was waiting for some initiative from Rome. He hoped that Avezzana would march out and attack the main Neapolitan column while he fell on it from the flank; but there was no sign from Avezzana, and there were indications that nervousness on the part of the triumvirate would soon cause Garibaldi to be recalled to Rome. On the other hand, Ferdinand was not anxious to fight his way into the city: he meant rather to feel his way in, trusting that where the French had failed he would succeed. On three sides, in Rome, in the French camp and in the Neapolitan army, there was a disposition to wait and see; and only on Garibaldi's side was the opposite tendency noticeable. His main idea now was to have a slap at the Neapolitans before he was recalled: but he was too experienced a soldier to lose his head. He knew Bomba was no fool. Accordingly, while drill went on in a meadow outside Palestrina, scouting parties of about twenty men under an officer scoured the country and occasionally picked up a few prisoners. Three waggon-loads of greatcoats intended for Bomba's army were intercepted and distributed among the garibaldini on May 8. It was a small triumph, but it helped the morale.

The following day was cloudless and immaculately beautiful. From Tivoli the movements of the enemy around Valmontone were clearly distinguishable. A small detachment had pushed forward and occupied a hill near a church about two miles distant from Garibaldi's positions. The movement looked too obvious, as if it was intended to attract observation. From his own view of the position as it had been developing in the last five days as well as from statements gathered from prisoners, Garibaldi thought that an attack was due.

The country suited him. There could have been no better site for hole-and-corner fighting than this terrain slotted by deep lanes and ravines; no ground less suitable to the operations of barrack-trained troops and more favourable to men prepared for guerrilla warfare. Palestrina itself was pitched on a hill, the surrounding ground sloping up to the inner walls and to the pinnacle on which stood the castle of San Pietro. The lower ground, too, was partly ringed by a wall which in some places was sound and which afforded everywhere good vantage to the defenders. Immediately inside the town walls were massive buildings separated by narrow alleys, from which, if necessary, a desperate resistance could be prolonged. Outside, hedges, trees, vineyards enclosed by walls completed the natural fortifications. Nevertheless Bomba had hopes. And it soon appeared what they were. A column was to cut in on the north side between Palestrina and Rome, making it impossible for Avezzana to join forces with Garibaldi. If this operation were successfully conducted Palestrina would be threatened with isolation and Garibaldi induced to evacuate it.

It was about two in the afternoon that the nature of the enemy's operations became clear. By that time from the Monte San Pietro two columns could be seen advancing along two roads which joined at Palestrina under the Porta del Sole. The columns were advancing slowly; and presently, as if to declare their intentions, a couple of four-pounder field pieces sent a scattered volley of flint shot in the direction of the gate. Colonel Manara, commanding a detachment of bersaglieri, had taken up his station on high ground above the Porta del Sole, and his orders to the defenders were conveyed by trumpet calls. Two companies of Garibaldi's Legion had gone out in scouting order to meet the enemy on the difficult ground in the valley. When the latter had got to close quarters they were met by a hot fire. The Neapolitans were still in column and refused to deploy, although their officers could be heard shouting to them to do so. They clung together like frightened sheep, and at the first bayonet charge turned and ran helter-skelter. The column on the left was the first to go. The second column had been allowed to come within pistol-shot and had taken possession of two houses which served them as strong points. A general charge ordered by Garibaldi dislodged them. Soon the whole force, after an engagement lasting only three hours, was in flight, leaving its field pieces behind. There were about twenty prisoners, who were no sooner brought before Garibaldi than they fell on their knees and, with clasped hands, begged him to spare their lives. They were handsome fellows, slung with images, amulets, madonnas, and relics, all destined to protect them from the evil eye. They said that they had been ordered to take Palestrina and seize the person of Garibaldi.

The engagement could not be described in any sense as decisive; for the Neapolitan army was intact and, except that it seemed to have lost any desire to molest Garibaldi, its position was as sound as ever. It occupied the heights of Albano and Frascati and might at any moment effect a junction with the French for the purpose of an attack on Rome. But for the time being Garibaldi had succeeded in checking the enemy, and he had kept open the roads between Rome and Anagni and Frosinone by which wine, oil and corn were brought to the capital.

Nevertheless, instead of leaving him to harass the flank of the Neapolitans, the triumvirs ordered him to return to Rome, where it was feared a French attack would be launched on the Monte Mario. On the night of the 11th-12th May, Garibaldi's small force covered the twenty-eight miles in dead silence, passing within a couple of miles of the Neapolitan camp, only to learn on their arrival that Ferdinand de Lesseps, acting as ambassador extraordinary of the French Republic, had interviewed Mazzini and concluded an armistice.

XV

WHAT with the armistice and the return of Garibaldi's victorious troops, the new Republic was beginning to feel its feet. It occurred to Avezzana, the Minister of War, that the time had come to deal effectively with Bomba, not by an expedition conducted precariously by the guerrilla leader, Garibaldi, but by an official exploit in which the regular troops and staff officers would be engaged. Garibaldi expressed no disapproval. He said he was willing to serve in such an expedition, as a private soldier if need be; and that he would take his orders from anyone the Republic cared to appoint. In the end the Republic committed the care of the expedition to General Roselli, and preparations began.

Hoffstetter and his fellow-officers were at breakfast on the morning of May 16, when news came in that a division was being formed, consisting of three brigades, one under Garibaldi and the other two under Colonel Masi and the cavalry general Galetti, respectively. At the last moment Manara's bersaglieri had received no orders to move; but after the other troops had set out, a mounted orderly arrived with a hot enquiry why he had *not* marched with the others; and it was explained to Manara, who overtook the main column at midnight after a furious march, that Roselli, the general commanding, thought Garibaldi would transmit the order to march to the bersaglieri, and Garibaldi was under the impression that this would naturally be done by Roselli.

At Zargarolla it was discovered that there was no food to be had. The Neapolitans had evacuated Zargarolla only the day before, and nothing could be obtained from the inhabitants; even wine, without which an Italian army could not be expected to sustain the hardships of a campaign, was exceedingly scarce. There was wheat: but no one had thought of converting it into flour; and, to complete the tale, the men had been allowed to march without an iron ration. But for Garibaldi they would have starved. He arrived driving along a number of cattle which were cut up, apportioned and roasted in the approved fashion.

So far as could be judged, the intention of the expedition was to drive southward and threaten the rear of the Neapolitan army which lay, about twenty thousand strong, in the neighbourhood of Velletri. And in this purpose it would certainly not have succeeded had the Neapolitans not been in worse condition than their attackers. The Roman expedition was amateurish; and, above all, it violated the principal condition of success, which was secrecy. But the Neapolitans suffered from a desire not to fight. They were feeling far from home and indifferent to the military purposes of their leader, King Ferdinand. As Garibaldi estimated the position, they had every kind of superiority, of numbers, of position, of artillery and of cavalry. Their left wing was protected by the sea and their right by the Apennines. Further, they had occupied Palestrina and so dominated the valley road to Rome, by which alone any massive force could be moved against them. The Roman force counted only eight thousand men, of which only about a third was to come into effective action. But the Neapolitans had against them their enfeebled morale.

On May 18 Garibaldi found to his astonishment that the Neapolitans had evacuated Palestrina and Valmontone, as well as the higher ground of the Monte Fortino. They were in full retreat on Velletri; and, at the rate of progress of the republican force which was toiling in disgruntled sections along the narrow Apennine passes, it looked as if the Neapolitans might escape altogether. He at once sent forward a detachment to reconnoitre the outskirts of

Velletri. 'I did not hope', he says in his memoirs, 'that with fifteen hundred men I should be able to beat the twenty thousand of the King of Naples; but I did hope to lure them on and, while keeping them busy, to give the main body of our army time to come up and join in the battle.' It was on the 19th that this characteristic project was put into execution: and, sure enough, a battalion of light infantry was seen to leave Velletri and to deploy. Acting on their instructions, the republican outposts gave away their location readily; and, when the Neapolitans advanced they retired.

Up to this point Garibaldi may be said to have conformed to military tradition as well as to his own inspiration. And having drawn the enemy he ought doubtless to have consulted Roselli, his commander-in-chief, as to the extent to which he should commit himself to battle.[1] But Garibaldi's purpose, or his instinct, was to commit both sides to battle, his own as well as the enemy's. Hoffstetter was in the thick of administrative difficulties when the sound of firing reached him on the 19th, and a messenger came from Garibaldi asking that the bersaglieri should be sent up in support. Roselli replied that this was impossible as the men 'had not had their soup'. This inspired answer was dispatched without the cognisance of Manara, who demanded authority to march at once; and after an hour permission was given.

The Neapolitan cavalry had followed the opening skirmishing movements of the infantry. At first repulsed by a steady fire from Garibaldi's outposts, it gathered for a headlong charge along the road. They were five hundred men: and for reasons best known to himself, and certainly not to be explained by any military text-book, Garibaldi elected to meet them head on with his own mounted men, who numbered not more than fifty. They met like Crusader and Saracen; but the sheer weight of numbers

[1] All the authorities, including Trevelyan, *Defence of Rome*, p. 154, who speaks of a 'gross breach of discipline', are agreed that Garibaldi was guilty of something like calculated (or inspired) disobedience.

carried the Neapolitans right through the small body of horsemen, and when they had passed Garibaldi, the latter found himself on the ground at some distance from his horse.[1] He sprang to his feet, hacking at the enemy to keep them off until he could mount again. And no sooner had he succeeded in this than he stuck his hat on his sabre and waved it in the air to let his men know he was not dead. They recognised him easily, as he was the only man on the field to wear a white poncho with a red lining.

The Neapolitans had done too well. Their charge had carried them through to Garibaldi's second line, which lay ambushed on the high ground on both sides of the road. Finding that they were being shot at and could not shoot back, they turned and made for their own people. At this stage of the fight Garibaldi sent for help and did not get it. The artillery on both sides was just coming into action and the battle settling down to an exchange of missiles from opposite hills when, at last, Manara's bersaglieri came up, their black plumes waving in the wind. Bit by bit the Neapolitans were being driven back. A band was playing a lively tune. And such was the elation of the bersaglieri at being near a fight that they stopped short and started dancing to the music. A cannon ball accounted for two of the dancers.

Manara was of opinion that they should take Velletri by assault; which was exactly what Garibaldi wanted to do. But, he said, with two thousand men and two cannon, how can we take a town perched like an eagle's nest and defended by twenty thousand men and thirty cannon? Through his glasses he could see there was a breach in the wall to the right of the gate. It was stopped with osiers which a couple of shots would send flying. The cover on the hillside was not of the best: but there were trees that would afford some shelter while the men worked their way to the breach, and the sappers would break down any

---

[1] The accounts of this incident differ. According to Lœvinson, i. 186, Masina's lancers were routed by the Neapolitans, and it was in an attempt to hold them that Garibaldi was overridden. He received two slight wounds, on the hand and the foot.

fortifications that might have been erected by the enemy. The enterprise required, however, a minimum of five thousand men, in other words, the whole of the force under the command of Roselli; and Garibaldi dispatched a message to this effect, asking for immediate support so that the attack could begin while the Neapolitans were still demoralised. But the support was not forthcoming. When Roselli did at last arrive with reinforcements, Garibaldi judged that the favourable moment had passed. So the day ended unsatisfactorily, the bersaglieri amusing themselves sniping at the enemy on the ramparts, and the Swiss gunners of King Ferdinand returning the compliment with artillery fire from the Capuchin convent.

About midnight Garibaldi sent an officer and forty men to see how matters were in Velletri. Sub-lieutenant Emilio Dandolo, the officer in question, first encountered two peasants who said the Neapolitans had gone. The town gate had been destroyed by gun-fire and was replaced by a barricade which Dandolo and his men scaled cautiously. There was no sentinel and, but for a handful of stragglers, there were no Neapolitans. Dandolo knocked up the inhabitants, and was informed that the retreat had begun almost at the first sign of night.

There were many things which might have been done and which, thanks to the cumbrous organisation of the expedition, had not been done. But at any rate Garibaldi had the satisfaction of sleeping on the night of May 20 in a magnificent bed in the Palazzo Lancellotti in Velletri; he was not partial to luxurious beds, but this one had been occupied only two nights before by King Bomba himself, and the circumstance gave him a republican feeling which was agreeable.

On May 20 he planted a tree of liberty and pronounced a speech. There was a madonna in one of the Velletri churches reputed to be miraculous. With some ostentation he paid a visit to the church and delighted the populace. But the local clergy were not pleased. Almost to the last nun and monk they vanished overnight.

When he went to sleep on the night of May 20, Garibaldi had already given up hope of being able to do further damage to King Ferdinand. But in the morning he was optimistic again and wrote to the triumvirate suggesting that he should be allowed to prosecute the expedition. As Roselli wrote at the same time saying that he thought such a course would be unwise, the triumvirate of Rome recalled Roselli and left Garibaldi to his own devices. They were not averse from gathering in any profits that might come from the adventures of their brilliant servant.

At the same time they left him only a skeleton force, Masina's lancers, Manara's bersaglieri and a regiment of Roman volunteers under Colonel Masi. But it was soon evident that Garibaldi, even with this handful of men, proposed to do something. He requested from the treasury enough money in gold and silver to pay seven thousand men for a fortnight; although, be it noted, he did not specify where the seven thousand men were to come from. The treasury responded, after a second request to the same effect, by authorising the dispatch of 35,000 scudi, part in gold and part in silver, the remainder to be made up as necessary, in paper money. Whether Garibaldi ever received this sum we do not know.

The seven thousand men were to be recruited from the deserters of the Neapolitan army and from the well-disposed of the countryside. But these sources proved disappointing. The clergy spread rumours as they went: and in some places Garibaldi found that the population had actually fled before him. On May 23, at three in the morning, Garibaldi left Velletri and reached Frosinone on the 24th, remaining there until the 26th. On the following day he proposed to give himself the satisfaction of invading the Kingdom of Naples. He lunched under an oak tree at Ceprano at a matter of twenty minutes' march from the little bridge and column that marked the frontier, surveyed the ground before him in his usual careful manner; and, on the 27th, crossing the frontier with some of his Legion and Manara's bersaglieri, ascended a spur of the

Abruzzi, from which he could continue his observations. He had just decided to advance by Aquino and San Germano when a courier arrived from Rome with an order recalling him at once. Bologna had fallen to the Austrians on May 15, after an heroic defence; and the Austrians were threatening Ancona. It was to be feared that they might cut off Rome from Umbria and the Marches whence some part of the capital's supplies were derived, as well as press on to the Abruzzi to join the Neapolitans. This last eventuality was not very probable, as the Pope's friends showed little inclination to co-operate with each other. But the order from Rome left Garibaldi no choice, except as to the route by which he would return. He chose the Abruzzi. For, of a sudden, his old hatred of the Austrians had flamed up, and he hoped only that on his way back he might find a few and hack them to pieces. They touched him on the raw; and it was a very raw Garibaldi who wrote on May 29 to Masina, telling him to prepare his men for meeting the Austrians, 'the most terrible and abominated of our enemies'. 'Tell the legionaries', he wrote, 'to get the idea well into their heads, let them think of it all day and dream of it at night. Let them think of a charge with cold steel (*a ferro freddo*) and of sticking a sharp bayonet into the flank of a cannibal.... Give an order of the day making the following prayer obligatory: Oh God! grant me the grace that I may put all the steel of my bayonet inside a Tedesco, and not deign to pull the trigger but keep my shot to kill a second Tedesco at not more than ten paces.' The Neapolitans were children, sorry relatives who made Garibaldi ashamed but who inspired no hatred; the Austrians were *stranieri*, foreigners who awoke in him a lust for killing. With this idea Garibaldi ordered 8000 rations to be held ready at Sora against his arrival. However, a second message came saying he must suspend all operations and return to Rome with all speed: in response to which he re-entered Rome at eleven in the morning on May 31, prepared to collaborate in the defence of the city.[1]

[1] Guerzoni, i. 301.

Mazzini was to have his dream, a few weeks of the perfect republic, with peace and goodwill and Christianity operating inside the walls, and at the end of them Rome was to be crucified as an example to Europe, its garrison of enthusiasts offered in a single mouthful (*in un sol boccone*), Garibaldi said, to the French.

But whatever the latter thought he gave no sign, and the Romans, seeing the poncho again, were aware of a sensation of security, as if, not the Holy Father himself, but a deputy father had come among them, beside whom they would come to no harm. Hoffstetter himself, when Garibaldi offered him a cigar, felt like a man living a dream.[1]

XVI

Hoffstetter had returned to Rome a couple of days before Garibaldi. He found the city very cheerful and peaceful. Shops and cafés were full; and there was a marked absence of uniforms in the streets. It was generally thought that the negotiations with the French would mark the end of hostilities.

On these grounds Hoffstetter made up his mind to go home. But Manara dissuaded him. Even if all went well in the French negotiations, he said, the Austrians had to be held off, and there was likely to be plenty fighting for any man who wanted it. Hoffstetter was not entirely persuaded, but he decided to wait and watch the turn of events. On June 2 he read a notice which said that a truce had been concluded with the French, subject to denunciation on either side after a period of fifteen days. On the evening of the same day a second notice was posted alongside the first. It was signed by the French commander Oudinot, and declared that Lesseps had exceeded his instructions in concluding the truce. The French would attack Rome on the morning of June 4. The 4th was a Monday. And between

[1] I have used Hoffstetter's narrative principally for the foregoing pages, as well as Lœvinson, Guerzoni, Trevelyan and others.

two and three on the Sunday morning Manara dragged Hoffstetter out of bed with the news that the French attack had begun.

The officers of the Legion, and indeed of all the units which composed the army of defence, were quartered in comfortable billets all over Rome. Garibaldi was in the Via delle Carrozze, near the Piazza di Spagna, in a modest house (number 59) where the surgeon-major, Pietro Ripari, was attending to the wounds the general had received in the Velletri campaign. The greater part of the Legion was billeted in the convent of San Silvestro, but its officers were scattered in private houses and inns, not all even in adjacent streets. The men of Masina's cavalry were in one place and their horses in another. The first result of the alarm was to send officers scurrying through the streets of Rome looking for their comrades and spreading the incredible news of the attack. It was five o'clock before Garibaldi could get his men to the scene of action. He had pleaded only two days before to be given complete command of the defence. But Mazzini had refused. Nothing had been prepared. During the truce not a single earthwork had been constructed. The day before the attack commenced Roselli exhorted an outpost to take as much rest as possible. When the French attack began the whole of Rome, including the garrison of defence, was asleep.

Garibaldi's orders to the bersaglieri were to assemble at once in the Piazza of St. Peter's. Accordingly officers and men clattered over the cobbled streets to the Forum, and were all ready to march to the rendezvous when an orderly officer brought a second order, this time from Roselli, to the effect that the bersaglieri were to stand by at the Campo Vaccino (Forum). It was plain that there was no reasonable connexion between the second order and the first; and Hoffstetter was dispatched to make contact with Garibaldi and tell him that Manara was ready to disregard the second order and join him at once if he would take the responsibility. It was no small distance to the north of the city. At the bridge of Sant' Angelo Hoffstetter was informed that

Garibaldi had already left the Piazza of St. Peter's and was on his way to the San Pancrazio gate. The information conveyed nothing to Hoffstetter except that he would have to chase the general still further: but, in fact, it meant that Garibaldi had been obliged to give up his first plan, which was to sally from the Porta Cavaleggieri and fall upon the French flank. It was too late to do anything scientific. The French had gained the high Villa Corsini, opposite the San Pancrazio gate, and held the key to the capture of the city.

Hoffstetter abandoned his tired horse and drove in a vetturino through the crowd that thronged the approaches to San Pancrazio. Adjutants and mounted orderlies were galloping this way and that, while wet sand was flung under the feet of their horses to give them a grip on the cobbles. The cab-drivers of Rome were all on their way to the battle, ready to do their share by transporting the wounded to the hospitals. Columns of troops were converging from the side streets. And, while the alarum bells tolled, the populace turned out to witness the spectacle of the siege. There was no lack of zeal on all hands and no lack of confusion. At the Piazza San Montorio Hoffstetter left his carriage and was about to climb the last lap of hill on foot when he heard the horns of the bersaglieri blowing behind him. A third order had reached them in response to which they had proceeded to San Pancrazio. A vetturino trotted slowly past. In it was Staff-Captain Bixio, wounded in the body. He said with a smile that he had got as far as the drawing-room of the Villa Corsini when his horse received nine bullets and himself one. He was very sorry, because the horse was English and a present from Prince Canino.

Garibaldi's poncho and hat were riddled with bullet-holes, but he was unhurt. Nevertheless, after something like an hour's fighting, the casualties were terrible. Daverio, Garibaldi's chief of staff, was killed. Manuli was dead. And three officers, including Bixio, were wounded. The casualties among the men were in proportion.

Oudinot had picked his position. No doubt he had decided on the Villa Corsini after adequate reflection. Once in possession of it he was master on both sides. He was safe on the side of the sea and could cover his own base at Civita Vecchia. And further, as the Corsini was higher than the walls of the city, he could entrench himself there and on the surrounding high ground and reduce the defence at leisure. The only difficulty in the way had been that of gaining possession of the Corsini, and this he had overcome by a stratagem which the Romans called treachery. He said he would not attack Rome before the morning of June 4. 'I am deferring the attack on the place until Monday morning at the earliest', he had written to Roselli. The Romans took that to mean that he would not make any attack of any kind before that time. But in Oudinot's judgment the occupation of the Corsini was not an attack, but the preliminary to an attack. He was manœuvring for position. Whether he was entitled to or not, the Romans should have been in force on the high ground outside the city, with guns in position and sniping posts well covered; instead of which the early morning attack found the Corsini, as well as the adjacent villas Valentini and Pamfili, only lightly held. With this calamitous blunder the defence of Rome began.

The bersaglieri took up their station behind the San Pancrazio gate, while Manara and Hoffstetter joined the general at the gate itself. Presently the latter, with the few officers of his staff who remained, rode forward in order that Garibaldi could explain to Manara the nature of the position. It was a difficult one. The Villa Corsini had to be retaken. But the privileges were all on the side of its present occupants; to such an extent that the most pressing problem confronting Garibaldi and his staff was how to collect troops in sufficient number to make an attack possible. Behind the Corsini on the western side the ground sloped away out of sight; and in the folds of the ground the French were at liberty to assemble and make what preparations they liked. The troops who had already been in action could rest there in complete calm. Neither cannon nor rifle could touch them. And, on the other hand, the French from the walls and windows of the Corsini villa looked down on a gentle declivity which culminated at the walls of Rome. The Romans had to fight uphill and without cover. They had clung to a villa on the right of the Pancrazio gate, the Villa Vascello; and to three houses in advance of the villa. Somehow or other these inadequate vantage points had to be made to serve. But the Vascello itself was dominated, not only by the Corsini, but by a third, and nearer villa, the Villa Valentini; and at the moment of Hoffstetter's arrival a lively fire was dropping from the Valentini into the gardens of the Vascello and about the outlying houses. To reach the Corsini at all, the attackers, after having overcome the initial difficulty of assembling under fire, had to charge along a narrow path enclosed by high boxwood hedges on either side into which, at the proper moment, the French could shoot a few hundred bullets every minute. Hoffstetter knew the ground well and he was all for caution. He wanted to stop and think. The odds were heavy; first the harassing before the attack and then the murderous bottle-neck into which men were to be poured from one end while lead was poured in from the other. Even as the reconnoitring party scanned the positions from the relative security of one of the outlying houses they could see a company of French creeping along the walls of the Corsini and crouching behind the ornamental orange-tree tubs with which the inner wall was dotted. After a brief survey, Garibaldi ordered Hoffstetter to occupy one of the houses with a detachment of men and keep the enemy's fire down as much as possible while Manara got his men ready to charge. They were somewhat demoralised. A detachment coming out of the San Pancrazio gate suddenly took to its heels and ran back to the walls. The battle thus became a test of blind courage. With a little more confidence in the morale of the Italian troops and a little more patience on the part of the leaders, some scheme might have been worked out. There was no reason, for example, why the Villa Corsini, now in the

possession of the enemy, should not be blown sky-high by
the three batteries in position on the walls of Rome. But
for better or for worse, Garibaldi had got it into his head
that the Villa Corsini itself had to be retaken because it had
been taken. The French had taken it from the Romans:
therefore the Romans must take it again from the French.
In this resolve he was confirmed by the distrust of his own
countrymen. Their courage had to be tested and hardened
under fire. Manara, in a passion of rage at seeing his men
fly back to the gate, ordered a fresh attack to be made at
once; while Hoffstetter, having ensconced himself according to orders in the outlying house, hastened to ply the
windows of the Corsini with a sharp fire. In such a case the
covering fire could not be too good; and Hoffstetter did
his best to send word to the Vascello and the other two
houses which were held by a handful of students, so that
they might support the attack in the same way. But
Manara was in such a hurry to settle the *point d'honneur*
that his men were being murdered between the hedges before their friends realised what was happening.

The designer of the Villa Corsini could not have been
more happily inspired if he had intended to make this
pleasure house a fortress. There were four storeys of it, of
which the two lower were blank wall on the side of Rome,
and the third was reached by a double stairway of stone
from the hedged path which we have mentioned. In addition the park surrounding the villa projected at an acute
angle in the direction of Rome, so that the defenders of the
Corsini could not only make any approach extremely difficult; but when some remnant of the attacking force had
got as far as the wall of the villa, they had only to make a
half turn to fire into their backs. There is no record in history of a more impossible proposition in the military sense
than that which Garibaldi proposed to tackle now; and in
his own eventful career he had never seen before, and was
never to see again, such terrible slaughter. This paltry
place, he called it; this wretched place! But, he added, 'I
have seen very terrible fights,—those of Rio Grande, the

Boyada, the Salto San Antonio, but I have never seen anything to equal the butchery of the Villa Corsini.' It was a battle in a cockpit, waged with all the nasty concomitants of a civil war, a battle that began as soon as the Italians left the San Pancrazio gate, which continued along the deep lane that ran alongside the park wall, which gained in intensity on the path between the box hedges and which culminated in the shattered drawing-room to which the double stairway gave access. There the inexperienced soldiers of the new Republic met the trained soldiers of France. The first attack to get as far as the drawing-room had taken place about six o'clock in the morning. Then the French recaptured the position. At seven it was again held by Garibaldi, who at half-past seven sent a proud report to the Assembly: 'Seven-thirty a.m. Have recovered the positions outside Porta San Pancrazio. Garibaldi'. And while the message was being read the position was lost again. The Villa Corsini was as easy to retake from the French side as it was difficult to take, and to hold, from the side of Rome.

The walls of Rome were for the moment quite useless. They were fine and substantial, with that backward slope characterising the defences which had gradually been evolved during the sixteenth and seventeenth centuries to resist the diabolism of gunpowder. There were three bastions facing the Corsini, with emplacements and siege guns in position. But obviously these could not be used while friend and foe were struggling in the lanes, the terraces, and gardens of the Corsini. In the meantime they afforded a fine view-point for those curious to study the tide of battle; and more than one artist laid himself alongside the sociable defenders and peered through the sandbags. Every time the Italians could be seen on the steps of the Corsini there came a burst of cheers from the walls of Rome: and again as the struggling figures dropped to the ground or turned and ran, a silence came among the spectators. It seemed that out of the chaos some sort of system was being evolved. As men could not be massed in numbers, they were sent to the attack in batches of about twenty. They crept up as far as they could under cover and then rushed. Sometimes they got to the villa; and sometimes they did not. One of these attacks had just concluded when Hoffstetter met Bixio at the San Pancrazio gate. And now the attack in which he found himself involved repeated the same tactics.

Manara's attacking party got as far as within thirty paces of the Corsini under a withering fire that now came mostly from the villa windows. These windows fairly spat fire, says Hoffstetter; and he was not given to exaggeration. The Italians were brought to a halt but not driven back. They knelt down in little groups in the garden and endeavoured to reply to the fire from the windows. The officers with their gleaming epaulettes stood upright in the midst of them, offering a fine target to the bullets of the enemy. The advantages, as always in this day's fighting, were on the side of the French. Behind the solid masonry of the villa and the well-filled earth-tubs of the orange trees they discharged their rifles carefully and with full effect. The two brothers Dandolo, Signeroni, Mangini, and others fell wounded. But Manara was still unhurt after ten minutes of this cross rifle fire. Hoffstetter, who had run over to one of the houses to order the garrison to keep as heavy a fire as possible on the Corsini windows, returned to find him leaning casually against the garden wall. On the way he encountered wounded men crawling away from the scene of action or seeking some patch of cover inside the garden. Manara asked Hoffstetter whether he thought he should sound the charge once again; and to this the Swiss answered: 'We are wasting time here in any case. The very worst thing you can do is to charge. We are not likely to get the villa now; and if we did we could never hold it'. The horn was blown for the retreat, and at this signal the bersaglieri, who had stood their ground admirably, turned and bolted for the gate, where they went down like ninepins, tumbling as they ran, so that Hoffstetter thought they had merely tripped over the roots of the vines that grew in the grounds. Manara made a point of walking slowly. And having by a miracle reached the first covering house with Hoffstetter, he called the latter a *cuore duro* because he showed no sign of emotion.

There was a pause after this attack. The sun was now rising high in the heavens, and it was evident that the Corsini, taken by cunning, could not be recaptured by heroism alone. Indeed there was a prospect that worse might befall. Inside the Vascello was a scene of confusion. No one was in command there for the reason that it was used as a refuge for the troops who had returned from the successive attacks; and there were men of all regiments, with and without commanders. For the time being the French seemed content to let the Italians do the attacking: but sooner or later they would burst from the Corsini and follow the defeated attackers to their base. The Vascello was substantial, bounded by a high wall which at any rate prevented the French from seeing the chaos inside. The inexperience of the Italians was so great that they did not even know how to shoot out of the windows. They crowded into the aperture a dozen at a time and let off their guns in a hurry; and it was clear to Hoffstetter that one good sniper working from the corner (the left-hand corner of the windows in this case) could do more damage than was being done. He saw to this matter; and to some others. Manara was put in command of the fortress. The wounded, instead of being carried into the Vascello, there to lie in the courtyard cumbering the ground, were directed to the San Pancrazio gate. A number of men were detailed for police duties inside the fortress, sharpshooters were posted at the windows, unattached men were returned to their units, and the main body of bersaglieri hidden behind the building until it should be decided how to use them. From the most advanced of the outlying houses Manara and Hoffstetter took another good look at the Corsini through the glasses and saw some movements which seemed to indicate that a battery was being got into position to fire on the Vascello. From the bastions on the left-hand side of the San Pancrazio gate this observation was confirmed. The Italian batteries opened out and dropped a heavy fire on the opposite hill, and for the time being the danger was averted.

Hoffstetter still clung to his plan of systematic attack. With the approval of Garibaldi he had the guns trained on the wall of the Corsini park to the left of the building; and at the same time he threw forward a company to take advantage of the cover on this side and creep towards the Corsini. He hoped that when the artillery preparation was adequate and the wall broken down, his men would rush in from one side and another detachment from the other. His plan required a good understanding between the scattered units from which this double attack was to emanate; and he did not spare himself. In the midst of his exertions he was overcome by the heat and had to lie stretched out on a mattress in one of the houses for a period of half an hour. He stood up, drank a glass of wine and was making for the Vascello when, to his consternation, he saw the garrison charging out in the direction of the Corsini in another forlorn attempt. There were bersaglieri, students, legionaries, infantry of the line, all mixed together and all yelling at the pitch of their voices. Apparently a relief had taken place at the Corsini; and the Italians thought the French were retreating. Garibaldi himself seems to have thought so. As the Italians streamed forward he followed up from the San Pancrazio gate with a detachment of dragoons. In the main particulars his more florid account agrees with that of Hoffstetter: only it does not appear in Garibaldi's narrative that the outrush was the outcome of an ill-considered inspiration.

'I left the Vascello', says Garibaldi, 'with a troop of dragoons. At sight of me, cries were raised on all sides: "Italy for ever!" "Long live the Roman Republic!" The cannon thundering from the walls, and bullets whizzing above our heads, announced a new attack to the French. Then, all together, without definite order, pell-mell, with Masina at the head of his lancers, Manara at the head of the bersaglieri, and myself at the head of them all, we hurled ourselves at that, I shall not say impregnable, but untenable, villa.

'When we reached the villa we found all entrance impossible. The torrent broke forth again to right and left. Those who were thus scattered spread themselves as snipers on either side of the villa; others scaled the walls and leapt down into the garden; whilst some others pushed on as far as the Villa Valentini, took it, and made some prisoners.

'I beheld something that I should have deemed incredible before my very eyes. Masina, followed by his lancers, was at the head of the column. The intrepid horseman simply flew across the ground, cleared the terrace and reached the foot of the staircase. Then, putting spurs to his horse, he made him gallop up the stairs, with the result that, though only for a moment, he appeared on the landing leading to the grand salon, like an equestrian statue. The apotheosis was only of an instant's duration. A shower of bullets, fired at close range, brought down the rider, and his horse fell on top of him, pierced by nine balls.

'Manara was following him up, leading a bayonet charge which nothing could resist. For a while the villa was ours. That period was brief, but it was sublime. The French, having brought together all their reserves, made a concentrated attack on us. Before I had any opportunity of rectifying the state of disorder which is inseparable from victory, the combat had begun again, more pitiless, more bloody, more deadly.'[1]

It had the usual result. Within ten minutes the Italians were again crowding back into the Vascello.

From Hoffstetter's notes of the battle Garibaldi's official account was drawn up. And there is some textual evidence that the narrative found in Garibaldi's memoirs is amended in some degree from the same witness. Garibaldi says that he had no time to rectify the state of disorder inseparable from victory; and for that reason was unable to hold the Corsini after the Italians had gained possession of it. But

[1] *Memoirs of Garibaldi*, by Dumas. The quotation is from R. S. Garnett's translation, p. 252.

at the outset of his description Hoffstetter remarks coldly that amid the yelling and enthusiasm of the onset no provision was made for the eventuality of victory. If a company had been kept behind ready to occupy the Corsini when the storm troops had taken it, Hoffstetter would have been better pleased; and instead of trailing back to the Vascello the Italians might have consolidated their victory. Even Masina's act of heroism had its terrible consequences; for when his horsemen saw him fall they turned about and rode through their countrymen as the latter fled to the gate. As they fell under the hail of French bullets they were trampled underfoot by the retreating cavalry. Throughout, Garibaldi preserved his legendary calm. He was the last to re-enter the Vascello. And, like Manara, he took his time. There were more holes in his poncho: but he had not a scratch.

The doors of the Vascello were swung to and barred. The returned attackers helped themselves to a gulp of wine from the barrels standing in the courtyard; then, once again, sharpshooting was resumed from the windows, and the rattle of the rifles was punctuated by the occasional boom of the heavy guns on the bastions. The batteries were firing on the Corsini now; but though their fire chipped the masonry and shook out a few stones here and there, the fortress remained. The covering guns at least held the French in respect. It was late in the afternoon, and both sides were ready to welcome the coming of darkness. So far as the Italians were concerned the position was as it had been at dawn. They held the Vascello; and the three houses in advance of it exactly as at five o'clock in the morning. But out of a total of something less than four thousand men, about one thousand were casualties, dead and wounded; and of the wounded no less than a hundred and fifty were officers, a heavy proportion, but one which testified to the courage and recklessness of the Italian leaders. There was one last sally. As night fell a young officer, Emilio Dandolo, and Goffredo Mameli, a poet from Milan, asked permission to take a hundred men for a last attempt. They had no military motive or special knowledge. And presently, permission having been given, they dragged back, both shot in the leg, with only fifty of their hundred men. There was nothing to be done but fortify; and on this task Garibaldi spent the better part of the night. Munitions were brought up, field pieces disposed on the walls of Rome, and earthworks thrown up around the Vascello. Hoffstetter went forward to set an outpost under the wall of the Corsini: but no sooner had they got reasonably near the sharp angle of the wall than a crackling broke out above their heads and the earth puffed up around them. The French were not to be caught napping. Hoffstetter got his men down behind some cover and, as he says, returned the compliment before proceeding to accomplish his object by a more circuitous route.

The bells that had been ringing all day were silent. A band which, with a fine Italian irony, had been blowing the Marseillaise beside the San Pancrazio gate, had sheathed its instruments. But Rome was illuminated as usual. It was a habit of the new Republic; and it was not to be discontinued under trial. Also it was a habit of the Romans to go to sleep at nightfall: and Hoffstetter, as he strode through the Trastevere quarter, making for the Babuino café, was surprised to perceive that the Romans were all in bed. They had had a busy day; for as the wounded were borne through the San Pancrazio gate the stretchers were taken from the hands of the military and carried by the citizens to the hospitals where the Princess Belgioso had organised the work of relief. Only at the doors of the hospitals was there still any sign of activity; there were pitiable scenes as women who had sent their sons off gaily in the morning, came to find them shattered or dead. Hoffstetter looked in at the hospital where the bersaglieri were housed and found a cheerful and cleanly row of beds, and very small outward sign of tragedy. He was himself in no tragic humour as he entered the Babuino and found the surviving officers of his regiment drinking merrily and discussing the perfidy of the French. Except for these officers the Babuino was empty; and this emptiness gave the late visitors opportunity for technical conversation as they ate a good dinner prepared with unabated skill by the renowned chef of the establishment. There was no sign of Garibaldi at the Babuino. He was going from outpost to outpost; and his white poncho twinkled in the night.[1]

XVII

In spite of the disaster the Romans still had certain advantages. They had to defend a circle from the inside, and they needed to defend only a segment of its circumference. They had short, internal communications; whereas the enemy had long and scattered and vulnerable ones. On the north side the Vatican walls jutted forth in precisely the same manner as those of the Corsini garden, making an acute angle from which a whole length of wall to the south could be enfiladed. This angle was bound to cripple the attack by holding it at a distance; and for this reason the French, instead of rushing the walls, settled down to a month's bombardment. The general scheme of defence was evolved by Roselli in consultation with Avezzana and Mazzini; and this triumvirate decided that it was their duty to cover the total circumference of the circle. They distributed the forces of the defence north, west and south;

[1] Guerzoni (i. p. 309 ff.) throws out a rather sinister hint that Roselli deliberately withheld support from Garibaldi on the occasion of the attack of June 3, saying that 'after considerable research' he was unable to discover where Roselli was and what he was doing on that day. The implication is that Roselli sought to provoke disaster in order to discredit Garibaldi: but I do not think this view is tenable. The blame for all the events of June 3 must be shared between Mazzini, the virtual dictator, Avezzana, the Minister of War, and Roselli, general officer commanding. They jointly gave Garibaldi his impossible task and failed, let us say from ignorance and indecision, in backing him.

The reader may find it of interest to read a French account in Bittard des Portes (*L'Expédition française de Rome*), from which it appears that Oudinot, the French commander, was blamed for not using all the twenty thousand men at his disposal, with whom he could undoubtedly have taken Rome instead of merely holding on to the Corsini. When the Italian and French narratives are compared it seems clear that mistakes were made on both sides and that the vigour of the Roman riposte served to hold the French general in awe.

and, having done this, confidently awaited the fall of Rome. They were sure it was coming. But with elaborate futility they ordered the fortification of the thin and lengthy line as if they believed the defence would prevail. Mazzini, who considered the affray under the walls of Rome as due to a misunderstanding between two sister republics, eagerly read the reports of his spies in Paris, inserted some propaganda in the French newspapers and hoped from one day to the next to hear that the French Republic had changed its mind.

It was not altogether a vain hope. Lesseps had returned to Paris with his treaty in his pocket on June 5, and almost simultaneously there arrived the news of the bloody conflict at the gates of Rome. These two facts, the treaty signed in black and white by a French plenipotentiary and the assault on the city with which the treaty had been made, required some reconciling. The ministers of the right endeavoured to explain the discrepancy by hinting that De Lesseps had had a touch of sunstroke, and was not responsible for the things he went about saying; but this explanation did not satisfy the left of the Chambre des Députés. However, by a careful concealment of the real facts, Odilón Barrot, the Minister for Foreign Affairs, managed to satisfy a stormy assembly that the friendly and helpful expedition had been flouted and war forced on the French. The quickest way to peace, he said, was by the conquest of Rome, which, if left to itself, would become a prey to irresponsible demagogues. The arguments were specious but they served, and Ledru-Rollin, who had been loud in protest, had to fly to England. In our country the intervention of France in the affairs of Italy was regarded with extreme suspicion. But Palmerston, while well informed of the real motives of French policy by his own and Mazzini's agents, was not warm enough to act in time to save Rome.

The attack on the Corsini had not been the only action on the night of June 3. Reconnoitring to the north-east of Monte Mario, the French general Vaillant had decided

to get hold at the same time of the bridge-head at Ponte
Molle; and a detachment of chasseurs had crept along the
banks of the Tiber about one o'clock in the morning and
shot the sentry guarding the bridge. As the Romans
tumbled out of the houses adjoining the bridge-head and
began to reply to the attack, the chasseurs kept them under
a heavy fire, while a party swam the river and barricaded
itself in one of the towers which stood at the end of the
bridge. Engineers then replaced an arch, which the Romans
had previously blown up, by a pontoon; and the main
body of chasseurs crossed the bridge and took possession,
while the Romans retreated to the Porta del Popolo.
Thereafter it lay with Oudinot whether he would pursue
the siege of Rome by this way, or by the front which he
commanded from the Corsini. And on this point the defenders
of Rome were naturally curious. In the one case
the battle would have to be fought by way of the Porta del
Popolo, street by street, to the heart of the city; and in the
other it would be a duel between opposing generals and
opposing lines of fortification. Oudinot chose the latter
course, not entirely out of kindness of heart, to spare the
monuments and the citizens of Rome, as he said in his reports
to Paris; but because he was not inclined to have
more fighting at close quarters than was absolutely necessary.
The French soldiers had been on the run once already,
with Romans whooping victoriously at their heels;
and Oudinot did not wish to take any risks of such a thing
happening again.

The doubts of the defenders were soon set at rest. There
was no movement from the Ponte Molle: but at night on
the slopes of the Pamfili, the camp fires of the invaders
could be seen pricking the darkness. At about eight o'clock
on the evening of June 4 some twelve hundred French infantry
silently lay down in the pleasant Pamfili garden at a
distance of some four hundred and fifty metres from the
walls of Rome. They had explicit orders. Each man had a
pick and a shovel, as well as his greatcoat and rifle; and at
the command 'Haut les bras!' they lifted their picks and

dug until one o'clock. By that time each man had dug one metre deep, one metre across and the length of his shovel; and a fresh twelve hundred then relieved them and deepened the trench to two metres. Hoffstetter, scanning the gardens on the morning of the 5th, could see a long brown scar, shaped like a crescent, which ran roughly from a point opposite the third bastion south of the San Pancrazio gate to the Villa Corsini.[1]

Garibaldi's task was to counter these works by artillery fire and by strengthening the opposing parallel formed by the walls of Rome. It was a game in which the defenders learned a good deal from the attackers; but in which they were handicapped by temperament and inexperience. The Italian troops liked war but they did not like work; tired by long vigils on the walls, they did not wish to spend their hours of rest digging. Civilians volunteered in small numbers; and at last had to be driven up for this purpose at the point of the bayonet. They dug without enthusiasm and leaned at frequent intervals on their shovels. The Italian artillery had a habit of scattering a few shots impartially over the opposite slopes in the hope that something might be where their shots landed. Hoffstetter spoke about the matter to Manara, who referred him to Garibaldi; and at last the enthusiasts were taught to fire on one objective until it was demolished. Thanks to Garibaldi, the inexperience of the Italians was partially concealed. The French were impressed to see the ground before the walls swept clean of every bit of masonry by means of which they could take cover. They were eager to take the Vascello, the one remaining villa on this side to which the Italians still clung, but they found that the Vascello had been made into a fortress. A covered way led from it into the San Pancrazio gate, and it was garrisoned by Medici, who instructed his men that they were on no account to lose the position. Manara did good work organising supplies of food and munitions, and in securing reinforcements for the Legion.

[1] Bittard des Portes, p. 249, and Hoffstetter, p. 143 f.

Probably Mazzini, Roselli and Avezzana would not have prolonged the defence of Rome at all but for the presence of Garibaldi. He was dangerous; for since the first hour of the attack he had taken no rest, and thought of nothing but the fight. With such a man near, they had not the face to give in, especially as the populace was madly enthusiastic about him. He had taken up his quarters in the high Villa Savorelli immediately behind the walls, whence he looked down over the San Pancrazio gate into the Vascello and over the Corsini and Villa Valentini. The fact that he was within half a carbine shot of the French snipers only added to the charm. He was visited by a stoutish man with a blonde beard that was turning grey. This was Ciceruacchio, the wine merchant who had formerly been noticeable among the crowds under the Vatican. He offered his wine to tempt the lazy citizens to work in the trenches and indulged an unlimited admiration for the guerrilla leader. Another admirer of Garibaldi's was Ugo Bassi, a young priest who had been active during the revolution in Bologna and who became attached as chaplain to the Legion. Garibaldi ate and slept at the Villa Savorelli; and at dawn and dusk each day he received the reports of the officers from the outposts and ramparts. His temper had been uncertain on the day after the attack, but now he was serene again.

The Savorelli offered a good mark to the enemy artillery, which occasionally sent over a shell; but during the early part of the siege the French had few guns in position, and used these sparingly. The inhabitants of the villa were more nervous of snipers. They were in high humour, having recovered from the fatigue of the first onset, and being abundantly fed with rations brought in tins from an adjacent restaurant. The Savorelli was crowned by a gallery round which ran a wooden balustrade, and on this gallery Garibaldi took his morning coffee, putting down his cup to look through his glasses at the enemy positions and discoursing pleasantly on the art of war. His staff was impregnated with his good humour and would occasionally run up an improvised flag bearing the inscription in big letters:

> Good Day, Cardinal Oudinot!

a pleasantry by which the Roman mind sought to convey to the French leader that his machinations with the Pope were well known. Garibaldi seldom descended from Savorelli to visit the city. If Avezzana or Roselli wished to consult him they had to come to his stronghold and listen to what he had to say. He made a point of escorting Avezzana to the belvedere, and the two stood looking at the French lines while the bullets whistled about them. Avezzana behaved well. But he sent sandbags to reinforce the wooden gallery.

It was said that if an officer was invited to share Garibaldi's *risotto*, the chances were he would not survive the day. Vecchi, having accepted an invitation, was sent out afterwards with twenty men to open fire on a French working party. The French replied with shells, and presently someone said to Garibaldi that poor Vecchi had been killed. Half an hour later Vecchi walked in, soiled but alive.

'For the love of God, let me embrace you!' said Garibaldi. 'I thought you were dead.'[1]

A shell had ripped open a row of sandbags, and these had tumbled on Vecchi, one after the other, covering him completely; and the same shell in ricocheting from the parados broke the back of a young soldier who died as he was being laid on a stretcher. A young officer named Pozzio threw himself on the body, kissing it tearfully; and it became known that the dead soldier was a woman, Colomba Antonietti, wife of the officer Pozzio. A woman's dress was drawn over her uniform and she was buried at Catinari in the church of San Carlo, in the chapel of Santa Cecilia.[2] The young women of Rome were hard to discourage, and Colomba Antonietti was not the only woman on the ramparts. There were five or six in the Legion. Two

---

[1] Dumas, p. 260 ff.
[2] Curàtulo, *Garibaldi e le donne*, 1913, p. 70 f.

girls who were considered too frail for soldiering were allocated to the canteen. One of them, Caroline, was pretty and took to serving hot coffee at three each morning in a half-military toilette, which displayed the charms of her figure. The officers of the Legion were soon scowling at each other, and Caroline was given her pay and returned to her family.

On the whole the defenders were not dull. The civilians who ventured as far as Savorelli and gazed timidly at the French lines through the legionaries' glasses, went back to their beds swelling with pride and heroism. Finding their defenders so cheerful they became cheerful themselves. It was a mood worth encouraging; and Garibaldi, who understood his countrymen very well, saw to it that a band played in the salon of Savorelli (against a background painted by Salvator Rosa). The soldiers danced and vendors from the city plucked up their courage and pushed their barrows up the slope. 'We are fighting on the Janiculum', wrote Garibaldi to Anita, 'and the people shows itself worthy of its former greatness. Here men live, die and suffer amputations with the cry of *Viva la Repubblica!* One hour of our life in Rome is worth a century of life! Congratulate my mother on having borne me in an age so splendid for Italy!'[1]

That was too much for Anita. Unkind critics have said that she heard of her husband's popularity with the young women of Rome. She set out from Nice and arrived at the Villa Savorelli on June 26. Garibaldi was astonished and not overjoyed, as she was pregnant. But he put his arms tenderly about her in the presence of his officers, and said to them:

'Here is my wife. We have another good soldier.'

It was characteristic of Roselli to do things just after they should have been done. He had shown this characteristic at Velletri; and now he sought to persuade

[1] Curàtulo, *op. cit.* p. 120. Also Lœvinson, ii. p. 214, and Trevelyan, *Defence* p. 205.

Mazzini that the Villa Pamfili should be retaken by a *sortie en masse* of the Roman garrison. Mazzini agreed that such a demonstration might produce its effect in Paris.[1] But Garibaldi objected, saying that an advance against experienced troops might well end in disaster. He consented, however, to a night sally with a solid body of about three thousand infantry; and the plan for the expedition, to take place on the night of June 10, was drawn up by Garibaldi in consultation with Manara. The major argument in favour of the undertaking was not its military utility but the possibility that it might affect the French elections. A French reverse under the walls of Rome might, Mazzini thought, swing popular opinion in France away from the clericals to the left. In the military sense the purpose was to hinder the elaborate siege preparations being made under the orders of the French engineer Vaillant. If possible the Villas Pamfili and Valentini were to be retaken.

Hoffstetter spent the greater part of a day watching the French positions from St. Peter's, and had the satisfaction of seeing the reliefs take place and counting the garrisons. In the square of the Vatican on both sides of the fountain the men paraded, two battalions of bersaglieri, three cohorts of the Italian Legion, four battalions from Roselli's command, as well as lancers and dragoons and two hundred of the Polish legion, who were to act as vanguard. It was eight o'clock. Ammunition had to be doled out, the lines inspected by Garibaldi, the password and instructions given to sectional commanders. In addition, Garibaldi took a peculiar precaution. He ordered the men to put their shirts on over their tunics, which they did with much laughter, because when the undergarments were brought to the light they were not always a credit to their wearers. By the time these preparations were accomplished it was ten o'clock, and the moon was up. The officers were getting impatient when at last the Cavaleggieri gate swung open on oiled hinges and the Polish legion led the way

[1] Lœvinson, i. p. 239.

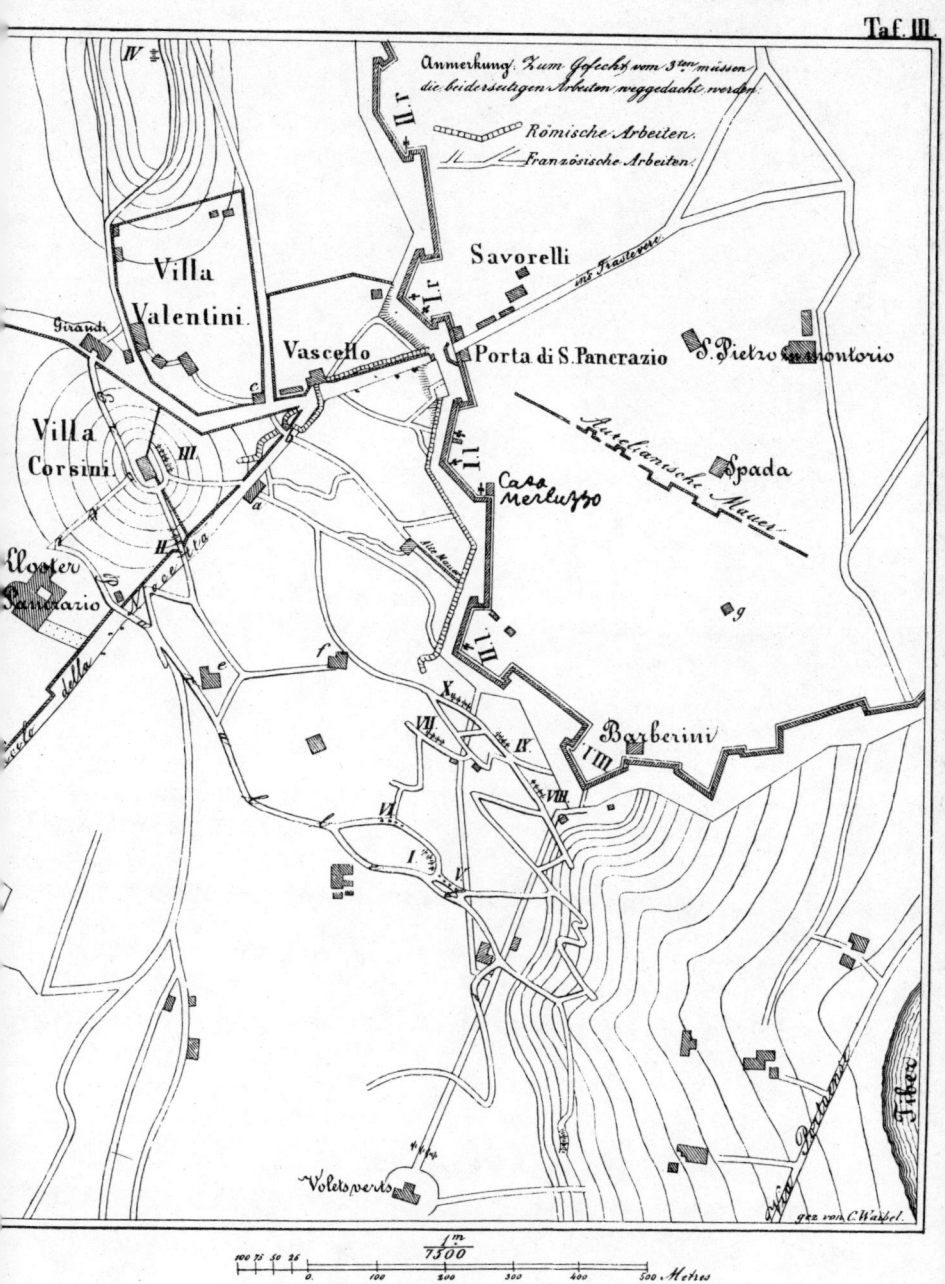

HOFSTETTER'S PLAN OF THE SIEGE OF ROME

through. They marched with broken step over the straw that had been put down on the drawbridge to deaden the noise of their exit. Beyond the walled-up Porta Fabrica an officer called down from the walls the password for the return. Then unexpectedly Garibaldi ordered the column to march along the wall to the San Pancrazio gate. They moved silently in the direction of the convent of San Pancrazio. But the dirty underwear of the soldiers gleamed with a strange purity under the moon and a halt was made while the shirts were removed. Garibaldi had thought that the disguise would prevent his men shooting at each other in the dark: but it was evident that it was more likely to make targets of them for the enemy. With some curses at the caprices of their leader the men did what was required of them. Not a soldier, says Garibaldi, took the trouble to restore his shirt to its proper place. Because of this curious episode the expedition of June 10 became known as the *incamiciata*, or sally of the shirts.

The advance guard under Hoffstetter, consisting of the Poles already mentioned, now found itself in the marshy ground to the left of the convent, and had to thrust its way through reeds that grew man high on all sides. The Italian Legion halted while the Poles went on. But while Hoffstetter with a small advance party had got clear of the reeds and was consulting with a guide to fix their position, he heard a tremendous crackling behind him, as if a detachment of enemy cavalry were riding his men down in the swamp. His small advance party fixed bayonets and waited. The crackling went on for a time. Then all was silent. Making his way back to see what had happened, Hoffstetter came upon rifles and shakos lying on the ground as if they had been thrown away by men in flight. The Poles had decamped; and when Hoffstetter came up with them he found Manara picking himself up from the ground, cursing the flying Poles, who had overthrown him as he tried to stop them. Garibaldi swung his horse across the road and lashed right and left with his whip. But the Poles were in such a panic that they would have fled back to

Rome had the bersaglieri not brought them up on their bayonets.

There was some excuse for them. While they were groping in the reeds a party from the Italian Legion had placed a ladder against the wall of a villa to see if it was as empty as it seemed. With the zeal which characterised the undertakings of the Italians, half a dozen men mounted the ladder at the same time; the top rung broke, the men tumbled on top of each other, and one or two rifles went off; a sequence which no doubt appeared as an unmerited misfortune, but which was liable to occur to troops who mounted ladders six at a time, who used ladders that were breakable and who did not take precautions against their rifles going off at odd moments. The noise of this mishap set the Poles on the run, and the expedition was brought to an untimely end. Hoffstetter begged to be allowed to carry on; but Garibaldi said with some scorn that troops who were so frightened of each other were not likely to frighten the enemy. 'Canaille', he remarked briefly. At one o'clock in the morning the whole division was back on the square of St. Peter's, where Garibaldi threw himself down on the stones and slept or appeared to sleep. Manara did likewise. And Hoffstetter, having tried the same position, and found the stones too hard and cold, leaned against his horse and came near crying.

It was given out in Rome that the advance guard had made a reconnaissance and found the French standing to; after which it had been withdrawn with the rest of the column. But visitors to Villa Savorelli saw a change in Garibaldi. A deputation of the Legion which waited on him to request that they might be permitted to wipe out the shame of the unlucky expedition by another, of which the bersaglieri would form the advance guard, was greeted with complete silence.

On the afternoon of the 12th, a French officer came to the walls under a flag of truce and was escorted to the Monte Cavallo to confer with Mazzini. He had come to say that the French batteries were in position and would begin bombardment next day unless the Romans preferred the alternative of immediate capitulation. The following day, this offer having been rejected, thirty guns opened out against the Roman bastions. They were still firing on the night of June 13. They fired all day long on June 14, and all the night. So it went on for seven days and seven nights.[1]

XVIII

THE French shells whined gently, then whistled and crashed; sometimes on the bastions and sometimes beyond the bastions in the narrow streets of the Trastevere, where the citizens nodded to each other and remarked: *Ecco un Pio Nono!* They were impressed, but they retained a childlike good temper, while those responsible for the defence became more bitter each day.

Garibaldi's temper had sharpened after the failure of the *incamiciata*. And the disappearance of his good humour was not due to the fact that the Polish legion had proved to be *canaille* so much as to the uncongenial character of the French offensive measures. Vaillant's trench system was slow and implacable. Garibaldi could see it, and he could see that it was like nothing he had ever met in warfare before. It was, in fact, the work of one of the greatest military engineers of the nineteenth century; and it negatived Garibaldi's qualities of individual courage and initiative in no small degree. The raid, a military genre in which he excelled, might temporarily succeed. But, as a reply to the French measures, it was futile. For this reason, from June 10 onward, and notwithstanding the consoling presence of Anita, Garibaldi was not a comfortable man to have dealings with. He was touchy on the subject of his own scheme of defence.

[1] Cf. Hoffstetter, p. 177 ff. Guerzoni, i. 319. *Memoirs* (Dumas), p. 264 ff. Trevelyan, i. 204. In the French accounts (Balleydier, *La Révolution de Rome*, ii. 176) the date is erroneously given as June 17-18 (also Bittard des Portes, p. 313); and the costume of the *incamiciata* is explained as a 'reminiscence du seizième siècle'.

Avezzana had nominated a young man called Amadei as engineer-in-chief. But he did not specify whether Amadei was to act on his own authority or under that of the generals commanding the line. In the upshot he did something of both, making a judicious mixture of Garibaldi's ideas and his own; and this arrangement worked for about a week in spite of occasional friction about working parties. There lay the great difficulty. Amadei could make a scheme. But he required men to do the digging; and for these he had to apply to Garibaldi. He needed about three thousand men, a number which, with the best will in the world, Garibaldi could not supply, even with the help of Ciceruacchio. At a critical moment Garibaldi called up all the men with Amadei to take part in the *incamiciata*; the fortifications came to a standstill, Amadei complained to Avezzana, and the fat was in the fire. Garibaldi said no headway was being made with the fortifications: Amadei that he could not get on because Garibaldi took away his men. On the morning of June 12, while Amadei was on the ramparts, some men of the Unione regiment made a sally without orders and were driven back with heavy losses. Thereupon Garibaldi, assuming that Amadei was responsible, put his engineer under arrest and sent him to Avezzana with a chit to the effect that he should at once be shot for neglect of duty.[1]

In due course, however, after a brief incarceration in the Castel Sant' Angelo, Amadei returned to the line, fully exculpated; and his presence did nothing to sweeten Garibaldi's temper. Up to the last day of the siege the general and the engineer were at loggerheads. Meanwhile the French, while awaiting the hour for the main attack, were doing small and useful jobs in the neighbourhood of Rome. They had not forgotten that Rome was open on three sides; and, although they could not attempt a complete blockade, they sent squadrons of cavalry to scout on the main roads, and in this way caught many waggon-loads of provisions and war material. On June 13 a French frigate

---

[1] Lœvinson, i. p. 243 ff.

cast anchor off the little port of Porto d'Anzio, some fifty kilometres to the south-west of Ostia. A detachment of marines with a couple of mortars took their station on the shore while Captain Castelnau, escorted by some men of the 66th regiment of the line, made a call on the director of the local munition factory. After some protest, the director, a plump Belgian, allowed Castelnau's men to dismantle the machinery and destroy the furnaces; which being done the French party proceeded to the adjacent fort in which the munitions were stored and there awakened the commanding officer, a young Roman, in the midst of his siesta. 'Vous êtes malade, monsieur; le soleil vous aura troublé l'esprit', the latter replied when ordered to deliver his stores. But when Castelnau had taken the young Roman by the arm and shown him from the window the French frigate *Magellan* lying in the bay with her two batteries cleared for action, the keys were given up without further difficulty, except that the still sleepy Roman was under the impression he should have a receipt. With a smile the Frenchman explained that the transaction was not of a strictly commercial character.[1]

The French left nothing to chance; especially in such minor matters as were likely to help towards a bloodless victory. For Oudinot was well aware that he might be praised for capturing Rome; but not for killing its heroic defenders. The exchange of letters between Mazzini and Oudinot still went on, and in it Mazzini had all the advantage; he proved, not only adequately but magnificently, in sentences which are memorable for their beauty and heroic spirit, that Rome was betrayed by her sister republic; and proved it with as much courtesy as firmness, as if in astonishment that such gentlemen as the French could have so far forgot themselves.[2] But the more perilous the state of Oudinot's conscience, the more carefully he was bound to perform his task. The place, as he called it, had to be taken

[1] Cf. Bittard des Portes, p. 291 f. (quoting from the *Historique* of the 66th Regiment).
[2] *Ibid.* p. 301 ff.

in such a way that the Romans were given as few opportunities as might be for spilling their own blood. They were keyed for great deeds; not only the Italians but volunteers from many nations. Poles, Americans, French, Spaniards, whose death was likely to echo afar and bring down a punishment on those responsible for it. Accordingly the French pursued their considered policy. And in the course of the day of June 10, the Romans discovered (even as they were preparing for the *incamiciata*) that the water from Paola had been cut off.

It was only one of Rome's sources of supply: but it fed, among other places, the Villa Savorelli; and on and after June 10 water had to be brought up to Garibaldi's headquarters in carts. The Romans had had ample notice of this possibility. As early as May 6, the municipal council of Rome had warned the Ministry of War that this source could easily be cut by the enemy; and the Ministry of War had done nothing. The water in itself was not so important, as there was other water in plenty: but from this particular aqueduct came the power to drive the mills on the Janiculum, where the wheat for Rome's bread supply was ground. To replace the water the mills had to be adapted for steam, a change which was effected after some time and labour. In the meantime Garibaldi had studied the lie of the aqueduct and discovered that it led to the Corsini; and, being now dry, might be used as a sap to undermine the French fortifications. The French may have heard the Italian sappers at work; or may have found the shortage of water inconvenient themselves. At any rate, on June 23, they let the water through again, washing out the Italian sappers and almost drowning fifty Italian soldiers who had elected to take their siesta in the basin of the Paola fountain.[1]

Before this date, however, events of importance had occurred. The French bombardment accounted for a daily total of about fifty casualties, of which a fair number were among civilians; and this total did not include casual-

[1] Lœvinson, i. p. 247 f.

ties incurred in sallies or occasional hand-to-hand fighting. There were signs that the Romans would not stand much more of the treatment, while the soldiers themselves, worn down by long vigils on the ramparts, had lost some of the spirit they had shown on June 3. Even more than Garibaldi they disliked the method of the French attack; probably both they and the inhabitants of the Trastevere would have preferred a street to street battle in the slums of the Trastevere. But the French went on from day to day; and by June 20 they had achieved one notable objective. The two villas, Spada and Savorelli, were crumbling about the heads of the defenders, to such an extent that even Garibaldi could hold out no longer. He wanted a few hours of peace to think and rest; and as these were no longer to be had at the Savorelli, he moved his headquarters to Villa Spada. Seven batteries had concentrated their fire on the second and third Roman bastions. By June 20, not only was the Villa Savorelli untenable, but three breaches had been effected in the city wall. It was a bad sign for Rome. Yet Garibaldi was not displeased. 'I hoped to show them yet what war waged to the knife and dagger was', he comments in his memoirs. A breach to be bolstered up and held in breast-to-breast conflict was a thing more to his mind than the long worm-like trench that crawled tortuously over the slopes of the Pamfili gardens.

Hoffstetter had a suspicion that Garibaldi's plans of defence were communicated to the French by someone inside the walls. The Romans had been strengthening number three bastion as circumspectly as possible; and it was while they attempted the repair that the French dropped one hundred and eighty shells there within twenty-four hours.[1] In the same way while Hoffstetter was inspecting the Casimato convent with a view to strengthening the fortifications, four shells burst in the church in ten minutes. At the time there were many women in the building removing the property of the nuns; and when the first

[1] Hoffstetter, p. 212.

shell crashed through three storeys and burst in the sacristy they threw themselves on their faces, screaming. Then, when the dust had subsided, they rushed about dragging their children at their heels. A second shell followed the first, and the painful scene continued. No doubt these incidents were due to the close observation kept by the French, whose outposts now lay at the foot of the slope, and picked off the Roman sentries almost as soon as they showed their heads above the sandbags: but to the defenders the French knowledge of what was going on in the city was uncanny, and with one accord they attributed it to clerical spies. An old man who was caught lowering a letter over the wall was shot. A similar fate befell a priest who was said to have grown a beard as a disguise to facilitate communication with the enemy. It was only too likely that the Pope's friends were still active within the city, and that their activity increased as the fall of the city became certain. But it is equally likely that in the tension of the last days the innocent suffered for the guilty. Tempers were very strained. Even good friends like Manara and Hoffstetter snapped at each other in a humour very different from that which had prevailed at the beginning of the siege.

The French artillery had shot three breaches; and it looked to Hoffstetter as if they would soon be practicable. In fact they could be mounted by a scaling party with very little effort; and the guard on the breaches was warned to shoot at the slightest sound. It was posted on each of the three breaches, a sentry keeping watch on the high sides of each breach and a party lying at the top hidden by a crest of rubbish and crumbled masonry. Before the guard was a huge heap of dry sedge, ready to be lit as a signal and as a defence; for, in the event of an attack, the orders were to fall back to the sides of the breach, leaving the enemy to face the wall of flame while the Romans poured their shot into the flanks. On the night of June 21-22, the guard was posted by Hoffstetter over the three breaches. He had just returned to the Villa Spada to snatch a few hours rest, and was unbuckling his sword when an adjutant rushed in with the news that the French had taken the wall. The news went about quickly; and Manara and Hoffstetter both advised Garibaldi to make a counter-attack at once to regain the lost position. But, for once, Garibaldi was more cautious than his lieutenants. It was still dark, and no one really knew the extent of the French victory. Garibaldi gave orders to secure the line of defence on the Janiculum, so that, at all hazards, a last stand could be made. Then he sent forward Colonel Sacchi with a party to ascertain the position on the second bastion. This party was hotly welcomed by the French and driven back with about twenty casualties. As the day broke the French were on the walls of Rome and the Roman batteries firing from the rear were directing their fire on a point which a few hours earlier had been a keypoint of the defence.

How the surprise had been achieved was a mystery to the Romans; and the explanations that were forthcoming were not very satisfactory, as they were provided by soldiers of the Legion and of the Unione regiment whose contribution to the battle had been of a most elementary character. They had run away and allowed the French to take possession without firing a shot. This fact they explained in various ways, of which the most plausible was that the French had debouched from a saphead between the sedge and the wall; they had risen out of the earth in a solid mass, as it were; whispered in the ears of the defenders that they had better run for it, and caught Lieutenant-Colonel Rossi who was coming back on his round of inspection from the Porta Portese. *Colonnello—ronda*, the latter shouted as he neared the bastion: to which the French, by that time in possession, replied, *Avanti, colonnello!* A moment later Rossi was surrounded and disarmed.[1] In the French narrative of the event there is, however, little mystery. 'Les postes romains s'étaient retirés dans leurs abris, un peu en arrière du front, et ils étaient plongés dans le sommeil.'

[1] Dandolo, *Italian Volunteers*, p. 253 f.

Mazzini had meantime been conducting affairs on the publicity front with that combination of earnestness and duplicity which was characteristic of his genius. The newspapers of Rome recorded the damage done by French shells to the monuments of Rome, as well as the casualties amongst women and children. In the course of the day of June 19 the rumour got about that a revolution had broken out in Paris and the French provinces. The army had joined the revolutionaries, the President and the ministers of the government had been arrested, and Ledru-Rollin had been elected chief of a new democratic Republic. Mazzini had a shrewd suspicion that it was too good to be true. But he saw to it that the news was distributed. On the evening of June 19 the bells were rung, military bands played and a part of the garrison's gunpowder was expended in fireworks. The rejoicings were marked by the usual illuminations. But it was very soon known that the news was false. At last the fact of Ledru-Rollin's flight to England became known: the knowledge of it coincided in point of time with the disastrous loss of the key positions on the walls.

'In the following night (of Friday, June 22)', wrote Arthur Hugh Clough to his friend Palgrave,[1] 'an immense number of bombs were thrown; they fell chiefly in the Piazza di Venezia, Piazza Sant' Apostoli, and Via del Gesù. I do not think much harm was done, and the people took it coolly enough. I found a crowd assembled about nine p.m. in the north-east corner of the Piazza Colonna, watching these pretty fireworks. "Ecco un altro!" One first saw the "lightning" over the post-office; then came the missive itself, describing its tranquil parabola; then the distant report of the mortar; and finally the near explosion, which occasionally took place in the air. This went on all night. But it has not been repeated in the same degree. The Consuls have remonstrated with Oudinot, but he, I believe, pleads "orders". The operations meantime, till yesterday (*i.e.* June 27), were unimportant, *e.g.* four can-

[1] *Prose Remains*, p. 158 f.

non were got up on the breach, but the Roman batteries say that they upset them. On Sunday night, however, the 26th, there was another general attack, and under cover of this the French got their guns planted on the breach, and were playing with these all yesterday upon *our* batteries of S. Pietro in Montorio, which I fear will not be long tenable.

'This morning (June 28) I hear nothing I can rely on, and considering the bombs, I forbore to visit my look-out of the Ara Celi. As for the feelings of the people, I can of course say little. I fancy the middle-class Romans think it rather useless work, but they don't feel strongly enough on the matter to make them take steps against a government which I believe has won their respect alike by its moderation and its energy; perhaps, too, they are afraid of the troops, under which term however do not understand foreigners, unless you choose to give that name to the levies of the Papal States in general. Visiting the Monte Cavallo hospital the other day, where there are, I think, 200 men, three Poles and one Frenchman were especially pointed out to me, that I might say some words of French to them. All the others I saw were Italians, from Bologna, Ferrara, Ravenna, Perugia and so forth. There was one Swiss. Most of them had received their wounds on the 3rd. Nice fellows they seemed, young, and mostly cheerful, spite of their hurts. One had lost an arm and a leg; another had a ball in his hip, yet to be extracted; and the like. On the whole I incline to think they will fight it out to the last, but *chi lo sa?*'

The combined effect of the loss of the bastions and of the bad news from France was to throw Mazzini into an ecstasy of heroism. The tocsin had been sounded by his orders when the news of the taking of the wall became known; and while Garibaldi was endeavouring to gain reliable information in the confusion and semi-darkness of the early morning of June 22, he was assailed by a shouting crowd which had followed Mazzini, Avezzana and Roselli, and which, with Mazzini's full approval, clamoured to be led against the French. There is no very clear account of this interview: but Mazzini must have been told pretty briefly to go to bed and take his rabble with him; to which suggestion the small triumvir replied with a positive order, confirmed by Roselli and Avezzana, that Garibaldi must retake the lost positions. The latter declined to obey; for which course he had ample reason of a military nature. Garibaldi had had painful experience of the mixed quality of the Italian troops. But the military argument was not the determining one. It was the fact that the position had been lost which decided him. It should never have been lost; and it was with the bastions as with the Villa Corsini. They were lost by stupidity and ought, in Mazzini's view, to be retaken by heroism. But Garibaldi thought differently. He considered the incident as a culminating argument against the interference of civilians in military matters; they bungled the issues and caused the lives of good men to be sacrificed uselessly. He could see that the French were fine soldiers; and that they were doing their job in a soldier-like way; while he, in his efforts to make good against them, was cluttered with the views of this man and the next man. He agreed with Mazzini about the news from France. It was fatal to Rome. He shared Mazzini's opinion that the Italians should fight to a finish. But there was a clash as to the manner. Mazzini wanted a grand fight to lose, a magnificent gesture of sacrifice, so that the Republic should go down in a curve of flame, like one of its fireworks. Garibaldi was prepared to fight with equal desperation, but to win, for a purpose which he could see clearly and which was sanctioned by his instinct as a fighting animal. He was tired of the walls of Rome. Let the French come in, he said; at the same time we shall go out and take with us only those who are real soldiers. The French, when they have taken Rome, will find that they have taken nothing. Garibaldi was not in a mood to carry this point of view by persuasion. He allowed it to be seen that he thought Mazzini a fool; and Mazzini retorted petulantly with a letter (June 22) to which Garibaldi made no reply at all. The question of nominating Garibaldi as dictator cropped up. He had only to ride through the streets of Rome to be nominated by popular clamour. A wave of his hand would have produced civil war in the streets. But that, of all the courses open, was the least desirable. He sulked magnificently. And then, relenting somewhat, he tried to explain to the Assembly how the situation looked to him. He would try another flank attack, he said, with the old idea of menacing the French communications with Civita Vecchia. Or, a course which seemed to him much better, the triumvirate and the army would take to the Apennines and proclaim that wherever they were, there was the Republic of Rome.

Mazzini swung round. At last the two were agreed. For, although Garibaldi could not see Mazzini's point of view nor understand his manner of thinking, Mazzini could understand Garibaldi's. The heroic in Garibaldi appealed to the heroic in Mazzini. There were faint hearts in Rome and in the Assembly, ready to open the gates at any moment. Among them was Roselli. In opposition to them Mazzini and Garibaldi found to their astonishment, that they had something in common. They were both men above the common run, who were to share between them in equal measure the glory of the last days.

There had been a lull in the firing during the diplomatic episode alluded to by Clough. The English consular agent in Rome was interested in the art treasures of the city. He spoke to the representative of the United States and to the consular agents of other Protestant Powers, and a joint letter was sent to Oudinot protesting against the bombardment. As Clough says, it had no effect except that Oudinot dispatched a reply to the effect that the bombardment would cease as soon as the city surrendered. The Roman guns were still firing, and they were marking well. The French held on to the walls, but they could not get their artillery mounted on the breach, so strong was the fire from the Roman bastions; and it was plain that only prolonged and concentrated fire on all the strong points of the city could end the siege. The French batteries were silent on June 26. Then, on the following day, there broke forth a terrific bombardment. 'The streets', says Garibaldi, 'were strewn with wounded. The sappers no sooner took pick or shovel in hand than they were cut in two by a cannon ball or mutilated by a shell. All our artillerymen—I really mean *all*—had been killed at their guns: artillery duty was being carried out by soldiers of the line. The whole of the National Guard was under arms; and—unbelievable as it may be—it had a reserve composed of wounded soldiers who, despite their still bleeding wounds, were doing duty. In contrast with all this, however, during the whole time the Assembly, calm and undisturbed, in permanent session at the Capitol, carried on its deliberations amid the bullets and cannon balls.'[1]

Hoffstetter bears out Garibaldi's account. June 27 was a hard day for the defenders: and at the end of it occurred a curious incident. When Hoffstetter had finished arranging matters for the night he returned to the Villa Spada, where Garibaldi asked him if any part of the Legion was still out on special duty. Hoffstetter said no, whereupon Garibaldi gave Hoffstetter his hand and said: 'Adieu, Hoffstetter, I hope to see you again at midnight or at the latest, early to-morrow morning. General Roselli is taking over the command'. And at that moment Roselli came in with his adjutants, greeted Hoffstetter cordially and enquired whether he would be good enough to remain in order to explain the disposition of the troops and the position of the fortifications to his chief of staff. Hoffstetter was bewildered, but he led the chief of staff over the strong points and, with a disregard of the enemy's fire which the latter did not altogether approve, gave the needed explanations. As they returned, Hoffstetter blurted out the question that had been on his lips ever since Garibaldi's extraordinary farewell. 'Colonel', he said, 'what is the meaning of all this? Has there been a quarrel between Garibaldi and the government? Where is he going? I tell you frankly *your* general

[1] *Memoirs* (Dumas), p. 274.

is not popular enough to bring the defence to an honourable conclusion.' But the colonel knew no more than Hoffstetter; and the latter excused himself in order to find Manara and ask him what was going on. The officers of the Legion were standing by, and the Legion was under orders to move out of the line. At last Hoffstetter found Manara as the latter was saddling his horse to return to duty. There could be only two possible explanations. Either the government wanted to negotiate and Garibaldi had resigned rather than be a party to the proceedings: or Garibaldi had proposed to carry on the defence elsewhere and had not been able to get a majority for this proposal. This last was the truth. Garibaldi's proposal to withdraw from Rome and continue the defence elsewhere had been rejected by the Chamber in spite of the fact that Mazzini was in favour of it. The news was brought to Garibaldi in the course of the day, and he had forthwith resigned command of the sector, the Legion going into billets in the Trastevere and the officers quartering themselves according to custom, in adjacent hotels. In one of these Manara found Garibaldi. He sat with him for an hour, and at the end of it persuaded the irate general to go back to the line. The San Pancrazio gate, said Manara, was Garibaldi's gate. It belonged to him and to the Legion. He must stand or fall with it. Also, he said, if the Legion withdraws, Rome will be at the mercy of the French, and they will impose any conditions they like. The last argument, presented with Manara's exquisite tact, was decisive. Garibaldi said he would return to the line the same night.

He was back on the fortifications behind the gate before dawn. Roselli blandly retired. The rival general had not left the shelter of the villa all night, and had spent the intervening hours conning the enemy positions on paper. There, thought Hoffstetter, you saw the difference between a *real* general and an imitation one; for Garibaldi was no sooner there than he was off on foot peering into the trenches and talking to the men. The legionaries had come back in a strangely conspicuous garb. During their brief absence they had exchanged their blue blouses for the red shirt, which up to this point had been worn only by Garibaldi himself and his staff. Henceforward the men of the Italian Legion wore the garb that was to become familiar to history. It saw the light of day on the morning of June 28, 1849, two days before the final battle which preceded the fall of Rome; and it was given out that the Legion had withdrawn from the line for a few hours so that it might be equipped with the new uniform. The general's temporary absence was explained in the same way. He had wished, it was said, to be present at the transformation.[1]

XIX

THE evening of June 29 was sultry. The preceding days had been dry, and dust clouds in the Pamfili gardens marked the movements of the French troops. It was the festival of St. Peter, and with circumspect regard for the traditions of its predecessors and a particular eye to the mutable inhabitants of the Trastevere, the Republic had ordered the usual illuminations. As dusk fell the cupola of St. Peter's blazed out in a splendour that could be seen for miles around. A nearer view showed the square of the Vatican coloured red, emerald green or pure gold by the Bengal lights. But the spectators soon scattered as drops began to patter gently through the dusty air. The clouds were gathered close above the city, and just before midnight the distant rumbling culminated in a clap as if the palms of a giant's hands had been struck together. There had been a great quietness. And now the wind rose in heavy, sobbing gusts, rattling the shutters in the Trastevere; and the silence was broken by a steady sizzling noise as the rain began to fall. It fell gently at first, then the weight of the overhanging clouds seemed to collapse and stream towards the earth in long shafts of drenching water. It dripped from

[1] Cf. Lœvinson, p. 258 f., and Hoffstetter, p, 265 f.

the greatcoats of the Lombard volunteers as they stood awaiting the order to take their posts for the night. They moved off at last to occupy the breach in bastion number 8, sinking up to their ankles in the turned-up earth round the trenches. The company was led to its position by a few flickering lanterns. But soon there came another light, a parabola of flame in the sky which came from the French side, curving flatly and touching the ground at the feet of the volunteers. There came a moment of darkness while the light sputtered faintly, and then a crashing explosion sent the men grovelling on their faces in the mud. The French were throwing grenades at bastion number 8. When the post was reached only a few men of the company remained, enough to relieve the sentinels. The remainder had been struck down or had slunk off to find a warm bed in Rome. There was small heart in the new sentries. They were sodden with rain and sunk to the knees in the trampled mud. After the storm came a cold wind that moaned over Rome like a dirge.[1]

The French were standing to. A column had been dispatched to create a diversion by bombarding with field pieces in the region of Ponte Molle. They were to fire anyhow and anywhere, to make a noise. And when the thunder had ceased the guns could be heard answering from the Porta del Popolo. The main attack was to take place against bastion number 8, and it was to be made by six companies, of which three were to assemble silently at two in the morning at the foot of bastion number 7, ready to charge on bastion 8. Their orders were explicit. They were to enter the enemy trenches and *kill* the defenders; 'tueront tout ce qui s'y trouvera'. The other three companies were to act as a reserve, while a further detachment would consolidate. The company commanders spent an anxious day inspecting arms and walking the length of the saps to make sure there would be no mistake. Oudinot's temper was short. He was informed from Paris that a general was soon to be sent to replace him because the siege of Rome had lasted

[1] Dandolo, *The Italian Volunteers*, p. 267 f., and Vecchi, *La Italia*, ii. p. 293.

too long. The engineer Vaillant had himself a warrant to take over full command. But he had kept it in his pocket and said nothing about it. A detachment of cavalry examined saddles and waited in the darkness ready to fall on fugitives who attempted to make good their escape. At 2.30 a.m., when, the storm having ceased, the citizens of Rome had retired to bed to forget their republican cares, came the signal, three separate cannon shots, terribly audible in the early dawn. Two minutes later the column of assault was moving from below bastion 7 towards bastion 8. The French infantry carried their rifles with fixed bayonets at the charge. They were led by a swarthy, lean-waisted colonial, Lieutenant-Colonel Espinasse, who held his sabre high in his left hand and used his knees and elbows to clamber up the escarpment of bastion 8. The Roman sentries were awake and a crackling of musketry greeted the attackers.[1]

It is as difficult to get a clear account of this incident as of the previous taking of the triple breach. The Italian accounts tend to be romantic rather than precise, and it is as well to turn again to Hoffstetter, who, as one of Garibaldi's staff officers (for, in effect, he fulfilled this function), directed the precautions for the defence of bastion 8. Some time before the attack he had made his round of inspection and found General Carogni, who was in command of the bastion, comfortably rolled in his cloak and sound asleep. He made some remarks to Carogni and told the men to fire at the least sign of trouble; after which he withdrew to Garibaldi's headquarters at Villa Spada. 'We had left the doors of Villa Spada open', writes Hoffstetter in his diary, 'in order to hear every sound.... I was too uneasy to sleep. ... The rain had stopped, but it was still pitch dark. Suddenly there was a shot, followed as usual by a volley. We were on the line on the instant—but all was silent again. Not a leaf stirred. I had called to the others, "Quickly, gentlemen, they mean business this time!"; and when I came back the others said I was too warm to-day.

[1] Bittard des Portes, p. 359 ff.

'It must have been one a.m. when the staff officer who had made the round came in with the report: nothing new. All the same I did not unbuckle my swordbelt as I lay down; and scarcely had I shut my eyes when the cry came: *all' armi, all' armi*. I heard no firing, but the sound of men running past the villa. We rushed out of the door, and I did not even take time to pick up my pistols.

'Outside everyone was running. No shouting or clang of weapons. I thrust through the fugitives to the exit through which the men from the outposts were rushing in. ... At the same moment a dark mass moved along the trench towards me. My men whispered to me: *i Francesi, i Francesi*, and wanted to fire at once. But I pushed down the barrels of their rifles with my sword, thinking it might just as well be some of our own people. Only when they were right on our bayonets did I see by their epaulettes they were French chasseurs. I commanded, "Fire!" and half a dozen of the intruders fell while the others took to flight.' Pushing his reconnaissance further, Hoffstetter was met by swarms of Frenchmen escalading the front and flanks of the bastion and threatening his retreat. He retired on the Villa Spada, where he met Garibaldi. 'A damnable scare, General', he remarked, 'should we not occupy the Villa and hold it?' 'That's what I'm doing', he said in a voice which showed how the flight of his men had affected him. 'Do you and Manara remain in Villa Spada and hold it. I will go back and collect the men who have run away and take up a position behind the street as far as the Villa Savorelli.' With the coming of daylight the courage of the Italian troops returned. They fired steadily from the windows of the Villa Spada. Garibaldi himself was like a man possessed. He says in his memoirs that he does not remember what happened. 'What happened next I could not tell you. For the space of two hours I struck and struck without respite. When day broke I saw I was covered with blood, but I had not a single wound. It was a miracle.' Vecchi, who was with him, says: 'His sword was like lightning. Every man who had the temerity to come near bit the dust. He reminded you of Leonidas at Thermopylæ or Ferrucio at the Castle of Gavinana. At every moment I feared to see him fall, but no; there he remained immovable as destiny'.[1] Even the man of destiny, however, would not have survived that day but for a message which arrived from the Assembly asking him to come at once. The Assembly was debating whether or not Rome should surrender, and required the advice of the defender of the line. He took Vecchi with him and, bloodstained as he was, rode off to the Campidoglio.

The French party which had taken number 8 bastion had met the supporting column, which had entered to the right by the most southerly of the three breaches: and both now concentrated on the attack on the Aurelian wall, of which the two strong points were the villas Savorelli and Spada. The defence of these last was conducted by rifle-fire and bayonet only: for all the Roman batteries were silent. Except for the Vascello, which was still held by Medici, the Romans now had no outpost at all from which to enfilade the enemy; and the Vascello was a heap of ruins. Medici had obeyed his instructions to the letter. Storey by storey the villa had been hurled to the ground. A great part of it crashed, burying some twenty men. But Medici accommodated himself among the ruins, hugging the ground more and more closely as the days went on. The Vascello was certainly a thorn in the enemy's side: every attempt to retake it at the point of the bayonet failed. It was the one point of the Roman line that was impregnable. Artillery fire could destroy the masonry: but it could not break the heroic spirit of the defenders. Alone of all the improvised fortresses of Rome, the Vascello could be trusted not to go to sleep. Now the French by their advance beyond the walls threatened to cut the Vascello off altogether. It looked as if it would still be puffing smoke at the French after Rome itself had surrendered. With a heavy heart Garibaldi sent word to Medici that he must get his garrison out and bring it back to Villa Spada.

[1] Garibaldi, *Memoirs*, p. 276; and Vecchi, *loc. cit.* p. 295.

In Garibaldi's absence the fight went on. The Roman blood cooled too quickly. But when it was up it was the blood of heroes. The Italian sun was too hot for the French, whereas its increasing heat affected the Italians scarcely at all. Hoffstetter found he could get volunteers for an attempt to retake the lost bastion and set out with a party which soon, however, ran short of ammunition. He crept back to the wall of Villa Spada and shouted to Manara to throw him some ammunition down. When he came back after an unsuccessful attempt, he found Manara dying from a carbine shot in the body. 'Does it pain you so much that I die?' whispered the bersaglieri leader as he saw the tears of those about him. 'It grieves me also. . . .' By the time Bertani, the surgeon, arrived, Manara was scarcely able to speak. 'Oh Bertani', he said, 'let me die quickly. I suffer too much.' He did not linger long; and as the last shots were fired his body became cold. It was said of Manara that he was the finest gentleman of all Italy's defenders.

Mazzini had put to the Assembly the three possibilities, surrender, a fight *palmo a palmo* in the streets of Rome, or the withdrawal of the government and the army from the city. General Bartolucci, speaking for Garibaldi, declared further fighting in Rome useless. It would mean the destruction of the city, he said. In the end no military purpose would be served since, sooner or later, a capitulation must come. But the Assembly wanted to hear this from Garibaldi's own lips. As Garibaldi set off for the Campidoglio with Vecchi he heard that Aguyar, his negro servant, had been killed. He strode into the Chamber and stood still in astonishment as the members cheered and shouted. Then, looking down at himself, he saw his uniform covered with dust and blood, and his sword, bent double, sticking half-way out of the sheath. He mounted the tribune and spoke briefly.

It was a characteristic speech; and it was not without bitterness. He said plainly that he had proposed, as early as February 9, a dictatorship whose main function would be to enlist an army of 100,000 men and train them for the fight. Such an army, he said, would have changed the face of Italy. But that proposal was not adopted; and there was no use reviling each other now over what had been done or not been done. The fire was masters of them and not they of the fire. They could hold their heads high. They could go forth from Rome. *Dovunque saremo, colà sarà Roma*, he said: where they were Rome would be. As to himself, his mind was made up. Whatever decision was made by the Assembly, he would go with whatever men would follow him. *Io nulla prometto. Tutto farò quanto è dato ad uomo di fare.* He would promise nothing, but what a man could do he would do. Having delivered his speech he rode back and conferred with Hoffstetter about the defence of the houses behind the Aurelian wall. At midday the white flag went out from Rome, and a truce was proclaimed for twenty-four hours, while both sides collected their dead and cared for the wounded. As if to emphasise the unusual stillness, the moon rose and swam in a clear sky.

The three triumvirs who had been responsible for the defence of Rome resigned and were replaced by three others who put their signature to the conditions imposed by the French. Hoffstetter supped in the evening with Garibaldi at the Palazzo Corsini, and was introduced to Anita. 'She was a woman of about 28, of a very dark complexion, interesting features and slight build. At the very first glance you see she is an Amazon.' Garibaldi spoke to her, as Hoffstetter noted, politely and tenderly. Next morning, July 2, the horns of the bersaglieri blew a lament as Manara's body passed over the Tiber bridge. It was a strange procession. Of the 900 men who composed the two battalions who had come to take part in the defence of Rome, there remained 400, who dragged along languidly in front of the bier. On the bier lay Manara's bloodstained tunic and his sword; and behind it came a straggling procession of wounded, some of whom had been lifted from their beds to pay their last respects to the fallen leader. In the church of San Lorenzo in Lucina the young priest

Ugo Bassi celebrated the funeral rites and pronounced the oration. The same day Garibaldi addressed the troops on the square of the Vatican. Those who were willing to endure hunger, thirst and death for the sake of Italy, he invited to be ready to follow him. The others could stay in Rome. He had no further use for them.

The volunteers met on the piazza by the Lateran gate, about four thousand strong. Among them was Anita, come to accept the conditions her husband offered to her as to the others; hunger, thirst and death, for a country that was not her own. She wore the uniform of an officer of the Legion, and was brought to the piazza by Vecchi, who delivered his charge and took farewell of the general. The column moved off towards eight in the evening and soon there was nothing left of the faithful men but a little dust that hung in the damp air and settled back on the ground.[1]

Colonel Niel, on behalf of Oudinot, had journeyed to Gaeta with the keys of Rome. 'France', exclaimed Pius IX with tears in his eyes, 'promised nothing. Yet I had always confidence in her. I felt that when the time had come France would give to the Church her treasure, her blood, and, a thing perhaps more difficult for her courageous sons, the slow endurance and patience to which I owe the preserving of Rome, my city, a treasure belonging to the whole world, a much loved and sorely tried metropolis towards which in my exile my anguished eyes were ever turned.'

The Pope himself was not to return for another nine months. But the re-establishment of his authority was celebrated by a ceremony in which the power of France and the glory of the Papacy were commingled. The Romans were given a week to swallow down their republican fervour. Then, on July 15, the town being decorated, the French and Papal troops were drawn up with fixed bayonets between the Piazza of St. Peter and the bridge of Sant' Angelo. It was a nice day, the shops were shut and

---

[1] Hoffstetter, p. 307 ff.; Lœvinson, p. 265 ff.; Vecchi, p. 299; Trevelyan, p. 230 ff.

the citizens and their families turned out to see the ceremony, which passed off peacefully. At three in the afternoon Oudinot and his staff cantered on to the square before the Vatican and took their station at the head of the troops; a cannon was fired, the yellow and white flag of the Pope rose above the Castle of Sant' Angelo and the Capitol simultaneously, the French batteries fired a thumping salvo of a hundred guns, the bugles shrilled and the drums rolled and, with one movement, the troops presented arms. It was expected that the Roman crowd would do its part. And it did. With compunctious fervour the citizens shouted, *Evviva Pio Nono! Evviva nostro Papa!* while the commander-in-chief, two French envoys, the generals and superior officers filed into the basilica, followed by a cortège of selected Roman magistrates. After the *Te Deum* had been intoned by Cardinal Castracani, a sermon was preached by Cardinal Tosti; and again after the service the cardinals offered the thanks of the Pope to the deliverers of the holy city. Oudinot replied modestly, alluding to the care with which the besieging army had preserved the monuments of Rome.

In the evening there were illuminations.

GOVERNO PONTIFICIO
Direzione generale di Polizia in Ravenna
Re Discovery of body of person unknown

MOST EXCELLENT AND REVEREND,

I consider it my duty to make urgent report to you concerning the discovery of the body of a person as yet unidentified.

Last Friday 10th, on the Guiccioli estate at a spot about one mile from the port of Primaro and about eleven miles from Comacchio, some children noticed a human hand sticking out of a heap of sand. The Curia, being notified, at once proceeded to the spot, where it was seen that the hand and a part of the forearm were in some degree decomposed and devoured by animals. The sand heap, about half a metre high, was then opened and disclosed the body of a woman whose height was approximately one and two-third metres and whose age would seem to have been thirty to thirty-five. The body was stoutish, the hair which had parted from the scalp and lay in the sand, was dark, rather long and had been dressed *alla puritana*.

The eyes projected, as also the tongue, which was thrust out between the teeth, the trachea was severed and there was a bruise round the neck; clear signs of strangulation. There were no other lesions on the body; two molar teeth were missing on the left-hand side of the upper jaw and one molar on the right side of the lower jaw. The body being opened was found to contain a fœtus about six months old. The clothes on the body were a chemise of white linen, a petticoat of the same and a *bournous* of purple cambric with white flowers. The legs and feet were without covering, and there were no ornaments on the fingers or neck; the ears, however, were pierced for earrings. The feet would appear to be those of a person not of the peasant class, as there were no callouses on the soles. None of the people who came from Primaro, Sant' Alberto and other nearby places recognised the body. The natural colouring was not ascertainable, owing to the condition of the body; and for this reason also it was not considered advisable to expose the body for purposes of identification. For reasons of public health it was reinterred.

The facts lead us to infer that the body is that of the wife or woman who followed Garibaldi and was reported to have landed in this district. The inference is borne out by the condition of pregnancy. It is not clear how the woman came to this precise spot nor how she was done to death. Inquiries are being made and the result will at once be communicated to Your Most Reverend Excellency.

I have the honour to remain the most obedient servant of Your Excellency.

Ravenna, 12th Aug. 1849.

A. LOVATELLI,
Delegate.

GOVERNO PONTIFICIO
Direzione provinciale di Polizia in Ravenna

TO THE MOST EXCELLENT AND REVEREND MONSIGNOR THE EXTRAORDINARY COMMISSIONER—BOLOGNA.

MOST EXCELLENT AND REVEREND,

Further to my respectful communication of 12th inst. I reported to you that as a result of inquiry by the police and of information obtained through secret agents posted in the neighbourhood I was in possession of the facts relating to the discovery of the aforesaid body. There is no doubt that the body is that of the woman who accompanied Garibaldi. She was brought in a dying condition on a handcart by Garibaldi himself to the cottage of the brothers

Ravaglia, factors for the marchesi Guiccioli on one of their properties at Mandriole. The woman was declared to be suffering from malignant fever by a doctor, Nannini di Sant' Alberto, who happened to be there at the time and felt her pulse. She was laid on a bed and given a glass of water but died soon after drinking it.

Garibaldi was present and gave way to uncontrollable grief; soon after he took to flight, requesting the family to give the body an honourable burial. These events occurred on the 4th of this month towards evening in the presence of more than twenty people, the labourers on the farm having then assembled to receive their weekly pay.

I immediately sent a warrant for the arrest of the brothers Ravaglia, which was duly executed and the charge is now being formulated. It would seem that the above-mentioned farmers, fearing punishment because of the help given to Garibaldi and because of the death of his wife in their house, sought to conceal the occurrence by burying the body at some distance in the country.

It will be my duty to inform you of the result of the case; and meanwhile I remain Your Excellency's Most Devoted servant,

A. LOVATELLI,
Ravenna, August 15th, 1849.   Delegate.[1]

Such was the end of Garibaldi's great adventure. Chased by French, Austrians, Neapolitans and Spaniards, he disbanded his followers on the soil of the neutral republic of San Marino, where no harm could come to them. But, disdaining safety for himself, he descended with a remnant of two hundred men on the port of Cesenatico and embarked in thirteen small ships to take part in the defence of Venice against the Austrians. He had not calculated on the fact that the knowledge of his heroism was now public property, and that his move to Venice was as easily predictable as the ambit of the moon in the sky. An Austrian fleet lay at hand and scattered the little fleet while Garibaldi with Anita ran his bragozzo ashore and fled inland.

The foregoing documents show in what manner the flight ended for Anita. As she died and he cast himself sobbing on her body, he was warned that the Austrian police were approaching the door.

[1] Documents quoted by Guerzoni (i. p. 367 f.) from *Il Governo pontificio e lo Stato romano*. Not translated before into English.

REFERENCES

Trollope, T. Adolphus, *Pius IX*. 2 vols. 1877.
Gallenga, A., *The Pope and the King*. 2 vols. 1879.
Martinengo-Cesaresco, E., *The Liberation of Italy*. 1895. *Italian Characters*. No date.
Goddes de Liancourt, A. de, *Pius the Ninth*. 1847.
Trevelyan, G. M., *Garibaldi's Defence of the Roman Republic*.
Bolton King, *The Life of Mazzini*. (*Everyman's Library*.)
Maguire, J. F., *Pontificate of Pius IX*. 1870.
Legge, A. O., *Pius IX*. 1875. 2 vols.
Clavé, F., *Vie de Pie IX*. 1848.
Costa de Beauregard, *Jeunesse de Charles-Albert*. 1889. *Les dernières années du roi Charles-Albert*. 1890.
Romussi, *Garibaldi nelle medaglie del Museo del Risorgimento in Milano*. No date.
Sforza, *Garibaldi in Toscana*. 1897.
Lœvinson, *Garibaldi e la sua legione nello stato romano*. 3 vols. 1902-1907.
Memoirs of Margaret Fuller Ossoli. Vol. iii. 1852.
Clough, *Prose Remains*. 1888.
Guerzoni, i.
Hoffstetter, *Tagebuch aus Italien*. 1860.
Bittard des Portes, *Expédition française de Rome*. 1849. 2nd ed. 1905.
Balleydier, *Histoire de la Révolution de Rome*, 1851.
Bourgeois et Clermont, *Rome et Napoléon III*. 1907.
Dandolo, *The Italian Volunteers*. English Translation. 1851.
Gaillard, *L'Expédition de Rome en* 1849. Paris. 1861.
Guerrazzi, *Assedio di Roma*. 1864.
Torre, Federico, *Memorie storiche sull' intervento francese in Roma nel* 1849. Turin. 1851-1852. 2 vols.
Vaillant, *Le Siège de Rome en* 1849. Paris. 1851.
Vecchi, C. Augusto, *La Italia*. Turin. 1856. 2 vols.

III

XX

GARIBALDI FOUND the time heavy. He spent it meditating on the inconvenience of heroes while his restless hands rolled cigars or mended fishing tackle. It was the autumn, and at last he was in safety in the house of the Sardinian consul at Tangier, wondering whether it might be possible to resume his old trade as a master mariner. He knew he would not be allowed in the Mediterranean. It had been made abundantly plain to him in the past months that he was not wanted: for having with great pains escaped from Italy where a number of loyal gentlemen had passed him from house to house until he got to the western coast at a point opposite to the isle of Elba, he found that his troubles were only half over. Piedmont had agreed as a concession to the protest of the left side of the Chamber not to put him under arrest: but it would not have him near. He had tried Tunis; but the Bey, being in league with France, had warned him off. And he had tried Gibraltar, where the governor was polite and told him he might stay six days. Finally he had come to Tangier, where at any rate, he had peace to think. The red shirt was discarded, and he wore instead a garb of black velvet which symbolised his mourning for Anita and for Italy. He wished to sail a ship under Italian colours; but, after seven months at Tangier, he came to the conclusion that the business end of Italian shipping was in America. With secret misgivings at leaving Italy so far behind, he proceeded by Gibraltar to Liverpool and there took ship for the new world.[1]

It was a decision that cost him a good deal, and on the

[1] He arrived at Liverpool on June 22, 1850, and left for America on June 27. *Nuova Antologia*, 1910, p. 648.

voyage across, which lasted a full month (the *Waterloo* being a sailing ship), he fretted himself into a sickness. At Staten Island he had to be carried ashore like a piece of luggage, *com' un baule*. His body was racked by rheumatic pains: but they were the physical expression of the misery that had seized him. He wanted to see no one, and, instead of making himself known in New York or seeing to the business which had brought him to America, he lay in hiding for about a week. He gave up the velvet costume and the remnant of romance that went with it, and prepared to settle down in New York in 'a sort of blue cloth surtout, with frogs for trimming round the buttonholes'; with which went baggy trousers, tightly buttoned round the waist in sailor fashion. Also, in order to cover a scar from an old gunshot wound, he was in the habit of winding a black scarf round his neck. It took the place of a tie, and possibly covered defective linen. On ceremonious occasions he donned a frock coat with a turn-down collar, in which he looked curiously like a Chelsea pensioner drafted prematurely out of the forces.[1]

The *New York Tribune* of July 30 had announced the arrival of the 'world-famed Garibaldi', the hero of Montevideo and the defender of Rome. It said that the famous Italian would be met as befitted one who had served the cause of liberty in the old and the new world. Arrangements had been made some time before his arrival to escort him from the Battery to the Astor House Hotel, which had placed a suite at his disposal, and hoped to recoup itself by a banquet like that which had lately been offered to Avezzana, the erstwhile Minister of War of the short-lived Republic of Rome. But Garibaldi declined these honours gently. He said he was not well, that he admired the American Republic, the last bulwark of liberty, but for himself desired nothing except to be allowed to live quietly as an American citizen. The committee which had taken in hand the business of his reception was loath to let the

[1] *Century Magazine*, 1907, p. 180, and *passim, Garibaldi in New York. Nuova Antologia*, 1910.

GIUSEPPE GARIBALDI (1807-1882)—ASTRIDE HIS FAVOURITE HORSE. A SIGNED PORTRAIT

Photo E.N.A.

lion go so tamely, and particularly to relinquish the banquet: but Garibaldi was firm. He begged the committee to leave him alone, which at last it did. But the New York citizens who had been so anxious to offer him champagne made no move to help him to get a living. Felice Foresti, ex-prisoner of Spielberg and now professor of Italian at Columbia, sought to interest the authorities in Garibaldi's plan for procuring a ship. But in vain. For some weeks the latter lived in the house of Michele Pastacaldi in Irving Place and met the more distinguished of his compatriots, Avezzana, Foresti, Filopanti (late secretary of the Roman triumvirate). His name figures on the list of patrons of a concert on behalf of the Italian exiles at which Adelina Patti was one of the singers. But in a short time he went back to Staten Island. Evidently Irving Place did not suit him.

He could not stay there without either spending or borrowing money; and, having none, he was not willing to do either. A sum of a few thousand lire administered by a cousin in Nice brought in a couple of hundred lire per annum. He could not live on that, much less support his family. When it was apparent that he was not likely to get a ship at once, he determined to earn money in some other way; and, having transferred his domicile first of all to the Pavilion Hotel on Richmond Terrace and later to the house of his Florentine compatriot, Antonio Meucci, he co-operated with the latter in organising a sausage factory, of which the employees were Italian refugees. Meucci looked after the commercial side, while Colonel Bovi, who had lost an arm at Rome, was foreman. The sausage factory did not pay and was reorganised as a candle factory.[1] There are no very accurate details. But it seems that Garibaldi laboured as a workman, carrying barrels of tallow from the quayside to the factory, and endeavouring, by the expenditure of physical energy, to sweat his rheumatism and his misanthropy out of himself. He had no need to work, inasmuch as any one of his richer compatriots would

---

[1] See *Century Magazine, loc. cit.*, and *Memorie*, p. 327.

have been proud to give him food and houseroom: but he worked as an example and as a protest. Behind his diplomatic politeness he was not very pleased with New York.

He was disappointed about the ship. But that was a private matter. He may have thought it strange that the Americans were so ready with their banquets and so unliberal with work; but he did not say so. His grudge against America was a secret one and concerned the effect it had on his fellow-countrymen. Their condition was in contrast to his own misery; for although they talked largely about Italy they were well on the way to foreswearing their native country and becoming citizens of this new republic. He himself had asked for citizenship—but in order to qualify under the law which provided that masters of ships registered in American harbours must be of American nationality. The adoption of America with him went no further than that; whereas many of his compatriots had nibbled round holes in the American cheese and liked it very much. They were pot-bellied and garrulous; and they flourished by virtue of those talents which Garibaldi most detested, by the dexterity of their tongues, the smoothness of their wits and the unsteadiness of their virtue. Garibaldi did not conceal his disgust. He deliberately turned from the rich Italians to the poor, to whom he put the matter into words: 'Here we are', he said, 'a colony of Italian exiles with nothing to do but talk. Now, our talk is never going to free Italy—it's this', he remarked, thrusting out his fist. 'We must await our opportunity and get to work.'

It is on record that Michele Pastacaldi commissioned an oil portrait of Garibaldi about this time, to be done by a young painter, Daniel Pelton, who, as he painted, discovered in the features of his subject a likeness to Christ: 'But', he remarked to the sitter, 'with more of the serpent's wisdom in the eye'. 'The Christ type, as you call it', answered Garibaldi, 'is not uncommon on the Ligurian coast where I was born; and perhaps it may be accounted for by the wives of sailors in peril going to pray before pictures and images of Jesus. As for the serpent's wisdom, or wariness, that undoubtedly was induced by the danger in which the population, including my own ancestors, has stood for centuries past from Algerian pirates.'

Foresti wrote to Mazzini that the general was receiving visits from many distinguished Americans and foreigners, as well as a large number of letters from all parts of the States. A good number of these were love letters sent by admiring women. Tuckerman, the American writer, noted that he had a quiet way of sitting without speaking in the corner of the room.[1]

Garibaldi had given up his military costume. His red shirt went to Meucci, who bequeathed it to a lodge of freemasons, where it was still being exhibited with other Garibaldi relics in 1907.[2] But the reformer's purpose was signified by his hair and his beard, which he had not allowed to be cropped during his flight from Cesenatico, although by so doing he could have disguised himself cheaply and thoroughly. His hair and beard were symbols of his own manhood and of the strength by which he meant to save Italy. They distinguished him from his own countrymen and from the citizens of the American Republic; for, although, as Tuckerman had observed, he was a quiet man, his modesty was a positive rather than a negative virtue. He was silent because he preferred not to talk; and for that reason only. It affirmed, just as much as did his speeches in Italy, that he was Garibaldi.

His mind was torn by problems that it could not solve. The world puzzled him, a world that had been panting a year since with the noblest passion for liberty, and was now lying still like a beaten dog; afraid of freedom and afraid of anyone who still proclaimed it. There was an inconsistency he could not fathom; nor could he understand why it was that men came in thousands to do the bidding of the Pope while, at the lifting of the Pope's finger, millions, who

[1] *Nuova Antologia, loc. cit.* p. 654, and *North American Review*, January 1861.
[2] *Century Magazine*, 1907, p. 180.

would not stir an inch for freedom, knelt down in prayer. As a commander of men Garibaldi marvelled at the phenomenon and, because of his present misery, he repudiated it violently, with the violence of a man who feels he has been beaten with his own weapons. His weapon was not a sword; it was faith, and faith was that by virtue of which the Pope also summoned the world to defend him. Garibaldi could not solve this problem, but he was willing to discuss it; and Dwight, the American who was to edit his memoirs, found to his astonishment that Garibaldi was less willing to talk about the siege of Rome than about the principles of Christianity. 'To my surprise I found my thoughts turned, in part, from fields of battle, the siege of Rome and the sortie of San Marino, to the philosophic principles of the Italian revolution and the true doctrines of Christianity, perverted by the enemies of liberty.'[1]

Garibaldi got Meucci to manufacture three special candles which looked like altar candles and were not. They were red, white and green, the colours of Italy, and he said he would set them up to illuminate the Campidoglio the day an Italian army entered the Eternal City.

Meantime the habits of the future saviour of Italy were plain. He bought his vegetables in the Stapleton market, played a game of bowls of an evening or at week-ends, borrowed a boat to go fishing or a gun to hunt on the Dongan hills. On one occasion he had to appear in the police court to answer a charge of trespass and was discharged by acclamation when it was known who he was. On another, again in court, he gave evidence in favour of a small fellow who had been set on by a larger man. He said 'It was cowardly to pitch on the little fellow....' Sometimes he played dominoes at Ventura's, a café near the Park Theatre where journalists, actors and foreigners met. Round the corner was Anderson's tobacco-shop, famous because Mary Rogers had been employed there before she was murdered and her case brought to the notice of the public in Edgar Allan Poe's *Mystery of Marie Roget*.[2] He was nearly always

---

[1] *Century Magazine*, 1907, p. 175.   [2] *Ibid.* p. 182.

with Italians by preference, though he endeavoured to feel towards the Americans those sentiments of gratitude to which occasionally he had to give public expression. But what he principally wanted from America was a ship.

Life was empty for the time being, all but the hope of a better future. He was neither an exile nor a hero any longer, but an uncommercial man in a country of commerce where men talked of dollars all day long. He would have been very willing to love America and to believe it was the home of freedom, its bulwark, as he had said, but if it was the home of freedom, then freedom as understood by an American was not freedom as he understood it. He had no money, or little. And if he had had it, he would have given it away as useless; with a fishing line he caught his own dinner; if he spent the better part of the day catching it, it was no matter. There was the next day. In a city one must have some money to pay for the room one slept in. But he did not care for cities. He liked the country where one could spread a cloak and lie down. Withal, he managed to do as he pleased in spite of the civilisation about him. But the sight of so many men doing things he did not understand made him feel lonely, particularly because they did them with enthusiasm. They had as much enthusiasm about shutting themselves up in ugly houses as he had in getting out of them. The complexity of humanity puzzled him. If he had allowed himself to dwell on it long he might have wondered by what authority he was to save Italy, from what he proposed to save her and what would be her lot after she was saved. But his thought stopped short; and, rather than venture on speculations essentially hostile and self-destructive, it turned on his own life on which he looked back tenderly. 1849 had been a climax. If he considered what had happened since, he felt like a man who had tumbled from the top to the bottom of a hill. But if he went back again, beyond 1849 to his youth and early manhood, he saw that year as the climax of a long ascent which had begun on the plains of South America, if not before; for there was no moment in his life in which he did not seem to be beginning the great adventure. 1849 was the apex, the crest of the hill.

What went before was dear to him, how dear he could realise only when he saw what had been taken from him. And he thought suddenly of Anita, of how he had wooed her, of how she had fought beside him, ridden beside him, slept beside him and was now dead. The sense of her heroism, which he had taken for granted, came to him and he wondered if he had used her rightly. He thought it might be a good thing for himself if he tried to remember her clearly and write down what he remembered of the adventures on which they had been engaged. He began a sort of memoir, and into it the portraits of his late companions-in-arms fitted naturally. Already at Tangier he had tried to write. He went on now and got so far as to confide his manuscript to Theodore Dwight for publication. But he repented and said he had thought better of it and was of opinion that the time had not come to print these matters. The manuscript did not appear until ten years later (1859), when Dwight seems to have heard of other editions in preparation and to have hastened to put his own on the market.

As Garibaldi wrote, the distress came on him more sharply. He was a good speaker and took pleasure in speaking: but he did not know how to write. The attempt robbed him of that feeling of power and competence which made life possible to him. In action his mind was vigorous and clear: he saw life as a picture clarified by his field-glasses, with the situation and detail of every object unambiguous; and, moreover, caught in a circle which coincided with his will. For what he chose to see he saw and nothing else. But writing was a form of action to which he was unsuited, in which no doubt the spirit of a man might expend itself, but in solitary fashion, so that if it did influence the minds of others it was by creeping on them from behind. He had some happiness recalling Anita and his companions of Rome, but he found himself at last in a greater solitude, with a feeling of weakness to which he was unaccustomed. His memory strayed back to his boyhood when he had learned mathematics willingly enough and discarded all other forms of learning to haunt the old port of Nice. His walks took him now along the wharves of New York and sometimes a Genoese captain would invite him aboard and a few Italians would meet in the cabin and discuss the newspapers, the *Eco d'Italia*, published by a New York Italian for the refugee colony, or Mazzini's paper, the notorious and much persecuted *Italia del Popolo*. His thoughts of himself were shed quickly, and he came to ask himself and his companions whether the next assault on the rotten fabric of tyranny would not best be made from the south, from Sicily; and on that point a great deal was said.[1]

He had been waiting for a letter from Carpanetto, a friend at Genoa, who had promised to see if he could not raise enough money in that port to buy a ship of which Garibaldi would be the captain; and when at length the expected letter came it said that the writer had secured a promise from three merchants who would each subscribe 10,000 lire, but that no others had come forward. Such a sum was inadequate for the purchase of even a small ship, for prices ran high in New York, and even if Garibaldi himself, with some of the workers of the candle factory, bought the materials and did the building themselves, the money was still not enough. It seemed that the late admiral of the Montevidean navy was not likely to set foot on his own deck again for some time; but he felt driven to the sea more and more and knew he must get on a ship if he were to lose the sensation of constant humiliation that came over him in America. He had no disdain for the Americans. He did not feel that he was right and they were wrong: but his feet took him to the docks and he looked for likely ships, and where he saw a vessel loading he offered to give a hand and said he was willing to sign on. There was no response

[1] *Nuova Antologia, loc. cit.* p. 657 and note.

at all, and wearily he came back to Ventura's and played dominoes. At John Anderson's there was talk of a revolution brewing in Cuba. Then a second letter came from Carpanetto saying he had loaded up a ship, the *San Giorgio*, for Lima, and he himself was coming first to New York and would go on to Lima afterwards. Would Garibaldi like to come?

Thus, on April 28, 1851, after much waiting, he got back to the sea, sailing on the *Prometheus* with the faithful Carpanetto, who was mindful to combine business with patriotism. The *New York Tribune* (April 29) announced their departure and wished the travellers luck. Carpanetto's business took him to the isthmus of Panama and presently to Lima, where the Italian colony was all Italian. They made a handsome fuss of him and, at once, Pietro Denegri put him in charge of the *Carmen*, 400 tons, with cargo for China.

The joy of the departure was marred only by the behaviour of a Frenchman who, while the cargo was being stowed, thrust on the new captain the French view of the siege of Rome. An encounter took place in the Frenchman's store, from which the Christlike Garibaldi emerged, somewhat bloody but unbowed, leaving inside the prostrate bodies of the store proprietor and his assistant. As the *Carmen* was about to sail there came a threat that the captain might have to go to prison: but the Italians of Lima waited in a deputation on the chief of police and persuaded the latter to ignore the incident.

The *Carmen* sailed on January 10, 1852, and a steady wind blew her across to China in ninety-three days.[1]

XXI

THE *Carmen* took in a fresh cargo at Canton or Hong-Kong and returned to Lima by the southern route, passing north of Tasmania, where the islands clustering in the strait took the captain's fancy. He mentions them in his

[1] *Memorie*, p. 336.

memoirs and, according to his habit when the subject interested him, he spent some time writing down his recollections. Garibaldi's memoirs, like a fairy tale, have an erratic completeness. They deal at length with matters which seem to have no importance and skip others which the historian may consider vital. But he knew very well what was important to himself.

The ship had passed through between Australia and Van Diemen's Land, when it had to call at one of the Hunter Islands for water. It was an agreeable spot. As their boat ran ashore a flutter of partridges rose in the air, and at once they found a gush of fresh water running through luxuriant vegetation to the sea. They lay down to quench their thirst and fill up the water-barrels; after which Garibaldi went for a walk. He had not gone far before he came on a gravestone bearing an inscription which he took to mean that an English settler and his wife had erected the stone in memory of a fellow-settler who had died; and that after his death they themselves had left the island for Van Diemen's Land. At a little distance was their house, complete with tables and chairs, just as it had been abandoned, a plain one-storeyed building, evidently built with such materials as they could find by the colonists who had gone. Long after the *Carmen* had resumed her voyage to South America, Garibaldi remembered his discovery; and when he thought of the island he was overcome by a sort of homesickness as if he had seen the place for which he had been longing, and had passed it by. For as he had sat on the little beach of the island he realised that more than a ship he needed an island, a place in which at last to anchor his life, and which would be his own. He reached Callao at the beginning of 1853, and touched at New York in the autumn of the same year; and by then he had had enough of circling round the world. His idea had been to run between New York or South America and Italy. But his present job took him too far away, into parts where he heard no news. He feared that he would come to port and be told that Italy had risen in revolt, and he had not been there. Besides, he was like his father. His place was the Mediterranean, a human and kindly sea along which a master could jog from day to day and from port to port, watching the sky and the newspapers at the same time.

The Signora Rosa was dead. He had known it before the news was brought to him. In the midst of a storm he had dreamed of the quiet of his native land, of the 'paradisal' air of Nice. And as he dreamed the air became all gloomy and he saw a procession of women who moved towards him, and in the midst of whom was a bier. He could not move in his bunk and the procession came nearer, set down the bier by his side and disappeared. He attempted to rise, but he was held down as if by the weight of a mountain; until he saw in the bier the face of his mother. When he awoke he fancied he could feel the touch of her icy hand. He noted the date of the dream. It occurred on March 19, 1852; and it was confirmed that on that day the Signora Rosa died. She had been the best of mothers. With her went that peculiar sensation that Garibaldi had always enjoyed, the sensation of being protected by her saintliness. It was to her and to her prayers that he attributed his good luck in battle. Not until she was dead did Garibaldi dare to proclaim himself a freethinker.[1] He was the more willing to do this now as he had, with this last disaster, reached the veritable bottom of life. It was fitting that Anita and the Signora Rosa should go together, the glory and the sweetness of life. Nevertheless there were his children. They were still at Nice and had reached an age when they required attention. Accordingly he took ship for England. The *Commonwealth* was bound first for Newcastle and then for Genoa. Thus, by stages, he would reach home.

In March, 1854, the *Commonwealth* cast anchor in the Tyne. She was the property of an Italian syndicate of Baltimore and was captained by an Italian, Figari. Before

[1] See Mario, *Supplement*, p. 119 f., for the text (in English) of Garibaldi's dream. It was originally printed in Italian by Guerzoni from a MS. page of Garibaldi's memoirs.

many hours had passed the news spread that Garibaldi was aboard, and a penny subscription was organised among the working men of Tyneside. They were not sure whether the hero was soldier or sailor, so they gave him gifts suitable to either condition, a gold-hilted sword inscribed 'To General Garibaldi, by the people of Tyneside, friends of European freedom', and a telescope of Newcastle manufacture. The gifts were delivered, along with an address handsomely written on fine parchment, by Joseph Cowen, son of Cowen of the Blaydon Burn brick manufactory. Joseph Cowen was himself a political figure of more than local importance. He had been to Edinburgh University, and had acquired such an enthusiasm for the cause of Italy that he hid copies of Mazzini's addresses in the insides of the bricks his father exported to the Continent. Joseph Cowen made it plain to Garibaldi that he was being welcomed by working men. 'The sword is purchased', he said, 'by the pennies of some hundreds of working men, contributed not only voluntarily but with enthusiasm, and each penny represents a heart that beats true to European freedom.' Garibaldi accepted the gifts on the deck of the *Commonwealth* and replied in a speech which, as the first delivered to Englishmen, is worthy of reproduction:

GENTLEMEN,
    I am very weak in the English language, and can but imperfectly express my acknowledgments for your over-great kindness. You honour me beyond my deserts. My services are not worthy of all the favour you have shown me. You more than reward me for any sacrifices I may have made in the cause of freedom. One of the people, a workman like yourselves, I value highly these expressions of your esteem, the more so because you testify thereby your sympathy for my poor, oppressed and down-trodden country. Speaking in a strange tongue, I feel most painfully my inability to thank you in terms sufficiently warm. The future will alone show how soon it will be before I am called to unsheathe the noble gift I have just received, and again battle on behalf of that which lies nearest my heart, the freedom of my native land. But be sure of this: Italy will one day be a nation, and its free citizens will know how to acknowledge all the kindness shown to her exiled sons in the days of their darkest trouble. Gentlemen, I would say more, but my bad English prevents

me. You can appreciate my feelings and understand my hesitation. Again I thank you from my heart of hearts; and be confident of this —that whatever vicissitudes of fortune I may hereafter pass through, this handsome sword shall never be drawn by me except in the cause of liberty.

The health of Joseph Mazzini, the 'illustrious compatriot of Garibaldi', was drunk and, on the following day, the *Commonwealth* lifted anchor and sailed for Gravesend.[1]

Garibaldi saw that there was a change in the political situation. In England the feeling was not what it had been when, five years since, the defender of Rome was allowed to wander from port to port in search of shelter. And in London he perceived that this change was not peculiar to the working classes, who, in England, had always been loyal to Italy; London and Newcastle were alike in this matter. For about the same time as Sir Robert Peel was thrown from his horse and died, the Austrian general, Haynau, who had been responsible for whipping the insurgents of Milan, visited London and took it into his head to inspect Barclay's brewery. He was set upon by the workmen and so severely hustled that he had to fly for his life, to save which the police locked him up in a cell at the police station (September, 1850). A protest to Lord Palmerston called forth the reply that the draymen ought to have 'tossed him in a blanket, rolled him in the kennel, and then sent him home in a cab, paying the fare to the hotel'.

Mazzini had returned to London in 1851, a grayer and a sadder man. His beard, which had been black, was white. He was wasted and so pale that tears came to the eyes of Carlyle and his wife when they saw him again. But his spirit was the same, and at once he set about organising propaganda in England. The 'Friends of Italy', a society founded at his instigation, pledged themselves to 'promote a correct appreciation of the Italian Question in this country'. He found an unexpected and powerful supporter

[1] April 12, 1854. Cf. Mario, *Supplement*, p. 124.

in Gladstone who, having recently visited Naples to take a holiday from politics, found himself assisting at the drama of the trial of conspirators implicated in the Neapolitan and Sicilian rising. The conspirators were almost all condemned; and from the courthouse Gladstone, in his methodical and thorough way, proceeded to the prison and saw in what filthy dungeons the poor men were to expiate their crime. His comment was not long in coming. He spoke as a man moved by the truth; not as a politician, but as a human being who found it hard to believe that human beings should be capable of such cruelty. By a strange turn in the wheel of political fortune the cause of Catholic Italy (for, whatever the political situation, Italy was Catholic), was confided for good and all to the hearts of Protestants in England. Gladstone's comment[1] was found to be undiplomatic at Vienna and Naples. But Palmerston retorted to this by informing King Bomba that a copy had been sent to all English diplomatic agents in Europe.

The fortunes of the Liberal Party fluctuated. But now the 'correct appreciation of the Italian Question' was common both to Liberal members of the upper classes and to the working men who discussed European politics at their meetings. Mazzini had always had a way with women. He did not know what attracted them; and he made no effort to attract them. But they came, drawn, no doubt, by that higher purity in him which made him so like a priest. He gave them nothing but good advice; and in return they formed the nucleus of a powerful circle from which he obtained quick and reliable information about the political situation in England and abroad, as well as enthusiastic help in the cause of Italy. Garibaldi found many ladies about Mazzini when he went to see him in London, among them one who, somewhat to his astonishment, seemed to find charm in himself.

This was a wealthy widow named Emma Roberts, who proposed marriage to Garibaldi and considered herself as accepted. It was given out publicly that the general and

[1] *Letters to Lord Aberdeen*, July, 1851.

she were engaged; and for a matter of two years she was referred to as his fiancée. She represented in a pleasant way the change which was taking place in the public estimate of the exile. But he could not get accustomed to her habits. She had many servants and spent a long time over meals, this last thing being a fact which he mentioned later as one of the causes which led to the breaking-off of the engagement. The principal reason was, however, that Mrs. Roberts wished to annex the hero and add him as a final exhibit to her collection of trophies; and this proved to be impossible.

The ladies in the entourage of Mazzini soon understood that although Garibaldi and Mazzini both loved Italy they did not love each other. Mazzini considered Garibaldi as a man to be used. And Garibaldi was not eager to be used by Mazzini. He listened to what the great plotter had to say and departed without having committed himself. A few days later he was in Nice.

He lived in his cousin Augusto's cottage by the Lazzaretto at Nice, while Mrs. Emma Roberts occupied the house in which he had been born. She was accompanied by a young Englishwoman, Jessie White, who was one of Garibaldi's (and Mazzini's) most devoted followers. The two boys, Jessie White records, stayed with their father in the cottage. 'Menotti attended the royal military college; of Ricciotti he himself took entire charge, washing the squealing urchin every day under the pump, and teaching him to write by tracing copies in pencil on carefully ruled paper. Up with the lark, he walked for four hours with his gun over the mountains; dined at twelve; slept; played at bowls with anyone who chanced; paid every day a visit to his daughter Teresita, adopted by his old friends the Deideri; came in the evening up to the "Garibaldi house" rented by the English lady (Mrs. Roberts)—whose guests we were—to whom he was engaged, to listen to her wondrous music and play at draughts. A quiet, thoughtful, unpretending gentleman, was the first impression he made on you, fairly up in the politics of the day, with a very decided opinion on the burning questions of the hour—the suppression of monastic corporations, the participation of Sardinia in the Crimean war against Russia.'[1]

The government of Piedmont did not object to his return. It was now in the hands of Cavour, who, like Mazzini, considered Garibaldi a man who might be useful when the time came.

He sailed about the coast in a little ship called the *Esploratore*, touching at neighbouring ports. Once he ventured as far as Marseilles, where the French police took no notice of him. But his favourite place of call was Sardinia. He thought of settling there, but could not make up his mind, until a storm cast him into the strait of San Bonifacio and compelled him to take refuge on the coast of the Isola della Maddalena. He had been there before, five years earlier: but this was the first time he had been able to see clearly the adjacent island of Caprera. The storm waylaid him three days. When he returned to Nice he had decided that the island for which he had been seeking was found at last. He had about sixty thousand lire, part derived from his savings as master mariner, part inherited from his brother Felice, who had just died. With this sum he purchased a corner of the island.[2]

It was a curious spot, a mere hump of rock that rose above the waters of the Mediterranean and dwindled back into them. Obviously it was not chosen for its pleasantness. A stranger viewing it from a passing ship might have thought it pretty; but those who, like Garibaldi, knew the coasts of Sardinia, were aware that it was wind-blown at most seasons of the year, and at other times was liable to be visited by the malaria which prevented Sardinia from being an earthly paradise. Garibaldi chose Caprera because it was an island on which he was not likely to have many neighbours. At the time of his arrival there were only a few herdsmen and an English couple of the name of Collins, who occupied the southerly half of the island. The de-

[1] Mario, *Supplement*, p. 132.   [2] Guerzoni, i. p. 401, note 1.

marcation between Garibaldi's property and Collins' was not very clear, and Collins complained that his neighbour's cows ate his grass, a considerable crime, as grass grew only in the rock crevices and on the back of the island. The compliment was returned by Collins' pigs, which strayed northward and grubbed up rows of cabbages and potatoes recently planted by the new colonist. Both Collins and Garibaldi were hot-tempered and took the depredations to heart.[1] But a sunstroke killed the Englishman; and Garibaldi was left undisputed master. He built a fourroomed square house in a niche overlooking the little port of Stagnarello, and devoted his days to primitive agriculture, reclaiming the land in the immediate vicinity for fruit trees and vegetables. The roof was flat and constructed so that rain-water ran down a pipe to a well below the house. It was such a house as might have been built by a settler in South America, and to complete the illusion, he had his daughter, Teresita, sent out to him from Nice. She had his own fair hair. But her skin was olive like her mother's. Her body was supple like Anita's and, climbing among the rocks, she began to use a sling with the dexterity of the born huntress. Her features were straight and regular like Garibaldi's. To look after Teresita and himself he employed Battistina, a Nice woman who is described as being 'small and rather ugly'.[2]

There was a certain amount of classical allusion in the withdrawal to Caprera. Garibaldi had read of Cincinnatus and drew a comparison between the noble Roman and himself. In part, his new passion for agriculture was a means of keeping in health, and in part it expressed his view that the time was a time for waiting. The sword was turned into a ploughshare in order that the edge of it might be kept keen and that the arm that held it might retain its strength. Garibaldi went to bed early and got up early. When he was in bed he read the newspapers. They arrived in piles by the boat from Maddalena, and Battistina was

[1] Vecchi, *Garibaldi at Caprera*, p. 26 f.   [2] Melena, *Garibaldi*, p. 26.

forbidden to destroy them until he had read them through. In this way, and on his own behalf, he kept his eye on events in Europe. Ricciotti, his younger son, had hurt his leg by a fall and was taken to England under the wing of Mrs. Roberts. But Menotti, the eldest, remained with him, a broad-chested lad, who looked as sturdy as a fisherman. With him, also, were a few companions who had elected to share his exile. It turned out to be a very relative one. Presently Caprera became a place of note, and in the course of time had many queer, and some distinguished, visitors.

Garibaldi's chief interest was still politics. But, in addition to politics, there was also that which inspired his interest in politics, his continual hope that something would turn up—a man to be saved, a lost sheep to be found; for he required as well as the major adventure of saving Italy, a reasonable amount of incident. And in this respect Caprera was disappointing. His enthusiasm for digging the soil was in great part artificial, as was also his zeal for building. He built, or helped to build, dry-stone walls around the house and across the frontier of his property. But he was a bad mason (or so it was whispered). And when he was gardening his temper was uncertain. He reproved Vecchi sharply for cutting a bean-stalk when he was hoeing. These occupations were a substitute for something better; and in themselves they were too monotonous for him. So it came about that in spite of his good resolutions he went to Genoa sometime in 1855 to discuss a plan for the liberation of the Neapolitan prisoners.

The plan had been mooted in high circles in London. The Liberal Party, influenced by the conspiratorial atmosphere of Mazzini, had decided to charter a ship and carry these prisoners off from their island prison of San Stefano under the nose of the Neapolitan government: and although the action was unofficial, it was sponsored by Gladstone and the vessel subscribed for by numerous persons in London. One end of the plot was in the British Museum, where the Modenese exile Panizzi was librarian, another end was in the hands of Sir William Temple, ambassador at Naples, and a third led from Sir James Hudson, British minister at Genoa, to Garibaldi on Caprera. The first attempt failed. The *Isle of Thanet*, the ship chartered for the purpose, foundered off Yarmouth; after which the money subscribed had to be recovered from an insurance company. Garibaldi himself was to be in charge of the second attempt. He came to Portsmouth in February 1856 to look out a likely vessel, and there the shipwrights discovered that there were few things about ships that he did not know. He did not look up the arch-conspirator Panizzi at the British Museum, a fact which surprised the latter: but Panizzi was informed from Genoa that Garibaldi was ready. Garibaldi undertook to keep himself free for a year if need be. But the affair came to nothing. Sir William Temple fell ill, and wrote that the attempt should be abandoned as an amnesty was probable.[1]

Garibaldi was disappointed. It was another lesson from which he drew his own conclusions. A year later he was asked to support a plan for a rising in Sicily, and replied that he saw no prospect of success, and would have no hand in it. The expedition was the ill-fated one in which Pisacane met his death. In Garibaldi's opinion such adventures were worse than useless. He judged that Italy had already spent too much blood at the command of dreamers. The day of Mazzini was over. That of Cavour was coming.

Meantime he was at war with 'nothing but stones'. He was waiting until the machinations of Cavour should have reached some conclusion. Gradually Piedmont was acquiring an army, trained for the undertaking that lay before it. The only argument which would achieve Italian unity was power. By a natural process, power linked with power. And therefore, if there were power in Piedmont, then power would come to Piedmont in the form of allies, and when these allies had come, Austria could be driven back over the mountains. With a grave and satisfied smile Garibaldi learned that Cavour had taken the first step in this matter

[1] Mario, *Supplement*, p. 134 ff.

of obtaining allies by offering the help of Piedmont to France and England in the Crimean war. Some people thought that a ridiculous thing to do. But Garibaldi did not. He gave Cavour to understand that he was his (and Victor Emmanuel's) man.

XXII

GARIBALDI kept his promise to be handy in case he was required to command the San Stefano adventure; but by mid-year 1856 it became evident that nothing was likely to happen. He was not quite sure why he had come to Caprera, to escape from the world or to be near Italy. But in the course of 1857 that doubt was solved. Cavour invited Garibaldi to talk with him.[1]

Cavour knew the kind of man he had to deal with; and he was a little afraid that the condottiere might get himself embroiled before the time was ripe. He enjoined on him to avoid all the proposals of Mazzini and to hold fast to one simple and radical plan. There would be no difficulty about having a war with Austria when war seemed desirable. The Italians must bide their time and collect their forces. The minister did not disclose the rather comprehensive scheme by which he meant to achieve his end, but he made it plain to Garibaldi that the King of Savoy would not strike until he had a weapon in his hands. Garibaldi was half inclined to become a sea-captain again, if only to keep himself out of mischief while the great adventure was preparing. The Piedmontese government was still nervous of him, and suggested that he might, for the time being, take command of a ship plying between Genoa and America. But he was afraid he might be on the wrong side of the water when the little 'trouble' that Cavour was brewing came to a head. After some reflection he declined.

He remembered this period as one of tedium, dismissing it in his memoirs as of 'no interest'. 'In part I spent it (*i.e.* the period from 1854 until the spring of 1859) sailing,

[1] *Daniele Manin e Giorgio Pallavicino*, Milan, 1878, p. 172.

and in part cultivating a small property I had acquired on the island of Caprera', he says. But it was during this time that he met a lady who played some part in his later life. She herself exaggerated that part and found little favour with Garibaldi's family. 'Donna isterica e fantastica', she is called by Ricciotti, the second son of the general. Nevertheless, small or great, she did play a part in his life; and it is the duty of the biographer to make mention of it. Her relations with Garibaldi did not exist solely in her own vivid imagination; for Giacomo Curàtulo, an Italian scholar of an enquiring turn of mind, discovered seventy-two autograph letters from Garibaldi to the lady, and they, together with some thirty from the lady to Garibaldi, go to prove that a good deal of what she wrote of him was the truth. The pen name of this lady was Elpis Melena.[1]

She had abundant leisure. In fact she had nothing to do at all except travel over Europe looking after her health and adding to her considerable knowledge. She was a blue-stocking of an uncommon variety; for, although she spoke many languages and knew Latin and Greek as few women do, she also rode a horse competently and went about accompanied by two greyhounds. She was young, twenty-six years only, at the time she met Garibaldi; also she was the mother of a son and had left two husbands by the wayside. With some precocity she had married in 1837, when she was only sixteen, a *mariage de convenance* apparently; and this first husband having committed suicide, she took a second, a banker of the name of Schwartz, whom she promptly divorced. She retained his name. In private life she was Madame Schwartz, or more fully, Marie Espérance Schwartz, which, being translated into Greek, gave her pen-name Elpis (espérance), and Melena (schwartz or black). Her passport declared her to be English; and indeed she was so legally. But she was of foreign blood, her maiden name having been Brandt. Her father appears to

---

[1] Cf. Elpis Melena, *Garibaldi. Recollections of his Public and Private Life.* English version published 1887.

have been a Hamburg banker who settled in Southgate, where Marie Espérance was born in 1821. He may or may not have been a Jew. At any rate, he was wealthy, and she inherited from him ample private means. Curàtulo, making enquiries about 1911, ascertained that Elpis Melena died in 1889 at Ermatingen in Switzerland. Her son provided the Italian scholar with a photograph of his mother, but had little or nothing to say concerning her relations with Garibaldi. Seemingly it was a subject of which he had no cheerful recollection. We have only a photograph on which to base an opinion of her features: but from that it may be seen that these were not distinguished. Her nose was snub and her nostrils somewhat eager; her brows jutted in masculine fashion, suggesting the headstrongness which characterised her actions. But her eye was luminous and intelligent; and her hair, trained in the romantic manner which had just then reached England, fell in ringlets on her shoulders like that of a heroine of Dickens. She was impressionable and inquisitive, and she seems to have inherited from her banking parent a knowledge of the procedure of business. Her first visit to Garibaldi in 1857 was for the purpose of securing the rights of publication of his memoirs.

She was very pleased when Garibaldi himself fetched her in his skiff from La Maddalena and treated her with his usual gallantry. He was so kind, so simple and so sincere that she at once placed him in the first rank of her enthusiasms—even before the Pope, for whom she had a romantic weakness. At the same time she did not neglect her business, and made a point of writing down her impressions of Caprera.

'This island', she wrote, 'differs wholly from Maddalena. Its port is not enlivened by the movements of boats and fishing-smacks; one sees no villages nor country houses on its shores; nor are its heights crowned by ruined fortifications. From the beach the ground rises amphitheatrically; it becomes precipitous; bold rocks intervene, and diversify the acclivities; and these at length combine in one majestic chain of mountains. There is a sublimity here, as if Nature had predestined for the Cincinnatus of our age a solitude in harmony with his character. Lentisk, arbutus, myrtle, heather, and a multitude of aromatic shrubs grow among the rocks, and form clusters here and there in the patches of greensward, ascending more or less precipitously from the sea to the General's house. After barely half an hour's walk, we came to an enclosed *parterre*, extending in front of the house. And here several hounds ran bounding and barking towards their master who lavished caresses upon them.

'On entering the enclosure, a sort of shed was seen to the right. "The remains, no doubt, of your first residence here?" I remarked.

'"The second", replied the General. "The first was a mere sail, which I used as a tent. And now, if you will allow me, I will escort you into my present house. It is built of granite, has but one storey, as you see, and, like the South American houses, it has a flat roof, used as a terrace, and crowned by a cupola."

'The handsome appearance of this building made an agreeable impression upon me, and entering it, I found that the exterior accorded with the interior: there was simplicity, space, airiness. The harmony of the proportions proved that the designer and builder had considered comfort rather than rules of architecture.

'In one of the rooms, occupied by one of the two friends who for several months had shared Garibaldi's rural life at Caprera, I noticed a little collection of standards, banners, weapons of different countries, etc., but when I asked the General for an account of these souvenirs of war, he managed to excuse himself; for he was not a man to enlarge on his own successes. These objects, which I carefully examined, were trophies of his different engagements, illustrative of the most brilliant episodes of his heroic life. Amongst others, I saw the flag which Montevideo had offered to her brave defender, after the battle of San Antonio.'

Madame Schwartz took advantage of the momentary absence of the general to scan the shelves of his library and found a number of works on navigation and the art of war, the 'best works' on natural science, Shakespeare, Byron and Young, Humboldt's *Cosmos*, Bossuet's *Discours*, Plutarch's *Ethics* and La Fontaine's fables. After which scrutiny she was introduced to Teresita who, to honour the occasion, had put on a spencer of white piqué and a muslin petticoat. In the course of her conversation with Garibaldi, Madame Schwartz noted that 'his choice language was not much seasoned with Attic salt'. She herself was rather given to quotation. But she forgave the general his plainness because of the sound of his voice, the voice of a man accustomed to command. 'His sonorous voice, strong yet sweet', she wrote. She missed the waving plumes and the poncho, of which she had heard, but she admitted a certain grandeur in his 'common peasant's gown'.

Garibaldi was very pleased to see her. They talked as he showed her over the island, and Garibaldi agreed that as he had nothing much to do he might as well accompany her in a tour of Sardinia. But he wrote at once to say that that promise was imprudent, and they did not meet again for a year. She sent him letters frequently, however, and occasional gifts, dresses for Teresita, slippers, cigars and an engraved gold watch for himself.

On her second visit Madame Schwartz felt she knew Garibaldi better. He had thanked her in cordial terms for the watch: 'a magnificent piece of jewellery', he called it. He proposed that she should come in August and enjoy the bathing. A room was specially prepared for her, a yellow and white counterpane which had belonged to Anita laid on the bed, which was of an 'orthopedical hardness'. In spite of this she spent a good night and came down to breakfast. Garibaldi was talkative. He had had a bathe in the sea and was dressed with 'peculiar care'. After breakfast he proposed a visit to his young plantations, and threw his poncho over his shoulders 'with a remarkably picturesque effect'. He displayed in the course of their conversation 'an inexhaustible wealth of knowledge about natural history in all its departments', and, as they were on their way back to the house, he begged her to walk more slowly, 'as he wished to lay a certain proposition before me while we were alone together'.

This was the prelude to an event which had better be given in the narrator's own words. 'We paused', writes Madame Schwartz, 'under the shade of a luxuriant fig-tree, and then Garibaldi asked me whether or not I could determine to join my fate to his, and take the place of his Anita, by being a second mother to his children. A thunderbolt could not have startled me more than this overture, and I could only elicit from myself an expression of the profoundest gratitude for the honour he did me, with, at the same time, an assurance that I would give serious thought to his important proposal.'

When Garibaldi had anything to propose, he did it in this manner. He had been thinking for some time of his children, especially of his daughter and her upbringing, and his reflections had convinced him that it was desirable that he should have someone to look after his family. He liked Madame Schwartz. She was romantic, talented, feminine; and with all the prestige of independence and wealth. In many respects she was more interesting than the brilliant Mrs. Roberts, from whose tutelage Garibaldi had been glad to escape to the solitude of Caprera. Madame Schwartz was obstinate, but she was not highhanded. There was a certain amenableness about her that suggested she might be an agreeable companion. And for himself he looked for nothing more. Women had always 'made a dead set at him', at all stages in his life, as much before he was known as a hero as after. They came to him like moths to a flame, and he did not bother about them at all. He liked women who, like Madame Schwartz, had some music about them, who could play a flute or a violin or a piano, and so add to the grace of life; and he liked them very much when to their sweetness they added the spice of courage. He was not sure, indeed, in which respect a woman was more pleasing to him, by showing the high spirit which he had valued in Anita or by bringing into life the things that a soldier does not readily find at hand. But, one way or the other, his need of them was temporary and simple. Had his mind not been otherwise occupied it might have exalted them; but his mysticism was concerned with Italy, the supreme inspiration, and he, therefore, took from them only what he needed immediately. As he had briefly told Anita, many years before, that she was to go with him as his woman, so he explained to Madame Schwartz that he required her as a mother for his children.

No doubt she would have accepted. But as they walked home Garibaldi withdrew his hand from Madame Schwartz's arm, saying, 'The women of the house are very fond of observing everything through a telescope'. Madame Schwartz knew there were only two women on the island, Garibaldi's daughter, Teresa, and the maid, Battistina. But at table it was soon evident to whom he referred. Whenever Garibaldi showed his guest any attention Battistina 'fell into a passion' and refused food and drink, while the host was noticeably embarrassed by the maid's behaviour. Madame Schwartz drew her own conclusions.

'Garibaldi's fear lest he should be seen arm in arm with me, strengthened my suppositions, and convinced me that his principles tallied in more than one respect with Terence's well-known line: *Homo sum, humani nil a me alienum puto.*'[1]

Their correspondence continued on a tender note. Garibaldi addressed Madame Schwartz in his letters as *Speranza amatissima*, a superlative which Jessie White Mario declared to mean nothing, but which, with due regard to the personages involved, may be taken as indicating at least the beginnings of affection. In response to Garibaldi's

[1] *Op. cit.* p. 26.

letters Madame Schwartz assured the hero of her soul's devotion and of her readiness to follow him to South America. It was not her fault if suddenly the idyll was brought to an end.

He had told her, as he told many people, of the pleasures of life in South America; and he said that perhaps they might visit that country together, a plan which Madame Schwartz cordially approved. But in January 1859 he wrote to say that the South American voyage was off. He did not say why, but she was soon to learn the reason.

The 'little trouble' was beginning, and Garibaldi was recruiting officers in Turin.

XXIII

THERE was at least one noteworthy resemblance between Cavour, the new director of Italy's destiny, and Mazzini. They both studied the map of Europe before applying their conclusions to the problem of their own country. Both had subtle, Italian minds in which lodged a strange mixture of idealism and unscrupulousness, the like of which was to be found in the medieval courts of Italy, but which was not common in the nineteenth century. Mazzini's plan for the redemption of Italy had been and still was a plan based on the sympathy of European democrats; and he hoped to realise it by connivance with the many societies, secret and public, by which the new democracy sought to affirm itself in Europe. He depended on diplomacy. But by his own choice his diplomacy selected as its field of action working men's clubs and those brotherhoods of one variety or another in which the enthusiasts of the educated middle classes voiced their grievances. Mazzini's usefulness to Italy seemed to come to an end, therefore, when, after 1848, the national chancelleries decided that the interests of such democratic societies were not identical with national interests. Italian unity thereafter could not be realised from below, by a process of internal fermentation stimulated by outside assistance. It was not to be a gift contributed by a victorious and enlightened European democracy in its march of progress. It was to be taken by a statesman whose idealism on behalf of Italy was not less than Mazzini's, but who used his cunning in the traditional courts of international diplomacy.

Cavour used the same methods of intrigue. But with different people. His first step was to dispose of Mazzini and make it plain to Europe that Piedmont was a good, old-fashioned, constitutional monarchy with no dangerous revolutionary ideas at all. He had Mazzini condemned to death *par contumace*, a gesture universally satisfying to the reactionaries in power and which did no harm to Mazzini, as Cavour had made sure that his victim would not be caught. His second move was to call the democrats of northern Italy to heel, which he did successfully in the course of 1857. His third was to buttonhole Napoleon III at a secret interview at Plombières (July 21, 1858) and persuade that disciple of 'la guerre pour une idée' that a professional supporter of righteous causes owed it to himself to support Italy if that country were attacked by Austria. His fourth and last move was to provoke Austria to attack, an event which duly occurred at the end of April 1859, after Baron von Kellersberg's ultimatum to the Piedmontese government had been allowed to expire. 'The responsibility for the grave consequences that must ensue would fall', said the Austrian ultimatum, 'on the government of His Majesty the King of Sardinia', a sentence of very fine unconscious irony, as the responsibility for these consequences certainly did lie at the door of the statesman who had led Austria by the nose to the trap he had prepared. When war was declared, Cavour breathed relief. He had taken no man into his confidence and he had made servants of all his masters. Most difficult of all had been to hold the young son of Charles Albert in check until the time was ripe. Victor Emmanuel was straining like a hound on the leash. In his speech at the opening of the Chambers he had said that the nation must 'await with firmness and prudence the decrees of divine Providence'. But it had not been easy to keep his military boot out of the spider's web so delicately and patiently forged by his chief minister. At last, however, the day was come. As the army of Piedmont advanced to cover the approaches to the towns, the French expedition ary force arrived as Napoleon III had promised.[1]

Cavour was no figure of romance. He looked and behaved like a lawyer; and his habit of keeping his own counsel made him an object of suspicion, even among those Piedmontese politicians who were in agreement with his policy. But, as Victor Emmanuel said, they had to put up with him because they could not do without him. And although, up to the very last moment, it was doubtful whether his intricate plans would end in disaster or in triumph (it is said that Cavour was ready to commit suicide when it seemed as if France might back out), the events which he had prepared arranged themselves in excellent order. He had timed the outbreak of war for the first week of May, and it occurred only a few days before the date he had scheduled. The staff work in the war ministries was less brilliant. Both the French and Piedmontese scrambled somewhat late into the field, the first French division reaching Turin on April 30, whereas Count Gyulai, the Austrian general, had crossed the Ticino on April 29. There, however, the latter halted to think what he ought to do next, and the French and Italian troops had time to get into line. In respect of general military inefficiency the opponents were roughly equal. But the Italians had enthusiasm on their side and the French a natural gallantry. At the village of Montebello these allies scored their first victory.

Garibaldi had seen Cavour. But the conditions under which he was to fight puzzled him. Although he was given extraordinary rank as major-general, his pay came direct from the Piedmontese government, not through the Pied-

[1] A more particular account of Cavour's activities will be found in Martinengo-Cesaresco, *Liberation of Italy*, p. 182 ff. Cf. also Trevelyan, *Garibaldi and the Thousand*, p. 82 ff.

montese war office, which would have nothing to do with him. Also his instructions were to recruit *volunteers*, not soldiers, a corps to be styled *Cacciatori delle Alpi*, and which apparently was to enjoy as little official recognition as its master. From these facts Garibaldi drew the conclusion that he was not so much wanted as feared. His presence insured that the democrats of northern Italy (who were liable to take their directions from Mazzini) would not fall foul of Victor Emmanuel and his undemocratic minister at a moment when all was staked on a national victory. Cavour played craftily. He had played with a courage in which there was some recklessness; for he had calculated in terms of men, judging them carefully in order to estimate what, in certain circumstances, their behaviour might be, and while such a calculation, conducted by a cunning man, was likely to be accurate in the case of one man or two, it was less likely to operate where half a dozen men were involved, each a magazine of destructive possibilities. At any rate Cavour was leaving as little as possible to chance. Although he was far from confiding his real thoughts to Garibaldi, he meant the latter to neutralise Mazzini.

The general was supremely useful, as well as supremely dangerous. He was like the pied piper; he had only to appear and crowds followed him; so that, by attaching this prestigious individual to the king's service, the crowds, with their revolutionary possibilities, were tethered and held harmless for the duration of the adventure. Cavour may have had other thoughts about Garibaldi, but this was the principal one. It had as its corollary that Garibaldi must be as inconspicuous as could be managed. Napoleon III was in supreme command of the allied armies, and with him was General Vaillant, the same who had organised the siege of Rome. As a matter of tact towards the French, the hero of Italy must not be flaunted too openly in case old memories flared up on one side or the other. With devious tact Cavour conveyed the necessary to Garibaldi, who emerged from the interview somewhat dazed. He had to *far capolino*, to be the dot on the *i*; to appear and not to appear, to collect volunteers and make no noise about it, to handle the provinces and make them rise in support of the cause and yet avoid becoming a nuisance himself.[1]

The conditions would have discouraged a vain or self-seeking man. Garibaldi did not pretend to like them, but he gave his word, engaging himself irrevocably until peace came, and with him the thousands who were his slaves. After all, he feared only one thing, that there might be no fight, that something might occur at the last moment to destroy the hopes on which he had lived for years. So long as Cavour and Victor Emmanuel fought there was nothing he would not do to help. Besides, he perceived advantages in not being the servant of the Piedmontese war office. He was free. All he had to do was to make himself unpleasant to the Austrians, stirring such a hornet's nest in the northern provinces that the *Tedeschi* would be glad to take themselves off over the mountains.

Madame Schwartz received a note from him dated April 12, to say that he would be glad to see her in Turin at 31, Via San Lazzaro. After waiting fourteen hours at Leghorn for the Genoa boat and spending an uncomfortable four hours in the Turin train, she arrived to find a crowd of young men outside the general's lodging. They told her he was out. But he called on her the same evening and talked with great enthusiasm of Victor Emmanuel. Madame Schwartz was anxious to return to the subject of their last conversation at Caprera, which Garibaldi seemed to have forgotten; he seemed also to have forgotten why he had summoned her to Turin. She asked whether he wished her to look after Teresa; but he said no, Teresa was with the Signora Deideri at Genoa and well bestowed. Madame Schwartz then hazarded a question about Battistina. She also, he explained, was provided for. Garibaldi had left her all the money he had, a sum of five hundred francs. Also he had asked Battistina to take care of his dog. Battistina would remain at Caprera and a woman from Maddalena would keep her company. This information Garibaldi gave

[1] *Memorie*, p. 342.

with crisp assurance. He pulled out his watch and was gone.

However, at half-past nine the following evening there was a noise in the street outside the hotel, and presently he appeared again, explaining that he had been obliged to get into a cab in order to escape the attentions of the crowd. From dawn to dusk he was so harried that he had not had time to wash his hands. She suggested he might remedy this omission in the adjacent toilette and, when he returned, she moistened his fingers with blüthentau, her own favourite perfume. After that she gave him tea with milk and sugar and some bread and butter.

He talked abundantly and kindly. After some persuasion Madame Schwartz obtained permission to take off the worn black ribbon from which the gift watch hung perilously, and replace it by a heavy gold chain which she unclasped from around her neck. Once more the idyll was shaping happily.

Whether she hoped to lead him captive or not, she was disappointed. Two days later he had gone to Brusaco.

The recruiting offices in Turin took the cream of the volunteers for the Piedmontese regular army; and left the rest for Garibaldi. But there was such a stream of men filtering in from Lombardy (where they had to run the gauntlet of the Austrians in order to get to the recruiting station), as well as from more southerly parts, that in a twinkling the Cacciatori numbered 3000 men. Among the other signs that he was to be prevented from being too powerful or too conspicuous, Garibaldi noted that when the 3000 figure was reached, a second corps was formed from additional recruits; and these, the Cacciatori degli Appennini were not given him. They were promised by Cavour, and Garibaldi asked for them. But they went elsewhere.[1]

The red shirt of Rome was also forbidden. The new volunteers wore a grey overcoat, dark blue trousers, a beret of the same colour, and a black leather belt to which was

[1] *Memorie*, p. 343.

attached a cartridge pouch. In the beginning they also wore the official haversack. But it was not long before Garibaldi told them to stuff their rations in their pockets so that they should march light. The Cacciatori were well officered. Medici, the hero of the Vascello, had charge of one of the three regiments into which they were divided, Cosenz, a veteran from Venice, had another; and in the third was Nino Bixio, tougher and more impetuous than ever. The men were mixed, but for the most part came from the professional classes, lawyers, artists, students, business men; but they were cheerful and marched along the roads singing a soldier's song, 'Addio, mia bella, addio'. Garibaldi himself was not over comfortable in the kit of a Piedmontese major-general. His beard did not go well with the elegant képi he wore on his head; nor was the képi any more wearable because it was copiously ornamented with silver braid. He was seen to remove it several times. Then he pushed it into a saddle-bag from which he extracted a black felt hat with a wide brim. In this ambiguous attire he rode with the Cacciatori to Casale.[1]

He watched his men keenly. At Papolo, Menotti Garibaldi, who was now beginning his career as a soldier, brought in the news that a patrol of Austrian cavalry was following close on the heels of the column. Accordingly, Garibaldi disposed twenty carabineers at both sides of the road, ordering them to hold their fire until the enemy had come right amongst them. But a musket went off too soon and the Austrians wheeled about and vanished. Next day Garibaldi issued an order of the day in which he said, 'Our Italians have incontestable bravery, but they lack that calm masculine courage which characterised their forefathers.... On the next occasion the Cacciatori delle Alpi will, I hope, show themselves worthy of the cause they are defending'.[2] It was not the Austrians who had to be defeated in order that Italy should be free, but the very nature of the Italians themselves and their habit of mingling courage and fear in equal doses. Garibaldi was the more anxious that the Cacci-

[1] Dumas (Garnett), p. 321.   [2] *Ibid.* p. 323.

atori should behave well, as he had the bersaglieri on his flank. The Cacciatori redeemed themselves promptly at Casale, where they held the bridge-head skilfully against a company of Tyrolese infantry and captured a field piece and a supply of ammunition. The first two weeks, however, were not very eventful. Garibaldi was on the left flank of the Piedmontese general, Cialdini, covering the approaches to Turin while the French troops disembarked at Genoa. But by May 12 he was left to his own devices and, like an arrow released from a bow, he flew along the left flank of the allied armies in the direction of the Lombard lakes. On May 17 he was at Biella, on May 20 at Gattinara, on the 21st at Borgomanero and on the 22nd at Castelletto.[1] His campaign had begun.

Among Garibaldi's volunteers were some fifty horsemen who acted as scouts. They were captained by Francesco Simonetta, a gentleman who owned an estate at Varallo Pombia and knew all that region and the banks of the Ticino River very well. Garibaldi conferred with him at Biella and arranged a plan of campaign. While Simonetta with a few men went secretly to Castelletto to prepare the crossing of the river, Garibaldi indulged in one of his characteristic feints. At Borgomanero he ordered provisions to be held ready against his arrival with the Cacciatori at Arona; and towards evening on May 22 the Cacciatori arrived, and quartermasters made a great show of inspecting billets for officers and troops so that the Austrian spies should not fail to convey the information that Garibaldi was proceeding along the northern shore of Lake Maggiore. But after this demonstration Garibaldi turned sharp about and moved south to Castelletto, where he found that Simonetta had surmounted all difficulties and awaited him with a small fleet of barges well hidden on the Piedmontese side of the river. Medici's regiment was shipped across safely in spite of the swift current that caught the heavy barges and dragged them downstream.

[1] Mario, *Supplement*, p. 177 f.

On the far bank they assembled and walked silently into the village of Sesto Calende, on Lombard soil, where they surprised and captured a number of Austrian gendarmes and officials who were sleeping peacefully in their beds. At dawn the next day the remainder of the Cacciatori crossed the Ticino, light in baggage and in heart. With the exception of a few mules to carry ammunition and one or two ambulance carts, they had no encumbrances of any kind. The exact nature of Garibaldi's plans was known to no one but Garibaldi himself; and that was perhaps just as well. His intention was to escape from the Piedmontese generals and put the Ticino between himself and any possible order of recall. For he still feared he might be baulked. Once across the Ticino he would be his own master.

He had three thousand men against whom the Austrians could detach any number they thought might be required; and there was no hope, if disaster occurred, that any help might be forthcoming from the French or Piedmontese armies. But this situation appeared to Garibaldi ideal. Leaving De Cristoforis to defend Sesto Calende with a company of Cacciatori and dispatching Bixio northwards to Laveno, on the Piedmontese shore of Lake Maggiore, he marched on to the town of Varese and there celebrated his entry into Lombardy. The troops entered towards nightfall under drenching rain, while the whole population came out to welcome them. Young girls and women broke through the ranks and clung on the necks of their deliverers. It was a scene that moved Garibaldi deeply, one which seemed to him to afford a lesson to the cold egoists who thought government could be established and maintained in defiance of the wishes of the people. Moreover, it was a relief to him to find that the second part of his programme was likely to be easily fulfilled. In spite of their long subjection the Lombards were more than ready to raise the flag of revolt. News was brought that in the outlying parts where the Austrian garrison was weak, the peasants were rising and throwing the Austrian officials into jail. This step had already been taken before Garibaldi's arrival at Varese, where the mayor had affixed the following proclamation:

Towards midnight a column of the Italian army is to arrive amongst you, under the command of Giuseppe Garibaldi, a general of the magnanimous Victor Emmanuel. The municipality is pleased to be able to make this news known to its citizens. It shares with them their joy and emotion in beholding the renaissance of their country. The emblems of the foreign oppressor are thrown down. We see the return of the sacred tricolour, the emblem of order, union, liberty and things to come. Blessed be those who restore it to us! Fellow citizens! let us receive them with enthusiasm. Let us follow the dictates of our hearts, and let our shout of welcome be: 'Long live Italy'.

Garibaldi lost no time in reporting his progress to Cavour, who approved of these bold and dangerous operations in a brief message: 'Insurrection, general and immediate'.[1]

The insurrection proceeded briskly and recruits poured in from all parts of Lombardy. Garibaldi received reports which said that General Urban with 40,000 troops was moving in the direction of Varese, and that other Austrian contingents were likely to set out from Laveno and Milan. It proved that Urban's army was only 10,000; but such a force, if properly handled, could dispose of the small band of Cacciatori. Austrian proclamations promised fire and sword to all villages and townships that made common cause with the revolutionary movement, and this promise gave Garibaldi much anxiety. It would have been easy to play hide and seek in the mountains with an Austrian army, or with several Austrian armies. But it was not so easy to protect the inhabitants of Varese against the consequences of their own enthusiasm. They were eager to fight; and on the evening of May 25, a notice was posted up by the king's commissioner, Emilio Visconti Venosta, saying that the Varesini had been the first to salute the tricolour flag in Lombardy and that they would be the first to defend

[1] *Memorie*, p. 349 ff.; Dumas, p. 327 ff.; Guerzoni, i. p. 440 ff.; Trevelyan, *Garibaldi and the Thousand*, p. 90 ff.

it. The following morning at eight o'clock Urban's column appeared on the Como road and the fight began. The 10,000 mentioned in the reports had again dwindled. Urban was attacking with about 2,500 men, having left the rest of his army in reserve at San Salvatore, while a detachment had gone north in order to come down on Varese by the Iduno road. Evidently Urban's intention was to take the bull by the horns; and it seemed he did not consider the undertaking difficult. At about a mile's distance from the city Captain Nicolo Suzini exchanged shots with Urban's advance guard and then retired. The Austrian sharpshooters advanced along the road, while Garibaldi, who expected that Urban would attack from several points simultaneously, went up to the southerly eminence of Biumo Superiore, whence he could see what was happening. But Urban had no complicated plan. His infantry was met by a withering fire under the walls; and the fire was followed by a bayonet charge which sent the Austrians running back on the road to Como. At this point Garibaldi judged that Urban had no further trick up his sleeve, and released a flank attack which completed the demoralisation of the enemy. For the time being, without much loss, Varese was safe. The day after, leaving the Varesini to look after themselves, Garibaldi advanced by the Cavallasca road until he had reached a point whence he could look down on the valley and uprising hills which protected the approaches to Como. He had been informed that large bodies of troops had been coming into that city; and he assumed that Urban would secure the key positions in the mountains, a barrier penetrable only by the high passes of San Fermo and Camerlata. Of these San Fermo to the north was the higher; and Urban judged that it was high enough to look after itself. He sent up a small garrison to hold San Fermo and concentrated the main body of his troops at Camerlata and in Como itself, where they were quite useless. To Garibaldi's experienced eye it was plain that whoever had San Fermo had Como; and he accordingly gave instructions for a triple attack on the hill. It was entirely successful, except that the gallant De Cristoforis lost his life. The Austrians precipitately drew into the city.

The Cacciatori had set out from Varese in the morning, sighted the enemy at noon and fought him until dusk. Now, instead of allowing them to rest, Garibaldi ordered a silent march down the wooded slopes towards Como. There was a halt at San Vito in order to pick up news of the enemy. As if by magic all the inhabitants seemed to have vanished and it was impossible in the darkness to discover what had become of the Austrians. Not a light was to be seen in Como itself. But when the Cacciatori entered the city, shutters were cautiously opened, lamps were lit and the triumph of Varese was repeated. It was a substantial triumph in every way. From the military point of view, Garibaldi had fully succeeded in harassing the flank of the Austrian armies and threatening their rear. He had roused the civilian population. And he had captured important stores of arms, food and money. He was badly in need of all these; for, although the liberated citizens of Lombardy were prodigal of huzzas, they bated not a penny on the price of their goods.

The capture of Como by Garibaldi occurred on May 27. It was followed by other less successful operations, in which Garibaldi was hampered by the necessity of defending Varese and Como against Austrian reprisals, an undertaking in which he did not entirely succeed. Before the end of the month Urban entered Varese and imposed a fine of three million Austrian pounds. But the French and Piedmontese armies had not been inactive. The battle of Magenta, fought on June 4, drove the Austrians out of Lombardy and ended the first phase of the campaign.

XXIV

WHATEVER the French and Piedmontese armies had done, Garibaldi had achieved the kind of victory dear to the Italian heart (and indeed to any), appearing unexpectedly in places where no sane soldier would have risked his neck, and disappearing with the same mystery and celerity. When he was hard pressed he disbanded the Cacciatori and ordered them to reassemble at a certain spot, a procedure which might have been fatal at another time (in the retreat from Rome it had not proved very successful), but which, in the general mood of exaltation, served its purpose very well. In this rôle, as general and conjuror, he was completely at his ease and, to the astonishment of his lieutenants, who saw him eating little and snatching only a few hours of sleep out of the twenty-four, he was becoming fatter and more placid. There was no word of his rheumatism. The correspondent of a London newspaper found him at the Angelo inn at Como, looking surprisingly like an Englishman and surprisingly insignificant. The popular imagination had run riot in the description of him. The Austrians were not far from believing that he ate his prisoners; and the Lombard peasants who had seen him on his white horse in the market place of their villages, said he was a tall man, exaggerating his undeniable five-foot-seven to the proportions of his reputation. It seemed incredible that this oldish-looking burgher was the man about whom all Europe (and now even *The Times*) was talking. A child, said the correspondent, would have stopped him in the street to ask the time; and obviously Garibaldi would have taken out his watch from his waistcoat pocket (Madame Schwartz's watch) and given a conscientious answer, without thinking there might be any reason why a child should not ask him the time. In the same way, and by virtue of the same smooth processes which were characteristic of him and which surprised people who allowed their imagination to play tricks with them, he would parry a blow aimed at him and, in the completion of the same reflex, knock his assailant down. While the Austrian rifles were firing against his outposts on the railway line, he kept up an easy conversation in which, for the benefit of some ladies in the correspondent's party, he obligingly described his adventures in South America and his travels in China. He chatted easily and without diffidence about himself, in a way that showed he was not ashamed of heroism and did not in any way seek to conceal the fact that he was a brave man. He thought that men should talk of such things and women be entertained by them; and it was by the manner of his narrative, by his insistence on technical points, that the listener could understand that he was not boasting, but speaking of things that interested him. He spoke of the adventures of war and of the curiosities of the world much as an Englishman speaks of passes in a football match. The game was the thing.

He had no objection to being visited in this way, either by men or women. He did not hold that war was an exceptional or horrible thing, but, on the contrary, that it was a thing in which all citizens should be interested. He liked to think that his little army was a part of the people, and that the people should come to him in the same way as his soldiers. He had still his old habit of propping a blanket on a couple of rifles, using his saddle as a pillow and going to sleep while a couple of sentries held off the curious until he should be awake again. The campaign, for him at any rate, passed happily, and there grew in him the certainty that Italy was going to be free because the Italians he met were sincerely resolved on it; some more and some less, for it could not be denied that a great number looked on the matter as one which was to be solved over their heads, and which would affect them as a thunderstorm affected their vineyards, with the same fatality and finality. They did not know properly where they belonged, to Austria or to Italy, and they prayed God only that they might not have to suffer in their goods and bodies if they nodded their heads in one direction or the other. It was not thus in Varese, where the inhabitants declared openly for Garibaldi: but it was so in Como, a commercial town which bobbed on one side or the other, according to the bulletins. When Garibaldi turned his back on Como he had an uneasy feeling that the opinions of the city swung round gently to the other side; and in this he was not wrong.

It was on June 1, 1859, in the midst of the campaign, that he halted at Robarello after his troops had sustained an unexpected defeat in an attempt to take the lake fort at Laveno; and because the Cacciatori had been beaten back and had turned and run before the enemy, he was for the time being not fit to speak to until he had slept on it and made up his mind what he should do. 'This cursed fear', he said as he rolled himself in his poncho and fell asleep under a tree between a map and his sword. Later, with some officers of his staff, he set off on the road to Sant' Ambrogio, and they were proceeding in silence when from the direction of Como there appeared a calèche in which were seated a young woman and a priest. 'The enemy,' remarked one of Garibaldi's staff, 'has charming spies'; for, as the calèche came nearer and drew up beside the party of officers, it was seen that the young woman was beautiful. She said she brought word from the king's commissioner at Como, Visconti Venosta, that if Garibaldi did not make an appearance soon it looked as if the city would go back in sheer fright to the Austrians. The man at her side, she explained, was Don Luigi Giudici, coadjutor of Socco and well disposed. As for herself, she was Countess Giuseppina Raimondi, daughter of the Marquis Raimondi, of Fino, on Lake Como. Her father was an old liberal who had been plotting for Italian liberty for many years.

The young woman did not appear to Garibaldi inappropriate. He thought the city of Como could not have done better than send warning by this charming messenger. She was the embodiment of youth, which in itself was the spirit that inspired Italy to refuse servitude and clamour for freedom; she was an epitome of the beauty of those village maidens whose modesty had been forgotten for a moment as they hung on the necks of the Cacciatori. He took the countess as seriously as she desired to be taken, and sat down in the inn at Robarello to write a note for Visconti Venosta. When she was gone he remained sitting.

She was eighteen, and he was fifty-two. A whiff of South

America came in with her, bringing memories of days when he would have put a hand on her shoulder and claimed her. He sat for a long time dreaming.[1]

Garibaldi had not seen Madame Schwartz since the pleasant interview at Turin, when she had hung the gold chain across his waistcoat and given him tea. She was annoyed to find he had gone so abruptly, but she sent a comfortable saddle after him, searching the city for a saddler who would make one on the South American model. Then she went to Rome, where she came into possession of a fine six-year-old horse, a strongly-made Arab of irreproachable line and action, a trifle lively for a lady, but with eyes so tender that she could not refuse to buy him. She called the horse Frontino, and thought it would be a nice thing to go to Garibaldi with him and share the dangers of the campaign: for she had moods when she thought she would be happy to give up everything for his sake. But the weather in Rome was treacherous, and on the morning of her proposed departure she fell ill. The doctor said her lungs were affected and advised her to give up the journey. She had rejected this advice and got as far as Ruta on her way to Genoa, when a hæmorrhage convinced her he was right. Instead of joining Garibaldi she travelled south to the Pyrenees, and it was not till past midsummer of 1859 that she returned to Nice to hear of the battle of Solferino and the peace of Villafranca.

The operations of the French, Piedmontese and Austrian armies had been in strange contrast with those of Garibaldi. While the guerrilla leader, still on the left flank, buzzed like a fly from Como to Lecco, from Lecco to Bergamo, and from Bergamo to Brescia, these cumbrous machines manœuvred solemnly for position. Garibaldi was preparing to accompany the Austrians in their retreat into Venezia, when an order from Piedmontese headquarters relegated him to the Valtellina in northern Lombardy, whither he went, grumbling that he was being sent out of the scene of

[1] *Memorie*, p. 371; Curàtulo, p. 294 ff.

war so that the glory of the final triumphs should belong to Piedmont's regulars and Napoleon III. But, as things turned out, there was small glory in the fighting that followed.

On June 24 the war machines collided on the battlefield of Solferino. It was a distinguished occasion in one sense, for Napoleon III led on one side (thrusting Victor Emmanuel aside), and Francis Joseph, the young Emperor of Austria, on the other. A great part of the day was spent by the Austrian staff searching for their leader, and by the time liaison was established between the Austrian troops and their high commanders, it was two in the afternoon, and the French were on the heights of Solferino. In the course of the day, also, Count Clam Gallas mislaid the Austrian artillery and General Zedwitz lost touch with 15,000 men, including six regiments of cavalry, which might have been useful. Nevertheless, although the French had fought well, they were exhausted, and both sides were preparing to retire when a sulphurous wall of yellow cloud rolled over the battlefield. The French thought the cloud contained Zedwitz's cavalry. But it was rain, a pelting storm that fell on French and Austrians alike. That storm put an end to the war.

Not long after, having found that in this stupid encounter 10,000 French had become casualties as well as 13,000 Austrians, Napoleon sent a private messenger asking for a truce, and by July 6 the second and last phase of the campaign was at an end and negotiations began. These negotiations were completed at Villafranca a fortnight later by pourparlers between Napoleon III and Francis Joseph, while Victor Emmanuel looked on in helpless rage. Madame Schwartz gleaned some account of these events. Garibaldi, she learned, was at Modena fanning the flame of insurrection in the duchy (from which the duke had fled after the battle of Magenta). All Italians, including Victor Emmanuel, Cavour and Garibaldi, were agreed that Italy had been betrayed and must look after herself.

Garibaldi proceeded from Modena to Ravenna in the

Papal States, leaving word that Madame Schwartz and the Deideris were to follow him; and a rumour having been spread in Ravenna that the *famiglia del prode generale* was likely to visit him, the vetturino in which the party was conveyed from the railway station was saluted by a dense crowd. They entered the Piazza del Palazzo at a gallant trot and rattled under an archway, to find Garibaldi at the foot of a staircase holding out both hands in welcome and looking ten years younger. That evening they dined with the Marquis Rora, the *intendente* appointed by the Piedmontese government to nurse the new political conscience of the Pope's subjects; and scarcely had they been seated half an hour at table when the cheering outside became so loud that the marquis advised Garibaldi to appear. The cheering became a perfect stillness as he stepped on the balcony. He spoke briefly, in a soft, yet sonorous voice that seemed to fill the air. The wind fell, the flags hung limply from their staves, and it seemed as if every man in the crowd was holding his breath. As Garibaldi finished his address and withdrew from the balcony, the cheering broke out afresh, lights blazed over the piazza, torches flared against tricolour flags, processions tramped this way and that, military bands played in odd corners, and out of the clamour a clear voice rose now and then praising Garibaldi, the son of the people. Madame Schwartz looked up to the stars and down at the rich commotion of the square and was strangely moved. She thought of the ancient glories of the city of Ravenna, of the Pineta or pine forest which supplied the masts of Venice, and whose glories had been sung by Dante and Boccaccio and Dryden and Byron. All the dead glories of Ravenna seemed small compared to the glory of that moment, to the mystery of this man who, ten years since, had crept from farm to farm, from thicket to thicket, hiding from the Austrians, and who, by virtue of his faith, stood on the same ground triumphant.

They drove next day through the Pineta, and Garibaldi told Madame Schwartz that the campaign had been 'magnificent', an adjective which he used unblushingly because it did not refer to himself but to the fact that few men had been lost and great results achieved. The Cacciatori had behaved like soldiers. Presently, after a drive of thirteen miles, they stopped at a farmhouse, and Madame Schwartz discovered it was the house of the steward of the Marchese Guiccioli, and the room in which they were sitting was the same in which Anita had died. Guests were expected. They were offered a splendid country banquet, and an officer proposed the health of Garibaldi and recounted the chief exploits of his life. Then Garibaldi rose and spoke while Madame Schwartz scribbled notes discreetly:

You have just narrated my history (said Garibaldi), and it is now my part to tell you how proud and happy I am to find myself again among this brave people, of whose courage and attachment I have experienced so many proofs. I repeat to you that, to the last moment of my existence, I shall be devoted to my country, body and soul. For fourteen years I have served the cause of liberty in foreign lands without pay or reward. What then will I not do for my native country? Events are progressing favourably, but there is still much to be done. The day is come when Italy shall regain her complete independence. This time it must be accomplished, and from the Alps to Sicily she must be free. Providence has given us the man we needed to re-knit us together. It is round Victor Emmanuel that we must rally to repulse the stranger from our soil. We will no longer bear the foreign yoke. Let but our oppressor retire and leave us to enjoy our possessions in peace, and we will at once welcome him as a friend; but so long as he desires to subject us to his dominion, he has nothing to expect from us but the fire of our artillery. It is only by union and strength that we shall obtain our freedom. When we can attain strength, believe me, no one will dare attack us. Before everything, it is imperative that we should all be soldiers. Our entire nation must form one army; and if domestic duties keep a few of us round the family hearth, let them remain there like soldiers, musket or sword in hand. Fifteen days are enough to transform a brave Italian into a brave soldier. A man's worth is not dependent on an embroidered uniform. Look at the Zouaves, for instance. In their simple, easy dress, they are the finest soldiers in the world. I remember once finding myself, during my American campaign, in the midst of a vast plain, where our wants could be supplied neither from the interior nor from the seaports; indeed the latter were blockaded by the enemy. The herds of this plain were our only resource, their flesh our nourishment, their skins our protection from the heat at noon, and our covering at night! yet I assure you our soldiers, armed with the musket alone, performed prodigies. We were the terror of the Imperialists, and my few hundreds of brave men put thousands of the enemy to flight. But we, my friends, want arms; and that this need may exist no longer, I have proposed that Italy should form a subscription to purchase a million muskets. Think only how many wrongs we have to get redressed. Bear in mind the number of years we have been under a foreign yoke.[1]

There was a peculiar accent about this speech which Madame Schwartz was quick to understand. 'He did not speak', she says, 'as an orator seeking to astonish his auditors by eloquent periods, but as a chief, an adored friend, in open-hearted converse with his faithful adherents, awakening in them sentiments of patriotism by the recital of acts of heroism.' She herself performed a very useful service by recording that speech and her impressions of it.

On the way back to Ravenna they stopped at a wayside church where a priest gave each member of the party a little wreath of fresh flowers and led them to a recess by the altar, where there was a tombstone.

They laid their garlands down and stood in silence. It was the tomb of Anita.[2]

Next day the general's party moved to Bologna, passing through Bagna Cavallo, Lugo and Medicina, where the people unharnessed the horses from Garibaldi's carriage and drew it along amid a storm of joyous shouting, lengthening the way by detours, in the course of which they displayed their idol in as many villages and at as many cottage doors as possible; until after seventeen hours of such travelling, they entered Bologna to the music of clanging bells and military bands. They city was illuminated with Venetian lamps, at intervals a cannon boomed a salute, and there descended on the carriage a mixed rain of

[1] Elpis Melena, *Recollections*, p. 69 ff.

[2] The ashes of Anita were later in the same year removed to Nice and placed in a niche in the cemetery chapel. In 1931 they were again removed and placed in the Janiculum. Cf. Sfinge, *Anita Garibaldi* (*Nuova Antologia*, 1905) and Curàtulo, *Anita Garibaldi*, p. 202.

flowers and cigars, the latter tied round with tricolour ribbons. It was an exhausting journey for the women, who were lifted, pushed and pulled more than they desired. Also they had to partake of ruinous meals at each halt, where coffee, chocolate, lemonade, confectionery and fruit were handed up with bewildering regularity and had to be consumed. They were very glad when at last they found themselves in their rooms at the Hotel Brun in Bologna. 'Such days as this', said Garibaldi to Madame Schwartz, 'are really infernal.' But he took the demonstrations very coolly and never forgot Teresa and her companions. At the many banquets and feasts, while toasts were being drunk to Italy and to Victor Emmanuel, he peeled fruits and passed them to his daughter, to Madame Deideri and Madame Schwartz.

At Lugo they had made a longer halt than usual, as numerous deputations had to be received from various districts of the Romagna; and as the mission of stirring up the Papal States was one which had been entrusted to Garibaldi by Victor Emmanuel himself, he was anxious to show what he could do. There were processions, speeches, crowds of country people in their best attire, speeches by distinguished citizens and replies by Garibaldi, so many that the ladies retired to a private room in the prefecture to wait until it was all over. A band was playing the Garibaldi hymn, and Teresa, excited by the music, caught the stout Madame Deideri and waltzed her round. But Madame Deideri was preoccupied. She shook Teresa off and whispered to Madame Schwartz. 'She began to represent to me', says Madame Schwartz, 'how desirable it was for Garibaldi and his children that I should ally myself with him, and be a mother to Teresa and her brothers.

'"Only think how you might save the whole family from misfortune!" she continued, when I made no remark upon her words.

'"But what do you mean?" I asked, somewhat surprised.

'"Surely", she replied, "you know that Battistina had a child by the General five months ago—a child christened

Anita Garibaldi, after his late wife; that he has promised to marry her as soon as possible—that is, when he has obtained the certificate of his first wife's death; and lastly, that he received this very document, enabling him to marry again, just before the requiem service in the Pineta yesterday?"

'"And, knowing these circumstances, you can yet think me capable of marrying Garibaldi! Do you think I would accept happiness and historical renown at the price of perfidy towards a poor woman? . . ."

'"But", interrupted Madame Deideri, "it will not have escaped your notice that Battistina is a low-minded person, and you must admit that it would be best for the General to come to terms with her at some small pecuniary expense."

'"It is too late now to discuss Battistina's character", I replied. "She is the mother of a child by Garibaldi, christened after him. Moreover, he has given her a sacred promise of marriage, and this poor woman shall never, never, be plunged into misery through my agency."

'I will say nothing', concludes Madame Schwartz, 'about the feelings which stirred me while I uttered these words. I will only add that they were to me a vow, made solemnly before God and my conscience, to persist in my resolution.'[1]

Madame Schwartz had no opportunity to discuss these matters with Garibaldi. She wanted to get him alone, and hated the continual processions and addresses. In order to convey to him that she at least was not his servant she sat beside Teresa in the carriage, knowing that Garibaldi wished her to sit beside Madame Deideri. He was silent when he saw what she had done. But presently he vaulted over Teresa and the sulky lady, and landed on the driver's

[1] Elpis Melena, *op. cit.* p. 72 ff. The child referred to, Anita Garibaldi, was born in May 1859, and registered and legitimised by Garibaldi himself. She was for some time tended by Madame Schwartz, but came to live with Garibaldi on Caprera in 1875, where she died soon after of fever (August 25, 1875). Cf. Mario, *Supplement,* p. 449 note.

box, whence he looked down with a triumphant smile, tapped Madame Schwartz on the shoulder and sang her a Spanish song, no doubt a memory of South American days, in which a certain majo, having offended his morena, besought her pardon.[1] She was not mollified but, as a woman who knew men, she marvelled that after seventeen hours of public worship he was as vivacious as ever. For herself, whatever her intentions had been, the visit was a failure. She could not get near Garibaldi. In the Hotel Brun the general was visited by innumerable government officials. The women could not go out unless at night for fear of being mobbed, and if they opened their doors to pay each other a visit, the bersaglieri on guard in the antechamber sprang to their feet and presented arms. At meals Garibaldi showed Madame Schwartz some kindness, placing her at his right hand and passing her tit-bits. But these were not what she wanted. 'Familiar conversation', she says, 'was impossible.' Every meal was a banquet, at least in numbers; and it was plain that Garibaldi's real companions were the men, Medici, Cosenz, Bixio, to whom she was a stranger. When the meals were over she was called on to play on a spinet the national airs of Italy and Spain, and what fragments of operas she could remember.

One day, however, Garibaldi called her into a side room, saying he wished to show her something beautiful. In the room were two splendid banners, one of three thicknesses of heavy silk, in the Italian colours, the other a heavy white moiré on which the coat-of-arms of the house of Savoy was embroidered.

' "These banners", said Garibaldi, "are sent to me as a present, and as the work of their own hands, by the daughters of the Marquis Raimondi. The Marquis has repeatedly invited me pressingly to spend some time with him at his villa on Lake Como. We will go there as soon as I am somewhat more free." '[2]

---

[1] Elpis Melena, *op. cit.* p. 81.   [2] *Ibid.* p. 82 ff.

XXV

THE diligence for Florence left at three o'clock in the morning, at which hour the whole of the Hotel Brun, including its officious sentries, was asleep. Madame Schwartz had to light herself down the stairway with a candle and find her way to the diligence herself; and when, being safely inside that vehicle, she reached the city gates, an official, hawking and grumbling alternately, required her passport, which she had left at the bottom of her trunk at Nice. Her explanations were disregarded, and she was ordered to descend: but as the official opened the diligence door and flashed his lantern on her face, he recognised Garibaldi's English lady, and with an astonished *Affè di Dio*, began profuse apologies, and put her inside again. At Poretta on the summit of the Apennines, she stopped to dine and was again recognised. The landlord of the inn would take no money for the meal she had just had, but presented her, instead, with a bouquet of flowers. The name of Garibaldi was enough in itself to lock and unlock the gates of a city and to act as a passport in the whole of northern Italy.

Madame Schwartz's relations with Garibaldi would have been happier if she had been able to forget herself, as he did, in a cause. But, like Mrs. Roberts, she would have liked to make a gentleman of the hero and cut him off from such inferior people as the Deideris, who travelled in third-class railway carriages amid hen coops and odours of sweat and garlic. She was beginning to find she could not change him. He had a natural nobility that took the place of fine manners. His self-possession in all circumstances was perfect. This last was a quality that really provoked astonishment, and made one wonder whether it was due to his being superior to the circumstances or inferior to them. At any rate, it was instinctive, and not due to any wilful hold over himself; for Madame Schwartz could see the same self-possession peeping out in Teresa, and was not sure whether she liked it or not. It seemed that the education of Garibaldi had been begun and completed by nature, and that a civilised woman like herself could not interfere with it; she felt held at a distance and seemed to be eternally walking round the base of an unclimbable pyramid. She alternated between admiration and dislike; and these alternations were strictly determined by the amount of attention Garibaldi paid to herself. Sometimes he paid her more and sometimes less than he paid to other people, and she could not make up her mind to this, being ever ready to resume her enterprise of love, to take him in hand with all his family and entanglements, and make a home in which the general would be rescued from the vulgarity of life. She was grieved that he had allowed her to go without a sign of affection; and the more grieved because her departure was the result of no necessity but was in the nature of a demonstration against the courtiers by whom he was surrounded. She hoped the general would appear and beg her not to go. Instead of that the household was asleep.

She had only a vague notion what Garibaldi was doing riding in a carriage through the states of Central Italy. These states were the scene of an interesting struggle in which the allies who had lately been united to fight Austria were on opposite sides. Napoleon had held up his finger and said the war should stop; but he might as well have pointed at the thunder clouds that had hung over the battlefield of Solferino and declared in the midst of the downpour that there must be no more rain. By the agreement of Villafranca it was declared that the Emperor of Austria and the Emperor of the French would favour the creation of an Italian Confederation under the honorary presidency of the Holy Father; and it was also stipulated that the Grand Duke of Tuscany and the Duke of Modena would return to their states. To these clauses there were several objections, of which the chief was that they were in flat contradiction with the desires of the Italian people; and in signing the agreement Victor Emmanuel solved the difficulty by a Jesuitical addendum, *pour ce qui me concerne*, by which he meant that he would not prevent the agreement from being effective, but neither would he do anything to help it. Cavour was more honest, being in a wild rage at having been tricked, as he said, by Napoleon III; and he declared with unusual emphasis that 'never, a thousand times no, never', should the treaty be executed. The matter, however, as the rulers of Piedmont were quick to perceive, was no longer in their hands. They had sown seed and the crop was coming up.

The people of the provinces in question had long been tired of their stupid and inefficient rulers who, thrust out in 1848, had crept back again under the shelter of the Austrians. They were not disposed to be written over to Austria again or to a confederation of which the Pope would be the honorary chief and Austria the real one; and it was their evident sympathy with the national idea represented by the King of Piedmont which suggested to the latter that their hearts should be warmed to the cause by the appointment of commissioners who, in effect, were agents of propaganda. Farini was sent as commissioner to Modena, Cipriani to the Romagna, and at Florence Ricasoli seized control of affairs in Victor Emmanuel's interest. A plebiscite taken in August showed that Modena, Reggio, Parma and Piacenza were almost unanimous in desiring to be united under the government of the King of Savoy. But their desire now appeared embarrassing to the latter, inasmuch as he had just signed the agreement by which these states were to figure under the honorary control of the Pope in an Italian federation. Victor Emmanuel decided to wait and see. And meantime Cavour officially withdrew the commissioners from their posts, but instructed them to stay where they were as private citizens. They could always allege, in view of the popular movement, that the tail was wagging the horse, and not the horse the tail.

The Pope meantime was bridling with the hope of recovering for himself the debated provinces, as well as with the fear that the malady of freedom or of nationalism or whatever it might be, should spread all over the Papal States. His army was ready to deal with such a situation.

And in response to this attitude Piedmont slipped an army into the Central provinces, ostensibly to defend them against the menace from the south; but possibly, according to the trend of events, to carry the insurrection with all its vague possibilities of disruption and reconstruction through the length of Italy. Neither Victor Emmanuel nor Cavour was sure that he desired this to happen, or not to happen. They were both somewhat dazed by the miscarriage of their plans and inclined for the moment to allow events to bear them along.

They had, however, forgotten Garibaldi. He had been dismayed no less than Cavour by the sudden end of the campaign; and when he was instructed to go about the Central provinces and Papal States and prepare the people there for a plebiscite in favour of annexation to Piedmont, he took this task very seriously. He was still better pleased when, on the rumours of the Pope's activities, he was placed second in command (under Fanti) of a nice little army of twenty or twenty-five thousand men; and, once more thirsting for battle, he waited from day to day for word from Victor Emmanuel. At the first sign he was ready to take this army over the frontier to Rome. But the days passed and no word came. Victor Emmanuel was talking of European complications, a phrase which Garibaldi did not pretend to understand, but which he associated, since the recent débâcle, with confusion and disaster. His own view was that some straight fighting by Italians for the things in which Italians were interested would put an end to complications once for all.

Instead of a command from Victor Emmanuel there came a series of hints which emanated from Mazzini's agents. Mazzini had predicted that no good would come of the collaboration between France and Piedmont; and now he recalled his prediction, pointed out how exactly it had been verified, and suggested that his advice should be taken for the future. Mazzini attributed the inglorious end of the campaign, not so much to the failure of France, as to the inefficiency of conservative diplomacy; he believed very sincerely that it was not likely that a modern Italy could be made by the machinations of a king of the house of Savoy with a minister who derived his inspiration from the Italian courts of the Middle Ages. And as these machinations had failed (or seemed to have failed), he put it to Garibaldi that whatever the king and his minister might be thinking, however they might be hesitating, Garibaldi was the master of twenty thousand men. Mazzini knew very well that Garibaldi could not be induced to use these men against the orders of the king unless in very special circumstances—if, for example, it could be made to appear that immediate action was in the king's (or Piedmont's) interest. If news came from the other side of the frontier that the people of the Roman Marches were favourable to Piedmont, or, better still, that they were in revolt against the Pope, then nothing would prevent Garibaldi from marching on Rome. Towards the beginning of November it was apparent that Victor Emmanuel was not likely to do anything. Simultaneously a report reached Garibaldi that insurrection had broken out in the Marches. The report may have been genuine or it may have been fabricated to get Garibaldi on the move. At any rate it achieved its object. On November 12 he made up his mind to invade the Marches and gave orders accordingly.

The same day, however, he was visited by his superior officer, Fanti, and by Farini. The latter was inclined to be peremptory and narrowly escaped being thrown via the balcony into the street. But between them they persuaded a puzzled and irate Garibaldi that he was being fooled. He did not entirely believe them. But he agreed to abandon the invasion.

The incident served to make one point clear. It was not safe, while Piedmont was engaged in its intricate political reflections, to have a man of Garibaldi's simplicity of mind at large. All the unhappiness and discontent that came from the abortive campaign found its way to him at last, blowing about until it came to the shelter of his simple convictions and the protection of his high courage. Both Cavour and Victor Emmanuel began to see the obverse of

Garibaldi. He was a threat held over them, a warning that they would not be allowed to fail. And as it seemed for the time that they were only too likely to fail (and indeed did not know whether to continue their enterprises or leave them alone), it was imperative to get Garibaldi out of the way. *Unico mezzo*, wrote the wise Cavour to Rattazzi (November 12, 1860), *per soffocare la nascente discordia invitar Garibaldi a deporre il comando*.

They had loosed the lion on the plains of Lombardy, and now he was crouching uneasily, deciding which way to spring. Someone had to lock him up, a task which promised to be of the utmost difficulty. He was in one of his worst rages, as Farini had discovered.

But the task proved easy. As Mazzini said, one man in Italy could do what he liked with Garibaldi. Victor Emmanuel sent for the latter on November 17, put his hand kindly on his shoulder, and two days later the general resigned.

In a public manifesto he condemned the 'miserable vulpine politics' that troubled the fair stream of Italian progress, but he did not involve Victor Emmanuel in the condemnation. On the contrary, he expressly invited all loyal Italians to hold themselves in readiness until they should again be called by the king. 'The day when Vittorio Emmanuele once again calls to his side his warriors for the redemption of the fatherland, I will find a weapon and my post beside my brave companions.'[1]

Garibaldi, meantime, had dispatched Madame Schwartz to Sicily. She was at Florence when, to her great delight, she received a telegram from Bologna (dated October 1) saying that the general wished to know if she was still in Florence, as he had an important communication to make. Three days later a delayed telegram reached her.

SPERANZA MIA,
    Tell me if you can go to Messina on a very delicate mission. I would fly to Florence to kiss your hand, but it is impossible. Reply telegraphically yes or no. Yours for life, G. G.

[1] Guerzoni, i. p. 504.

The next message from Garibaldi said that a 'person' was leaving Bologna on the afternoon of October 5 in order to hand over instructions. Madame Schwartz waited all day in her room at a Florence hotel, expecting to see one or other of Garibaldi's henchmen, Deideri, perhaps, or Bixio; and she gave orders that no one was to be shown up except a friend whom she expected from Bologna. Just after sunset there was a light knock and, in response to her *favorisca!* there entered a pretty woman of about thirty-five, fair and dressed in black. This stranger was the 'person' to whom Garibaldi referred; and after some conversation, in the course of which Madame Schwartz sought to hide her annoyance, the lady produced a paper which was signed by Garibaldi and which said that the bearer was a true friend of Italy. Presently the messenger unpinned from an inner lining of her dress a proclamation from Garibaldi to be used by the Sicilian patriots, and a further paper which instructed Madame Schwartz to go to Messina and 'come to an understanding with the committee'. 'Be cautious', this document said, 'but proceed boldly towards the goal because the matter will have a fortunate issue.' While Madame Schwartz was reading the proclamation the visitor produced from her pocket-book yet another document, a letter from Garibaldi.

Bologna, 4th October, 1859.

SPERANZA MIA,
  I have received your letter of yesterday, and regret infinitely to cause you so much disquietment (*sic*). I have full trust in your angelic soul. The mission with which I charge you is sacred, but very dangerous.
 . . . Before undertaking it, make serious estimate of your strength.
. . .
 If you accept it, remember that there is much to be done not only in Sicily, but also in Naples and in Rome. You will doubtless find several friends of Italy among your fellow-travellers: use the opportunity, and stimulate them on behalf of the sacred cause. Yours for life,
        GIUSEPPE GARIBALDI.[1]

[1] Elpis Melena, p. 94 f.

Madame Schwartz had a feeling that Garibaldi was being very inconsiderate, thrusting on her a task which he esteemed dangerous and using as his go-between a pretty woman completely unknown to her; and in her account of the matter she does not disguise a certain petulance. This very human and unheroic note in her narrative makes its general authenticity tolerably certain. If she had sought to impersonate the heroine we should be sceptical: but she appears here in her normal rôle, that of a lady of intelligence who had not enough to do and who enjoyed romance most when it was consistent with her personal safety. However, once she had made up her mind, she was cool and practical. She spent her last days in Florence making a cipher transcription of the documents confided to her; after which she destroyed the originals and selected a large trunk in order that she might pass for an English tourist of the normal, globe-trotting kind. She was joined on board the *Vatican* (a French ship belonging to the *Messageries maritimes*) by the fair-haired lady, who struck up a swift acquaintance with the handsome captain and, this friendship prospering, had occasion to use the cabin, which she shared with Madame Schwartz only in the morning when she entered 'to repair her disordered toilette'. As the ship called at Naples, Madame Schwartz suggested that this conception of the art of conspiracy would be best employed in that city on the susceptible Prince Colonna; and, this advice having been accepted, she had the pleasure of seeing Garibaldi's emissary go ashore.

The *Vatican* continued her voyage to Messina, where the customs' officials scrutinised all the passengers closely to see if they bore any resemblance to Mr. Gladstone. Madame Schwartz's English passport was not helpful, as the English were in bad odour since their discovery of the conditions in Neapolitan dungeons. The traveller's cold cream and the spurs of her riding boots were minutely discussed, and it was two hours before she was free to go to an hotel. But she found a pleasant one with a room overlooking the harbour. Without delay she went in search of

Mr. Joseph Richards, the British vice-consul. He was not at home, but the clerk in the office promised that the vice-consul himself would wait on her later.

Mr. Joseph Richards came that evening, and at once Madame Schwartz's practised eye saw that he was not English, but a born Levantine, in spite of his name. She talked vaguely of Garibaldi's victories until he caught the drift of her conversation and said abruptly: 'Madame, if you suppose that Her Majesty Queen Victoria will favour an insurrection in Sicily on behalf of your friend Garibaldi, you are mightily in error'.[1] Mr. Richards was a commercial man who had money to lose and left revolutions to paupers who had nothing better to do. The country, he said, would not be ripe for a more liberal form of government for many years. Whether this was bluff or not, Madame Schwartz did not know. Mr. Richards came again and brought her passport, with a request that she should not set foot in the English consulate again.

She had no desire to do so. The immediate result of her two interviews with Mr. Richards was that she at once booked a passage on the next ship to leave the island for Genoa. But this ship did not sail until October 17; and while she was pondering on her indiscretion during the intervening days, a little courage came back to her, and she called on certain members of the revolutionary committee. Her story would be more authoritative if she gave the names of these members; but she does not, and we must conclude that they were put out of her head by what followed. Two nights before her ship, the *Quirinal*, was due to sail, she was arrested and thrown into prison.

Whatever may be lacking in her story on the political side, it is abundant in all that strictly concerns herself, a fact which is not as annoying as might appear, since, by her natural egoism she restores a normal perspective through which it is useful to look on the great events in which she was superficially involved. In her description of the *oubliette* into which she was cast, there is a superfluity

[1] Elpis Melena, p. 102.

of quotation; *nunc animis opus—nunc pectore firmo*, she said to herself as the prison door closed, shutting out the legend which she was sure must be inscribed over the fatal portal: *Lasciate ogni speranza, voi ch'entrate*. 'I saw that the walls of my prison were of unhewn stone streaked with lines of damp, and that its furniture consisted of a dirty sack of straw, a wooden stool, and an earthen water-jug. There was no window, only a grated aperture affording passage to some foul air, and perhaps, at certain hours of the day, a feeble ray of light. Pointing to me, the gaoler exchanged a few words in the Sicilian dialect with the officers, and then they all left me and closed my prison door. I was to experience the pangs of a *sepolta-viva*, perhaps a sentence of death. My one consolation—if under such circumstances any comfort could exist for me—was the fact that, mindful of a maxim of my father's, I had with me a good round sum of money, by means of which I hoped to procure my deliverance.'[1]

Her fears were exaggerated; for the same night the gaoler passed her out into the street, where his brother-in-law took charge of her and brought her to his wife, who gave her a bed and warm soup. This was an aspect of Sicilian tyranny that a perusal of Gladstone had not led her to expect; and she was still more astonished when the incalculable authorities took no notice whatever of the escape of their prisoner, and allowed her to embark without difficulty on the *Quirinal*. A few days later she arrived at Bologna, eager to tell her tale to Garibaldi.

He was at Rimini, torn between his desire to invade the Marches and his loyalty to the King of Piedmont. He welcomed her with a lightness which she thought ill in accord with the dangers she had been running for his sake. 'So here you are again', he said. 'I hardly expected it, really, because you had no sooner started than I learned that a traitor to the cause had laid a trap for me, into which, alas! I stept all too credulously. I was afterwards assured that it

[1] Elpis Melena, p. 107.

was all up with you, that you had been put out of the way, like so many more victims to the Bourbons.' When she dwelt on her 'terrible adventures' and her 'wonderful salvation' Garibaldi merely said, 'I thought as much', tapped her on the shoulder playfully and added with a laugh that she would be reckoned with the bravest of the brave and have the right to wear a red shirt.

On one point she was relieved. Garibaldi explained that he did not know the fair lady in black. He had met her at dinner and thought she might be useful. Nevertheless, in spite of this explanation, Madame Schwartz was chilled by her reception. She endeavoured to explain it to herself, and at last reached the just conclusion that 'having staked his own life for his country a hundred times, he considered that others who underwent a similar test were the happiest of people'.[1]

She contented herself with this explanation for a time, saying to herself that Garibaldi belonged to Italy. But in January 1860 she read in the *Galignani* a paragraph which showed how little she knew of her hero:

On the 24th instant (*i.e.* of January 1860), the marriage of Garibaldi with the eldest daughter of the Marquis Raimondi was celebrated in the villa of the latter.[2]

Then in a flash she remembered the silken banners of Italy and Savoy. Garibaldi's last letter to her had been written after the incident with Farini and Fanti, and was dated November 26. It said only that he had 'withdrawn from active service' and proposed to spend his time in writing.

Evidently there was much, very much, she did not know.

XXVI

GARIBALDI had not promised Victor Emmanuel he would go to Caprera. But that was the only place to which he could go. He felt a little ashamed of himself in a vague

---
[1] Elpis Melena, p. 131.   [2] *Ibid.*

way. He had, as his friend Medici said, talked too much in the last months, written too many proclamations, listened to too many people who were bent on using him. Now he realised that he was not equal to the cunning of his fellow-countrymen. Unlike himself, they seemed to talk in order to conceal what was in their minds; his own impulse was genuine, messianic; his art in moving the people a natural poetry. But the vulpine politicians saw in him an instrument of propaganda, considering Garibaldi as a showman who, by reason of his success, was put up for their bidding. They conspired to possess him. And, in certain moods of disappointment or irritation, he was an easy victim. As Madame Schwartz had learned, he had no talent for conspiracy. Anyone who sat down beside him and expressed a passionate interest in the affairs of Italy could worm a secret out of him. As always after a surge of high impulse, Garibaldi plunged in the late autumn of 1859 into a trough of despair. Like a dark cloud the *malinconia* which lurked on the other side of his energetic nature settled upon him. He did not know what to do with himself. He tried a few days at Caprera. But he came back to the mainland again uneasy in mind.

And then, one day, as he was still in this mood, a letter came to him from Giuseppina Raimondi, the girl of Como. She said she loved him and wished him to be her husband. He remembered her as he had seen her that day, *coraggiosa ed aveniente*, courageous and beautiful, a vision that had come upon him in the midst of war, and it seemed to him that here at last was the solution of the difficulties that beset him.

'Towards the 3rd December 1859', he records in a few pages which he afterwards deleted from the manuscript of his memoirs,[1] 'I received at Sestri from the beautiful girl, Giuseppina Raimondi, a letter dated November 28 which opened up a new phase in my life'.

---

[1] The MS. pages were recovered and printed by Curàtulo, *op. cit.* p. 302 ff. They are here translated for the first time into English. They appear in the 1932 edition of the *Memorie* (Milan MS.), p. 278 ff.

'I have already said that I was struck, as by a vision, by the sight of that dear creature, and her image was carved in my heart indelibly, ever since the day when she appeared to me in a light carriage of which she herself was the driver, while a priest, a friend of her house, accompanied her.

'I had not been able, on the occasion of my rare visits to the pleasant villa at Olmo, to hide the interest she inspired in me; and when once I met her alone in the Angel inn at Como by the shore of the lake, I knelt down and kissed her hand and exclaimed: "Oh that I might belong to you in some way!"

'These words did not appear to me to have touched her, and I despaired of inspiring in her the love I felt in my heart.

'On another occasion I was invited by her father, the Marquis Raimondi, to a night's fishing on the lake, and flattered myself I would spend a pleasant night under the same roof as the lady of my heart; but I reflected that this might not be agreeable to her and, although I was sad, I fortified myself with the pride and male dignity which I retain in such circumstances and decided to forget the angel!

'The regiment of the Appennini was at that time in Como, about to embark for the Valtellina. I took advantage of one of the steamships transporting the troops, to proceed in the same direction and rejoin my brigade, which I had left for the time being. The Marquis Raimondi, who had shown me the most exquisite friendship, came to the jetty to see me off, accompanied by his charming daughters. And there was Giuseppina more adorable than ever! I looked furtively at her from the ship, after I had taken my leave; but I had decided to forget a lady who showed no sign, or small sign of returning the love she awakened in my heart. I suffered indescribably but I was strong; and I told myself that our different ages were the obstacle between us. The ship moved off and I made it my duty to forget the fair daughter of the lake.

'Months went by. The war, and still more, the intrigues of my enemies, kept me busy. Occupied as I was in Central Italy and disgusted as I was by the difficulties placed in my way by the enemies of Italy and by timorous doctrinaires, plunged, too, in a certain melancholy to which I have always been subject, I yet did not fail to remember the beautiful girl who had captured my heart on the shores of Como. I saw the marquis at Bologna, and the news he gave me of Giuseppina was balm to me. But my love was all the time an ideal love based on no well-founded hope. I had no proof that she loved me, and I was content to remember her as a happy dream. Then when I was at Sestri in the house of Signor Gastaldi, I received a letter from her in which she said she loved me and asking me to marry her!

'In an ecstasy of happiness I lost not a moment in going to Fino, where I found her with her family. I left Sestro with my friend Deideri and reached Fino the following morning.

'I had a short conversation with her father and then wrote her, explaining my position exactly, my age, my poverty, my obligations to other women and lastly my melancholy, which made me an unsuitable companion for a young woman. She replied that she had considered everything and was still of the same mind. Thereupon I forgot all the irking cares of life and gave myself up to the joy of being with the lady of my heart.

'An accident, which might well have been fatal, occurred to me a few days after my arrival at Fino. I was riding beside my fiancée, who was as graceful and firm on her mount as an Amazon, when my horse bolted. I did not know the animal, so I let him have his head along the road; then after some miles, I turned him off at right angles into a side opening at the end of which I saw a house, where I hoped to be able to stop him. But he would not be pulled up; so I drew him to the left again, but, as I did so, my leg was brought against a wall and the right knee-cap fractured.

'It was midday, and the people of the house were in

church, all but one woman who fled shrieking and hid herself. The horse kicked furiously at everything it saw before it, and finally came to rest in a stable between the doors of which we had passed as by a miracle.

'Once outside the stable it took the side-road again, and there waiting for me in a carriage was Giuseppina with the rest of the household, her two sisters, Deideri, etc.... Mortified at not having been able to master the beast, and thinking it was tired by its escapade, I put it to the gallop, but the fiery animal took the bit in its teeth again, and once again I could not stop it. We came full tilt up to the crossroads where the company was waiting, and I could not pull the beast sufficiently round to avoid hitting the carriage-pole; then, looking round and seeing first a stone bench and beyond that a circle of poplars so close together that there was no hope of passing safely between, I resolved to jump off, and did so more successfully than I dared hope, landing on my feet without being thrown to the ground, in spite of my bruises and broken knee-cap. I was proud of my leap in the presence of the spectators, and especially because the lady of my heart was present.

'Indeed I was so proud that I made to mount once again, but Giorgio, the young brother of my fiancée, would not hear of it, and insisted on my taking a seat in the carriage.

'The carriage was certainly better for me, as I was severely bruised. We returned to the house at once, and I spent eighteen days in bed recovering from the hurt to my knee. I could have found no place more pleasant nor more suitable for curing wounds than the house of the Marquis Raimondi; and the appearance of my beloved in my room (a thing which would not have been permitted had I been well) made me forget my pain. Woman is an angel at the bedside of the sick; a man, however kind, can never equal her exquisite care, especially when the woman is so dear.'

The manuscript does not go any further. It was presumably written at Como while these events were still fresh in Garibaldi's mind; and the last sentence suggests that he was still being nursed by Giuseppina when the phrase on the excellence of women was composed. We can see, at any rate, from this fragment that Garibaldi had risen from the depths of despair to a bridegroom's gaiety. And we can see how, apart from this intimate stimulus, the proposal of Giuseppina had a practical advantage. It gave Garibaldi an excuse for remaining near the scene of war. He told himself that he had finished with war; and, with some insistence, he described himself to Giuseppina as an enemy might see him, poor, ill-tempered, ailing and old. She said she had considered everything and still wished to marry him. As if by a miracle the deep sources of his manhood were suddenly renewed, and he found himself, in the intervals of his strange courtship, looking eagerly forward to a resumption of the war which would, once for all time, deliver Italy.

His sojourn at Fino beside his fiancée was no secret. While he was still in bed suffering from the effects of his fall, he received deputations representing the National Guards of Como and Milan. On January 1 he talked at length with Alexandre Dumas (whom he liked). On the 14th of the same month there was performed in his honour, at the most important theatre in Como, a choral work by Bartolommeo Gatti. Finally, on January 6, the *Corriere del Lario* announced the forthcoming marriage in these words: 'We are in a position to state that the family of General Garibaldi's fiancée has made all arrangements for the wedding to take place at an early date. The General is at Fino, and is staying with the father of the bride'.[1] This sequence of happy events was brought to a climax by the marriage which Madame Schwartz had seen announced in the *Galignani*. It took place, as the journal said, on January 24, at Fino. Some local notables were present at the ceremony, as well as the Count Giulio Porro Lambertenghi and the Governor of Como.

No sooner were they out of church than a note reached Garibaldi saying that Giuseppina was already the mistress of a young officer, Luigi Caroli, of the Piedmontese regular

[1] Curàtulo, p. 300.

army. On her knees in the bedroom she confessed, or is said to have confessed, that the contents of the note were true. Some say that she wrote it herself. At any rate Garibaldi told her father to see that she did not bear his name, and rode away.

The story, as it has found its way into the biographies and histories, is pieced together from fragments of hearsay; for, of course, no one was in the room at the time of the rupture except Giuseppina and Garibaldi. The father's behaviour affords no enlightenment. In classical Italian fashion he ordered his daughter off to a convent to expiate her sin. As for the lover, or alleged lover, Luigi Caroli, he found himself so unpopular in his native land because of the part he had played in this drama, that he took himself off to Poland to fight for the freedom of that country. He died in Siberia without having said anything that adds to our meagre knowledge of the event of January, 1860. The accounts of biographers who were personally acquainted with Garibaldi are melodramatic and vague. 'In January 1860', says Jessie White Mario, 'Garibaldi married the daughter of the Marquis Raimondi, and, for reasons best left between her and himself, an hour after the ceremony he led her back to her father, saying, "This is your daughter, but not my wife".' Guerzoni, who was Garibaldi's companion-in-arms during the spring campaign, is so ashamed that he specifically warns the reader that no 'erotic anecdotes' are to be had from him.[1]

It was said that Giuseppina Raimondi was with child by Caroli and that her marriage with Garibaldi was designed to cover her lapse. Giuseppina answered this accusation, but not until she was an old lady of seventy-eight years, when the slander was rebutted in court. Her tale, as she then explained it to the newspapers, was that she was young and simple and had been allowed more freedom than most young Italian girls, a fact borne out by the manner in which Garibaldi first made her acquaintance. Going freely

[1] Guerzoni, i. p. 508 f.; Mario, *Supplement*, p. 450.

about the roads in war-time, she encountered Luigi Caroli, with whom she fell in love: but, although she would readily have married him, he did not wish to marry her. And at this point Garibaldi intervened. Her father, an enthusiastic patriot and politician, seeing the hero's admiration for his daughter, made it plain that he wished her to marry Garibaldi. If she had been able to plead that she was already engaged to Caroli all would have been well, for Caroli was wealthy and a suitable match. But Caroli was not to be cajoled. And while her father continued to insist on the marriage with Garibaldi, she fell ill with typhoid, and in the weakness that followed allowed herself to be overwhelmed by her father's arguments.

She speaks also of a plot. There were men, she said, who hung on the heels of Garibaldi and made a living out of the cause of freedom which he represented, and who feared that their livelihood would go if a shrewd wife took over Garibaldi's financial concerns. Alternately (or simultaneously) there were men about Garibaldi who feared that he would retire from politics after the marriage and who, to prevent this, hatched a deep scheme for Giuseppina's ruin, waiting with the note till after the ceremony, so that Giuseppina's silence should be inexplicable and lead inevitably to a rupture. For there was a chance, if the conspirators spoke too soon, that the girl would justify herself and lead Garibaldi to the altar.

In all these explanations there is, on the lowest reckoning, an element of truth. Whether or not there was a plot to ruin Giuseppina, there certainly were many men about Garibaldi who did not favour the marriage, and who, no doubt, spoke their minds about it. Very likely Deideri and Medici told Garibaldi he was making a fool of himself. But it is also true that such emphatic disapproval came from these men only, and not from hangers-on of one kind or another. The disapproval of Medici and Deideri, if it was expressed, went no further; and it is still less likely that the parasites in Garibaldi's entourage would trouble to destroy the marriage by a plot. If they had observed their man they must have known that, married or unmarried, he was exploitable: and that, married or unmarried, the affairs of Italy would have first place in his heart.

However that may be, Giuseppina Raimondi proffered her explanations in perfect good faith. She believed she had been betrayed: and if her explanations of the manner in which this was accomplished do not appear convincing in the cold light of history, that is not her fault. She, of all the people involved in the drama, understood least what had happened; not so much because she was young and perhaps innocent, as because she was young and very much wrapped up in herself. Of course the story of her being with child by Caroli was a fabrication. She was probably not even his mistress. But she was in love with Caroli. And that being the case, she was, although she did not know it, at the mercy of the first genial gossip who knew her affairs. In due course, full of the knowledge of her own sacrifice and the virtue of her intentions towards Garibaldi, she encountered the blast of his disillusion. It was such that she spent the rest of her life wondering why a poor girl who had done her duty should be rewarded in such a way.

There was no one to tell Garibaldi what was going on in her mind. It did not occur to him that she found suddenly a number of contradictory duties laid at her door. There was her love for Caroli which she maintained out of loyalty to herself. There was the duty of obedience to her parents, who made her union with Garibaldi appear as a matter of patriotic obligation. And there was the affection and admiration in which she held Garibaldi. With the obstinacy of youth she clung to these mixed obligations, being faithful to Caroli, faithful to her parents and faithful to her noble admirer until, in the bedroom, the consequences of her multiple consenting dawned on her. Then she knew she did not love Garibaldi. And, with this paper in his hand, he asked her: Did she love Luigi Caroli? A cunning girl could have lied herself out of the dilemma. She had before her a man hot with desire, ready to be played by her guile. No plot could have kept him from her if she had been minded to coax him. He wanted her, and if, as her detractors said, she was already no stranger to love, she had the night in which to persuade him. But suddenly she was a child in tears, sobbing the name of the man she loved. By the time she had recovered her wits he was gone.

In that moment she had revealed to Garibaldi a vision of himself as he appeared to her: not Garibaldi the condottiere, the saviour of Italy, but Garibaldi, the fool of fifty-two, uncouth, clumsily ardent, in whose veins the blood boiled so urgently at the sight of her that he must show his gaucho tricks to the gallery and come to grief in the performing of them. That was nothing. But in the picture was a parable of the last months. She was Italy, winking at unworthy lovers over the shoulder of her hero: and he appeared, as his enemies described him, as the man with the heart of gold and the brains of an ox, the orator of the silver tongue whose audience tittered behind his back; an intolerable picture, this, which he glimpsed but for a moment. He was not a man to dwell on it. He thrust Giuseppina from him; and in the same gesture obliterated it. She who had been the bright vision of victory on the Como road had turned what was left of his victory to ashes.

Garibaldi's friends breathed freely. He had been a fool and he had got over his folly. But, foolish or not, in no action of his career had he been more honourably inspired. In no action does Garibaldi appear more like himself, loving beauty as the source of life and bringing to it the tribute of his manhood, with all the prompt energy and conviction of his character.

He saw now the utility of Caprera and understood the secret instinct which had prompted him to secure for his idealism a safe refuge from the treachery of men. He sat in front of his cottage and watched the sea foam on the rocks and ride away again. And there, as he meditated, he discovered why he loved Italy. He loved her as he loved Giuseppina, because she was part of the beauty of the world. Deep below his love was the love of earth, of the sea and air and sky and all the mystery of which the world

is composed, a great harmony resolving the petty contradictions of men, making a peace out of their strife. As he thought about this, his own peace came back to him and he remembered his own dictum: Why bother about one woman—there are so many.
Smiling grimly, he set himself to dig in a row of potatoes.

XXVII

THE conference of Zurich, which had begun its labours soon after the peace of Villafranca, sat quietly until November 10, and once again Victor Emmanuel put his signature to a document in which the twin aspirations of Napoleon III were satisfied. Italy was, in part, made free and in part also, so far as the thing was possible, handed over to a hypothetical Papal federation. In the course of the negotiations it occurred to Napoleon that Victor Emmanuel had something up his sleeve. His royal cousin wanted the provinces of Central Italy and seemed to be waiting only until the French armies were out of Italy to stretch out his hand and take them. Napoleon could not prevent this development and cared very little about it. He imitated Victor Emmanuel's diplomatic silence, from which the latter understood that his consent was to be had, at a price. Probably there had been very little duplicity in Napoleon III when he came to fight for Italy. But before he left again for France there was a good deal, not a little of it absorbed from the people with whom he was dealing. He behaved at Zurich like a not unapt pupil of Cavour, emerging from the council room with an idea which he divulged to Lord Cowley. If Victor Emmanuel meant to have the Central provinces, then he would like to have his share of cake also, Savoy and the town of Nice. He arrived at this decision in what seemed to him an innocent and natural manner; but to the suspicious eyes which had been watching from London it appeared otherwise. 'My dear Lady John' (wrote Sir James Hudson from Turin to Lady Russell on April 6, 1860),

'You mention in your letter the name of that scandal to royalty—Louis Napoleon. What can I say of him? Hypocrite and footpad combined. He came to carry out an "Idea", and he prigs the silver spoons. "Take care of your pockets" ought to be the cry whenever he appears, either personally or by deputy.'[1] The queen was of the same opinion. 'We have been made regular dupes', she said.

Whatever were the rights and wrongs of the matter, it had begun to excite public opinion in this country; for it was soon perceived that if Louis Napoleon had done nothing else, he had broken some of the bonds by which Italy had been attached for centuries. She was set free among the nations of Europe, to drift among them until by alliance or otherwise she was tied to some dominant power. The Italian question involved, therefore, the greater question of the balance of power in Europe, a fact which in London we were quicker to understand than Louis Napoleon. Although, on the face of it, he appeared to have been rather wily in his sparring with the Italian diplomats, he was content to prig spoons when it would have been more to the point to have brought a lorry in honest British fashion and removed the sideboard. The importance of Savoy and Nice was military. On the assumption that Italy did one day become united and hostile they were likely to prove useful. But that day was still far off; and, in the meantime, the petty theft (as it was called) made the ruler of the French appear in the guise of a dangerous hypocrite. Having recovered from our temporary irritation, we saw that Louis Napoleon in his haste had dropped more than he had picked up, and, with a graceful gesture, we stepped into the rôle he had vacated, that of friend of Italy, a rôle in which there was now nothing to lose and possibly much to gain. We moved obscurely. But henceforward the whole prestige of England was thrown on the side of Italian freedom. Without fighting for Italy, we contrived to make ourselves awkward to those who fought against her. The Austrians said our banknotes wrapped up many mysteries.

[1] Trevelyan, *Garibaldi and the Thousand*, p. 173.

Journalists, meantime, were waiting in their hotels in Genoa and Turin to see what the next move would be. In the latter city the newly elected parliament had just met and was waiting to have Cavour's explanations of the cession of Nice and Savoy. The treaty had never been submitted to parliament, and it was not likely that it would be, except for a formal ratification: but, in order to give an appearance of legality to the transfer, it had been arranged that the people of Savoy and Nice would vote on the matter. This also, it was assumed, would be a formality, because precautions had been taken to see that they voted the right way. The King of Piedmont withdrew his troops while the French brought in theirs. In case the hint was not broad enough, the Governor of Nice, Lubonis, put up a proclamation: 'All uncertainty is at an end. By a treaty of the 24th of March last, the valorous King Victor Emmanuel has given up Savoy and the territory of Nice to France. Before the august word of the King, all uncertainty as to our future is dispelled. All opposition must break and become powerless against the interests of the country and the feeling of duty; nay, more, it would meet with an insuperable obstacle in the wishes of Victor Emmanuel. Let us hasten and confirm with our votes the annexation of our country to France—let us range ourselves round the throne of the glorious Emperor Napoleon III'.[1]

In view of this attitude on the part of the authorities, the citizens of Nice, who had little experience of the privileges of democracy, were resigned to their fate. But they had not forgotten their great fellow-citizen, Garibaldi, whom they elected as their representative to the new parliament of Piedmont. The French press pointed out that since Nice belonged henceforward to France (the result of the forthcoming plebiscite being a foregone conclusion), it could not elect a representative to the Piedmontese Chamber. But in strict law the election was legal and valid until the plebiscite had been taken. Garibaldi, at any rate, arrived in Turin to take his seat. He was no lover of parliaments, and

[1] Chambers, *Garibaldi and Italian Unity*, p. 32.

an ordinary convocation would not have fetched him at the present juncture in his life from the healthful solitude of Caprera. But the occasion was not ordinary. It had seemed that no humiliation could be added to what he had already suffered publicly and privately. But the terms of the treaty convinced him of his error. The lawyers were now going to take from him his birthplace, to sell the tomb of his mother and the ashes of his wife; and he had come to protest.

According to *The Times* correspondent he sat motionless until Cavour entered and went to his place on the government bench. Then, at once, with a loud *Domando la parola*, he sprang to his feet and asked leave to put a question. Cavour was nervous, as well he might be. He moved the previous question, explaining that the Chamber was not yet properly constituted, and adding that in any case he would not answer. Two deputies rose to the support of Garibaldi, and pointed out that the House had been sworn on the previous Monday, the king had addressed the members; what more, then, was required? Obviously Garibaldi's question might be inconvenient, but it could not be called improper or irrelevant; and seeing that if the debate were allowed to open up and take a democratic turn, a discussion of the treaty might ensue, Rattazzi hastened to support Cavour by smothering the interpellation in a long argument on parliamentary precedent. He talked long enough to confuse the House; and when a division was taken it was found that the legislators had left Garibaldi and Nice in the lurch and proposed to adopt the previous question by a large majority. His first attempt having failed, Garibaldi tried again on April 12. He came primed with precedent and read out the fifth article of the constitution, which provided that no sale or barter of any part of the State could take place without the consent of parliament. His speech was fairly long and not in his usual style. Evidently he had taken advice and had had it prepared for him. He was eminently reasonable, his calm behaviour contrasting with his violence on the earlier occasion; and, after the statement of the case, he asked that the plebiscite of Nice should be postponed until the treaty, of which the cession of Nice was a consequence, had been debated in the Chamber. Only when this motion, too, was lost did his anger become visible. In high indignation he left the House.[1]

His prompter in this second speech was the English journalist, Laurence Oliphant, who, by virtue of his nationality, was accepted as an authority on constitutional procedure. Oliphant had found a Nizzard committee assembled in a large upper room in Turin under the presidency of a 'red-bearded, slightly bald man, in a poncho': the latter, Garibaldi, was advising direct action, a riot, by means of which the population would be stirred from their apathy and the vote perhaps postponed. *Sempre interpellazione!* said Garibaldi disdainfully, when Oliphant suggested a further question in the Chamber. But he submitted. As he emerged from his second defeat, he said to Oliphant, 'There, I told you so; that is what your fine interpellations and parliamentary methods always come to. I knew it would be all a waste of time and breath'.[2] The crowd outside the House cheered at the sight of Garibaldi. They picked him up and carried him on their shoulders; and in answer he spoke to them and said that there were too many literary celebrities in the Chamber for a poor soldier who could only talk with a rifle.[3] The same night, according to Oliphant, it was arranged by the Nizzard committee that the following Sunday they would take ship from Genoa, land at Nice with two hundred men and smash the ballot-boxes. Thus they would achieve by force what the Piedmontese Chamber refused to concede to justice.

They took the train from Turin to Genoa. A special compartment was reserved for the general, who was accompanied only by his aide-de-camp and Oliphant, the latter eager to see the end of the adventure. Garibaldi was

---

[1] Chambers, p. 33.
[2] Oliphant, *Life of Adventure*, 2nd edition, 1887, p. 171.
[3] Chambers, p. 33.

silent and preoccupied. Presently he untied a packet which apparently contained his morning mail, and he spent the rest of the journey reading letters and tearing them to pieces. When they reached Genoa the carriage looked 'like a gigantic waste-paper basket'. It was arranged that Oliphant was to go to the diligence office in Genoa, looking as much like an eccentric milord as possible, and there require the use of a diligence for an indefinite number of friends with their luggage. He expressed willingness to pay for sixteen places and six horses; but the clerk put him off for an hour, saying he must ask his superior. An hour later Oliphant secured the promise of a large carriage and went to report to Garibaldi at his hotel. It was a second-rate place on the quay. A number of young men were going in and out and, surprisingly enough, Oliphant's name was taken at the door. A few moments later he was shown into a large room where twenty or thirty men were at supper, with Garibaldi at the head of the table. '*Amico mio*', said the latter, making room for Oliphant beside him, 'I am very sorry, but we must abandon all idea of carrying out our Nice programme. Behold these gentlemen from Sicily. All from Sicily! All come here to meet me, to say that the moment is ripe, that delay would be fatal to their hopes.... Fond as I am of my native province, I cannot sacrifice these greater hopes of Italy to it.'[1]

The letters which Oliphant had seen Garibaldi tear up came from Sicily. Most of them came from young men who offered their services in the event of a Sicilian expedition; and some no doubt said that the island was ripe for rebellion, and that the campaign which had come to an end in the north could be resumed in Sicily and pushed to its logical conclusion. Garibaldi was accustomed to such letters and he generally did with them what Oliphant had seen him do. But as he returned from the Chamber muttering indignantly: 'Behold, what a fine Chamber we have', he found the shining faces of the Sicilian delegates waiting

[1] Oliphant, p. 176 f.

for him. They presented a pleasant contrast to the faces on which he had just been looking. He came from an assembly which had no use for him. And he found men who said that only he, Garibaldi, could knot the tiny insurrections of the island into a national revolution. That had always been his ambition, to discover the small fires of faith glowing in the darkness and fan them till their flames leaped up and united in a universal conflagration.

He liked their enthusiasm. But he was sceptical. Sicily was the happy hunting ground of Mazzini, the traditional home of futile insurrection and the paradise of foolish martyrs. If Napoleon had not usurped Nice, Garibaldi would have patted the enthusiasts on the back and told them to make their war themselves. The Sicilians were sure of success. But they had been on other occasions, and their opinion weighed little with him. They were not soldiers, and their conversation showed that they had little idea of the difficulty of the undertaking. Their theory, a very flattering one, was that Garibaldi would come and see and conquer; and the reason they advanced to support the theory was that, *per dio*, Garibaldi was Garibaldi. He smiled, liking their faith and believing not a word they said. But their faith was a familiar and necessary thing, a breath without which he could not live for very long. And as he put it away it came back to him, as the water came back to the rocks at Caprera, refusing to be repulsed. He thought, as a practical soldier, that the deliverance of Italy must come from the north. In spite of recent events, his common sense told him he ought to think so still; and he did think so. But the cession of Nice had hit him hard. It shook his almost impregnable faith in Victor Emmanuel, whom he exonerated only by transferring an immense and unjust hatred to Cavour. Without prejudice to practical issues, he thought of the north as the home of treachery and of the south as the home of faith. In this dubious frame of mind he met Sir James Hudson, the British minister at Turin, and asked him if the talk of revolution in Sicily was all wind. Hudson said no, it was not. He appeared to hint that Garibaldi should go. And the latter, feeling for the first time that the dream of a Sicilian revolution might possibly become a reality, told Bixio to get in touch with the Rubattino Steamship Company through their agent, Fauché, and secure a ship to take him and a few companions to Sicily. He had not decided to go but he was beginning to think it might be well to make some preparations in case, after all, he did go. For a few days the matter dropped. Then on April 12, after the second defeat in the Chamber, he took serious steps.

Sicily had suddenly become important; not only to Garibaldi, but also to Mazzini and Cavour. The three great protagonists of Italian freedom, at this important juncture in the history of their cause, were scarcely on speaking terms. Garibaldi said in public that Cavour was a rascal with whom he would have no further dealings; and as for Mazzini, he thought him, for the purposes of war, a fool. Mazzini was more than ever: *Quel Mazzini!* a man whose futility was summed up in a shrug of the shoulders. Nevertheless, in spite of their private differences, their actions at this stage showed a perfect unity, not because they were virtuously sinking their differences, but because all three were at last being manipulated by one compelling circumstance, so that their heads, so full of individual and ingenious ideas, turned in a fine synchronism towards Sicily. Each of the three looked towards Sicily in a manner befitting his character. Cavour blinked over an indifferent shoulder, Mazzini gazed with sad concentration and Garibaldi allowed himself to be persuaded to look thither in humorous contempt. This unexpected unanimity of gesture was explained by the complete checkmate in the north which dared not move against the Pope and had no wish to try a single-handed fight with Austria. The fires were extinct except at the far end of the peninsula, where the embers still glowed.

The Sicilians seemed to have only just heard of the triumphs of Garibaldi and the victories of Solferino and Magenta; and they seemed to have failed to hear of the lamentable negotiations that followed. They began by waving flags to celebrate these victories, and from flag-waving they passed to revolt. In the mountains armed peasants moved in *squadre* and caught a Bourbon soldier on the end of a hayfork when occasion offered. From minor demonstrations they passed to greater; and, having neither secrecy nor method, they were uniformly unsuccessful. But they were obstinate. Bomba, their king, was not, like the evicted dukes of Central Italy, an inoffensive relic of an outworn system. He was a tyrant of a sound model who knew that a little terror went a long way. His smile was warm and charming and his sudden revenges were bloody. His system of government, which consisted of patting and kicking alternately, had the important result of alienating the local nobility, who, instead of acting as a body-guard, were revolutionaries almost to a man. The Sicilian priests, too, were freethinkers in politics. They were far from the influence of Rome and lived in sympathy and understanding with the people. The executive of Bomba's government was made up of the army, the police and spies; of its kind it was efficient, but it was of a kind that was not liked. In May, 1859, Bomba died, leaving his system behind him. It was inherited by his son, Francis II, a lymphatic boy who left things as they were and hoped piously they would be no worse. On his accession he contemplated a holy alliance with the Pope and Austria to undo the work of the campaign in the north. But his inertia overcame him. And, as it proved, he was kept busy at home.

The insurrections in Sicily continued to fail. They were habitual, a part of the island routine; and the army was well prepared for them. It enjoyed these excursions, being conscious of a comfortable adequacy to all contingencies. Bomba had taken a pride in his army; for although his system might be a poor one, he knew how to make it work. He paid the men regularly. They were equipped with the best shoe-leather and the latest rifles; and they were well fed. They did not excel at long distance work, as the advance on Rome had proved. But within reasonable reach of barracks they enjoyed a man hunt in the mountains and an occasional disciplinary massacre in the towns. News of such events in Sicily was generally telegraphed to Malta, where the British squadron usually had the latest information. It was transmitted thence to Genoa and Turin. But as it came from revolutionary agents, it was frequently tendentious and could not be relied on. Not infrequently the telegraph from Sicily reported brilliant victories with no other purpose than to stir up sympathy and provoke action in the north.

Garibaldi was suspicious. If Sicily, which was reported to be 'in arms', was to play a large part in the destiny of Italy, the heavy garrison of regular troops had to be fought off the island. A few men might make themselves unpleasant, but they could not do much more. What was required was a proper expeditionary corps, properly equipped, amply provided with money and made up of trained soldiers. All these things Garibaldi could find except the soldiers. He did not want amateurs. And his own *Cacciatori* had been disbanded and absorbed into Piedmontese line regiments, whence they could not be recovered without the permission, or at least the connivance, of Victor Emmanuel. On this account Garibaldi paid two visits to the king. On the first occasion Victor Emmanuel agreed to let him have the men. On the second he cancelled this consent and said that Garibaldi must not take his veterans from the Piedmontese army. This, it was plain, was to be the official position. And a further condition was added. If there was an expedition, to Sicily or elsewhere, it must not set out from a Piedmontese port.

These instructions may have been accompanied by a portentous wink. Piedmont was not at war with the King of Naples. Yet money, arms and men could be had in Piedmont provided they were taken without public fuss and provided the government could turn a blank face on Europe and say it knew nothing about it. Enfield rifles were at the depot at Milan, and it was understood that Cavour had said that if they found their way to Genoa no amazement was to be notified to him. Recruiting offices were open all over Piedmont, and these also were tolerated. Lastly, although an expedition might not set sail from a Piedmontese port, a bold man might seize vessels *in* a Piedmontese port and take them where he wanted them. This being understood, Garibaldi arranged that two steamships of the Rubattino Company would be 'captured' by his men as they lay in port, the crews would be 'overpowered' and troops picked up at a place appointed.

The expedition, prepared in this way, was so little a secret that it was announced in Sicily and known to the authorities there long before it started.[1]

Garibaldi was not sure whether to go or not. He came to Genoa on April 20 and presently drove out to Quarto, on the coast, where he stayed at the Villa Spinola as the guest of his old friend and comrade, Augusto Vecchi, the same who had been at his side in the last days of the siege of Rome. The organising ability of Garibaldi's subordinates revealed itself of a low order. The ships were ready but the rifles were not. They were held at Milan. Other rifles, miserable, rusty old muskets (*cativissimi fucili*, says Garibaldi)[2] were made available. But though he was pledged to the expedition, he was of the same opinion as Cavour and Victor Emmanuel; it was a mad venture. The Piedmontese government hoped he would succeed and thought he would not. He himself, as a soldier, could not see how it might succeed. The Sicilians were represented by three committees who each had their own programme, and only as a measure of extreme necessity consented to work together. In the Central provinces, from which support for the expedition was coming in the form of men and money, there were also rival committees. Officially the missing Enfields were at the disposal of Garibaldi and the property of the *Million Rifles* fund. Finzi, the director, had gone to fetch them from Milan, with the secret approval of Cavour.

[1] Trevelyan, *Garibaldi and the Thousand*, p. 180.
[2] *Memorie*, p. 415.

But they were in the arsenal of Milan, and D'Azeglio, Governor of Milan, would not let them go. All day long enthusiasts tramped in and out of the Villa Spinola, always with news. But when one asked whether this had been done or that, it had not been done. At last, on the night of April 27, a telegram was brought in, dispatched the previous day from Malta. 'Complete failure in the provinces and city of Palermo', it read. 'Many refugees picked up by British ships have arrived in Malta.'[1] This sounded like real news, Garibaldi said the insurrection was not begun, it was finished. His conditions were not fulfilled, and he would not go.

Thereupon he became the most melancholy of all the volunteers. There is a strip of rocky beach at Quarto, whither he went quite alone to sit down on a rock and gaze out to sea. His eyes seemed to be fixed on some point on the horizon, 'as if', says Guerzoni, 'he could see through the mists the vision of the strife-torn island, and as if the waves brought to his feet the answer to the riddle of destiny'.[2] Oliphant who had seen him mazed over a simple interpellation, would have been surprised to see him now. Here sat Garibaldi, the dangerous man; the most dangerous in Italy, Panizzi had said. From him, of whom at another moment any child might inquire the time, there came such an atmosphere that human beings were repelled. The family of Vecchi kept in the villa and the Sicilians went to air their grievances in the cafés of Genoa. No one dared say a word to him. He had listened for a month to all they had to say; he knew their words were breath and that he must decide alone. These men were children to be gathered into his hand and sent to death if he judged that the thing was good and necessary. They were men who could undo their words with other words; but if he set his hand to this enterprise, he might make Italy or destroy her. His life was a little matter. He had risked it many times. But if the end was that he died in Sicily, there was no one who would see to it that Italy was saved. The prospect of

[1] Guerzoni, ii. p. 34 and note.   [2] *Ibid*. p. 35.

such a death, with the thing he had lived for undone, frightened him and he shivered with a fear he had never known. One night a deputation came to say that if he did not go to Sicily the expedition would go without him. Bandi, Garibaldi's aide-de-camp, conveyed the message and stood petrified as he saw the leader's face become red as a furnace. 'Show them in', Garibaldi said. He stood with his arms crossed and looked at them one by one. The youngest blurted out a speech. He listened without a sign. Then he spoke gently, with tears in his eyes, dismissed them with a wave of his hand and turned to lean out of the window.[1] He had decided. He would not go. But his soul cried for some compulsion that would tear up his resolution and set him free.

The Sicilians had reported how things stood with Garibaldi, and the telegraph was heard again. 'Insurrection still alive in the mountains above Palermo', it said.

His indecision was ended. 'We will go', he said.[2]

Towards midnight on May 5, Bixio boarded the *Piemonte* and the *Lombardo* in the harbour of Genoa and the recruits streamed out of the town by the Porta Pila. Garibaldi came down from the Villa Spinola to the shore. He was in a red shirt, sombrero and poncho, he was smoking a cigar, and it was noticed he was in jovial temper. A white moon got up and bathed the water. As usual there were delays. The *Piemonte* and *Lombardo* were stone cold and needed hours of stoking. In the process it was discovered that the engines of the *Lombardo* were out of order. By the time the volunteers were on board it was dawn. One accident led to another. Because the ships were late they missed the boats which were to put off with the ammunition. But now Garibaldi was young again. 'No matter', he said; 'we go without.'

A mad expedition. And with a leader who seemed suddenly to have become mad. *The Times* correspondent had had a word with him as he smoked a last cigar on the rocks below the Villa Spinola. 'The tone in which Garibaldi

---

[1] Bandi, *I Mille*, 1906, p. 18 ff.   [2] Trevelyan, *op. cit.* p. 193.

spoke to those who urged upon him the desperate character of his enterprise', the journalist reported, 'touched upon that sublimity which may seem akin to madness; to those who called his attention to the chances of meeting with the Neapolitan cruisers, he talked about the feasibility of boarding the Neapolitan frigates, and taking possession of them one after the other; he also remarked that a navy was the very thing he should want the most, and that they would be very useful. Those who well knew his devoted love and affection for his eldest son, implored him almost on their knees to spare the youthful Menotti. . . . The only response gained was—"I only wish I had ten Menottis, in order that I might risk them all ".'

The port authorities of Genoa were plunged in the most profound official slumber. The theft of the Rubattino Company's ships was duly reported and Admiral Persano was dispatched in pursuit. But he suspected that he was not intended to catch Garibaldi. To make sure he wired Cavour, asking him to reply *Cagliari* if it was really meant that Garibaldi should be arrested, and *Malta* if not.

'Il ministero ha deciso per Cagliari', telegraphed Cavour. An English admiral would have put on all steam and made a capture. But Persano read this telegram several times and reflected that 'the ministry has decided for Cagliari' did not mean that Cavour agreed with the ministry. He read it again and came to the conclusion that it meant that Cavour did *not* agree with the ministry. And with a brief 'Ho capito' (I have understood), this admirable servant proceeded leisurely in the wake.[1]

XXVIII

GARIBALDI had spent the day before the departure writing letters. One was addressed to Victor Emmanuel. 'I did not counsel', it said, 'the insurrectionary movements of my

[1] Persano, *Diario privato, politico, militare*, p. 14 ff.

brothers in Sicily, but from the moment that they have arisen, in the name of Italian unity, of which your Majesty is the personification, against the most infamous tyranny of our epoch, I do not hesitate to place myself at the head of the expedition. I well know that I embark on a perilous enterprise, but I put confidence in God, and in the courage and devotion of my companions. Our war-cry will ever be "*Viva* the unity of Italy! *Viva* Vittorio Emmanuele, her first and bravest soldier!" Should we fail, I hope that Italy and liberal Europe will not forget that this enterprise was decided by purely patriotic motives, entirely devoid of selfishness. If we succeed, I shall be proud to grace the crown of your Majesty with this new and most brilliant gem—on the well understood condition that your Majesty shall oppose any attempt on the part of your counsellors to cede it to the foreigner as they have done with my native province. I did not communicate my project to your Majesty, fearing lest the reverence which I profess might have succeeded in persuading me to abandon it.'

Like the other letters he wrote that day, this one was in reality a political document. It was simple and honest. The last sentence made clear to the world that Victor Emmanuel was not responsible for the expedition. And the remainder made clear to Victor Emmanuel that, although he was not responsible, he would share the profits. Garibaldi thus assumed generously the heavy task left to him by the Piedmontese ministry, and such comment as he made was directed at Victor Emmanuel's ministers, by whom he meant Cavour. But for Cavour, Garibaldi felt that Victor Emmanuel would have been at his side. And the letter, in which there was a great deal of human tact and political wisdom, made it possible for the King of Piedmont to link up again with Garibaldi at a future date. In the meantime it secured a more than benevolent neutrality.

There was also a larger claim. Garibaldi did not sneak off like a filibuster, with a promise of hush money to those who backed him. He was going on a national mission;

another letter, to Bertani, who had been active in organising the expedition, and who was now left behind to see that it did not lack further support, indicated that he considered himself the delegate of the nation, and explained what measures should be taken to make the expedition finally effective. 'I entrust the following mission to you', he wrote: 'To collect all the means that are possible to co-operate in our enterprise, to endeavour to make the Italians understand that, if we are properly assisted, Italy will be made in a short time and at small expense, but that they will not have done their duty if they limit their effort to sterile subscriptions; that Italy, free to-day, instead of 100,000 soldiers, ought to arm half a million—a number not disproportionate, surely, to her population, or to the armies of neighbouring States, which have not to conquer, their independence; that with such an army, Italy will no longer have need of foreign masters, who under pretext of liberating, gradually devour her; that wherever Italians are fighting against oppressors, our volunteers must be sent to aid, and provided with the expenses of the journey; that the Sicilian expedition must be aided, not only in Sicily, but in Umbria, in the Marches, in the Sabine territory, in the Neapolitan provinces—wheresoever there are enemies to be combated. I did not counsel the movement in Sicily, but, once the insurrection commenced, I believed it my duty to aid our Sicilian brethren. Our war-cry will be "Italy and Victor Emmanuel!" and I trust that, as in the past, the Italian flag will not be dishonoured.' On a separate piece of paper enclosed with this letter were the words: 'You will publish this letter four days after my departure. Vale!'[1]

Garibaldi proposed to draw Italy behind him. That was his purpose; and in his reflections at the Villa Spinola he had been less mystical than observers supposed. There was, after all, something of the serpent's cunning in him, as Daniel Pelton had noted, a cunning which, at close range, had a greater effectiveness than that of Cavour. He

[1] Mario, *Supplement*, p. 255 ff.

had been pushed into this enterprise. And his reflections did not begin to take shape until, seeing himself in a corner, he reacted in a spontaneous manner. He was being used as a tool. He saw that plainly enough, for although he appeared to take the telegrams from Sicily as authentic, he had, like other men of action, a layer of disbelief in things he had not verified himself; and his only guarantee in the matter of the news from Sicily was the character of the men who brought it. They were, he saw, conspirators, inspired after their fashion. What news he did believe, he took from Sir James Hudson, who was well informed and reasonably neutral. That did not go far. It left Sicily a possibility. On the other hand he preferred to do something rather than nothing; and this choice between something or nothing constituted for him the real dilemma. If there had been anything else to do, of more practical interest than breaking ballot-boxes at Nice (from which Hudson dissuaded him), he would not have gone. But there was nothing else. And therefore he had to think what he could make of the situation, so that, if he did go, he was not the helpless victim of circumstance, or, still worse, of the 'vulpine' politicians who divided Italy between them. Cavour had turned his back on him and was gently edging against him, pushing him towards Sicily. Mazzini had tightened the strings so that, if things went well, a tug would bring the revolution over to him. But they were in Garibaldi's hands. They could exploit his victory, if he gained a victory; but otherwise they were as bodies without a head. And, considering this, Garibaldi saw that it depended on himself whether he was pushed into an enterprise, of which the fruits would be taken by others; or whether he would seize the enterprise himself and drag the others behind him. The outcome of his reflections is seen in the letters he wrote. He urged Bertani to *publish* that he went to Sicily to win it for Victor Emmanuel; and this publication disposed of Mazzini, who did not recognise Victor Emmanuel. It also mobilised the people behind Victor Emmanuel, a people in whom hope and enthusiasm were high, so that, in the moment of victory they would rise and surge forward, carrying the king with them. In this way would be achieved, if all went well, a triumph greater and more thorough than that of the factions, an Italy united by the action of a soldier and placed, by his will, in the keeping of a soldier. There were those who said Garibaldi could not think. He could not think, if by thinking is meant the assembling and dovetailing of logical ideas. But he could think with great clearness in terms of action. And this particular piece of reasoning, achieved on the beach of Quarto, was the finest piece of thinking of the *risorgimento*.

It left him exhausted. He was going to take the matter of the salvation of Italy out of the hands of the doctrinaires, wrench it from the diplomacy of Europe in which Cavour alleged that it was entangled, make it once more a homely, simple problem, to be settled by strength and faith by the men whose business it was. So far as he was concerned the issue was clear before him; he must go to Sicily and fight, with the cunning of the fox and the courage of the lion, until the insurrection was blazing with a steady flame, and from Sicily he could send word to Genoa that the time was come. These thoughts were in his mind as he watched the *gozzi* of Genoa rowing the recruits over the moonlit water to the *Piemonte* and *Lombardo*. It was no moon for a conspiracy, but it was a moon for an enterprise of faith. 'O notte del 5 maggio, rischiarata dal fuoco di mille luminari, ... bella, tranquilla, solenne, di quella solennità che fa palpitare le anime generose che si lanciano all' emancipazione degli schiavi!'[1] He smiled at the young men as they stood in groups on the deck, a wary, paternal smile. And he noticed that some of his heroes were already beginning to be seasick. They did not know that, by the accident at the start, they were going to conquer Sicily without weapons or ammunition, nor that there was not enough food or coal on board to last the voyage. But these were practical matters which concerned the leader. He descended to his cabin to think them over.

[1] *Memorie*, p. 417.

Tuscany belonged now to Piedmont; and south of Tuscany lay the Patrimony of St. Peter. Somewhere on the coast of the first province Garibaldi must find the food, coal and munitions he needed: for neither the ships nor the men were equipped, unless the oil and tallow taken aboard at Camugli to coax the poor *Lombardo's* engines could be called equipment. Garibaldi had to choose a spot far enough on the way to make his arrest unlikely. It would not do to strain the courtesies and stop to coal outside Genoa, for, although the government of Piedmont was not anxious to hold him up, it had to be kept in countenance while it tricked Europe. The telegraph wires were already busy, telling Paris, London, Vienna and St. Petersburg that Garibaldi had set out. He decided to run for Talamone, south of Elba, where he would be near San Stefano and Ortebello. In one or other of these places he hoped to get what he wanted, as well as pick up some Tuscan volunteers. He navigated the straits of Piombino on the night of May 6, the vessels anchored off Talamone on the morning of the 7th, and Garibaldi went ashore. He had put on a slightly creased uniform dating from the previous year, which marked him as a Piedmontese general (although he no longer was one), and in this guise, uncomfortable and gravely smiling, he confronted the elderly commandant of the tower of Talamone, who apologised for the poorness of his stock, a few rusty rifles and an ancient culverin, to which he said Garibaldi was welcome. There were better munitions, he added, at Ortebello. Colonel Türr, a polite Hungarian, was sent to interview the commandant of Ortebello, and took a note from Garibaldi saying: 'Have confidence in my aide-de-camp, Colonel Türr, and help me with all means in your power in the expedition which I have undertaken for the glory of our King, Vittorio Emmanuele, and for the greatness of Italy'.[1] Major Giorgini, in command of the fortress, haggled, fearing a court-martial: but Türr's manners prevailed, particularly as he led Giorgini to understand that it

[1] Guerzoni, ii. p. 46.

might be a worse thing to defeat the hopes of the whole nation than to take the risk of an official wigging. At a pinch, Garibaldi was resolved to lock the major up and help himself, but this proved unnecessary. Türr's reasoning was so convincing that Giorgini, anxious to see the great adventurer with his own eyes, came himself with 100,000 cartridges, powder and a hundred Enfield rifles, an armament by no means generous for the task to be undertaken, but which had to suffice.[1] At the same time the volunteers were lined up ashore, counted into companies, drilled summarily and styled in an 'order of the day' *Cacciatori delle Alpi*, although not many had seen the last campaign. There were 1089 of them,[2] of the liberal professions mostly (many of them were already writing memoirs to meet the occasion): and when Garibaldi, in a flare of rage, had convinced the leaders of the Sicilian sections that their leadership was over, the recruits settled down to discipline and put the cartridges doled out to them (about ten apiece) in the pockets of their civilian clothes. Only one man in fifty had a uniform. A small body was detached and sent into Umbria to attempt a diversion in the Papal States. These measures were accomplished by May 9, when the ships' bunkers were full (with coal from San Stefano), the larder provisioned, the culverin and a few more serviceable pieces of artillery lashed on deck and the loose powder placed handy so that, under expert guidance, the volunteers could spend their time packing cartridges. The ships got under weigh and steered a course almost due south for the western angle of Sicily.

Garibaldi debated with the maps before him whether to come up from the south to Siacco (or, alternately, Porto Palo) or to make a straight dash for the nearest point, which was Marsala. A good deal depended on the Neapolitan war-vessels, which might be expected to be keeping a look-out for him. He hoped to discover, before he came

---

[1] Trevelyan, *op. cit.* p. 215.

[2] According to the *Gazzetta Ufficiale*, November 12, 1878, quoted by Trevelyan, *ibid.* p. 218.

to a final decision, how they lay; and, leaving the *Lombardo* behind, he steamed ahead in the *Piemonte*, which was a couple of knots faster. But he discovered nothing. And as night was falling he decided to lay to while the *Lombardo* came up. For several hours there was no sign. Garibaldi had muffled all lights and commanded silence. Meantime Bixio, in command of the *Lombardo*, had lost a man overboard and spent some time lowering a boat and getting him in again. He crept anxiously through the darkness looking for his partner and, at last, seeing a dark hulk ahead of him, concluded it was a Neapolitan. His instructions were explicit. He had, in such circumstances, to sail his ship into the enemy and board him; and he had shouted orders to the volunteers and was standing at the prow ready to spring at the moment of shock, when a warm, familiar voice came over the water: 'Oh Capitano Bixiooo! Do you want to send us to the bottom?'[1] A collision was avoided in the nick of time, and the *Piemonte* and *Lombardo*, once more in company, moved on towards Marsala.[2] It was the night of May 10-11. At dawn they were off the dangerous shoals of Trapani, keeping well out; and it was still unsettled whether they would sweep out in a circle and come up by the south or cut through the narrow channel between the little islands of Marittimo and Favignana. Garibaldi did not know these waters well enough to decide. A fishing boat was hailed and its master picked up. He said it would be better to run through between the islands. There was only a slight chance of meeting the enemy ships in the strait, and it was more likely that the islands would give useful cover up to the last moment, when the *Piemonte* and *Lombardo* would rush for the harbour of Marsala. By noon they had acted on this advice and left Favignana to the north, while the battlemented walls and white houses of Marsala rose against the sun-touched coast of Sicily. Garibaldi scanned the port

---

[1] Guerzoni, ii. p. 59.
[2] There are various accounts of this incident (cf. *Memorie*, p. 421 f.; and Trevelyan, *op. cit.* p. 228 and note).

through his glasses. It was full of small fishing craft. And just outside were two ships of war. But their luck was in. The ships looked to be British by the rig; and this was confirmed by a schooner which just then passed them on the way north. They spoke the schooner, which replied that the ships outside the port were two vessels of the British squadron.

Three ships of war were just visible to the south. They were Neapolitans, warned by the coast semaphore of the approach of Garibaldi's Legion. They were beating up at full speed, hoping to catch him.[1]

Captain Ingram, of the British Mediterranean squadron, had been stationed during April at Palermo, where the British merchants were uneasy at the prospect of disturbance. Prince Casteldicara, viceroy of the island, former officer of the 4th Dragoon Guards and more recently Neapolitan plenipotentiary at St. James's, had been recalled to Naples and replaced by General Lanza. The new viceroy was no younger than his predecessor, both being near eighty: but Lanza was a soldier. And it was thought that the change indicated that if there was trouble it would be dealt with firmly. So far as Palermo was concerned this anticipation turned out to be correct. An insurrection begun in the convent of La Guancia and abetted by the priests was put down swiftly, the troops sacking the convent and hawking its books in the streets.[2] Many young noblemen, suspected of being malcontents, were arrested; and the *sbirri*, or secret agents of the director of police, Maniscalco, promptly filled the prisons with conspirators, real or imaginary, many of whom were subsequently taken out and shot. But the country was full of armed bands of peasants. And the citizens of Palermo and Messina were sullen. An order was sent from the Admiralty that the British squadron in Sicilian waters was to be reinforced; and on April 20, H.M.S. *Amphion*, Captain Thomas

[1] Guerzoni, ii. p. 59 ff.; Trevelyan, *op. cit.* p. 230; *Memorie*, p. 423.
[2] Winnington-Ingram, *Hearts of Oak*, p. 194.

Cochrane, arrived at Palermo, superseding Captain Ingram on the *Argus* as officer in command. At the same time an American and a French man-of-war anchored in the bay and were shortly followed by a Sardinian frigate. Vessels of the Neapolitan navy patrolled the coast and carried troops from one point to another. The atmosphere was tense. Captain Ingram shot quail on May 6, 7 and 8: and on May 9, the cheerless inhabitants of Palermo, who, by order of the governor, were liable to be shot at sight if found in the streets in any number, were invited to a play on board the *Argus*. The play was the *Thumping Legacy* (with an ordinary seaman in the chief part), and the evening finished with a 'grand supper'. On May 10, H.M.S. *Intrepid* arrived from Messina, and Captain Ingram received orders to accompany her with the *Argus* to Marsala. The two British ships of war set out at 8.30 p.m. that evening, and on the morning of May 11 steamed between the islands of Levando and Favignana and Sicily, and finally anchored off Marsala in nine fathoms, about two miles from the town, the *Intrepid* being inshore of the *Argus*.

'About 11 a.m.', the diary of Captain Ingram continues, 'I landed with Commander Marryat (of the *Intrepid*), and we both called on our Consul, Mr. Cousins, and Mr. Harvey (manager of Mr. Woodhouse's wine establishment), to obtain information respecting the present political state of the country around Marsala, so that Commander Marryat might convey the latest news that evening to our Admiral at Malta. Whilst conversing with Mr. Edwards (Mr. Harvey's assistant), two Sardinian merchant steamers were reported to be coming in from seaward full of armed men. They steamed round the *Intrepid*, and then pushed on for the Mole. One of them got safely into the inner harbour, but the other grounded at its entrance. Shore boats came off to the latter vessel, and she commenced disembarking a number of red-shirted men, and landing them near the lighthouse at the end of the Mole. A Neapolitan war steamer and a sailing frigate were in sight to the eastward. The former, with signals flying, was rapidly closing with the Sardinian. It was a critical moment, and we asked each other's opinion as to whether she would open fire upon that vessel before the men were clear of her, for, if so, we might witness a fearful slaughter under our very eyes, and at the same time stand a good chance of being ourselves struck by a ricochet shot. A doubt seemed to occupy the mind of the Neapolitan commander, for he brought his vessel to a standstill close to the *Intrepid*, and hailed that sloop to inquire if those were English soldiers landing. He, of course, received a reply in the negative, but was told that there were English officers ashore, as well as the commanders of both British ships. Upon this, he requested that a message might be sent to recall those officers, as he was about to open fire upon the parties landing from the steamers. In the meantime, the Sardinians were putting ashore men, stores and ammunition as fast as possible. The gunner of the *Intrepid* now joined us, bearing the Neapolitan commander's message, on which we dispatched him at once to the town to warn our officers, and at the same time requested Vice-Consul Cousins to cause the British flag to be hoisted on all houses and wine stores appertaining to Englishmen in and around Marsala. Presently, a boat was seen to quit the Neapolitan war steamer and pull towards the grounded Sardinian. She had not, however, reached more than half-way to the vessel, when a panic appeared to seize those in her, and a retreat was hastily made to their ship, which now opened fire upon the Mole with her heavy guns. Commander Marryat, Mr. Cousins, and myself embarked at once in the gig of the *Argus*, and proceeded on board the Neapolitan to beg her captain to direct his shot and shell clear of the British wine establishments. To our surprise, we found that officer to bear the name of a fine old English Roman Catholic family, and to be complete master of our language. (He is now, 1883, Admiral Acton, and Italian Minister of Marine.) He seemed much impressed with the responsibility of his situation, but promised not to injure British property, pointing out to us that his guns were laid for the Mole only, and along which the red-shirts were seen making their way for the town as fast as encumbrances would permit them. We now left him, and were pulling for the *Intrepid*, when the Neapolitan sailing frigate came bearing down upon our boat, and her officers hailed and waved to us to pull faster. Hardly had they (? we) done so when a veritable storm of shot and missiles of all kinds, delivered from her broadside guns, passed over our heads, but fell short of the Mole. One of her shot, however, entered Mr. Woodhouse's wine establishment, and nearly killed Mrs. Harvey, the manager's wife. The next vessel to arrive upon the scene was the *Capri*, a hired armed steamer in the service of the King of Naples. She commenced firing, but we could not trace the course of her shot. An officer from her went on board the *Intrepid*, with the cool request that one of the latter's boats should go to the Sardinian steamers and demand their surrender. He received a very decided negative reply. I now returned to the *Argus*, and shifted her anchorage nearer the wine-stores for their better protection. The Sardinian steamers being completely deserted, the Neapolitans sent in armed boats to take possession of them. They succeeded in bringing out the one that had entered the inner harbour, but scuttled the other that had grounded at its entrance. The Neapolitan steamers continued, during this operation, to fire heavily at parties dragging guns and ammunition into the town, but we only saw one man knocked over. The patriots stood fire splendidly, and appeared to be altogether a fine body of men. Hostilities ceased at sunset.

'*May* 12.—At 5 a.m. the officer of the watch reported that the red-shirted troops were marching out of Marsala by the south road, and that they numbered about eight hundred. Soon afterwards Consul Cousins came on board with the information that Garibaldi himself was with the landed force, and had sent a message requesting that I would receive on board the *Argus* the crews of the Sardinian steamers he had run away with from Genoa. This I declined doing, as it would have appeared a breach of neutrality. Commander Acton, of the Neapolitan war steamer *Stromboli*, next paid me a visit, to say that his senior officer in the frigate *Parthenope* had ordered him to destroy the Sardinian steamer remaining aground by firing shot at her, and, as she lay in a line with the British wine establishments, if I would send and warn the people there to keep under cover. I requested him to destroy the vessel by some other means, as he would now have no enemy to contend with, as General Garibaldi and his men were in full march on Palermo. He seemed surprised and disconcerted to learn that the great revolutionary leader was present with the troops, and went away muttering that he must obey his commander-in-chief's orders. I sent an officer ashore to warn the residents at the wine-stores, and also a lieutenant to the *Stromboli*, with my official protest against the proceeding contemplated by her commander. This, it would appear, had the desired effect, for he sent boats in to destroy the Sardinian instead of firing at her. Much alarm was felt at the wine establishments at the reception of my message, and 3000 dollars (cash) was sent from Mr. Woodhouse's store for safety on board the *Argus*. The wives and daughters of the employers were also about to embark, when I was able to reassure them, and point out that their lives were no longer in danger. On landing, I found the crews of the Sardinian steamers and the Sardinian Consul waiting at Mr. Ingham's stores, to beg I would receive the former in my vessel. I explained that I could not possibly comply with their request, unless they could prove that their lives were in danger by remaining ashore. Failing to do this, I recommended them to follow General Garibaldi, who had—most certainly had—made himself their proper protector by taking them from Genoa against their will. I also found a Neapolitan government agent sheltering at Mr. Ingham's stores, he being afraid of returning to the town on the chance of falling in with the Garibaldians. When visiting Mr. and Mrs. Harvey at Mr. Woodhouse's wine establishment, I was introduced to the American Consul and his wife, who had taken refuge there, so as to be under British protection. They had, nevertheless, a narrow escape from the fire of the Neapolitan ships, a shot from them having passed close to the English flag flying over the stores, and another had gone through the wall of the latter and destroyed two large casks of wine. I put this damage down to the *Capri*. News reached us here of troops marching from Trapani. They turned out to be patriots *en route* to Marsala. At the same time, a Neapolitan steamer, full of soldiers, passed by Marsala. The *Stromboli* accompanied her, leaving the *Parthenope* frigate cruising in the offing. The town remained quiet. The names of the Sardinian steamers, bringing the Garibaldians, were the *Piedmont* and *Lombard*.'[1]

XXIX

UNLIKE his predecessors, Garibaldi did not lurk in the mountains, waiting to be exterminated. He fought his way over to Palermo and then, to the consternation of General Lanza, went right into the town and captured it while the Neapolitan ships of war, instructed by the governor, poured shells indiscriminately over the buildings. By the third week of June the Neapolitan garrison had completed its evacuation, under the eye of Menotti Garibaldi, who sat in youthful magnificence on a large black horse while the enemy filed out to the transports. Sicily was not yet conquered. There remained a substantial Neapolitan force at Messina. But the adventure had now changed in character. It was no longer a forlorn hope, but a victorious expedition which looked like sweeping all before it.

The British Mediterranean squadron had interrupted its intended manœuvres in order to follow the interesting happenings in Sicily. Rear-Admiral Mundy had brought four sail of the line from the Malta base and anchored off

[1] *Hearts of Oak*, p. 197 ff. The diary of Captain (later Rear-Admiral) Winnington-Ingram shows signs of having been written over. But it is the only neutral account of the landing from an eye-witness.

Palermo in the days immediately following Garibaldi's successful landing at Marsala. He thought so little of the latter's chances that he moved his ships close in so that refugees could get to them; while the *Intrepid* stood in so near that she was in danger from the gunfire of the Neapolitan ships. Garibaldi suspected that the intentions of the British squadron were benevolent. But he did not know that the *Intrepid* had picked a spot near the rocks by the Marina in case Garibaldi had in the end to swim for his life. What happened was quite different. At a quarter-past two on May 30, 1860, two Neapolitan generals and Garibaldi stepped on the deck of the flagship *Hannibal* and, after exclamations and protests on both sides, agreed to an armistice. The Neapolitans were stiff with decorations, while Garibaldi had sought to honour the occasion by putting on the general's uniform which had served at Ortebello. He did not look well in it, because, apart from the creases, it was too tight for him. But Mundy liked his behaviour. The Neapolitans blustered. Garibaldi kept cool. He was, in the Italian manner, politely ironic, allowing that his adversaries were, as they said, great generals and he himself only a poor amateur in the art of war. None the less he refused to sign a clause by which the inhabitants of Palermo were to refer their future destinies in a humble petition to Francis II. The day for such transactions had passed.

With the departure of the Neapolitan garrison for Naples, there occurred a relief in the tension which, even for the British squadron, had been considerable. Neutrality, in the circumstances, had become a fine art which Mundy practised with success but not without grave anxiety. It happened that June 20 was the date of the Queen's accession to the throne, and the British squadron dressed ship with flags, an example that was politely followed by the other vessels in the bay. At noon they united with the British in firing a royal salute; and Garibaldi, whose prodigious luck seemed to hold even in such small matters, was at that very moment getting into the barge *Maria Adelaide* to pay a friendly visit as the self-proclaimed dictator of Sicily. Rear-Admiral Persano of the Piedmontese navy, who since his arrival in Sicilian waters had been a benevolent spectator of Garibaldi's activities, welcomed the new official with a salute of nineteen guns which, taken with the previous general greeting intended for Queen Victoria but received by Garibaldi, marked the recipient as a political personage of the first order. The Sicilians gathered on the shore had no doubt that the navies of the world had combined to do homage to their new ruler.

Garibaldi came aboard the *Hannibal* dressed in his red shirt, grey trousers and broad-brimmed hat with black plumes. Mundy observed the long curved sabre that hung at his side, as well as the fact that the dictator's broad hips enabled him to wear his trousers without braces. In this garb he was a different man from the caricature of a Piedmontese general who had lately been negotiating in the *Hannibal's* cabin. But Mundy explained that he was still neutral. He could not acknowledge in any public way the dictatorship which Garibaldi had taken on himself, but must content himself with ordinary civilities. He was careful to return Garibaldi's visit two days later and, sitting in an apartment in the left wing of the Royal Palace, whence he could see the hills of Sicily and the blue water stretching to the north, he talked in a friendly way. Garibaldi discussed ordinary matters 'with the blandest manner'. But when the admiral began to give his views on Italy, he observed that the dictator 'became inaccessible to reason'. Mundy looked at Garibaldi with quiet curiosity. He was himself a man of action and of ability. And he perceived, or thought he perceived, that with the idealism of Garibaldi there went 'a deep astuteness of character'.

The matter on which Garibaldi refused to hear reason was Cavour. It was apparent that he hated him. Cavour, he said, had sold his birthplace; he had connived with the Emperor of the French to despoil his own country and, although he was sorry to say it, he could never forgive the first minister of Sardinia for the part he had played. He added that he did not think the Emperor of the French had any true regard for Italy; to which Mundy replied that 'there were always two sides to a question', and without the emperor Italy would not be in the position she now held. Mundy fancied he was discussing the past. But on the next occasion he saw Garibaldi he found him much changed, thinner in body and nervous in his movements. 'He told me he had received bad news from Turin. The Emperor Napoleon was decidedly hostile to Italian regeneration, and would never quit Rome unless the island of Sardinia was given up to him in compensation. This sacrifice Count Cavour was quite prepared to make, and a treaty was already in progress for the further humiliation of Italy, and for the aggrandisement of the French Empire.'

This news was untrue. But it contained the gist of the difference between Cavour and Garibaldi. While Garibaldi fought in the south, the lawyer continued his intrigues in the north; and Garibaldi feared that the outcome would be, as it had so often been before, that the adventure would be called off. But this time he had made up his mind that he was going to Rome, Cavour or no Cavour, diplomacy or no diplomacy. And he told Mundy, who had received orders to proceed to Naples, that in a short time he would meet him there.

'I remarked to him, in reply to this unexpected announcement, that His Majesty King Francis II had now entered his name upon the roll of constitutional monarchs, and was about to enter into an alliance with King Victor Emmanuel.

'Garibaldi gravely answered, "It is too late!"' [1]

It was obvious to impartial observers that the day of Italian liberation was not far distant. The fruit was ripening and must drop. For, whereas in 1848 the fires of revolution had been separate and had been separately quenched, now one stream of life ran up and down the leg

[1] Mundy, *Palermo and Naples*, p. 193.

of Italy and across the waters to Sicily, so that, when it became known that Garibaldi had landed at Marsala and gone on to take Palermo, the news throbbed through Calabria and Naples to Tuscany and Piedmont, through the Papal States and across Lombardy to Venetia. And whereas in the past news of such victories had meant the hanging out of flags and the ringing of a few bells, now, as Garibaldi himself had foreseen, citizens of all classes considered that still greater events were on the way. Piedmont had remained neutral, keeping up an elaborate pretence that deceived nobody. But the people of Piedmont, of Lombardy and of Central Italy, were not neutral. They were clamouring to be allowed to do their share; and insisting that the king should cast away the trickery of diplomacy and march to war. Things had turned out very much as Garibaldi had hoped they would. The cat's-paw was master. From Sicily he commanded the destinies of the new nation.

It was uncertain, however, in what sense he proposed to command them; and when Persano let off his nineteen guns he was expressing his fervent hope, on behalf of the Piedmontese government, that Garibaldi would remember the promise he had made, and frequently repeated, that all he did was, and would be, in the name of Victor Emmanuel. Garibaldi did remember. When he proclaimed himself dictator, he stated in his proclamation that he was the deputy of Victor Emmanuel. At the same time, while he exercised a perfect loyalty to his absent sovereign, he was omnipotent. Victor Emmanuel had no orders to give, and the dictator consulted nobody. Cavour's first fear was that he would consult Mazzini. He feared that that subtle politician must be on his way to Sicily, and sent agents to look for him everywhere in order that he should, at this critical hour of Italy's destiny, be safely under lock and key. Mazzini had reached Italy and was walking about in Genoa with his beard shaved off, completely unrecognisable because of this slight alteration. But even if Cavour had been able to lay hands on him, he would only have learned that Mazzini was as ignorant as himself on the subject of Garibaldi's intentions or, if not ignorant, powerless to affect them one way or another. Mazzini, too, was trembling for Italy; wondering whether the strange magician who could make an army of thirty thousand men run before a sixth of their number, was on the point of making his country or destroying it. Cavour, in his subterranean way, had solved Garibaldi's problem for him. Garibaldi would take Sicily. Cavour would apologise to the French Emperor for the zeal of Piedmont's servant. And then Piedmont would take over Sicily. That would be so much done. And the rest would be seen to later.

If, on the other hand, the Sicilian adventure went further, Cavour considered that the future of Italy would be gravely compromised. He was informed that Garibaldi proposed to use the island as a stepping-stone for the invasion of the mainland; with what purpose was only too clear. His goal was Rome. And, before he had got there, or half-way there, he would have brought on the country he loved a disastrous series of European complications, of which, in his simplicity, he could not be aware. The Pope would complain. The Emperor of the French would seize the opportunity to intervene again; and the Austrians would come flooding down from the Quadrilateral to recover what they had lost. Cavour did not blame Garibaldi. He admired him for what he had already done. But once again he thought the time was come to lock the lion up. And, having reflected on these matters, he sent La Farina to take over the dictatorship.

It was Garibaldi's treatment of La Farina that made Admiral Mundy think there must be a 'deep astuteness' in Garibaldi. He was polite to the new official, though somewhat tardy in receiving him (he allowed him to wait a fortnight before he arranged an interview); and he told him that the annexation of Sicily was a foregone conclusion. Of course, he said, it would be handed over to Victor Emmanuel. But he intended to choose his own time and method of making the proclamation; and to preserve his own freedom of action. If La Farina had had no secret instructions, this assurance would have been satisfactory enough. But La Farina had been told by Cavour that his business was to circumscribe the operations of Garibaldi and make sure they did not go beyond Sicily. Of that Garibaldi was quite aware. And when La Farina attempted subversive propaganda, he had him arrested and conveyed to Admiral Persano with a request that he should be returned to Genoa.

Thereafter it was plain to all the world, as well as to Garibaldi and Cavour themselves, that each of those two men wanted a different thing; or, wanting the same thing, wanted it in a different way; the lawyer wishing to nibble patiently at the cords that still bound the nation, to nibble them furtively under cover of darkness, and the soldier to use his curved sabre in broad daylight. Garibaldi did not like having Cavour as an enemy; not on any personal ground, but because he symbolised excellently the enemy he had always fought in his fellow-countrymen, that subtle faithlessness which expressed itself in their devious machinations, in their flourishing and perfidious politeness, the 'vulpine' quality which they had learned in centuries of subjection, of court intrigue where poison and the dagger disposed of enemies who might not be fronted with open force. Because of this characteristic the Italians had remained petty citizens of petty duchies and republics: they trusted each other too little to unite and were too selfish for sacrifice. Cavour made Garibaldi nervous because he was more than a man. He was a type, from whom Italy had to be wrested, if Italy was ever to be anything at all.

On July 14 Cavour wrote to Persano to say that *at all costs* Garibaldi must be prevented from crossing over to the mainland. But the phrase *at all costs*, coming from Cavour, meant nothing at all; it meant, perhaps, that Persano was to do his best to find out what Garibaldi's plans were, put traitors in his camp and hold him by treachery. On August 1, Cavour's tone was feebler. 'Do not assist the passage of Garibaldi to the continent. Try by indirect means to delay it to the uttermost.' But Cavour might as well have held up a straw before the wind. The whole will of Italy was in Garibaldi, sweeping him on. In spite of Persano's patrolling, the expedition crossed and marched northward. In the last days of August 1860, Francis II heard that the terrible condottiere was advancing through Calabria Citeriore upon Cosenza, and that the royal troops were laying down their arms or retreating before him.

He also heard through his spies that Cavour was paying out money in Naples in order to bring about a popular rising. It was one of many conspiracies, and the news of it left the young king only a little more bewildered and cold. Cavour was trying, in his habitual way, to get to Naples and forestall Garibaldi. He had been checkmated in Sicily and was trying again. But Garibaldi was playing his hand well. The next news was that he was at Eboli, twenty miles from Naples, with about twenty thousand men; while on September 6, just before seven in the evening, the King and Queen of Naples embarked on a Spanish steamer of war and fled, protesting against the 'unjust war', to the fortress of Gaeta. On September 7 Garibaldi entered Naples at noon. There was only one thing to be done. Piedmont must cast hypocrisy aside and enter the war. When the two armies were side by side, the pipeclay of Savoy beside the rags of Garibaldi's volunteers, then Cavour could cast his net over the lion and keep him out of harm's way.

Admiral Mundy had had some amusing passages with Persano in the Bay of Naples, where the navies of the world were again collected to witness the further stages of the drama. He was not impressed. But when, on the evening of Garibaldi's entry, he received a call from the Piedmontese admiral, he was inclined to listen to him. Garibaldi had turned over the vessels of the Neapolitan fleet in the bay to Persano, to be ranked as captures of the Piedmontese navy. At the same time he informed Persano that his stay in Naples would be short. He intended, he said, to march to Rome and then to Venetia; and, when Italy was 'restored to herself', to transfer the kingdom to Victor Emmanuel. It was a stupendous programme; and the admiral had instructions to beg Mundy to 'use his influence' to dissuade Garibaldi from it. The matter was indeed very grave, and Mundy turned it over in his mind as he drove through the city in plain clothes the next day. 'No words', wrote Mundy in his diary, 'can express the frantic joy of the people, or the madness of the scene. Hundreds of the best-looking young women that could be mustered, many of them of respectable family, and others perhaps not the most discreet, were dressed in the costumes of ancient days, when excess of drapery was not required, and, formed in voluptuous tableaux and mounted on triumphal cars, were drawn in state along the great thoroughfares of the Toledo and Largo-Castello. Men, boys and girls were also in requisition, in every imaginable garment, armed with swords, spears, and flambeaux; and following their train were the very dregs of the population, denouncing with hideous yells the hated rule of the Bourbon, and forcing everyone to join in the cry of "Evviva Garibaldi!"' It was a touching and disturbing spectacle. There was not a drunken person to be seen, and when word went round that the dictator slept, the revellers became hushed like little children.

The following day Mundy called on Mr. Elliot, the British representative at Naples, and found him holding a telegram from Lord John Russell instructing him to 'express to General Garibaldi the hope that no attack would be made on Venetia'. London, too, was becoming anxious. Mr. Elliot could not call on Garibaldi, being accredited as Her Majesty's Minister to the Court of Naples. He suggested that it might be well if Admiral Mundy had an informal talk; and the latter mounted the six storeys of the Palazzo d'Angri and found Garibaldi on a sofa, hastily dragging on a boot. He had been told that the British admiral was outside and remarked to *The Times* correspondent, who was with him, that it would be unbecoming to receive an admiral in slippers. 'I told you', said

Garibaldi, holding out his hand to Mundy and laughing, 'that we should meet again at Naples.'[1] There were no chairs, so the company, which included Lord Llanover, Mr. Craven and Wreeford of *The Times*, sat on the bed, and it was arranged that Garibaldi should meet Mr. Elliot at eleven next morning on the British flagship.

The meeting was of a more formal character than the encounter of the previous day. Garibaldi arrived accompanied by members of his staff, who did not seem anxious to leave their leader alone in the hands of a British diplomat. But Mr. Elliot was a good liberal and had no love for the Bourbons. He said how miraculous it was that Garibaldi should have accomplished such marvellous results with such trifling means; and in this remark he put a quite unusual sincerity because, to an Englishman, the phenomenon of an unequipped band of enthusiasts beating armies known to be equipped with munitions and accoutrement of the best British and French manufacture was impressive. He went on to say that, although he could not have official relations with Garibaldi until he received instructions from Her Majesty's government, he would remain at Naples, a piece of information which seemed to give the dictator 'great satisfaction'. After these courtesies Mr. Elliot came to business. He said he had been 'charged to express the hope that no attack would be made on Venetia', as, in the opinion of Lord John Russell, such an attack would be 'calculated to bring the greatest calamities upon Italy.'

If Mundy expected Garibaldi to adopt the tone he had used to Persano, he was agreeably deceived. With a singular dexterity the latter said what he had said to Persano. But he said it in such a way that the significance of it appeared to be completely changed. The 'deep astuteness' caused him to shift with an easy movement from one leg to the other. 'He intended', he said, 'to push on at once to Rome, and when that city should be in his hands, to offer the crown of a united Italy to King Victor Emmanuel, upon whom would then devolve the task of the

[1] Mundy, *op. cit.* p. 240.

liberation of Venetia, and in which he would himself be but the lieutenant of His Majesty. If this liberation could be accomplished by purchase or by negotiation, so much the better.' To Persano he had said he would go to Rome and thence to Venetia. As he stated the matter now to Elliot, he did not say he would not go to Venetia. But he caused himself to appear as the humble servant of Victor Emmanuel, to whose wishes he would defer. Elliot knew this deference of Garibaldi's was a very relative affair. Victor Emmanuel had twice told Garibaldi to stop, commanding him not to leave Sicily and not to come to Naples. And Garibaldi had replied that when he had crowned him King of Italy in Rome he would be his obedient servant for the rest of his life. Accordingly Mr. Elliot was cold. He told Garibaldi not to delude himself about England. England liked heroes and disliked European wars. If Garibaldi brought on a European war he would find that the citizens of England would have very little sympathy for him. The English diplomat warmed slightly as he discovered he was being handled diplomatically. 'In forcible language, he pointed out that if Garibaldi went to Rome and fought the French garrison there, he would bring about immeasurable disaster.' To that Garibaldi replied that Rome *was an Italian city*, and the French had no business to be there. It was a final sentence, delivered with such a blast of conviction that the Englishmen felt there was no more to be said. Using influence with Garibaldi was sometimes a vain undertaking. Moreover, though Mr. Elliot was not sure that Rome was an Italian city, he was inclined to agree that the French had no right to be there.

'This is the day', wrote the admiral in his diary on September 19, 'on which the miracle of the liquefaction of the blood of Saint Januarius is performed. It is the universal belief of the lower classes of the people that when the spirit of this holy man is satisfied with the administration of the government of the Neapolitan Kingdom, he makes it manifest to the faithful by the melting of a few drops of his precious blood which was collected at his martyrdom in the year 305, and has since been safely preserved in a small glass bottle. It may readily be imagined that during so long a period as fifteen hundred and fifty-five years this bottle or phial must have had many adventures and many narrow escapes from destruction. It was carried at various epochs to other cities in Italy, but in the year 1497 eventually found a resting-place in the Duomo at Naples, where it has continued to remain in quiet repose, by the side of the head of the saint, which had been also miraculously preserved.

'As the capture of Naples by an unrecognised adventurer was an event in every way likely to give displeasure to the saint, it had already been circulated by the chiefs of the Church that there was much probability of the non-fulfilment of the usual rite. Noon was the hour at which the process of change from congelation to liquefaction was generally completed. Great, then, was the astonishment of the pious inhabitants when, at 9 o'clock in the morning, salvos of artillery from the forts announced that the saint had approved the downfall of the Bourbon dynasty, by a three hours' advance in the time of the performance of the miracle.'

There were various explanations of the phenomenon. One was that 'orders had been sent from the dictator which admitted of no other solution than that which had occurred'. But Mundy, ironical Protestant though he was, wished to see the miracle with his own eyes. On September 27, being the Octave or last day of its performance, he entered the Duomo and found about a hundred people, mostly old women, within the balustrade of the chancel, while a priest carried round the phial so that it might be examined and kissed. 'An acolyte', says Mundy, 'accompanied him, with a lighted taper in his hand. This was held close to the bottle, by means of which the saintly blood was made transparent to the beholders. The bottle has a diameter of three or four inches, is circular in form, and quite flat at the sides, like a pocket scent-flask. As I stood outside the rails it was brought up for my examination, and as it was made to revolve in the priest's hands the liquefaction of the pitch-like substance it contained was made clear to the view. The priest wished me to kiss the bottle, which I politely declined.'

The power of Naples was breaking. In the autumn months the armies of Victor Emmanuel, assisted by the Legion of Garibaldi, defeated the stubborn remnant of the Neapolitan regulars. But the power of the Pope was not broken. All over Europe the faithful prayed that the Holy Father might be delivered from the hand of his sacrilegious son. Even in the worship of the lazzaroni of Naples, who kissed the hem of Garibaldi's robe and called him a god and a little father, the patriot could hear the accent of prayer. He blamed Cavour when, with a firm hand, his royal master took over the possession which his heroism had won, disbanded the *Cacciatori* and offered him a dukedom and the Collar of the Annunziata, the acceptance of which would have made Garibaldi and his children wealthy for the rest of their lives. He declined and, on leaving Naples, he came to shake the wise English admiral sadly by the hand. It was six in the morning and, from the stern verandah windows of the *Hannibal*, the English merchantman which had been chartered to take Garibaldi back to Caprera was seen blowing off her steam. 'Rome and Venice are not French and Austrian cities', he repeated. 'They are Italian cities.' As Garibaldi passed from the cabin to the quarter-deck he saw the admiral's visiting-book lying on the table, the same table on which, six months before, the armistice had been signed at Palermo. Mundy asked if the dictator would be good enough to sign his name: upon which the guest sat down and wrote one of those little certificates which, like cheques of nobility, he delivered to those he admired: the certificate was in French:

G. GARIBALDI,
    doit à l'Amiral Mundy par les preuves bien sincères et affectueuses d'amitié, dont il a été comblé dans toutes les circonstances, la reconnaissance la plus vive, et qui durera toute sa vie.

A few hours later the English merchantman could be seen rounding the island of Ischia and bearing north, on a direct course for Caprera.

November 9, 1860.

Garibaldi was going to dig up his potatoes.[1]

XXX

A WELL-WORN cart-track now led up to the cottage. On the left ran a dry stone wall which fenced in the cultivated patches and kept out the wild goats, donkeys, cows and the general's horses, all of which were turned loose to find their own grazing on the ledges of rock. The gate of the cottage was a movable pole. This displaced, the visitor found himself in a narrow strip of garden facing a small vestibule entrance. On the left was the room in which Teresita slept with Madame Deideri, on the right the general's room, where recent events had left some traces in the improved furniture. In the past the general's bedroom had boasted one chair which had no back. Now it contained some new maple-wood chairs, a gift from the officers and crew of the *Washington* (who had inscribed their names on the backs) and some walnut chairs imported by the Deideris. There was also a small plain iron bedstead with muslin curtains, a walnut writing table, and a chest of drawers. Beside the bed was a deal chest covered with books and letters. On a cord stretched across were the general's red shirts, drawers, trousers, and socks. He had now a greater variety of these than at any time in his life, for his ideas on costume were now fixed. He had brought back with him from his last campaign the Piedmontese uniform (preserved against the contingencies of the future), two red shirts, two pairs of grey trousers and about thirty pounds of unspent money. And he had decided that of this equip-

[1] The substance of this chapter is taken from Mundy's diary, *Palermo and Naples*. For an account of the events of the Sicilian and Neapolitan campaigns, as well as for political detail, the reader should consult Trevelyan, *Garibaldi and the Thousand* and *Garibaldi and the Making of Modern Italy*.

ment he required only the shirts and the trousers, with underclothes to match. In his simplicity he was not indifferent to luxury. He changed these several times a day according to his occupation. He looked wrinkled about the eyes, so that the sober cunning of them was more apparent. He was ageing. With his rather bent legs, the slight roll of his walk and his friendly smile he looked daily more like his father, a sailor-man of the Mediterranean.

The books in the bedroom were mixed, a few shipping annuals, some history books and some treatises (obviously unread) on military tactics. There were newspapers everywhere, on the floor and on every article of furniture, including the bed. Those that the general had read were stacked in a corner and removed to make way for others: for this was one of Garibaldi's occupations from which he derived a mingled irritation and delight. He retired to bed about ten o'clock and read the newspapers for an hour before dropping off to sleep. Then again, waking up early, sometimes as early as three in the morning, he lit a cigar and stretched out a hand for the nearest bundle. A shout brought his secretary, to whom he briefly indicated the answers to be sent to his innumerable correspondents. Augusto Vecchi, having volunteered to act as the general's secretary during a holiday he spent at Caprera, had to write forty letters at four o'clock in the morning, most of them short notes to letters begging for Garibaldi's autograph or a lock of his hair. The secretary had instructions to be polite, as these correspondents who wrote from all parts of the world were allies in the task which the general considered still lay before him. The most of the letters of admiration came from English or American ladies. Out of the forty answers written by Vecchi, Garibaldi selected one addressed to a Miss Kitty Johnson.

'Do you know this lady?' he asked.

'I never saw her in my life!' replied Vecchi.

'You have made use of such flowery language . . .', said Garibaldi.

'It will produce money and enthusiasm for the cause',

said Vecchi; whereupon the general laughed, patted Vecchi on the shoulder and took him out to *amuse* himself in the fields. The amusement was usually some form of hard work. But at times the visitor was allowed to escape and wander up to the ridge of the island where heather and asphodels were in bloom and trickles of water ran through the grass. There were some pine trees and dwarf oak on the ridge, their tops nipped by the wind. Below lay La Maddalena, glittering among its sister islands in the water, and, nearer, the rocky coast-line of Caprera itself, the white cottage on the slope, and beside it three patches of land which Garibaldi had begun to cultivate since his return from Naples. He had taken up his potatoes and was experimenting with vines, some of which straggled on the south side of the cottage. He was proud of his vines, and as he turned up the diseased bunches for Vecchi to spray with sulphur, he stopped to discharge himself of a surplus of philosophy. 'The great spirit of eternal *Life* is in everything!' he said. 'These plants, these fruit trees, even these hard granite rocks, have a soul. It may be rudimentary—but there it is. Do not geologists speak of affinity among metals? Botanists of love among plants? and do not we see them reproduce themselves before our eyes? We have speech; the brutes motion. Plants are speechless; stones motionless; but I believe they speak a language, although we are unable to understand it. . . . I feel happy', he said, 'because I can prop the plants laid low by the wind, tie the weak to a stick, bind up the wounds of those whose branches have been broken, and sprinkle sulphur over those attacked by the mildew.' Sulphur, a sovereign remedy, applicable, remarked Garibaldi, not only to vines which suffered from mildew, but to human institutions which, like the temporal power of the Pope, require the curative hand of the gardener. The cross, he said, speaking solemnly, has to be grafted on the crown.

It was a conversation like many others. Garibaldi's thoughts brooded over the problems of the spirit, seeking their roots in a kinship with the silent life of the earth.

And then they came to the surface in an allusion to Pio Nono. He was sorry for Pio Nono because of what would have to be done to him. It might be that, like the poor lad Francis II, he would be made an exile. But the abuses which he represented must be cured. Even the herdsman knew Garibaldi's thoughts on this point and belaboured one of the donkeys which rejoiced in the name of *Pio Nono*. He said in excuse that he had not beaten him. *Pio Nono* had run away, and when he was found on the mountain all the wild asses were pitching into him. They were fighting, declared the sly Sardinian, about the Immaculate Conception, and the other donkeys had bitten *Pio Nono* and kicked him. He was in sorry condition. His ears were torn, the end of his tail bitten off and half his mane plucked out. While Teresita washed his wounds in vinegar and water and tied him up with pieces of rag, Frusciante addressed him. 'It is quite right to take away your temporalities, but it is wicked to flay you', he said. 'In '49 we tried to make you understand, but you would not. You chose to be independent, with the Austrians on one side and the French on the other. See what has undone you! the indignation of the people. Thus have you lost the Legations, the Marches, and Umbria; are despised by the civilised world, and are given over to the stick of an unbelieving dog.'[1]

Garibaldi was passing through one of his periods of self-examination. They occurred regularly after his great adventures and coincided with a condition of melancholy which he tried to shake off by physical exertion. He had more acutely than ever the feeling of being divided, torn between this strange chemical affinity which linked him as a natural man to the plants of the earth and to the rocks of his island, making him feel that no sympathy with a human creature could be so profound and peaceful as that unity; and yet returning from this condition by stages, like a diver coming back to the surface by a succession of instinctive kicks. His tenderness to the animals of the island was noticed (as indeed it had been noticed in Naples, where,

[1] Vecchi, *Garibaldi at Caprera*, p. 36.

during the period of his dictatorship, he had fallen foul of the cab-drivers for beating their animals). He went out in the middle of the night with a lantern to look for a lamb that had strayed and came back with it silently, giving it warm milk from a sponge to quiet its bleating in case it should disturb the other members of the house. And while this tenderness went with his own self-possession and strength, expressing a natural pity which he felt for the weakness of all things in which flickered the flame of life, it was accompanied by a certain self-consciousness, as if he were aware that he was giving those about him a lesson. It appeared that he was a teacher who was convinced that the strength and tenderness in himself should be conveyed into others. The simplicity of his habits was not altogether a private matter. It was part of a gospel of which the immediate meaning was that those who were dedicated to the high enterprise of saving Italy must live simply. And whether or not Italy was to be saved, this was the way that any man must live if he wished to obey the spirit within him. There was self-consciousness in him but no hypocrisy. He was as completely unspoilt as ever, like a very wise and very experienced child. An English visitor, who wished to carry away a souvenir, asked for a pair of hob-nailed boots which he saw under the bed. 'No,' said Garibaldi, 'you may not have these. They are my only pair, and the cobbler who made them is in Nice, which is now a foreign country. But you may have one of these,' he added, taking down one of the red shirts from the line. He still drank only water. A jar of it stood in his room, covered by a sheet of paper. But the guests were provided with good wine and fed abundantly on the game and fish of the island. They came from many countries to look at him, some of them out of the merest curiosity. The little port of Maddalena became prosperous with the traffic.

Letters came every week from Maddalena reminding him that the eyes of the world were on him. Some were from cranks. The inventor of a new kind of artillery offered to communicate the secret by which the Austrian Quadrilateral could be destroyed. A Frenchman knew of a means by which an army of 200,000 men could be wiped out; he offered to share his knowledge with Garibaldi if the latter promised that the men wiped out should not be Frenchmen. A mad priest declared Italy to be possessed and invited Garibaldi to exorcise the country with fire and sword, driving out the Pope, who was the representative of Lucifer, along with the legions of demons, who were the cardinals, bishops and monks of every order.[1] There were New Year greetings from municipalities, along with offers of the freedom of many cities. As many people as could write in Palermo signed an address. The twelve commanders of the twelve battalions of the National Guard of Naples expressed their homage. Instead of making him vain, these signs of his power made him sad. He said he wished he were twenty years younger; and when he talked with Vecchi he spoke of death, saying he would wish to be buried at Caprera where the rising sun, as it rose above the hill, would salute his grave, and the thrushes would fill the air with their sweet notes, and the cheerful sparrows would chirp over his head. Often he had called Italy his lady and spoken of the kiss of the bridegroom which he would set on her lips; now he spoke of death in the same way, with a tranquil voice, as if he had discovered that beyond the salvation of Italy she awaited him, folded in the stillness of the earth. He talked, too, of America. The North Americans wished him to lead them in their war for the emancipation of the slaves. Vecchi, said someone, would go with him; and Vecchi would have a young black to keep off the flies and offer him tea in the shade of his tent, and he would return with half a dozen black boys and instal them as souvenirs of America in the Villa Spinola. Garibaldi listened without smiling. 'Four thousand two hundred miles, and more', he said, as if to himself, 'from New York to Rio de la Plata.' He was absorbed in thought and it seemed as if he were thinking of the emancipation of the American slaves. But he was not. He stopped and

[1] Vecchi, *op. cit.* p. 34.

looked at Vecchi as they had climbed to a high point on Caprera, and he said the island would be a paradise if Anita had been alive to share it with him. No woman would stay in such a solitude. There was no one like Anita.

In the spring of 1861 Teresita had married Canzio of Genoa, one of the volunteers of the Thousand. They came to pay a visit to Caprera in August and Garibaldi became more cheerful. He began to sing Azucena's song from *Il Trovatore*. In the evening there was music. The Maddalena boat had also brought a box for the general, inside which they found a case made of precious woods containing a sword. There was, as well, a book with the names of the subscribers, citizens of Melbourne, Australia, who sent their homage to the general and informed him that the sword had cost £300. The hilt was of solid gold and showed Italy arisen, her chains broken, brandishing a sword with which she was cleaving the coils of a serpent. On the guard was a brilliant representing the star of Italy. The scabbard was of green velvet.[1] 'This is the first sword', said Garibaldi, 'on which I have seen our revered Mother, Italy, represented as I always see her in my thoughts. "The Niobe of nations", sword in hand, animating her sons to redemption or death.'

From another parcel, opened some time before, had tumbled out three long candles, one red, one white and one green. They came from New York.[2]

The summer of 1861 had been very dry. For six months there had been no rain at Nice. But when Madame Schwartz embarked on the *Solferino* for Genoa a violent sirocco brought with it a deluge of rain; and at Genoa, where she went to get a berth on the steamer for Maddalena, Captain Dodero told her that the *Sardegna*, on which she would sail, was the worst boat in the world. She had small luck in her dealings with Garibaldi. He had imperilled her life in Sicily. He had, she thought, tricked her in the matter of his memoirs and he had said nothing

---

[1] Vecchi, *op. cit.* p. 129.   [2] *Ibid.* p. 58.

of his marriage. But some sort of force drew her to him. His publicity value was increasing, and she had in her pocket the honorarium for the first two volumes of the German edition of the memoirs, published by Messrs. Hoffman & Campe in the previous year; with this inducement to further effort she hoped still to come to some arrangement for a third volume. At Genoa, while she waited for the boat, she visited Colonel Deideri and a Signora Coltelletti, from whom she learned that Battistina was spending a great deal of money, and that Garibaldi had been obliged to remind her that he was not rich. On the boat there were a number of gentlemen all bound on the same mission. Like herself, they wished to see Garibaldi on one matter or another.

He seemed glad to see her, and left her in Teresa's room with the manuscript which he had been recently writing. He said he would not publish it in his lifetime, as he intended to leave it as a legacy to his children: but she was welcome to read it. Less than half an hour had passed when the door was abruptly opened and Canzio put his head in and asked, 'Do you want any dinner?' Madame Schwartz did. But she had hoped that Garibaldi would come to fetch her himself.

There were eight at dinner besides Canzio and his wife and Garibaldi's two sons. She had seen Menotti before, a tall young man who liked dancing and shooting and who was built strongly, like the fishermen of Nice. She hoped that Ricciotti, whom she saw for the first time, would be more genteel as he had spent some time at Nice and in England with Mrs. Roberts. Madame Schwartz, finding herself somewhat neglected, asked Ricciotti, 'How long have you been with your father?' But he did not seem to know, and advised her to ask someone else. Garibaldi was silent, for what reason she could not discover; and the others followed his example. The meal was dull. After dinner the men went to play bowls, while Madame Schwartz continued her reading. Then Teresa came to say that her father would like to see her. He was still melancholy. 'Do you know that it has gone so far', he said, speaking of the attitude of the Piedmontese government, 'that they will scarcely tolerate me here. God knows where they will banish me one fine day!'

Madame Schwartz presented the honorarium, along with a box of cigars and 'certain confectioneries', to which he paid no attention.

'You are forever giving me presents', he said, 'and I do not deserve them.'

She asked if she might keep the manuscript for a little, but he said she might lose it at Maddalena. Canzio, whom she asked to persuade the general, said angrily, 'The general is poor. When he dies his children will find themselves in the middle of the road'. A little later, as she was about to leave, Garibaldi referred to Anita, Battistina's daughter, saying he would rather she was in the care of Madame Schwartz. 'But', he said, 'there is no need to hurry, and we must try by gentle means to induce the mother to give up the child to us.' In the course of their conversation, Madame Schwartz could not keep her eyes from wandering to the place where her watch ought to have been, and at last Garibaldi noticed. 'I see it has not escaped your attention', he said, 'that the watch you gave me is not in its place. I have had the misfortune to break the glass, and had it sent to Genoa. But I do assure you that as long as I live I will wear no other watch and chain but those you have given me. Have you not recognised the chain on all the photographs they have taken of me?'

In spite of this assurance Madame Schwartz was sad, thinking of the third volume of memoirs which she had not succeeded in obtaining, and feeling that she had now a very small place in Garibaldi's heart. But next day she returned and again a dull meal was followed by a noisy game of bowls. She had learned her lesson and did not mention the manuscript. With feminine tact she induced the general to talk of his own concerns. 'He spoke freely', she records, 'about the burning difficulty of the Eternal City, and did not hide from me how bitterly he was irritated[1] by the different obstacles set in the way of the solution of the Roman question.' Although Madame Schwartz did not like to see the general surrounded by so many followers that she could not enjoy such têtes-à-têtes in any privacy, she was not above collecting as much gossip as possible. From Captain Roberts at Maddalena she heard with satisfaction that Garibaldi's wife, the daughter of the Marquis Raimondi, had been a visitor at Maddalena. She had come with a cousin named La Calcagna, and, accompanied by a servant, had gone to Caprera to see Garibaldi. But the attempt had failed. Garibaldi refused to see her, and had not answered a letter sent by La Calcagna. After an interview with Signora Deideri, the despised wife had been obliged to go as she had come. Signora Deideri was well informed. She said that Giuseppina used to put her love-letters to Luigi Caroli into a casket on the mantelpiece, from which they were taken by a servant and delivered. But her brother, with whom she happened to quarrel, took one of the letters and put it into the hands of Garibaldi. Signora Deideri also said that Garibaldi had gone about looking for his pistols and, not finding them, went to his wife's room. 'Have you written this letter?' he asked: and when she said yes, he said, 'Then see that you do not bear my name'. Giuseppina, continued Signora Deideri, with the omniscience of a matron, was at that time five months gone with child.

Not until eight months later did Madame Schwartz see Garibaldi again. At Milan she heard that the restless hero had been engaged in some sort of premeditated insurrection on the Austrian frontier, an affair which had apparently been unsuccessful. She found him resting in the villa of Signora Cairóli, a lady who had given all her sons to the cause of Italian redemption.

This time it was Garibaldi who wished to see Madame Schwartz. Would she, he asked, accompany him on an

[1] Elpis Melena, p. 147. In the text 'how bitterly he was *cajoled*'. I have altered the expression, which appears to be a mistranslation.

expedition to Sicily which was to be the prelude to a general rising for the conquest of Rome?

It was her last chance. There were many things in Garibaldi's mind when he put the question. But Sicily was a name that stirred unpleasant memories in Madame Schwartz. She replied that she had promised Lord Harrowby that she would address a meeting in London on the subject of cruelty to animals in Rome.[1]

XXXI

TERESA had grown into a graceful young woman. She had a small mouth with large regular teeth like her father's; and she had Garibaldi's auburn hair and straight nose. She was most like the general in her manner. She did not talk much, but when she spoke it was in a quiet musical voice that contained a curious suggestion of resolution. In the spring of 1861 General Türr had arrived with a package from the king which, when undone, was found to hold a glittering diamond necklace. Signora Deideri dissolved in tears and said a great deal about the honour paid to the daughter of Garibaldi. Garibaldi himself was touched. 'Pray express my gratitude to the king for this token of his friendship', he said. Teresa only blushed and said: 'Thank the king'. When Vecchi asked to see the necklace again, she told Signora Deideri to show it to him, cast a careless glance at it, and ran off to ring the bell for dinner.[2]

It may well have been that the sight of the necklace recalled to her the glories and wealth which her father had rejected. If he had chosen, he might at that moment have been a duke, safely adopted into the noble caste of Savoy and entitled to call Victor Emmanuel cousin. And she, with Menotti and Ricciotti, would have been attending splendid ceremonies in Turin. As it was, thanks to the peculiar constitution of their father, the children of Gari-

[1] Elpis Melena, pp. 141-153.   [2] Vecchi, p. 42.

baldi might soon be, as Canzio had said, in the street. In this obstinacy, too, there was danger. The source of it was pride. When this pride induced Garibaldi to refuse gifts for himself and his family while he conferred the kingdom of Sicily and Naples on Victor Emmanuel, he was testing the quality of his royal master in a very intimate way. Victor Emmanuel was a proud man, too, with the same mountain blood in him as ran in the veins of Garibaldi's mother. He had sense enough to see he had obtained his new kingdom in an inglorious, if not dishonest manner. All might have been well if the plot by which the kingdom had been obtained had been fabricated by a number of equally ignoble conspirators who could, in the sequel, forget their obliquity, absorb the honours and the profits and settle down to the virtuous life of established proprietors. They desired nothing better. But while Garibaldi was at Caprera it was difficult to forget the past. He not only refused the gifts of the king, but said that he awaited an opportunity to complete the work he had begun. Declining himself to be made a duke, he insisted that he would crown Victor Emmanuel King of Italy in Rome.

Garibaldi had not understood the behaviour of Cavour. He thought that Cavour stood between him and the king. And in this he was not wrong. Cavour interpreted Garibaldi to Victor Emmanuel, sometimes to the former's disadvantage and sometimes to his advantage; for Cavour cherished for Garibaldi the kind of affection that intelligent men have for magnificent animals whose primitive instincts can be trained for useful purposes. After the fashion of intelligent men, he forgot that primitive animals have their own kind of intelligence, and their own means of action. It was Cavour who suggested that the lion should be harnessed with the collar of the Annunziata and induced to take his food from the same trough from which the Piedmontese nobility were fed. No doubt he suggested the necklace for Teresa. He was a clever man, and knew the value of trifles. He insisted at the end of the 1860 campaign that Garibaldi's volunteers, men and officers, should be rewarded, a matter on which he had a 'hot discussion' with Fanti of the Piedmontese war office. Fanti wished to disband the Garibaldians with a simple dole; whereas Cavour wanted to take the pick of Garibaldi's officers into the regular army and to allow the *Cacciatori* to retain their name and a separate existence. Not until later did Garibaldi appreciate the large view taken by Cavour; and even then he was grudging. 'I am told so', he said. The fact was that such small matters could never bridge the gulf between them. 'By God!' said the man of intelligence emphatically, 'I could not bear the merited stain of having ignored services such as that of the conquest of a kingdom of nine million inhabitants.' But the rift between the soldier and the politician no longer mattered. Cavour was dying. Fra Giacomo was called on June 6, 1861, to administer the sacraments. Cavour said in his last lucid moment that he died a Christian. But when he fell into delirium it was clear enough that he died a politician. 'Rome, Venice, Naples', he muttered, '. . . no state of siege.' Such was his reply to the letter in which, on May 18, Garibaldi had stated his final view. 'Signor Conte', he had written, 'you ought to be the arbitrator of Europe and treat on a footing of equality the man (Napoleon III) who seeks to act as its master. Italy to-day represents the aspirations of the nationalities of the world, and you rule Italy. But to rule it you must not descend to the weaknesses inherent in present conditions. Kossuth, Manin, Guerrazzi, Mazzini, were overthrown rather by an inherent defect in their intrinsic conditions than by the power of their enemies. They were dictators, but not soldiers. . . . Leave others', he concluded, 'to govern by the miserable subterfuges of deceit, and the dynasty of the Re Galantuomo will last forever in Italy as an emanation of Providence. . . . In 1849, I quitted Rome with 4000 men, and was obliged to hide myself alone in the forests. In 1860 you have seen what could be done with a thousand. To-morrow we shall proceed in geometrical progression with the people who gave the Romans to the universe.'

Whether this doctrine was right or wrong, it no longer required to be explained to Cavour. Garibaldi took Cavour's disappearance from the scene with equanimity, thinking that no doubt he had been a well-intentioned and clever man, but a man also who was the main obstacle to his own plans for the freedom of Italy. He did not recognise with the same lucidity that he was just as much at variance with all the other authorities of Piedmont. He scorned the new parliament which had met at Turin after the war, and went there as an afterthought only once to complain of the treatment of his soldiers. In spite of the fact that Piedmont in its new form now had two armies, one in the north and another in the south (where the late Bourbon army had been taken over), he called for *volunteers* for the enterprise of capturing Rome. Although his homage to Victor Emmanuel was peremptory and sincere, it took the form of an injunction laid on those who obeyed him rather than a personal obedience. He claimed, in fact, complete freedom; from government, army and king. And by a stroke of unconscious irony he claimed this freedom in the name of Italy, which he proposed to save in spite of them.

In the year 1861 Garibaldi was the most popular man in Italy among the people of the country; his popularity extended through the length and breadth of Italy. Simultaneously, with those who held any kind of office, he was unpopular. He disclaimed Mazzini loudly. But by a process of *reductio ad absurdum* he found himself with the same followers and in the position of taking Mazzini's theoretical insurrection from him, converting it into a reality and handing it over to the king. There was no doubt that if he succeeded, this last gesture would also follow. But Victor Emmanuel disliked the prospect, with a very honest and instinctive dislike. He felt in his bones that if he got his power this way, as a gift from a demagogue with a streak of military genius, he might lose it by the same means. Mazzini was not displeased at the turn events were taking, and his smile was as enigmatical as ever.

As Garibaldi saw it, the position at the end of 1861 or in the spring of 1862 was the same as that in the spring of 1860, when he had set forth on the conquest of Sicily. It was the same, less Cavour; a better situation, therefore, in which Italy could be given the things it wanted. Italy, which, for purposes of action, was still Piedmont, wanted certain things and would not take them, being afraid of the bogey of European consequences. At the same time, he thought, Piedmont was still open to receive gifts which were pressed quietly into the palm of its hand while its face betrayed no knowledge of them. The thing most wanted was Rome. At the opening of the Chamber a year since, it had been discovered, almost with surprise, that by the action of Garibaldi (and the slight assistance of the Piedmontese regular army) that the new kingdom of Italy was in two parts, each as remote as it could be from the other. It consisted of Piedmont, Lombardy, the Central provinces, the Marches and Umbria recently filched from the Pope: and of the kingdom of Naples, which extended to the extremity of Sicily. Between these lay Rome, the natural capital, occupied by the Pope and held against the Italians and their nationalising enterprises by a French garrison. It was inevitable that, in the course of time, the junction would be effected. Cavour had been so sure of it that he spoke of Turin as a dead capital which he would quit with regret. The Chamber declared Rome to be the capital of Italy; and, having made this declaration, proceeded to other business. All that remained, in Garibaldi's opinion, was that Rome should be raided and handed over. The Pope, in spite of his *never, never*, was known to have made indirect inquiries and to have been told with great civility by the British government that in the event of his being in any distress, a British warship would be ready to take him off to a place of safety. In point of fact, the person of the Pope was in no danger. Garibaldi, a very dangerous sign, felt towards him as a man, very charitably. He was sorry for him as he had been for Francis II. In Garibaldi's mind there was no doubt at all that the enterprise which had been cut short in 1860 could be accomplished in 1862 with promptitude and complete success. He had dragged Italy so far on the way to victory. What she asked now was that she should be dragged the rest of the way.

It was a point of view founded on a contempt of his contemporaries who, like children, had to be given the things they had neither the sense nor the power to take for themselves. It rested on the axiom that Italy lacked courage, an ingredient it was his duty to supply; and it contained an implied insult that could be appreciated, especially by those who were proud enough to feel the truth of the criticism. But Garibaldi was not quick to see into other men's minds. He saw the history of Italy as a projection of his own destiny, the failure of Italy mixed up inextricably with his own failure. Always at the critical moment his action had been frustrated by that of the academic thinker, by the subtle, vulpine politician who, in the guise of Mazzini or Cavour, complicated issues which were simple, and halted the charge. He had two occasions in mind. Once Italy had been lost by Mazzini who, in Rome in 1849, had given command of the city to Roselli (*quel brav' uomo*, said Garibaldi ironically) when it ought to have come to himself. Again it had been lost by the intervention of Cavour in 1860. And on both occasions it was not only Italy which was sacrificed, but the purpose and heroism of Garibaldi and of the men in whom he had breathed his spirit. It is by no means certain that Garibaldi was wrong in this view. But, right or wrong, it was this vision of his past life, interlocked with that of Italy and frustrated by Italy's failures, that moved him now. He was alone, he thought, with the Re Galantuomo. The ruck of politicians did not count, now that Cavour was gone. He would take Rome, hand it over, take a scolding from Vittorio Emmanuele and, smiling gravely, return a satisfied man to Caprera. He had on some occasions acted on impulse. Now he acted with all the deliberation of a man achieving at last the great purpose of his life.

All the time he had a curious consciousness that it was

the Italians he was fighting for Italy, and no outside enemy. By the Italians he had been beaten. It seemed to him that he was holding in his hand a sword that had been snapped off short; he was taken back in mind to Sicily, the scene of his last completely victorious action, and, enveloped in a dream, he saw the future as the completion of an adventure which had been left unfinished. Instead of looking forward, he looked back, living through the days when the *Piemonte* and the *Lombardo* steamed silently southwards and the Thousand clambered on the mole at Marsala, while he smoked a cigar and joked with them under the eye of the Neapolitan cruisers. From that point, from Sicily, the adventure must be resumed and, like a drama, once misplayed, conducted to its full artistic finish. The vision he had seen on the beach in front of the Villa Spinola must be accomplished.

He had only to take a walking-stick and stroll into Rome. The Pope would have been in flight an hour later. But the memory of the unachieved masterpiece haunted him, and he went to Sicily.

On March 3, 1862, Garibaldi arrived at Turin. The ministry of Ricasoli, who had replaced Cavour, had fallen and a new cabinet was formed under Rattazzi. Ricasoli had been known as an honest man who openly proclaimed that when Rome was once more an Italian city, not only Italy would be free but the world also. Rattazzi was not generally held to be honest. It was said that he was the sigisbeo of the Princess de Solms, granddaughter of Lucien Bonaparte; he married this lady a year later, when she became a widow, and it was supposed that by this alliance the new minister fell unduly under the influence of Napoleon III, who was the chief supporter of the Pope. But Rattazzi was not openly opposed to Garibaldi. If he had been, his chances of remaining long as Prime Minister would have been slight. For Garibaldi epitomised the national will; and Rattazzi, like his predecessor Ricasoli, and like Victor Emmanuel himself, had to be careful not to rouse his opposition. But although the meeting of Rattazzi and Garibaldi passed off without any outward sign of rupture, the policy of Piedmont was now changed. Under Ricasoli it had been for a year a national policy, not a European one. Now Rattazzi returned to the Cavour tradition and proposed to play with the pawns on the European chessboard. He, too, like Garibaldi, was going to re-enact the imperfect drama of the past. His motives and intentions are still obscure: but the most charitable interpretation of them leads us to suppose that he was being cunning after the fashion (as he thought) of Cavour, and that he supposed that his cunning would inevitably be rewarded in the same manner. Garibaldi was not interested in his motives. He despised him. But it was the fact that Rattazzi had come to the ministry which determined his own line of action. Under Ricasoli there was no need for him to do other than Ricasoli; which was to support in an open manner the national programme. But when Rattazzi reverted to the policy of underhand negotiation, Garibaldi at once reverted also. He was cat's-paw again, as he had been in 1860. This time he would not stop until he got to Rome.

He told his followers that he had received pledges from the new ministry and that those pledges were to be redeemed immediately. In case Rattazzi changed his mind, Garibaldi began the dragging process at once, going from city to city in northern Italy and stimulating by his speeches the 'holy idea'. He assured Lord Palmerston in a letter that if England upheld the principle of non-intervention (by which he meant if England prevented the intervention of France), the Italians would secure the complete deliverance of their country *unassisted*. In general it appears to have been agreed between Rattazzi and Garibaldi (though there is no written evidence) that the latter would raise a corps of volunteers and use them as he pleased. Only Garibaldi must not openly declare that he was going to Rome. He might project an expedition to Greece, for example, and find himself elsewhere. Or he might begin with a sally against the Austrian Tyrol. Whatever he did the pantomime of official ignorance would be played as before. Piedmont would know nothing until the unexpected spoils were forced upon her.

For some reason or another there came a hitch in the plan. An expedition against the Tyrol was organised. But the participants were arrested by government order. Among them was Colonel Nullo, aide-de-camp to Garibaldi, whom the latter at once acknowledged as his agent. 'I consider it my duty', he wrote to the Milan *Gazette*, 'to declare that that officer acted exactly in conformity with my orders.'[1] The arrest had not been bloodless. There were killed and wounded at Brescia. The red-shirts had been fired on by the Piedmontese regular army. There followed a violent debate in the Chamber, and an enquiry was called for. But the affairs of Piedmont did not bear enquiry, and after some discussion the matter was suppressed. It may have given Garibaldi some hint of the real enemy. But it did not dismay him. He met the king's agent on June 15, at Belgirate, dined with him and took him for a row on Lake Maggiore. Then on June 28, Garibaldi landed at Palermo.

In a twinkling the news spread and the opera-house emptied. The sons of Victor Emmanuel, who were in a box, asked what had happened and were told that the great dictator had come. His courtesy towards them could not have been more exquisite, and next day they listened to him addressing a vast meeting held under the auspices of the National Rifle Clubs, and telling the crowd that there were two men in Italy who would never deceive them. 'They are', he said, 'Victor Emmanuel and myself.' The enthusiasm was tremendous. At Marsala there was a solemn service in the cathedral, and Garibaldi spoke again. His voice is said to have been calm and solemn. 'The time has come', he said, 'when we can no longer permit the stranger on our soil, holding in slavery a portion of our brethren. Italy can no longer abide this shame. . . . Shortly, yes, shortly, Rome is ours; yes, Rome, or death.'

[1] Chambers, *op. cit.* p. 183.

The Sicilians were alive to the poetry of the phrase. *Roma o la morte*, they shouted. Ever since his departure they had suffered from internal dissension, the secret propaganda of Bourbonist and Papal agents, as well as the ineptitude of Piedmontese officials. The one person they believed in was Garibaldi. In words which were no longer politic or wise he told them that Napoleon III was the enemy of Italy, that he schemed for the division of Italy, and had a prince of his own family ready to take the throne of Naples and another to assume power in Rome. The Pope he declared to be the enemy of true religion. 'I warn you', he said, 'to distinguish the true priests from the false, between priests who are ministers of God, and priests who are ministers of the Devil.' He was himself at the moment unable to distinguish between his function as the leader of an aggressive expedition and his mission as high priest of the national movement. The soldier had forgotten that the yelling multitude was his enemy. In the intoxication of the moment it seemed to him that it would be a glorious thing that Italy itself should march on Rome, a great procession of the young men of the nation proclaiming the faith that was in them, and proceeding to take up their inheritance by virtue of their strength and the justice of their cause. By the end of August the whole island was roused to fever heat, and once more the warships of the nations cruised expectantly in the waters of Sicily. Garibaldi was ready to embark. He had watched with amusement the panic of Rattazzi, who was now giving orders and countermanding them with a more than Cavourian fluency. He watched the great ships come one by one into the port of Catania.

The *Duke of Genoa*, of the Piedmontese navy, lay at anchor; and some said she would bombard the town if Garibaldi's expedition set sail. As before, a British frigate came up and worked her way in between, taking pride of place by natural right. Shortly after there came two postal steamers, one French, the *Général Abbalucci*, the other the *Dispaccio*, belonging to the Florio Steamship Company. It was Sunday morning, and the *Duke of Genoa* had left port for a short cruise, an event which occurred every day and which was always preceded by a warning to the harbourmaster that any ship leaving with volunteers would be fired on. No sooner was the *Duke of Genoa* out of port than Garibaldi stepped on each of the postal packets in turn and put their captains under arrest. The French captain protested and was rowed ashore and escorted to the French consulate, where, as Garibaldi said, he could make his protest in due form. At four o'clock the *Maria Adelaide*, another Piedmontese frigate which had joined the *Duke of Genoa* a few days before and now lay in the harbour, got up steam and, taking no notice of what was going forward, proceeded to sea. An hour later a seething crowd gathered to see the expedition off. The approaches to the harbour were gay with red-shirts. Flags flew and women waved their handkerchiefs from the windows. Boat-load after boat-load put off. The *Dispaccio* and the *Abbalucci* were chock full, and still more volunteers clamoured to be taken on board. The Piedmontese warships were obligingly remaining at sea. But it was ten o'clock before the two little ships staggered out of the harbour, with such a cargo of men as they had never carried before.

It was useless to command the surplus volunteers to disembark. They would not go. They were not soldiers, but zealots sitting at the feet of St. Joseph, ready to witness another miracle. And indeed it was a miracle that both ships did not founder with all souls. A puff on the water would have sent them to the bottom. But the night was calm. Outside, the *Maria Adelaide* spoke them respectfully and sheered off. They cast anchor not far off, while Garibaldi reflected what he had better do. He had been on many a full ship before, but never on one as full as was the *Dispaccio* at that moment. Darkness had fallen and he was uncertain whether to lie to until dawn or to pick his way east. At last he decided. The engines were started; they picked up a light, steady breeze, and at dawn the volunteers unshipped at Melito on the mainland. They were a little stiff, but none the worse. Every man had a red shirt and

GIUSEPPE GARIBALDI (1807-1882)
From a photograph

grey trousers. On the whole, too, they were indebted to the Piedmontese navy. It had behaved in the best Cavourian tradition.

On the beach lay the hulk of the *Torino*. For they had landed almost at the same spot as the volunteers of 1860, a desolate strip of beach behind which rose the mountains. Garibaldi remembered that fine ship and how he had spent nearly a whole day trying to float her after Bixio, with his usual headlong clumsiness, had run her aground. Just as Garibaldi thought he might succeed, some Neapolitan war-vessels hove in sight and pumped shot into her until she was quite destroyed; a silly, spiteful act, he thought, typical of the Bourbons. Now he could choose between three roads, eastwards by Gerace, the western road to Reggio or the road that lay between by San Lorenzo. He chose the road to Reggio because it was the one they had taken in 1860. This time, however, he noticed that the peasants were keeping out of the way. As they marched along by the coast they saw a Piedmontese cruiser, and presently they were surprised to hear a rattle of musketry and the whine of bullets. They were being fired on. There was just a hope that they might get into Reggio without mishap. At Sannazaro the column was greeted by a deputation of citizens from Reggio who had come to warn them that the town had been occupied by 4000 regulars, who had orders to hold Garibaldi. They implored him not to enter, and he agreed.

The column turned off to the right, following the bed of the San Nicolò torrent up into the mountains. In this way Garibaldi hoped to avoid an encounter with the Piedmontese troops. It was beginning to occur to him that they might not be so accommodating as the navy. But he thought that if he left them alone, they would leave him. He began to wonder, however, when on the 27th, as the column was straggling into the mountains, he heard a sound of firing from his rear. By the time he had ridden back to the end of the column it was all over, and it had been a mere skirmish. But there were dead and wounded on both sides.

He hoped by hard marching to distance his pursuers and give them a good excuse for losing him. But there was nothing to eat on the mountain. That day, the 27th, the column had only a few sheep which had been bought from a shepherd and which did not go round. Some of the volunteers ate nothing at all. They were, for the most part, very young, and a good number of them were town boys, wearing their town boots with the grey trousers. At the end of the second day they were footsore and desperately hungry. They did not know, nor did Garibaldi know, that the forced march had been in vain. Their guide either did not know his country or chose to mislead them; in reality they were not more than a day's march from their starting-point. The old soldiers kept to the head of the column with Garibaldi, while the remainder struggled on some way behind. On the 28th they reached Aspromonte, in the middle of the pine forests. They had been told there was some sort of chalet there where they would be able to get provisions. But it was locked and empty. They pulled up a field of potatoes and chewed them raw. Then a few dry sticks were lit and more potatoes roasted. They were, says Garibaldi, delicious. In groups of twos and threes the stragglers came up and threw themselves down. Some had cast away their equipment. But the majority, though dropping with fatigue and hunger, made a pitiful attempt to look like soldiers. They had faith in Garibaldi. Presently a few peasant women came with baskets of food. When the roll was called a little later it was found that five hundred men were missing, either lost in the mountains or cut off by the regular troops. No doubt, too, a few had found it easier to pull off their red shirts and slip down to the plain.

Garibaldi sent out officers to buy up provisions. They had good money with them, and there was little likelihood that they would be refused. But he was not sure what to do. On the next days his troops would be fed. Perhaps the missing five hundred would come up. And what then? He could make a two hours' march to Santa Eufemia, a small township from which he had received messages of welcome. He could divide his force in two and send half to Santa Eufemia and half somewhere else. Or, as he had often done before, he could scatter the men and tell them to meet somewhere farther north. Any one of these measures would have gained time. But for the first time in his life he could not come to a decision. There was an unreality about the situation which prevented his mind from grasping it effectively. Next day (it was some time before noon) he could see a column of troops moving through the trees below; it was about three miles off, but it was marching swiftly. In the nearer foreground he detected little groups and isolated figures which turned out to be women and boys bringing provisions.

Garibaldi lost his hesitation. Instinctively he drew his troops up to the highest point, extended them in a short semi-circle from which they could fire down on the attackers, while their flanks left and right were covered and the buttress of rock protected them from behind. Menotti was sent to command on the left wing, General Corrao on the right, while Garibaldi himself took the middle. From his position he could see the hostile troops on the opposite hill. It was beginning to look as if they really meant to catch him.

Rattazzi, like Cavour, had been obliged to take notice of the French protests, and he had sent General Cialdini from Genoa with orders 'to combat Garibaldi in Sicily'. These instructions were sufficiently vague, and Cialdini did not know what they meant. He left Genoa on August 24, believing he would find Garibaldi in Sicily. But at Naples he was informed by General La Marmora that the object of his instructions, 'contrary to all reasonable expectations',[1] had disembarked on the mainland near Melito. General Cialdini's mission was therefore over. He could not 'combat Garibaldi in Sicily' if Garibaldi was not in Sicily. But, to make sure, he went to Messina,

[1] *Report of General Cialdini to the Minister of War at Turin.* See Chambers, p. 235.

arriving on the morning of the 27th, and found all quiet. Instead of returning to Genoa, however, he took ship to Reggio, where he discovered an active officer whose 'first dispositions bore the stamp of the energetic resolution which is natural to him' in charge of the garrison. The officer in question was Colonel Pallavicini of the bersaglieri: and the dispositions concerned the manner in which Garibaldi had been warned off from Reggio. We cannot diagnose the actions of General Cialdini at this point with any certainty. But if he had been madly jealous of Garibaldi, and if he had suddenly perceived that here was the chance to humiliate a man who by his triumphs had so long humiliated the professional army of Piedmont, he would not have behaved differently. He had no right to take any action at all. He was not the officer in command of the district, which was under La Marmora. However, on his confession (which he seems to have made with some pride) he expressed himself as happy to meet Pallavicini 'so opportunely', and ordered the latter to set out with six or seven battalions. Pallavicini was 'to make every effort to come up with Garibaldi . . . and to pursue him constantly without giving him a moment's repose; to attack him if he sought to escape and destroy him if he accepted battle.' 'I ordered him', says Cialdini, 'not to treat with Garibaldi, and only to accept a surrender at discretion.' At the same time Cialdini arranged to send out other columns to close every road by which Garibaldi could make away into the interior. He knew Garibaldi, and he did not think that Pallavicini, able officer though he was, would succeed in catching him.

In this surmise Cialdini was quite right. The outcome of any immediate encounter did not depend on Pallavicini, but on Garibaldi. The latter was capable of taking care of himself for at least a few weeks; and of enjoying the experience. But his object was to go to Rome, avoiding, as he did so, the official attentions of the Piedmontese army, which was proving to be aggressive in an unexpected degree. Neither from Rattazzi nor from Victor Emmanuel had he been led to expect anything worse than the usual public demonstration of disapproval. In the stress of the moment he did not reflect that the regular army had a private grievance against him, and that the vacillations of authority gave it an opportunity to exercise it. But on this point he was to have sharp evidence. The bersaglieri on the opposite slope had no sooner extended into line than, without a word or challenge, they opened a murderous fire, to which, without order on Garibaldi's part, there came a brisk reply from Menotti's end of the line. The position, in spite of the vigour of the attack, was impregnable. It could have been held by 500 men against 5000. But the salvo of musketry brought Garibaldi to his senses. This was civil war. The men in front of him were the same who had defended Rome, sons of the same Mother Italy, men whose very faces he must know, and who bore wounds received under his command. He shouted to his buglers to blow 'Cease fire' and sent peremptory orders to the left, where Menotti's youngsters were beginning to warm to the fight. The fire of the bersaglieri continued, while Garibaldi's veterans took cover and waited explanations. The general stood erect in the centre of the line, turning frequently to repeat the order that there must be no reply. His officers sat down obediently. One of them saw him shiver slightly. He took two or three short steps and then he staggered. He continued to shiver as the officer held him. Then he raised his hat and cried several times: *'Viva Italia! Viva Italia!'*

He was lifted and carried into the shelter of the forest. But he turned in anguish, shouting, 'What do you do with my people?'

Colonel Pallavicini, who came up to say politely to the wounded prisoner that it was the 'unhappiest day of his life', found Garibaldi smoking a cigar.[1]

[1] The evidence for this account will be found in the *Memorie*, p. 491 ff.; Guerzoni, ii. p. 314 ff.; Chambers, p. 223 ff.; Martinengo-Cesaresco, p. 348 f.

CONCLUSION

GARIBALDI had received wounds in the right foot and left thigh. The wound in the thigh was a mere scratch which healed promptly, but it was discovered that a bullet was lodged under the instep of the wounded foot; and only after many months was it extracted. He had meantime been held a prisoner on a capital charge of treason, but popular indignation was so great that he was granted a free pardon and allowed to return to Caprera. There, after a time, he was able to leave his bath-chair and hobble about on crutches.

The adventure of Aspromonte had not damaged his fame in England. A Mrs. Chambers, delegated by an English committee, installed herself at Caprera and pestered Garibaldi until he consented to come to England. He did not understand why the English should be so eager to see him, but he thought the visit might indirectly be of service to Italy; in the spring of 1864 he came, landing on a rainy Sunday morning at Southampton and being whisked off to the house of the Seelys in the Isle of Wight. It was feared that his visit might be the occasion of political disturbance (although Palmerston was sure that Garibaldi himself would never 'lift a finger' to create trouble in England). He was carefully shepherded and taken like an Eastern potentate to see a broadside fired at Portsmouth and to visit Tennyson at Freshwater. There was an exchange of courtesies. Garibaldi planted a tree and listened to Tennyson reciting a few of his poems. And the visitor declaimed his favourite poem, Foscolo's *I Sepolcri*, although Tennyson did not understand Italian.

The government would gladly have kept Garibaldi in the Isle of Wight. But that was not possible. The committee of reception was clamouring for him; and on April

11, 1864, he took the train to Nine Elms Station, and there stepped into a carriage which conveyed him by Westminster and Trafalgar Square to Stafford House, the home of the Duchess of Sutherland. The crowd was enormous and its enthusiasm indescribable. The carriage took six hours to traverse five miles. By the time it reached Stafford House it was falling to pieces, and Garibaldi's right hand, which had been shaken thousands of times, was black with hospitable grime. He showed to the crowd the same courtesy as to the members of the nobility; indeed he astonished even those who knew him by his ease in all kinds of company. The Lord Mayor and aldermen welcomed him at a banquet, the inhabitants of St. Pancras sent a delegation to remind him that their patron saint was the same San Pancrazio whose gate he had defended at Rome, he shook hands with innumerable Oddfellows and Foresters and members of more than half the corporations of London; while at Chiswick, visiting the Dowager Duchess of Sutherland, he was seen to produce one of his long, cheap cigars and begin to smoke without invitation. No one had ever done such a thing in such a presence before, and the Earl of Malmesbury recorded the event in a letter.

It was a trivial event. But it was characteristic. It showed that Garibaldi could not be altered to suit local circumstances: and, for all their nursing, the distinguished hosts of the great Italian found they could do nothing with him. Gladstone emerged discomfited from a talk on religion. Palmerston suggested that the affairs of Venice could safely be left to time and diplomacy. 'It is never too soon', said Garibaldi, blushing a fiery red, 'for slaves to break their chains.' In great matters as in small, he had to be allowed to do as he pleased; for, while his condescension was perfect and his compliments sincere, he could not be drawn to this party or that. In the end it did not appear certain whether he was a joke played by the Liberals on the Tories, by the Tories on the Liberals, or by the New Democracy on both. The Duke of Sutherland, acting on instructions from the government, stepped in with an invitation to a cruise in the Far East: and Garibaldi, in some disgust at the political squabbles to which his visit had given rise, accepted. He suspected that the Italian Foreign Office had helped to bring his visit to a conclusion, and his friends told him secretly that the tour in the Far East was meant to keep him away from Italy. He insisted, therefore, on being set down at Caprera, whither he returned, with some relief, on May 9. A French journalist wrote in the *Courrier du dimanche* that the English had filled Garibaldi with turtle soup, plum pudding and sandwiches, but had not contributed a halfpenny to his Million Rifle Fund. It was a cynical view, but it was near enough the truth.[1]

This visit represented the climax and the end of Garibaldi's popularity in England. The government did not readily forget the roar that greeted him at Nine Elms Station and followed his progress through the civilised streets of London. It was a noise that had no relation to polite government, but was akin rather to the deep forces of nature, to the booming of the sea or the murmur of the jungle. It came out of the hearts of men who had fastened on Garibaldi all their dreams of power and freedom; who respected in him something that was greater and more real than the conventions by which they were bound. They did not see in Garibaldi the sailor who made kings: for the crowd did not know whether Garibaldi was the friend of Victor Emmanuel or his enemy. They did not applaud the enemy of the Pope, for there were Catholics as well as Protestants amongst them. They did not see in him the maker of modern Italy, for Italy was still to the majority of them, as Metternich had contemptuously described it, a 'geographical expression'. His significance transcended politics. It was human, poetical, religious. Garibaldi was, to them, the free man, bound only to the utmost loyalties of the earth, rooted like the trees in the soil, bearing, like them, a proud head towards a mysterious sky, a man great in his completeness and in his shortcomings. The sight of

[1] Guerzoni, ii. p. 391.

him shook them profoundly. They did not need to be told that Garibaldi was a humble man. Instinctively they knew that the man in the carriage was the son of the Signora Rosa. Had they known her they would have said that his purpose in the world was what hers had been. Only the mother had gone with a shopping basket and the son with a sword.

Garibaldi was beginning to perceive that he would shortly be excluded altogether from the Italian nation which he had created: and as this was in part the result of his own desire, he was not distressed. But he still wished to see Victor Emmanuel in Rome, to drag him there, crown him and apologise. It was a scheme set fast in his brain, one which dated back to the hopeful days of Montevideo, and no argument could convince him that it was now needless. But Victor Emmanuel managed to get to Rome without him. In 1866 the new Italian nation took advantage of Austria's embarrassments with Germany to declare war; and although it was badly beaten it secured Venetia. Garibaldi, still hampered by his wounded foot, took part in the campaign, and then, to complete what had been left undone, marched on Rome, from which he was driven off by the French garrison. Italy, however, had learned its lesson from Cavour. It bided its time. And in 1870 the Emperor of the French met his fate at the battle of Sedan. While the French allies of the Pope were engaged in a life and death struggle against the armies of the new German state, an Italian army respectfully took possession of Rome. It was less proud of being there than of having got there without the help of Garibaldi. The latter, like a compass needle seeking the true north, discarded the great purpose of his life, which he saw now fulfilled; he read with anxiety the news of the French defeats. Such things had not happened before in his lifetime; and all the memories of his youth rose up to tell him that, whatever might have been her recent behaviour, France was the cradle of such political liberty as the world enjoyed. With the abdication of the emperor she was what, in spirit, she always had been, a free republic. Garibaldi had seldom shown himself more sublimely obstinate. He set off for France and commanded an army of four or five thousand men in the operations of 1871; and, on his way back to Italy, he forebore to mention the matter of Nice. The Cavourian nuances of Italian policy always escaped him, and he said it was not a proper time to bring up such a matter.

His loyalty to Italy was too much of a habit to be discarded. But it mingled curiously with new gestures of thought. He perceived that the nations which had laboriously created themselves now fought with each other; and, seeking some escape from the cycle of error, he said that they must fight for peace amongst themselves and brotherhood. In part this conclusion was the outcome of disillusion; he saw that when Italy was stitched together, made one fabric by his sword, there was as much unhappiness as before and as many unsolved problems. He did not renounce what he had done, however, but conceived the future amalgamation of the nations as an extension and completion of his work. And this hope he found abetted by the less intelligible part of himself. The more he tried to realise national differences the less he appreciated them, except as matters of momentary passion and pride. On the other hand, he was conscious of an elementary sympathy which united him easily with other men, and still more easily with the inarticulate members of the creation. He remembered how, after a hard day's riding in South America, he took the saddle off his horse and led him to water, how he rubbed the sweat off the animal, fed him and watched him lie down; and he thought there could be no deeper happiness in a man than what he felt when he had done these things and rolled himself in his blanket to go to sleep. He remembered too, his dog Castor, which he had left with the English consul Murray at Tangier, when he left for his second sojourn in America. He thought that the dog would be best with the kind Englishman and be sure of its food; whereas he himself might have to starve. But the dog died of grief. In view of such circumstances, Garibaldi did not think that there was a case for the separation of created things into hostile categories. No quarrels could undo the bonds which made the life of humanity a part of the general life of the earth; and it seemed to him, when he reflected quietly, that quarrels which disturbed this deep unity were vain and foolish.

He did not esteem this thinking profound. Nor was he ever able to formulate his thought or extinguish its little contradictions. It was part of himself; even he could not dislodge it for the purpose of examination. It expressed itself in conversation, sometimes in letters, of which he wrote a great many; a little of it found its way into his memoirs, which he began to write out finally after his return from France: but mostly it revealed itself in his behaviour. He was not easy to get on with; for, in spite of his disabilities, he had not grown old. His body was that of an old soldier, marked with wounds and crippled with rheumatism. Arthritis frequently prevented him from writing. It twisted hands and feet. But while he could walk he walked; and when he could not, he pushed himself about in a chair, cursing the fate that held him. Only a modicum of the life that was in him could come out in what he said or wrote. The rest had to be expressed in what he did. And when at last he could do little, his body failing while his spirit remained exactly the same age as it had always been, the task of those about him was not easy. He consented to take a little wine to warm his blood. But his diet remained as simple as before, fish rather than flesh, and fruit rather than fish. His doctor told him he should not take baths so frequently. But that was one of his habits, and he stuck to it. His Italian admirers could not understand why a man should want to wash himself so much. They understood more readily his other tricks, the care with which he brushed his hair, for example. It was thin on top of his head and quite white. But at the back and sides it was still abundant. The mane of the lion remained to the end.

His family was baffled by the complete integrity of his

old age. He was compliant and helpful in things which concerned them; but obstinate in things which concerned himself. Like Victor Emmanuel, they were not sure whether it was Garibaldi's virtue or the lack of it that was the trouble. No state could have been more admirably managed than were the affairs that Garibaldi administered himself. Yet no profit came out of the things he touched. No money grew out of Caprera for all the labour that was spent on it. It was like one of the hero's shirts, soberly patched, well mended, and growing more threadbare every year. To his sons, who had learned to spend money, his poverty was painful. They argued him into the belief that he ought to be providing for his family; and he, with that modesty which was the mark of the privacy of his thought, did not tell them what they might have learned from the study of his life, but remarked only that he had always had enough. To provide money for his family he began negotiations for the sale of his memoirs. And, after much persuasion, he agreed to accept a pension. They had, he said dolefully, made him a servant after all.

But not entirely. Sometime in 1866 Teresa and her husband Canzio brought a Lombard peasant girl to Caprera to act as nurse to their youngest child. Her name was Francesca Armosino, and she was about twenty-six, sturdy but not good-looking. When the Canzios' visit came to an end and they wished to take Francesca with them, Garibaldi refused to let the girl go; and in February 1867, Francesca gave birth to a daughter, Clelia, 'pale and not at all pretty', said Madame Schwartz of the baby when she saw her a year later. In order that Francesca's child should receive Madame Schwartz with proper ceremony, she was decorated with a pair of wings. But Madame Schwartz was not edified. She was already paying for the education of Battistina's daughter in a school in Switzerland and receiving small thanks for her pains. Anita had slapped Madame Schwartz's face and rolled on the ground when the latter took her away from Caprera; and Garibaldi, who thought that children could do no wrong, had not reproached his daughter. In the end Garibaldi and Madame Schwartz quarrelled over some such matter concerning Anita, who was brought back to Caprera and died there of fever in 1875. After that time Madame Schwartz did not see Garibaldi again.

Francesca was a good woman. As Garibaldi grew older he found in her an understanding of his way of life that he sought in vain elsewhere; perhaps she was not altogether unlike the first Anita. Madame Schwartz and Garibaldi's grown-up children thought she had too much influence over him; they certainly had little. It seemed as if the peasant woman had weaned the great man from the affairs of the world and begun a new life for him, a simple life circumscribed by the walls of Caprera. Another girl was born in July, 1869, and called Rosita: but like her namesake of Montevideo, she was short-lived, dying while Garibaldi was absent in France in 1871. Then in April, 1873, came a boy, Manlio.

Francesca may have told Garibaldi that it was not fair that these children of hers should not bear their father's name. They were the last happiness of his old age; as Francesca was the guardian of it. For Teresa came only once after the dispute over Francesca.[1] The obstacle in the way of Francesca's wishes was not any reluctance on the part of Garibaldi, whose naturalism in love was always accompanied by a sense of responsibility. But he was married in law to Giuseppina Raimondi, and could not legitimise Francesca's position until that marriage had been dissolved. He moved heaven and earth to get this done. Giuseppina had no objections, but the legal problem was difficult. At last, however, after the civil tribunal of Rome had rejected Garibaldi's application in 1879, and Victor Emmanuel had declared he could do nothing to alter the course of the law, the court of appeal consented to the dissolution of the marriage in January, 1880, on the ground that the contract was made under the Austrian régime and that Austrian law permitted divorce when the marriage had

[1] Elpis Melena, p. 256, note 1.

not been consummated. No sooner had this judgment reached Caprera than Garibaldi hastened to acknowledge Francesca. The verdict of the court was promulgated on January 14; and on January 26 the Mayor of Maddalena came to Caprera to perform the ceremony.

Menotti brought his wife, Italia Bedeschini-Garibaldi; and Canzio was present with Teresa. A witness who wrote describing the occasion to Madame Schwartz said: 'The General's face shone with joy. He sat with the air of a patriarch in his rocking armchair, wrapped in a poncho white as snow, and with a red handkerchief round his neck. Donna Francesca was dressed in white. After the formality, in the course of which Garibaldi defined himself as a husbandman, a dinner took place, at which his family, his friends, and the Mayor of Maddalena assisted. Countless telegrams of congratulation poured in, and among them was one from King Humbert'.[1]

There was no telegram from Victor Emmanuel, who had died two years before and been succeeded by his son Umberto; and there was none from the great conspirator Mazzini, who lived just long enough to see Italy united before he, too, passed from the scene in 1872. Alone of all the greatest artisans of Italian freedom Garibaldi remained; and he, too, was near death. On his last visit to Milan in 1879 he looked as he sat in his carriage, white-haired and pale, like the figure of a saint taken from one of the churches. 'Pare Sant' Ambrogio!' the people said.[2]

He had heard from Captain Roberts of Maddalena, how the body of Shelley had been burned; and he asked Jessie White Mario to tell him the story more exactly, saying, when he heard it again: 'That is the right thing, and it is a beautiful and healthy thing also; you defy worms and corruption, you do not contaminate the air of the living'. For a man who had gone about the world like himself, he felt it to be a proper end also; because the world, as Galileo had discovered, was a dust in space, in each fragment of which lived the spirit of its creator, so that all things animate

[1] Elpis Melena, p. 325 and note.   [2] Guerzoni, ii. p. 600.

and inanimate were one, and there was no beginning and no end; but a scattering of dust and the spirit rising from it. He spoke to his friend Nuvolari a good deal on this subject, giving him precise instructions:

'You will make a pyre of acacia,' he said; 'it burns like oil: and place me, dressed in my red shirt, my face upturned to the sun, on an iron bedstead. When my body is consumed, put the ashes into an urn (any pot will do), and place it on the wall behind the tombs of Anita and Rosita. I mean to finish so.'

Having obtained a promise from a doctor that he would supervise the burning of his body, Garibaldi wrote to him:

You have kindly promised to burn my body. I am grateful to you. On the road leading from this house northwards to the sea, about three hundred paces to the right, there is a hollow bounded by a wall. In that corner build up a pyre, about two metres long, of acacia, myrtle, linden, and other aromatic woods. Place on the pyre an iron couch, and on that my open bier, with my body dressed in the red shirt. A handful of ashes preserved in any sort of receptacle should be placed in the little sepulchre where are the ashes of Rosa and Anita.

These instructions were given in 1877.[1] He was to be burned, he explained insistently, not cremated: 'I have no wish to be put into one of those ovens they call crematoriums'; his intention was that he should be burned in the open air and, fearing that it would not be literally carried out if it were left to strangers, he made Francesca promise that as soon as he was dead and *before* any news of his death was sent to the mainland, she would see that his will was obeyed.

He suffered a good deal now from senile catarrh, and on the morning of June 1, 1882, he complained of an oppression on his chest. He was much worse the next day. But he lay looking out hopefully to the sea, and asked Menotti if he could see the steam of the ship that was bringing a doctor from Palermo. Two finches who knew him played on the window-sill. 'Feed them when I am gone', he said. His blue eye clouded over and he sank into coma. At six o'clock, on the evening of June 2, he was dead.

[1] Mario, *Supplement*, p. 460.

They had not the courage to burn him. Francesca protested. But the body of the hero was taken and buried in a grave, while those elements of which he had known it as a part, protested in a raging storm.[1]

[1] Mario, *Supplement*, p. 461.

REFERENCES

In addition to texts already cited, see

Bandi, G., *I Mille*. 1906.

Bianchi, N., *Il Conte Camillo Cavour*. Turin. 1863.

Chiala, L., *Lettere edite e inedite di Camillo Cavour*. 6 vols.

Ciàmpoli, D., *Scritti politici e militari di G. Garibaldi*. 1907.

Bolton King, *A History of Italian Unity*, 1814-1871. 1898. 2 vols.

Mario, Jessie White, *Garibaldi e i suoi tempi*. Milan. 1884 and 1905.

Chiesa, J. della, *Noterelle Varesini*. Varese. 1906.

Falconi, A., *Come e quando G. scelse per sua dimora Caprera*. Cagliari. 1902.

Vecchi, C. A., *Garibaldi a Caprera*. Bologna. 1910.

Curàtulo. *Garibaldi, Vittorio Emmanuele e Cavour nei fasti della patria*. Bologna, 1911. *Il dissidio tra Mazzini e Garibaldi*. Milan. 1928.

Bidischini, F., *Garibaldi nella vita intima*. Florence. 1907.

Mazzini, *Scritti editi e inediti*. 17 vols.

Menghini, M., *La spedizione Garibaldina di Sicilia e di Napoli, nei proclami, nelle corrispondenze, nei diarii*, etc. 1907.

Mundy, Rear-Admiral Sir Rodney, *H.M.S. 'Hannibal' at Palermo and Naples*, 1859-1861.

Fagan, L., *Life of Sir A. Panizzi*. 1880.

Persano, *Diario privato, politico, militare*. 1880.

Thayer, W. R., *Throne Makers*. 1899.

Whitehouse, H. K., *Collapse of the Kingdom of Naples*. New York. 1899.

Winnington-Ingram, *Hearts of Oak*. 1889.

Luzio, A., *Garibaldi, Cavour, Verdi. Nuova serie di Studi*. 1924.

Cesari, C., *La Campagna di Garibaldi nell'Italia meridionale*, 1860. 1928.

Starritt, S. Stuart, *Garibaldi the Liberator*. 1929.

Fabietti, E., *Garibaldi. L'anima e la vita*. Milan. 1930.

Edizione Nazionale degli Scritti di G. Garibaldi. Bologna. 1933. *In progress*.

Trevelyan, *Garibaldi and The Making of Modern Italy* (now exists in several editions. My references are to the edition of 1928). In addition to the very complete bibliographies to be found in Trevelyan, consult Quarenghi, *Bibliogr. relat. al gen. G. Garibaldi* in *Rivista mil. it.* xxvii, 1882; Vismara, A., *Materiali per una bibl. del gen. G. Garibaldi*, Como, 1891; and Guerrini, D., *Saggio di bibliografia garibaldina* in *Garibaldi e i garibaldini*, Como, 1910.

APPENDIX A

GARIBALDI'S MEMOIRS AND OTHER WRITINGS

THE EDITIONS in which the memoirs of Garibaldi are to be found fall into two groups.

(*a*) Garibaldi began to compose a history of his life at Tangier in the autumn of 1849. He took the manuscript with him to America, where he continued it and completed it up to the year 1848 (departure from Montevideo). It was given to the American Theodore Dwight for immediate translation and publication. But for reasons which are not wholly clear, Garibaldi told Dwight to defer the work to a later time. It appeared in 1859 as *The Life of General Garibaldi, written by himself, with sketches of his companions in arms*. Translated by Theodore Dwight, New York. This version exists only in English and not in Italian.

Presumably Garibaldi retained either the original or a copy of this manuscript and brought it to Italy on his return from America. On this manuscript, more or less modified by himself, were based three further editions: *viz.*:

(1) In Carrano, F. *Cacciatori delle Alpi*. Turin. 1860.
(2) Dumas. *Mémoires de Garibaldi*. 3 vols. Brussels. 1860 (in French).
(3) Elpis Melena. Garibaldi's *Denkwürdigkeiten*. Hamburg. 1861. 2 vols.

All three editors had personal access to Garibaldi, and varied the text in places with his permission or on his advice. They also supplied the hiatus between 1848 and 1860 from MS. supplied by Garibaldi.

(*b*) Garibaldi took advantage of his enforced leisure after the collapse of the 1859 campaign to begin writing again. He was at this time in the house of the Marchese Raimondi on Lake Como, awaiting his marriage with the latter's daughter; and it seems that he carried forward his tale to the campaign of 1859 and had begun a chapter on his relations with Giuseppina Raimondi when the unfortunate conclusion of the marriage made him lay down his pen. He did not resume writing until after the conquest of Sicily, when, on his return to Caprera, he added the account of this expedition.

Not until after the French campaign of 1871, however, did he again think of publishing his memoirs, for which an offer had been made by the city of Palermo. The negotiations for purchase fell through. But Garibaldi completed the task of revision, and this manuscript passed into the possession of his sons Menotti and Ricciotti. On this final or revised version is based the first independent Italian edition: *viz.*:

Garibaldi, Memorie autobiografiche. Florence. 1888 (of which various translations were made, including an English translation by Jessie White Mario).

A second edition, based on the same MS., appeared for the centenary of Garibaldi's birth: *viz.*:

Memorie di Giuseppe Garibaldi. Turin. 1907 (edited by E. Nathan).

A standard edition of his works and correspondence is now in progress. Of this the two volumes which have already appeared deal with the memoirs. The first presents a text of the memoirs from a MS. anterior to the final redaction (Milan, Museo del Risorgimento): the second gives, once more, the text of the MS. of 1872.

There is no text presenting *all* the variants of the MSS. and printed versions. A critical edition would bring out the evolution in Garibaldi's thought on many matters and would be of great value.

Mr. R. S. Garnett's translation (*The Memoirs of Garibaldi*, Benn, 1931) offers the most complete text for the English reader. It was supposed that certain passages found in this (Dumas') version had been interpolated without authority by the French novelist. But this supposition was shown to be erroneous by A. Luzio in an article in the *Corriere della Sera*, September 15, 1907. Some of the passages found in Dumas and not in the Italian edition based on the revised MS. of 1872, were suppressed by Garibaldi for reasons of modesty or because they expressed opinions which he no longer held. Others were no doubt suggested by Garibaldi himself in January 1860 when Dumas visited him at Fino.

In 1870 Garibaldi began a versified autobiography but abandoned it. A fragment, dealing with the death of Anita, is preserved in the Biblioteca Classense at Ravenna.

After the unsuccessful attempt on Rome in 1867 Garibaldi wrote a novel, *Il Governo del Monaco*, of which the first edition was published in Milan in 1870, with simultaneous translations into English (Cassell, 1870) and German. A French edition, *La Domination du Moine*, appeared in Paris in 1873. The *Saturday Review* hoped that the 'stuff' was not really by Garibaldi. 'Garibaldi', it said, 'has suffered before now from the indiscretion of his intimates, and we fear he has on this occasion been flattered into an exhibition of weakness which will cause triumph to his enemies. He was never credited with much wordly wisdom; but we would scarcely have believed, except from his own mouth, that he was capable of talking such nonsense as fills the *Rule of the Monk*.... The book is like the first attempt of an enthusiastic and rather clever lad.... This strange mixture of absolute childishness with genuine heroism would make Garibaldi a far better hero than author, of a romance.' The story belongs more in type to the fiction of the first years of the nineteenth century, of which it presents the stock characters, the rich English young sculptor, etc.; and on this background is grafted the tale of 1867 in adapted form, fifty patriots defeating a thousand Papal troops and dying in Rome in defence of the Italian idea. From the psychological point of view, the story offers considerable interest, revealing the atmosphere of make-believe which, in one form or another, was the atmosphere of all Garibaldi's enterprises.

I Mille (Turin, 1874) is a mixture of fiction and history, but the historical element predominates. It is Garibaldi's own account of the Sicilian adventure.

The *Ricordi* which Guerzoni used for his biography of Garibaldi were published more fully by Ciampoli, D., as *Scritti politici e militari, Ricordi e pensieri inediti, raccolti su autografi, stampi e manoscritti*, Rome, 1908.

Garibaldi's verses were published by Carducci, *Versi e prose*, Bologna, 1907 (2nd edition): also by Curàtulo, *Poema autobiografico —Carme alla Morte: altri canti inediti*, Bologna, 1911.

Various papers are also enumerated by Curàtulo in *Autografi documenti storici e cimeli riguardanti Garibaldi e il Risorgimento italiano*, Rome, 1917.

APPENDIX B

SOUTH AMERICA

(1) RIO GRANDE DO SUL, the state on whose behalf Garibaldi first waged war in South America, constitutes the extreme southern apex of the Brazilian empire; and its function was to act, like the adjacent Banda Oriental or Oriental Republic, as a buffer between the Brazilian empire on the north and the Argentine Federation on the south. The Brazilian empire belonged to Portugal, while the Argentine was a sphere of Spanish influence.

In reality, both the north and south of the continent were bound by very slight ties to Europe. Discovered in the sixteenth century by Spanish and Portuguese explorers, the continent was subjected and colonised in the succeeding centuries, the original settlers intermarrying with the native Indians and forming a mixed race of creoles between whom and the Spaniards and Portuguese who continued to come from Europe there grew up a considerable racial hatred. The administrative posts were mostly held by the latter, while the creoles were responsible for the commercial development of the country. The wealth of Brazil was of varied character. But until the eighteenth century both Brazil and the other states of the northern part of the continent were considered merely as gold mines. Spain and Portugal required only that all the gold of the new continent should find its way to Lisbon and Cadiz. Other trade was discouraged. But, in fact, the development of gold and other mining in the north led to the need for food, and so to the discovery of another source of wealth, the cattle of the Argentine pampas. With the growth of cattle-rearing on the Argentine pampas and on the plains of the Banda Oriental and Rio Grande do Sul, the importance of the Argentine increased and the port of the Argentine, Buenos Ayres, began to take rank with Rio de Janeiro. Simultaneously rival interests began to covet the estuary of the River Plate. The English and the French were interested as well as the Spaniards. All these claimants were driven off, and a treaty between Brazil and the Argentine recognised and guaranteed the independence of the Banda Oriental which had its own port, Montevideo, on the northern side of the Plate estuary. When, in the course of the eighteenth century, the two great blocks of the continent established their right to trade freely with Europe, their independence became a matter of practical fact. Their problems were, thereafter, internal problems, in particular the adjustment of the relations between the coast cities and the vast hinterland which fed them. The cities were natural republics: whereas the feudal captaincies of the seventeenth century survived in the interior.

In the first half of the nineteenth century this process of internal adjustment was complicated by European relations. Buenos Ayres declared itself a republic in 1810: but it had to defeat the Spanish garrisons and then impose its own authority on rebellious local chieftains, a task that was not completed by the middle of the century. In Brazil a similar position was complicated by the arrival in the early part of 1808 of a few shiploads of Portuguese, among whom was the prince-regent of Portugal, expelled by the advance of Junot's French army. He was accepted as a constitutional ruler: but when news of the Spanish revolt of 1820 reached Brazil he was obliged to hand over the sceptre to his son, who granted all popular demands and in 1822 declared Brazil an independent empire. This son, Pedro I, had to deal with the same problem as faced the republicans of Buenos Ayres; having proclaimed a form of government, he had to impose it by defeating the remaining Portuguese garrisons and by coping with local revolts of one kind or another. In addition there was the question of the River Plate, which Pedro sought to solve by making war on the Argentine; as a result of this war he abandoned Uruguay (or Banda Oriental), which his father had conquered, and the independence of this state was recognised (1828). Pedro I proved to be reactionary and, on the outbreak of the 1830 revolution in Paris, he was met by a similar movement in Brazil before which he was obliged to abdicate in favour of his infant son. A regency followed (1831), during which there were revolts in nearly every province of Brazil. Of these the most obstinate and considerable was the revolt of Rio Grande do Sul.

Its immediate cause was the unpopularity of the Portuguese officials. The revolt was backed by the gauchos and estancieros of Rio Grande, so that the governor was obliged to flee from Porto Alegre. A new governor was not successful in restoring order; and an army was sent and defeated the republicans at the battle of Fanfa, where their leader, Bento Gonçales de Silva, was captured. With him was an Italian, Livio Zambeccari, a political exile from Italy, who had become acquainted with the republicans of Porto Alegre at the lodge of the local freemasons. According to Assis Brasil, the historian of the Rio Grande republic, Zambeccari supplied the intellectual ferment which led to the revolt.

It is not known in what precise circumstances Garibaldi met Zambeccari. A romantic legend declares that while the former was at Rio de Janeiro he saw a boat-load of prisoners being taken to the fortress of Santa Cruz and heard them speaking Italian. But probably through the Italian freemasons of Rio de Janeiro Garibaldi was enabled to negotiate with Gonçales and so to obtain the letters of marque with which, on May 4, 1837, he began his campaign.

Apart from Garibaldi's narrative in the *Memoirs* there does not appear to be any source of information of first-hand value on the Rio Grande war: but, although this part of Garibaldi's story was written with the object of arousing interest (and not, like the latter part, with a view of providing a text and a lesson for young Italians), its general accuracy may be taken as certain. Garibaldi had a very clear recollection of the sequence of events; only in matters of date is he approximate.

The war continued sporadically until 1845, when General Caxias, dispatched by the Emperor Pedro II, gained two victories over the Rio Grande rebels and followed these up by a promise of an amnesty. In the spring of 1845 Rio Grande accepted the terms of the amnesty by which the province was granted, as well as freedom from any punitive measures, a greater degree of autonomy than any other part of Brazil.

It is possible to corroborate Garibaldi's account of Moringue's attack on the shed by his official report of the affair, published in A. F. Rodriguez, *Homens e factos do passado*, and translated into Italian by Curàtulo, *Anita Garibaldi*, p. 23. It is as follows:

'To-day we were attacked by a body of more than a hundred men, according to my calculation, made up of cavalry and mounted infantry. As we had spent the night in continual alarms, I decided, as soon as the sun had cleared away the clouds and since there were no further developments, to withdraw the sentinels and advanced pickets in order to proceed with work on the ships. But clouds having come up, the enemy suddenly appeared at about half a pistol-shot, issuing from a wood at the side of the shed, in which there were only eleven men at the time. Nevertheless, after several hours of lively fire, the band of slaves and assassins retired, leaving six dead and taking with them many wounded, among the latter Moringue himself, wounded in the hand and chest. We had six slightly wounded, and we deplore the death of a comrade. It is my duty to draw attention to the fact that, as my men were scattered, I could not get them together during the fight, all the glory belonging, therefore, to the eleven brave men above mentioned, whose names I will bring to the notice of the government so that they may be suitably rewarded in view of the courage with which they faced death for the cause of the Riograndese republic against an enemy so much superior in numbers. This affair shows, moreover, that a free man is worth 12 slaves. We found some weapons on the field, equipment, cartridge-pouches and odds and ends. My money-box and all my accounts were taken by the enemy. It is necessary that Your Worship should send some cavalry in this direction, as we may receive another visit from the dogs, although we are not afraid of it.'

Brejo de Camaquà, 17th April 1839.

GIUSEPPE GARIBALDI,
Commander of the flotilla of the Republic.

(2) The siege of Montevideo is an important episode in the history of the Argentine. The establishment of a theoretical republic in 1810 was followed by a long period of civil war, conducted at first be-

tween the Spanish garrisons and the armies of the republic, and later between two parties, the Federalists and the Unitarians, representing respectively the gauchos of the pampas and the inhabitants of the cities. When the country was tired of this civil war, Juan Manuel Rosas stepped in and, in 1835, made himself dictator, his despotism being at first welcomed as a sign of a firm central authority. He was, moreover, a man of great intelligence. His control lasted until 1852, when he was defeated by Urquiza, governor of Entre Rios, and took ship for England. For the rest of his life Rosas lived on a farm near Southampton.

Montevideo naturally became, during the reign of Rosas, the home of political refugees. At the time of the siege it was essentially cosmopolitan. Out of a total of 31,000 inhabitants, there were some 6,000 French, 3,000 Spanish, over 600 English, 4,000 Italians and 2,500 Argentines. The remainder, about 11,000, were natives of the city or of the province of Uruguay, imported African blacks, Brazilians and others. The French contingent enlisted for the defence numbered 2,000 men, the Spanish 700, and the Italian 600, this number being increased as the siege went on. In 1847 Garibaldi was put in supreme command of the forces of the defence.

Early in the war the province of Uruguay was overrun by Rosas' troops. Only the city itself held out. But Montevideo, by reason of its position on the estuary of the Plate, was able to bargain with England and France, both of which countries were interested in trading in the port; and during the siege there were repeated diplomatic interventions from Paris and London, which failed because of the obstinacy of Rosas and because these interventions were determined by motives no less material and selfish than those of Rosas. The Italian Legion with the help of the French held the city until 1845, when an allied (French and English) fleet declared a blockade of Buenos Ayres. But this expedition brought no final result. In 1847 Ouseley, the British plenipotentiary, was recalled and replaced by Lord Howden, who, in turn, was replaced by Gore (1848). Finally, in 1849, Henry Southern was sent as minister to Buenos Ayres, and a treaty of peace was signed between Britain and the Argentine. A similar treaty was concluded in the following year with the French. By that time Rosas' power was seriously menaced by Urquiza and the nine years' siege was at an end.

In addition to references in the general histories of the Argentine, there are two first-hand sources for the internal history of the siege: that of Bartolomeo Mitre (in Spanish), which contains an interesting portrait of Garibaldi, and the rare *Anales de la defensa de Montevideo* (also Spanish) of Isidoro De-Maria (1883-1887, 4 vols, Montevideo), from which Curàtulo has extracted some letters of Garibaldi referring to the years 1845-1846. Sir William Gore Ousley's reports in British State Papers are also useful; as also the *Memorandum* addressed by Ouseley to Lord John Russell in 1859 on the subject of Garibaldi's qualities as a man and a leader (reprinted in *Cornhill Magazine*, 1910). Guerzoni also refers to an account in Italian of the Italian Legion: *viz.* C. Laugier de Bellecourt, *Documenti storici intorno ad alcuni fatti d'arme degli Italiani in Montevideo*, Leghorn, 1846. Dumas' *Montevideo, ou une nouvelle Troie*, was based on first-hand information supplied by General Pacheco y Obes to the writer in 1849, and affords the most easily accessible source of information for the general reader. The atmosphere is Dumasian but the facts are reliable. Cuneo's short *Biografia di Giuseppe Garibaldi*, Genoa (no date), contains first-hand information.

In Melena's *Garibaldi, Recollections of his Public and Private Life*, Appendix VI, p. 339, an account of Garibaldi's fame in Montevideo is given. The identity of the writer is not disclosed, but Melena declares that the account was sent to her by Lotte Kestner, sister of the Hanoverian ambassador in Rome and only daughter of Goethe's Lotte.

The portrait of Garibaldi's physical appearance in Book I of my text is based on Mitre's very circumstantial account. According to Mitre, Garibaldi did not himself wear the red shirt, but a blue tunic with narrow buttoned collar. His hat was a high white beaver of cylindrical shape with a broad brim thrown up at the front; and in battle his most characteristic gesture, says Mitre, was to bring his hand to this brim and turn it up still further. Himself a young man, Mitre encountered Garibaldi first among the Italians of Montevideo; he was eating a simple meal of bread dipped in garlic sauce and drinking water while, with other Italians, he sang the hymn of Young Italy. In his speech Garibaldi showed himself to be a man more richly endowed with feeling than with ideas. He expounded his theories of freedom to Mitre in brief dogmatic sentences. 'The impression he left me was that of a mind and a heart unevenly balanced; of a soul inflamed with sacred ardour and with an impulse towards sacrifice and greatness, a true hero in flesh and bones with a noble ideal and with exaggerated and ill-digested theories of liberty, and carrying in himself the seeds of great enterprises.'

APPENDIX C

ITALIAN RISORGIMENTO

(1) THE NEARER history of the Italian risorgimento begins with the making and breaking of the Napoleonic empire in the opening years of the nineteenth century. In the process of building up his empire Napoleon endowed Italy with a unity of which it had often dreamed but which it had never possessed. Although in fact he sold Venice to the Austrians and parcelled out the peninsula among his relatives, the authority by which Italy was held belonged to him alone. It was when this unity was shattered with the fall of Napoleon in 1814 that the problem of the risorgimento began: how to restore the unity that had been broken.

'Italy', wrote Napoleon in his jottings at St. Helena, 'is surrounded by the Alps and the sea. Her natural limits are defined with as much exactitude as if she were an island. Italy is only united to the continent by 150 leagues of frontier, and these 150 leagues are fortified by the highest barrier that can be opposed to man. Italy, isolated between her natural limits, is destined to form a great and powerful nation. Italy is one nation; unity of customs, language and literature must, within a period more or less distant, unite her inhabitants under one sole government. And Rome will, without the slightest doubt, be chosen by the Italians as their capital.'

Napoleon wrote before railway trains began to creep about the peninsula. They made the unity that he had foreseen inevitable. While they were slowly uniting the cities of Italy into one economic unit, the broken pieces of the Napoleonic empire were still further broken up.

The Congress of Vienna, by which the Napoleonic empire was liquidated, was chiefly eager to restore in Europe the authorities that Napoleon had laid low. It put back the Pope and the ancient dynasties of Hapsburg and Bourbon. Italy found itself in ten pieces. Tuscany was under Ferdinand III (a Hapsburg), Naples and Sicily fell to their former rulers, the Bourbons, Parma and Piacenza went to the Empress Marie-Louise, the Infanta Maria Luisa of Spain claimed Lucca and the reversion, after the death of Marie-Louise, of Parma and Piacenza. Monaco and San Marino remained independent. Modena was given to a Hapsburg, the Archduke Francis, while Victor Emmanuel I, of the House of Savoy, became sovereign of Piedmont and Sardinia. Austria took Venice and Lombardy, and at the same time, by virtue of its army and with the full consent of the Congress, was acknowledged as having a primary interest in Italian affairs throughout the peninsula.

The Congress of Vienna restored, therefore, the political diversity of Italy. Italy resumed its place as an aggregate of unimportant states in the feudal system of the Hapsburgs. In case it should have any desire to link up with France at any future time, the buffer kingdom of Piedmont was there to prevent it. There was no dynasty more ancient than that of Piedmont and no nobility more reactionary. Italy was thus doubly safe. It was held by Austria on one side and Piedmont on the other; and the safety of the south, of Naples and Sicily, was guaranteed also by Austrian arms.

These provisions were in flat contradiction to the general tendencies of the nineteenth century. And no sooner had they been made than their consequences began to become manifest. A sort of unity *à rebours* had been accomplished, a unity of protest.

It was a protest that extended beyond the frontiers of Italy. For what had happened in Italy had also happened throughout Europe. Old dynasties had been superimposed on countries in which new ideas of government had long been fermenting. Spain had gone through the same experience as Italy. It had been subject to Napoleon, absorbed new notions in contact with the French and then once again it had been handed over to the Bourbons. A revolution broke out in Spain which had for object to compel the king, Ferdinand VII, to grant a liberal constitution. This he did in 1820.

Ferdinand I, King of Naples, was an infante of Spain and had to swear allegiance to the new Spanish constitution. A paradoxical situation was thus created; for while he acknowledged the new Spanish constitution he remained an absolute ruler in his own kingdom of Naples. Not for long, however. The rising in Spain was followed by a rising in Naples and a demand for the *Spanish* constitution, to which the king was compelled to accede. He granted the constitution in July 1820 and then attempted to explain himself to Austria.

He held his power on condition that he governed according to principles which Austria approved; and Austria did not approve of constitutional monarchies. It placed an army at the disposal of Ferdinand and told him to abolish the constitution and make himself absolute ruler again. In March 1821 this army defeated a force sent to oppose its entry, and the revolution was crushed. Until his death in 1825 Ferdinand maintained a régime of extreme tyranny. His successor, Francis I, lived until 1830, when he was succeeded by Ferdinand II, who was to become known to history as Bomba.

The revolution of 1821, meantime, had repercussions in the north. In Piedmont a rising in March 1821 led to the abdication of

King Victor Emmanuel I. Once again the *Spanish* constitution was proclaimed; and again immediately repealed and the revolutionaries defeated. In the decade 1820-1830 it was evident that the constituent parts of Italy were firmly held in the grip of reaction. Lombardy, Venetia and the kingdom of Naples were kept in subjection by the vigilance of Austria. And Austria also saw to it that the Papal throne was occupied by a succession of Popes who had no liberal leanings. Pius VII was followed by Leo XII: after whom came Pius VIII and Gregory XVI. Nevertheless, the spirit of revolution persisted, being nursed by secret societies of carbonari and freemasons and encouraged by most of the noble families of northern Italy. The revolutions of 1821 had had a local character. But thanks to the action of Austria the scattered societies became aware of the unity of their aim, which gradually, from being the vague echo of libertarian sentiments of the eighteenth century, took on a national quality.

A good deal depended now on the action of Piedmont, which, although reactionary by tradition, was jealous of the power of Austria, to which it had indirectly to submit. On the abdication of Victor Emmanuel I an attempt had been made to bring the Piedmontese throne under Austrian influence by marrying one of the daughters of Victor Emmanuel to the Austrian Archduke Francis d'Este. This project would have given Austria complete sway over Italy, and for this reason was discouraged by France and England. The crown of Piedmont came to Charles Felix, Duke of Genoa; thereafter, as Charles Felix had no children, it devolved on Charles Albert, Prince of Carignano, who represented a younger branch of the House of Savoy. In his earlier years Charles Albert had given signs of being a liberal. He had passively approved the insurrection of 1821. The nationalists, therefore, hoped that with his accession three things might happen: (1) A more liberal form of government would be adopted. (2) The Austrian prestige in Italy would be impaired. (3) The kingdom of Piedmont would replace Austria at the head of Italian affairs.

Charles Albert came to the throne of Piedmont in April 1831, and was saluted by a letter of advice from the young Genoese democrat, Giuseppe Mazzini. But it was immediately seen that the king's views on government had changed. He issued an order of exile against Mazzini, who went to Marseilles and there founded the association of the *Giovine Italia*, or Young Italy, whose most active members were refugees from the recent unsuccessful risings and whose propaganda was spread chiefly by way of the Mediterranean seaports. Its membership was increased by refugees from the Romagna and Modena, where insurrections against the governments had been put down with the help of Austrian troops. It had been hoped that the abdication of the very ultra Charles X from the French throne (1830) would mark a turn of events favourable to the new ideas in Italy. But this hope was disappointed. The liberal pronouncements of Louis-Philippe, the new French king, were not borne out by his actions. A French expedition helped to restore order in the Romagna and left a garrison at Ancona.

Mazzini hoped to force the hand of Charles Albert by a timely insurrection. But in fact Charles Albert was a man of intricate and subtle character, and unsuited for political life. His hand was forced by many people; by his own Savoyard courtiers, who expressed the tradition of his house, by Austria and by the Pope, to whom, as a fanatical Catholic, he owed loyalty. He resented the multiple dictation to which he was submitted and tried to release himself from it by violent action. Naturally his violence was directed against the new party which claimed to tell him how he must rule. He had come, like most of the rulers of the duchies and kingdoms of Italy, to fear the people; and when he heard of a plot for a descent on Savoy by a band of patriots who hoped to bring the Piedmontese army to their side and proceed to the conquest of Lombardy, he arrested the chief conspirators and had them shot. The executions occurred in 1833 and made a profound impression on the minds of the generation to which Garibaldi belonged. Although there is no specific evidence on this point, it may well be that the executions of Corporal Tamburelli, Sergeants Miglio, Biglia and Gavolli, the death by suicide of Jacopo Ruffini in his cell at Genoa, the shooting in the same town of Luciano Piacenza and Luigi Turffo, finally determined Garibaldi on active conspiracy.

An account of the ill-prepared expedition led by the Polish general Ramorino in 1834 will be found interpolated by Dumas in the text of Garibaldi's memoirs (Garnett's translation, p. 40 ff.). The expedition consisted of two parts. One, under Ramorino (who was accompanied by Mazzini), crossed the Swiss frontier into Savoy. The other was stopped by the Swiss authorities on the Lake of Geneva; and Ramorino, hearing of this, recrossed the frontier and disbanded his force. It was to prepare the way for the patriots under Ramorino that Garibaldi was instructed to spread disaffection among the soldiers of the garrison at Genoa and the ships of the Piedmontese fleet.

(2) The second phase of the risorgimento coincides in point of time with the European unrest of 1848.

In the interval there was a gradual and general resurgence of reasonable liberal opinion which was particularly noticeable in France and England. The fear of revolution and the reactionary state of mind to which this fear gave rise died down and was replaced by a desire for constructive liberal government. Here, however, the powers found themselves confronted with the consequences of their own acts. The Congress of Vienna had put a premium on absolute governments and had provided pigeon-holes for incompetent princes. The unrest of 1848 was directly caused by the collision of these two factors, the absolutism consecrated in fact by the Congress of Vienna and the natural tendency to find a reasonable form of government. Some form of constitutional government was required by the social conditions of the century.

In Italy the contrasts were more acute than elsewhere, the middle and upper classes cultured and intelligent, and the form of government in nearly every part of the country obsolete, if not tyrannical. In 1844 the brothers Bandiera made an attempt to raise an insurrection in Calabria, but they were betrayed and shot; while the following year Pietro Renzi made a brief incursion into the Papal States which was so far successful that he was able to take possession of Rimini for a short time before being compelled to retire over the border to Tuscany. These protests against the form of government practised by the Papacy and by the King of Naples were noticed sympathetically in England; and in 1847 Lord Minto and Cobden visited Italy, the former seeking to implant in the minds of those in authority that some modification of absolute government was desirable, the latter preaching the economic doctrine of free-trade. In Tuscany their doctrines had some success. But in some of the smaller states the form of government was absurd. Charles Ludovico, Prince of Lucca, being pressed for money, offered Lucca to Tuscany in exchange for a guaranteed civil list. In Parma Marie-Louise took a succession of lovers, and these gentlemen in turn had the task of misgoverning Parma. As before, the maintenance of this system was guaranteed by Austria.

The accession of Pius IX to the Papal throne in June 1846 had the effect of bringing matters to a head. He was a liberal of the academic order. And his attitude gave sanction to the aspirations of European and Italian liberals. He initiated reforms in the Papal States; and these were loudly welcomed. But he did not take into account the peculiarities of his own position. His temporal power was guaranteed by Austria. And secondly there were other elements in the risorgimento movement besides pure liberalism. He committed himself by his liberalism to the Italian national policy and thus found himself at loggerheads with Austria. When it was too late he began to hedge and withdraw.

The year 1848 opened with a revolution in Sicily, as a result of which Ferdinand II precipitately granted all the constitutional reforms required of him, without, however, controlling the revolt, which went on in Sicily for fourteen months. As if the Sicilian revolt had set a light to the smouldering discontent throughout Europe, there followed in France the abdication of Louis-Philippe and the declaration of the second Republic; and in Vienna a similar movement resulted in the flight of Metternich from Vienna and the temporary suspension of effective Austrian authority in Italy. The constitution which had been granted by Ferdinand II was demanded in Piedmont, where Charles Albert accorded it with much misgiving; for he now found his dynastic and national aspirations to have ousted altogether the remnants of his former liberalism. The Grand Duke of Tuscany also granted a charter: and in the possessions of Austria the Austrian authorities were driven out and republics proclaimed. The Dukes of Parma and Modena took to flight and left their subjects to govern themselves.

Pius IX followed the fashion and granted a constitution for the government of the Papal States in March 1848. It seemed, therefore, that all the obsolete governments of Italy had been abolished or modernised, and that the only task remaining was the expulsion of the Austrian army from Mantua, Legnano, Peschiera and Verona, whither it had taken refuge in retiring from Milan and Venice. But it soon became apparent that these events had provoked widespread dismay. England, in particular, which had made itself the sponsor of constitutional government, feared that the French example might be followed in London. In the months that followed the institution of the Italian republics, opinion in governing circles swung swiftly back to the position of 1815.

While this movement of opinion was taking place Charles Albert declared a national war against Austria on March 23. The declarations of the Pope made it seem certain that Charles Albert would be assisted by an army from the Papal States; while it was also possible that the subjects of Ferdinand II would be able to compel their ruler to take part in the war. But the Pope had been profoundly shaken by recent events; neither he nor Ferdinand took part in the war, which Charles Albert had to fight alone. The latter was not sure whether he was fighting the Austrians to secure Italy for the Italians or for the better purpose of preventing the establishment of a republic in northern Italy. The campaign ended in the defeat of Charles Albert and the entry of the Austrians into Milan on August 6, an armistice being declared on August 9. The following spring Charles Albert attempted to make good the errors of this campaign. He denounced the armistice in March 1849 and was again defeated at Novara on March 23. He abdicated in favour of his son Victor Emmanuel II, who signed the treaty of peace. As

Pius IX had left Rome on November 25, 1848, driven out by the spread of the local revolution, the situation throughout Italy was now a simple, if a desperate one. The new republics and constitutional governments had to make terms with Austria. Ferdinand II of Naples, profiting by an incident in the streets of Naples, threw his troops on the city and tore up the constitution (May 1848).

There had been some hope that the new French republic might show its sympathy with the Italian cause by practical assistance. But that republic fell at the end of December 1848 into the hands of Louis Napoleon, and when the French did intervene it was not to support the Italian democracy but to restore the Pope to Rome. Whatever may have been Louis Napoleon's personal motives in this adventure, it fell in with the French ambition to play a part in Italian affairs. Had France not intervened Austrian domination would have been complete.

This ambition at least was gratified. While Austria went on with the task of reducing Lombardy and Venice, France attacked the republic of Rome. A more specific illustration of the chaotic senselessness of mid-century European politics could scarcely have been achieved. What had been done in Paris a year before was being done in Rome: a government was elected by universal suffrage and proclaimed a republic of which the executive power was delegated to a triumvirate, Armellini, Saffi and Mazzini. The siege of Rome was thus an event of international importance. It represented the second phase in the struggle between the new forces of the nineteenth century and the forms of government inherited from the past. Also it was to be an unforgettable episode in the progress of the Italian national idea.

At the date of the fall of Rome (July 2, 1849), however, it seemed that the reaction had completely triumphed. Venice held out heroically under Manin until July 24, when it capitulated. The conclusion of this second phase of the risorgimento history is marked by the death of Charles Albert at Porto in the summer of 1849.

The division of the national and democratic ideals which had become apparent in the spring of 1848 was now lost in defeat. Whatever the differences between liberals and nationalists, all Italians had the feeling that the solution of their private problems had been deferred by the intervention of the foreigner, French or Austrian. In the following phase of the struggle the national ideal comes at last to the surface.

(3) The third phase of the movement is associated with the name of Cavour, who became chief minister of Piedmont in 1852 on the

resignation of D'Azeglio, and remained in office, with the exception of short intervals, until 1861. He was himself a conservative and aristocrat but, for the purposes of the internal government of Piedmont, he encouraged friendly relations with the democratic party. Nevertheless he was aware that further progress in freeing Italy from Austria could only be made by help from outside. Hence his apparently ridiculous gesture in committing Piedmont to take part in the Crimean war. This gesture was only understood later. He had hoped for an alliance with England. But although Queen Victoria was enthusiastic for the Italian cause, Palmerston assured Cavour that England would not support an armed intervention on behalf of Italy. For this reason Cavour turned to Louis Napoleon. At the Congress in Paris in 1856 Cavour had the satisfaction of securing a general discussion of the problem of foreign occupation in Italy. For the moment, however, it led to no result, except a protest from the Austrian representative that this matter should be discussed at all.

The liberal movement was in abeyance. But the prevalence of the reaction had meantime brought out the extremist element. While, in Piedmont, liberals contented themselves with an attack on the privileges of the Church, the more desperate supporters of freedom planned expeditions against the kingdom of Naples which, under Ferdinand II, had lapsed now into a splendid isolation; for Ferdinand II not only held the democrats at bay, he also would have nothing to do with Austrian policy or with the advice offered frequently by England and France. In 1856 there was an attempt on his life by a soldier Ageslao Milano; in the same year (which was marked also by an earthquake at Naples) Baron Bentivegna headed a rising which ended in disaster. In 1857 another attack on the kingdom of Naples by Carlo Pisacane also ended in failure. In the meantime French refugees expelled from France by Louis Napoleon, who had made himself dictator, encouraged the notion that if Louis Napoleon were got rid of, the French nation would come to the assistance of Italy. Acting on this belief, Felice Orsini attempted to assassinate the French emperor on January 14, 1858. The attempt was unsuccessful and Orsini was executed. But after a bill had been passed through the Piedmontese Chamber for the more stringent supervision of revolutionary societies (Louis Napoleon had said that England and Piedmont were 'dens of assassins'), the French emperor suggested to Cavour that they might meet at Plombières to discuss Italian affairs. The meeting took place on July 28, 1858. In January 1859 Prince Napoleon, cousin of the emperor, was married to Clotilde, daughter of Victor Emmanuel. This public sign of the French emperor's interest in Italian affairs was followed by the French and Piedmontese campaign of 1860, in which Garibaldi took part.

The French emperor underestimated the strength of Austria; and the campaign was inconclusive. Its purpose on the French side was to substitute French influence for Austrian in the peninsula. But the campaign was too dubious in character to achieve this; and Italy escaped, by the failure of Louis Napoleon's arms, from the danger of passing from one master to another. The Italians were more alive to the fact that Louis Napoleon had left them with the job of emancipation half done; and on this count they pursued their unsuccessful protagonist with derision. In fact, however, by the failure of Louis Napoleon to triumph radically over the Austrians, the problem was simplified. It became clear that neither the Austrians nor the French had any right to be in the peninsula; and this point of view was henceforward supported diplomatically by England. The great powers cancelled out and left the Italians to work out their own destiny.

As in 1848 the internal unity of Italy was again demonstrated in 1859 by simultaneous revolutions which occurred while the French campaign was in progress. The Grand Duke of Tuscany was replaced by a provisional government controlled by a remarkable statesman, the Baron Ricasoli, who forestalled Louis Napoleon's claim to the grand duchy (in which it was suspected the latter would instal the Prince Napoleon) by instituting and maintaining a popular national policy. The Duke of Modena and the Duchess-Regent of Parma also left their states, while in the Romagna and the Marches the Pope's subjects rose and demanded to be annexed to Piedmont; a demand which the Pope answered by sending the Swiss Guards to crush the revolt. The Pope was resolved to defend his temporal power; but his severity at this stage was as fatal as his liberalism had been in 1847, for now that France had entered the lists on the side of Italy, he was deprived of his last effective supporter and dependent on the good will of his subjects. Instead of seeking to identify himself with the Italian national cause he clung desperately to the last vestiges of his temporal power. The Papal expedition gained Perugia and established control in the Marches of Ancona: but the Romagna succeeded in its wish to share the fate of Piedmont, the Marquis d'Azeglio being sent as administrator. Similarly Parma and Modena were administered by the Piedmontese agent, L. C. Farini. In May 1859 Ferdinand II of Naples died and was succeeded by his young and feeble son, Francis II. The latter declined Piedmont's invitation to join in the war against Austria, and so committed himself to follow the policy of his father. In this gesture he was supported by England which, along with Russia, was not eager to see an Italy consolidated by France; while France herself, whose object was not the consolidation of Italy but the establishment of her own prestige, discouraged the idea of Neapolitan intervention.

The checkmate of France at Solferino brought about a new position. While Louis Napoleon took Savoy and Nice to justify his intervention to those Frenchmen who did not believe in wars for ideas, he indulged his vanity as an arbiter of Italian affairs by suggesting that the Pope should be the head of an Italian federation. With this suggestion went a renewal of the protection which had been rendered doubtful by the alliance with Piedmont. By this continued French protection the Pope was enabled to retain his dwindling claims to temporal power until the collapse of France in the war of 1870. Thus, the final solution of the problems of the risorgimento was postponed some ten years by Piedmont's trafficking with Louis Napoleon. It might have been better, as Mazzini said, to have trusted only to Italians to do Italian work.

This view emerged definitely from the negotiations which led to the cession of Nice and Savoy. While these negotiations were still pending, it was affirmed emphatically in the states whose fate still hung in the diplomatic balance. The Piedmontese commissioner in Modena was relieved of his office by the Piedmontese government and reinstated as dictator by popular vote. Ricasoli held Tuscany against all eventualities; and the Romagna made Cipriani governor. Parma and Piacenza voted themselves under the same control as Modena. The diplomatic situation was delicate and uncertain. But the national position was now affirmed as clearly as it could be. Garibaldi who, in himself, represented this new unanimity and desire for action, acquired at this stage a maximum of power. Piedmont's rôle, by choice and by compulsion, was to hold up before the European powers a screen of diplomacy while such actions as were necessary for Italian unity were taken by Garibaldi. Had he not taken them, however, no one would: for Piedmont was tied up internally and externally in a mesh of compromise. It required such a man as Garibaldi to demonstrate flagrantly by the Sicilian and Neapolitan expedition of 1860 that the spiritual union of Italy was already an accomplished fact. It was not an expedition which took time by the forelock and brought about consequences before their time. On the contrary it was an expedition which had only military difficulties to surmount. These were considerable. But in other respects it was the celebration of a unity which had long been a spiritual reality, existing underneath and in spite of the vagaries of diplomacy. And the union was other than spiritual also; it was already commercial.

What was true of the general unity of Italy was also true of the secondary problem of the establishment in Rome of the seat of national government. Already all Italians agreed that Rome was to be the capital: and Rome itself was ready at any moment to assume the rôle. Garibaldi's Aspromonte adventure of 1861 failed only because he chose to go to Rome by Sicily instead of by the swiftest and surest route. But, in fact, it was assumed by the government of Piedmont that time and careful diplomacy would dispose of the remaining obstacles. In 1864 a convention agreed to by Louis Napoleon provided for the evacuation from Rome of the French garrison within a period of two years, and for the removal of the seat of government from Rome to Florence. It was felt that this last was only a temporary solution. But the change of capital was adopted in 1865. In the same year Bismarck proposed an alliance which offered an opportunity of taking Austria in the flank; and in 1866 Piedmont once again put her forces in the field against the old enemy. The Piedmontese army was beaten in a somewhat inconclusive manner at Custoza on June 24; and this defeat was followed by a panicky retreat to cover Milan. Nevertheless, in spite of this inglorious behaviour, the purpose of the campaign was attained when the Prussians inflicted defeat on the Austrians at Sadowa on July 5. The latter hastened to concede Venetia to Napoleon (by whom it was handed over to Italy). The campaign continued until July 25, when Prussia made a separate peace with Austria and left Italy to arrange her own terms. These did not include the ceding of the Trentino, so that this strip between Lombardy and Venetia remained after the constitution of the Italian nation as the Irredenta, which was to remain a bone of contention for many years.

Garibaldi's part in the campaign of 1866 was at the very least less inglorious than that of the official Piedmontese armies. He was excluded more rigorously than before from the main operations: but his troops played a useful part which was untimely brought to a conclusion by the cessation of hostilities. He had not approved of the September convention, as was made clear by his message from Caprera, in which he refused to be 'ducked in the mud' with the men who had signed the convention. For him only one convention was possible with Louis Napoleon: that Italy should be 'disinfected' by his departure, not in one year or two but at once. The Prussian alliance, in Garibaldi's view, was a means to this end and a step nearer the occupation of Rome. From Garibaldi's own account it is clear that many blunders were made by his volunteers in 1866, many of them due to the fact that he had to move about in a carriage owing to the state of his health and, therefore, was unable to exercise all the qualities of a guerrilla leader. But the spirit was the same. The Austrians were held on the Tridentine frontier, in spite of the very inferior equipment of the Italian volunteers, and the Austrian general's army would have been nipped between Garibaldi's force and that of Medici, who was advancing by way of the Venetian valleys in the direction of Trento, when Garibaldi received the order to withdraw on August 25. He replied with the famous telegram: *Obbedisco*, I obey. But his thoughts were conveyed to Jessie White Mario. The men who led Italy were sheep and had made Italy 'the laughing-stock of Europe'. He did not follow the suggestion of the Mazzineria (as he called Mazzini's followers) that he should proclaim a republic: but he resolved to organise an advance on Rome.

He did this publicly, with the result that he was interned in Caprera, the straits being patrolled by vessels of the Piedmontese navy and a fleet of fishing boats. He evaded their vigilance, however, paddling over in his *beccaccino* (small boat) to La Maddalena and thence reaching the mainland (October 1867). The expedition was too elaborate and was defeated under the walls of Rome by French zouaves. Garibaldi ascribed the numerous desertions which occurred to treachery; and the treachery to the followers of Mazzini, but it was, in fact, a venture requiring a different type of organisation.

APPENDIX D

CAMPAIGN OF 1870

GARIBALDI'S CAMPAIGN in France in 1870 showed that in spite of his age and physical disability his military genius was unimpaired. The issue was a purely military one, to harass the left flank of the advancing German army; and this task he performed with undoubted success. His own account of this campaign is quiet and lucid and gives full credit to the efficiency of the Prussian needle guns. But it also shows that if France had been served as well by her own generals as she was by her old enemy she would have held the Germans off Paris. Garibaldi was fetched from Caprera on a French ship, the *Ville de Paris*, and reached Marseilles on October 7, 1870. He found that there was no real intention of using his services: all that was wanted was his name. He was told to organise a few hundred volunteers from Marseilles and Chambéry; and after days had been lost in useless argument he went to Dôle to form a contingent out of odds and ends of volunteers of all nationalities. Dôle was already menaced by skirmishers from the German flank: but Garibaldi's volunteers took position at Mont Rolland and in the La

Serre forest, covering Dôle effectively. From Dôle Garibaldi received orders in November to protect the Creusot works in the Morvan, and established his headquarters at Autun. On November 21, 400 men under Ricciotti Garibaldi attacked about a thousand of the enemy at Châtillon and routed them, taking 167 prisoners, including 13 officers, as well as horses, munitions and gear. When Dijon was first occupied by the Prussians, Garibaldi sent a force to encourage the citizens to resist: but the city surrendered and the municipality forbade resistance, so that Garibaldi was obliged to withdraw. On November 26, Garibaldi attacked a column emerging from Dijon, defeated it at Lentenay and obliged it to re-enter the city. The following day the German commander Werder sent heavier forces to Lentenay before which Garibaldi retired to Autun. While the *armée des Vosges* was being reformed there, Werder launched a surprise attack which Garibaldi drove off (December 1), the victory being completed by the French general, Cremer, who crossed the mountains from Beaune to Bligny and fell on the retreating Prussians at Vendenesse, routing them. Garibaldi at Autun, meanwhile, was covering the movements of two French armies, Crousat's, which was moving from Chagny to Orleans, and Bourbaki's army, which was moving east and which, by menacing Dijon, brought about the evacuation of this city by Werder. Garibaldi sent a few companies of francs-tireurs to occupy the city. His troops, as well as those of Bourbaki and Cremer, suffered from the hard winter and the inadequacy of all supplies. An attempt by Garibaldi to prevent the junction of Manteuffel's army with Werder's by an attack in front of Dijon, had to be abandoned because of the vastly superior forces of the enemy. He was obliged to content himself with strengthening the fortifications of Dijon. A heavy day-long attack on Dijon was repulsed on January 21, Garibaldi saying that the Prussians were 'famous soldiers': for three days the Prussians persisted and then drew off from the city.

On January 29 the French government concluded an armistice, withdrawing to Bordeaux while the Germans occupied Paris. The armistice, however, did not apply to Dijon and the area occupied by Garibaldi's army, nor to the army of Bourbaki, which last withdrew into Switzerland, where Bourbaki shot himself. Garibaldi received a letter from De Freycinet advising him of the position and asking him to hold Dijon and cover the army of the east, which Garibaldi at once did, capturing Dôle from the Prussians and marching on Mouchard and Lons-le-Saulnier. His experience in fighting for the French had been very similar in some respects to the rôle to which he had been long accustomed as a volunteer ally of Piedmont. Here, as in Italy, arms and equipment suddenly became abundant just as the campaign was brought to an end. The effect of the armistice was to produce a tendency to panic, which Garibaldi restrained with firm discipline. By this time the troops under his command had increased to about 40,000: for at various times scattered units had been put under him until his force and authority were considerable. The Prussians were anxious to catch this force, which had proved itself so annoying. But Garibaldi was watchful. Having ascertained definitely that the armistice did not apply to his command, he decided to make an orderly retreat before the German forces could close on him. On January 31, the enemy began an attack on Dijon, and skirmishing parties were seen in the valley of the Saône, in the rear of Garibaldi's positions. The latter at once began his retreat in three columns; the first under Canzio followed the railway line by Lione and covered the heavy artillery and baggage, the second went by the valley of the Ouche towards Autun, the third followed the left bank of the Saône towards Verdun. Garibaldi made his new headquarters at Chagny. The retreat took place in the night of January 31-February 1, and was effected without mishap, the Germans occupying Dijon on the morning of February 1. Subsequently Garibaldi shifted his headquarters successively to Chalons-sur-Saône and Courcelles.

Grave discord having arisen between Gambetta and Jules Favre on account of the armistice concluded by the latter, a Constituent Assembly met at Bordeaux, to which Garibaldi was elected by Algiers. He left the army under Menotti (now a general) and went to Bordeaux, where he found that his presence added to the discord between right and left. He decided that, as the Constituent Assembly did not propose to continue the war, his rôle was finished; and he returned to Caprera, arriving on February 16, 1871. The question of the validity of his election to the French Chamber did not lapse with his departure, however, as Algiers insisted on the claims of its candidate; and Victor Hugo defended these claims in a speech which roused the right to fury, especially the sentence: 'Garibaldi was the only general who fought for France and was not conquered'. This was too near the truth to be tolerated, and Hugo was howled down.

Jessie White Mario (*Supp.* p. 421) quotes Manteuffel's opinion of Garibaldi's generalship in this campaign. 'Garibaldi's tactics', says Manteuffel, 'are specially characterised by the great rapidity of his movements, by the sapient dispositions given under fire during the combat, by his energy and intensity in attack, which, if partly due to the courage of his soldiers, demonstrates that the general never for an instant forgets the objective of the combat, which is to dislodge the enemy from his positions by dint of a rapid, vigorous and resolute attack. The proof of this, his special quality, we have in a combat which proves equally the heroism of our soldiers and the bravery of the Garibaldians. The Sixty-first Fusiliers had their colours buried under a heap of dead and wounded because it was impossible for them to escape from the celerity of Garibaldi's movements. The successes of Garibaldi were partial successes, and were not followed up; but if General Bourbaki had followed his advice, the campaign of the Vosges would have been one of the most fortunate of the war of 1870-71.'

The attitude of the French deputies may to some extent have been affected by developments at Nice, where it was confidently expected that Garibaldi would make good the claim he had made in 1860. Jessie White Mario's evidence on this point is first-hand. She was with him as a member of the ambulance corps during the campaign, and when he decided to leave for Caprera he instructed her to evacuate the Italian wounded. ' "Are we to get back to Nice or not, my General?" I asked point blank, for in truth I had promised many of our comrades to get at the truth if possible. There came a sad, hesitating, and troubled look over that face ... as he said: "Why, you see, Nice is my birthplace; the bitter days of France have just begun, Germany will be unmerciful, France will be rent in twain by civil war. How can I add to the troubles of this unhappy people? Besides, how can I, who came to help them voluntarily, ask for a recompense on leaving? No, it seems to me that we must be silent about Nice for the time being." ... Then, changing his tone, as if choosing to justify to himself his own renunciation, he said in sterner tones: "Tell them that 229 representatives of the Italian people voted for the sale of Nice: that that vote has never been rescinded nor the cession cancelled by any succeeding Italian parliament".'

APPENDIX E

TRANSLATION OF A LETTER FROM GARIBALDI TO GIUSEPPINA RAIMONDI

THE FOLLOWING letter was deposited in the Archivio di Stato at Mantua by the Marchesa Raimondi and is preserved there:

Fino 30 *November* 59.

GIUSEPPINA ADORABILE,

I am torn between two sentiments which trouble me inconceivably, love and duty!

I love you with all my soul, and would give all that remains to me of this painful life to be yours for one single moment. My duty forbids me to be yours! to make you mine, you whom I worship.

This is what the voice of duty says:

I have on the island a common woman, and by this woman I have a child—this would be the smaller obstacle—because I can have no further love for her and will never marry her!—

By uniting myself to you, most beautiful maiden, I would renounce that character of abnegation which in part explains a popularity to which I attach some value, and which may be useful to me in the service of my country if the affairs of Italy should once again call me to lead her soldiers, and it will be said of Garibaldi he looked after himself (*egli ha brigato la fortuna*)! . . . and he has abandoned the people whom he so often boasted he would serve until death.

That I am poor—your angelic and generous heart has already forgiven me; but that I am of an age too disproportionate and in health insufficiently certain—is an overwhelming objection which I cannot allow your indulgence and your sympathy to pass over.— Perhaps in a short time, no longer a fit companion for blooming youth, I shall be obliged to put constraint on myself! live a hopeless life! or find death! because . . . I could not certainly endure your indifference!

Reply to me quickly! I am not in a condition to wait! . . . Please do not be angry! against one who loves you with adoration! but permit me to go from you with your esteem, your friendship, and the consciousness of having done my duty!

For life and whatever you may decide, your!—

G. GARIBALDI.

APPENDIX F

GARIBALDI'S DESCENDANTS

THE ELDEST son, *Menotti* (1840-1903), was brought up at Nice from 1847 until 1856, when he joined Garibaldi at Caprera and took part three years later in the campaign of 1859, and in the following year distinguished himself in Sicily and in the kingdom of Naples, being wounded at Calatafimi and later driving the Bavarian mercenaries from the heights of Monte Caro, near Maddaloni. He again took part in the campaign of Garibaldi in 1866 as commander of the 9th regiment of volunteers, fighting with them at the battle of

Bezzeca. He led the expedition against Rome in 1867 (October-November) and accompanied his father to France in 1870, being nominated general before the end of the French campaign. From 1876 to 1900 was representative of Velletri in the legislature and president of the *Consiglio provinciale*.

Menotti had four children, Beppino, Giuseppe, Anita and Gemma, of whom the eldest predeceased him.

Ricciotti Garibaldi (1847-1924): brought up in Nice with Menotti until in 1852 Mrs. Emma Roberts took him with her to England to be educated. He also joined his father at Caprera in 1856. His first campaign was in 1866, while in 1867 he commanded a company under Menotti. In 1870 (November 20) he led a victorious attack on the Prussians at Châtillon and took part in the defence of Dijon. He was elected a deputy in 1887.

Endeavouring to live up to his father's ideals, he led a brigade of volunteers in the Greco-Turkish war of 1897, and again in 1912 recruited 10,000 volunteers to fight the Turks in the first Balkan war. He enlisted in the French army in 1914.

His eldest son, *Giuseppe* (or Peppino) *Garibaldi*, was born at Melbourne in 1879. He fought in Greece and Mexico and commanded the Italian Legion on the outbreak of war in 1914, returning to Italy to join the Italian army when that country joined in the war.

His second son, *Bruno Garibaldi*, was killed on December 26, 1914, while with the Italian Legion in France.

His third son, *Costante Garibaldi*, was killed in the Argonne on January 5, 1915, while with the Italian Legion.

His fourth son, *Ezio Garibaldi* (born 1884), took part in the Fascist movement and was made a general of the Fascist militia. He became a deputy in 1929.

Other children are Sante, Ricciotti, Menotti, Italia and Rosa and Anita. The last is the author of works on Garibaldi (see Bibliography, Book I).

There are also numerous descendants from the Canzio-Teresa Garibaldi marriage.

INDEX TO PERSONAL NAMES [1]

Abercromby, 71
Aberdeen, The Earl of, 54, 55
Abrecu, Colonel Juan Pietro de, 35
Abreu, shipwright, 37
Acton, Admiral, 268, 270
Aguiar, Manuel Duarte de, 41, 42, 46
Aguyar, 99, 111, 165
Amadei, 148
Antonietti, Colomba, 142
Antunes e Ribeiro, *see* Ribeiro, Maria
Anzani, 53, 59, 70, 71, 79
Apice, General, 76
Armosino, Francesca, 316, 317, 319, 320
Aspiazu, Don Zenon, 48 and 48 *n.*
Avezzana, General, 101, 106, 108, 114, 115, 117, 137, 141, 142, 148, 153, 156, 176, 177

Balleydier, *La Révolution de Rome*, 147 *n.*
Bandi, 257
Bandi, *Anita Garibaldi*, 42 *n.*
Bandi, *I Mille*, 257 *n.*
Barrot, Odilon, 138
Bartolucci, General, 165
Bassi, Ugo, 141, 167
Battistina, 192, 201, 206, 222, 223, 292, 316
Bedeschini-Garibaldi, Italia, 318
Belgioso, Princess, 109, 136
Bertani, Dr., 165, 260, 261
Bixio, Nino, 99, 126, 131, 208, 210, 224, 231, 252, 257, 265, 305
'Bomba', *see* Ferdinand II, King of Naples
Bonaparte, Carlo, Prince of Canino, 87
Bonaparte, Lucien, 300
Bovi, Colonel, 177
Brandt, Marie, *see* Schwartz, Mme
Brignardello, 7
Brown, Admiral, 47, 49, 50, 51

Cairoli, Signora, 293
Canabarra, General, 36, 37, 39, 43
Canino, Prince, 126
Canzio, 290, 291, 292, 295, 317
Carlyle, Thomas, 90, 188
Carniglia, Luigi, 38
Carogni, General, 162
Caroli, Luigi, 240, 241, 242, 243, 293
Carpanetto, 183, 184
Casteldicara, 266
Castellani, 85
Castelnau, Capt., 149
Castor, Garibaldi's dog, 314
Castracani, Cardinal, 168
Cavour, 194, 195, 202, 203, 204, 205, 206, 207, 210, 218, 227, 228, 229, 230, 245, 247, 248, 251, 252, 254, 255, 258, 259, 260, 261, 262, 273, 274, 275, 276, 277, 278, 283, 295, 296, 297, 298, 299, 300, 301, 307, 313
Century Magazine, 176 *n*, 177 *n*, 179 *n*, 180 *n*
Chambers, *Garibaldi and Italian Unity*, 247 *n*, 249 *n*, 302 *n*, 307 *n*, 309 *n*
Chambers, Mrs., 310
Charles Albert, *see* Savoy, King of
Cialdini, General, 209, 307, 308
Ciceruacchio, wine merchant, 92, 141, 148
Cincinnatus, 192
Cipriani, 227
Clough, Arthur Hugh, 102, 103, 104, 108, 154, 157
Clough, *Prose Remains*, 103 *n*, 154 *n*
Cochrane, Capt. Thomas, 266-7
Collins, 191
Colonna, Prince, 232
Coltelletti, Signora, 291
Corrao, General, 307
Cosenz, 224
Cousins, Mr., 267, 268, 269
Cowen, Joseph, 187

[1] References to Giuseppe Garibaldi are not included.

347

INDEX TO PERSONAL NAMES

Cowley, Lord, 245
Craven, Mr., 280
Cuneo (Giovanni Battista), 14 n, 15, 19, 22, 23, 24
Curàtulo, Giacomo, *Anita Garibaldi*, 41 n, 45 n, 143 n, 196, 197, 217 n, 221 n, 236 n, 240 n

Dandolo, brothers, 121, 131
Dandolo, Emilio, 135
Dandolo, *Italian Volunteers*, 153 n, 161 n
Daniele Manin e Giorgio Pallavicino, 195 n
Daverio, 126
D'Ayala, 84, 89
D'Azeglio, Marquis Massimo, Governor of Milan, 256
De Cristoforis, 210, 213
Deideri, 190, 231, 238, 242, 291
Deideri, family of, 219, 225
Deideri, Mme, 206, 222, 223, 284, 293, 294
Denegri, Pietro, 184
Diego, Signor, 11
Dodero, Capt., 290
Doria, Gino, Bandi's *Anita Garibaldi*, 42 n
Dumas, Alexandre, 240
Dumas, *Memoirs of Garibaldi*, edited by Garnett, 12 n, 17 n, 19 n, 27 n, 38 n, 134 n, 142 n, 147 n
Durando, General, 76
Dwight, 180, 182

Echagüe, Don Pasquale, 30
Eco d'Italia, 183
Edwards, Mr., 267
Elliot, Henry, 279, 280, 281
Espinasse, Lieut.-Col., 162

Faby, Capt., 107
Fanti, General, 228, 229, 235, 296
Farini, 227, 229, 230, 235, 276, 277
Fauché, 252
Ferdinand II, King of Naples, 24, 83, 109, 110, 111, 114, 115, 118, 121, 122, 189, 253
Ferreira, Manoela, 35, 36, 37, 39, 43
Ferreira, Paola, Dr., 35
Ferrucio, 164
Fieschi, 67
Figari, 186
Figueiredo, Araujo, 41

Filopanti, 177
Finzi, 255
Foresti, Felice, 177, 179
Forli, The Cardinal Legate of, 96
Foscolo, 310
Francis Joseph, Emperor of Austria, 218, 226
Francis II, King of Naples, 298
Frontino, Garibaldi's horse, 217

Galetti, General, 117
Galignani, 235
Gallas, Clam, Count, 218
Galleano, Giuseppe, Cap., 11
Gallino, 71
Gandolfi, Maria, *see* Garibaldi, Maria
Garibaldi or Garibaldo, *see* Duke of Turin
Garibaldi, Angelo Maria, 6, 7, 8
Garibaldi, Angelo, son of Domenico, 8
Garibaldi, Anita, 40, 42, 42 n, 44, 45, 46, 47, 48, 56, 58, 59, 69, 70, 80, 100, 101, 143, 147, 166, 167, 170, 175, 182, 192, 199, 201, 220, 221, 221 n
Garibaldi, Anita, II, 223, 223 n, 290, 292, 316, 317, 319
Garibaldi, Augusto, 190
Garibaldi, Bartolomeo, 6
Garibaldi, Clelia, 316
Garibaldi, Domenico, 5, 7, 8, 10, 12
Garibaldi, Domingo, 48 n
Garibaldi, Felix, 8, 9
Garibaldi, Manlio, 317
Garibaldi, Menotti, 44, 193, 208, 258, 271, 294, 307, 309, 318, 319
Garibaldi, Michael, 8
Garibaldi, Ricciotti, 45 n, 193, 196, 291
Garibaldi, Rosa, 7, 9, 10, 13, 15, 34, 48 n, 69, 186, 313, 319
Garibaldi, Rosita (daughter of Anita), 45, 58, 60 n
Garibaldi, Rosita (daughter of Francesca), 317
Garibaldi, Stefano Domenico, 6
Garibaldi, Teresa (child of Giuseppe), 8, 45 n, 190, 192, 199, 201, 206, 222, 223, 225, 284, 290, 291, 294, 295, 316, 317
Garibaldo, Paolo de, 5, 6
Garibaldo, Rubaldo, 6
Gastaldi, 238
Gatti, Bartolomeo, 240

INDEX TO PERSONAL NAMES 349

Gattina, Petrucelli della, 66
Gavotto, Marchesse, 71
Gazzetta di Firenze, 84
Gazzetta di Genova, 17
Gazzetta Piemontese, 18 n
Gazzetta Ufficiale, 264 n
Gazzoli, Cardinal, 94
Giacimo, Fra, 296
Gioberti, 72, 100
Gioberti, *Primato morale e civile degli Italiani*, 66, 71
Giorgini, Major, 263, 264
Giudici, Don Luigi, 216
Gladstone, 189, 193, 232, 234, 311
Gladstone, Letters to Lord Aberdeen, 189 n
Gonçales, Anna, 33, 34
Gonçales, Antonia, 33, 36
Gonçales, Bento, 22, 31, 33, 35, 43
Gregory XVI, Pope, 65, 68, 93
Griffini, General, 76
Griggs, John, 33, 37-38, 43
Guerrazzi, 86, 90, 296
Guerzoni, 241, 256
Guerzoni, *Garibaldi*, 8 n, 18 n, 102 n, 123 n, 124 n, 137 n, 147 n, 170 n, 186 n, 191 n, 211 n, 230 n, 241 n, 263 n, 265 n, 266 n, 309 n, 312 n, 318 n
Gyulai, Count, 204

Harrowby, Lord, 294
Harvey, Mr., 267
Harvey, Mrs., 269
Harvey, Mr. and Mrs., 270
Haynau, General, 188
Hoffstetter, 110, 111, 112, 113, 117, 119, 124, 125, 126, 127, 128, 129, 131, 132, 133, 134, 135, 136, 140, 144, 145, 146, 147 n, 151, 151 n, 153, 158, 159, 160 n, 162, 163, 165, 166, 167 n
Hudson, Sir James, 194, 245, 251, 261
Humbert, King, 318

Il Popolano, 89
Imola, Bishop of, *see* Pius IX
Ingham, Mr., general store merchant, 270
Ingram, Capt., 57, 266, 267
Isolani, Governor of Leghorn, 82, 83
Italia del Popolo, 183

Johnson, Miss Kitty, 285
Jornal do Commercio (Rio), 25, 26

Kellersberg, Baron von, 203
King of Piedmont, 91, 100, 227, 234, 247
Koelman, 104, 105; *In Rome*, 106 n
Kossuth, 296

La Calcagna, 291
Lainé, Admiral, 56
La Marmora, General, 307, 308
Lambertenghi, Count Giulio, 240
Lambruschini, 67
Lanza, General, 266, 271
L'Apostolato, 45
Latour, General, 97
Leblanc, Colonel, 103, 104
Ledru-Rollin, 138, 154
Leonidas, 164
Lesseps, Ferdinand de, 117, 124, 138
Levaillant, General, 107
Llanover, Lord, 280
Loano, parish church of, 7 n
Lœvinson, *Garibaldi e la sua legione nello stato romano*, 98 n, 99 n, 105 n, 124 n, 143 n, 144 n, 148 n, 150 n, 160 n, 167 n
Lovatelli, A., 169, 170
Lubonis, Governor of Nice, 247

Malmesbury, Earl of, 311
Mameli, Goffredo, 135
Manara, 110, 113, 115, 117, 119, 120, 125, 127, 128, 129, 131, 132, 133, 134, 140, 145, 146, 153, 159, 163, 165, 166
Manara, General, 76
Mangini, 131
Manin, 296
Maniscalco (Director of Police in Sicily), 266
Manuli, 126
Maria Theresa, Sister, 72
Mario, Jessie White, 7, 8 n, 11 n, 14 n^2, 17 n, 24 n, 45 n, 48 n, 58 n, 186 n, 191 n, 194 n, 201, 209 n, 223 n, 241, 241 n, 260, 318, 319, 320
Mario, Jessie White, *Supplement to the Autobiography of Giuseppe Garibaldi*, 6 n
Marryat, Commander, 267, 268

Martinengo-Cesaresco, *Liberation of Italy*, 204 n, 309 n
Masi, Colonel, 117, 122
Masina, 123, 125, 133, 134, 135
Mazzini, agents of, 228
Mazzini, Giuseppe, 5, 14, 15, 16, 17, 19, 24, 45, 74, 79, 90, 99, 102, 103, 104, 108, 117, 124, 137, 137 n, 138, 141, 144, 146, 149, 154, 155, 156, 157, 165, 179, 183, 187, 188, 189, 190, 193, 194, 195, 202, 203, 205, 228, 229, 230, 251, 252, 261, 275, 276, 296, 297, 299
Medici, Giacomo, 73, 74, 75, 76, 77, 78, 79, 80, 140, 164, 208, 209, 224, 236, 242
Melena, Elpis, *see* Schwartz, Marie
Melena, Elpis, *Denkwürdigkeiten*, 12 n
Melena, Elpis (Madam Schwartz), *Garibaldi, Recollections of his public and private life*, 192 n, 196 n, 221 n, 223 n, 224 n, 231 n, 233 n, 234 n, 235 n, 293 n, 294 n, 317 n, 318 n
Memorie Autobiografiche (Garibaldi), 27 n, 38 n, 40 n, 177 n, 184 n, 206 n, 208 n, 211 n, 217 n, 236 n, 255 n, 262, 265 n, 266 n, 309 n
Menichetti, Governor of Leghorn, 82
Metternich, Prince, 14, 312
Meucci, Antonio, 177, 179, 180
Micara, Ludovico, 66
Millan, Leonardo, 31
Mitre, Bartolomeo, 57 n
Mitre, Bartolomeo, *Ricordi dell' assedio di Montevideo*, 41 n
Modena, Duke of, 226
Molière, General, 107
Mondo illustrato (Turin), 70
Montanelli, 83, 84, 89
Mundy, Admiral, 271, 272, 273, 274, 276, 278, 279, 280, 282
Mundy, *Palermo and Naples*, 274 n, 284 n
Murray, 314
Mutru, Edoardo, 38

Napoleon I, 13, 66
Napoleon III, 203, 204, 205, 218, 226, 227, 245, 246, 247, 251, 273, 274, 276, 296, 303, 313
New York Tribune, 176
Niel, Col., 167
North American Review, 179 n

Notary, Carlo, 83, 84, 85, 86
Nullo, Colonel, 302
Nuova Antologia, 175 n, 176 n, 179 n, 183 n
Nuvolari, 319

Oliphant, Laurence, 249, 250, 256
Oliphant, *Life of Adventure*, 249 n, 250
Oribe, 26, 52, 53, 55, 56
Oudinot, General, 103, 107, 124, 126, 127, 137 n, 139, 149, 154, 157, 161, 167, 168

Pachecho, General, 55
Palgrave, 103, 154
Pallavicini, Colonel, 308, 309
Palma, Monsignore, 95
Palmerston, Lord, 138, 188, 189, 301, 311
Paris, Joseph, 5
Panizzi, 193, 194, 256
Papacin, Pio, 8
Pastacaldi, Michele, 177, 178
Patti, Adelina, 177
Peel, Sir Robert, 188
Pelton, Daniel, 178, 260
Pepe, General, 85
Persano, Admiral, 258, 273, 275, 277, 278, 280
Persano, *Diario privato, politico, militare*, 258 n
Pesante, Capitano, 10
Peuple Souverain, 18
Picard, Capt., 108
Pigli, Carlo, 87, 89
Pisacane, Carlo, 194
Pius VI, 95
Pius IX, 58, 59, 66, 67, 68, 71, 73, 90, 92, 95, 96, 100, 103, 104, 109, 110, 152, 167, 168, 179, 219, 226, 227, 229, 252, 253, 276, 283, 287, 289, 298, 300, 303, 312
Pocarobba, 49
Poe, Edgar Allan, *Mystery of Marie Roget*, 180 n
Poldi-Pozzoli, family of, 74
Portes, Bittard des, 140 n, 162 n, 147 n
Portes, Bittard des, *Historique* of the 66th Regiment, 149 n
Portes, Bittard des (*L'Expédition française de Rome*), 137 n
Pozzo, 142

INDEX TO PERSONAL NAMES 351

Radetzky, Field-Marshal, 73, 74, 75, 78
Raimondi, Countess Giuseppina, 216, 224, 235, 236, 237, 238, 239, 240, 241, 242, 243, 244, 293, 317
Raimondi, Giorgio, 239
Raimondi, Marquis, 216, 235, 237, 238, 239, 293
Raimondi, Rosa, *see* Garibaldi, Rosa
Rattazzi, 230, 248, 300, 301, 303, 307
Ravaglia, brothers, 170
Ravenna, Prolegate of, 96
Ribeira, José Aranjo, 22
Ribeiro, Bento, 41
Ribeiro, Maria Bento, 41
Ribera, President, 47
Ricasoli, Bettino, 227, 301
Ricasoli, ministry of, 300
Ricci, General, 73
Richards, Joseph, 233
Righetti, General, 94
Rini, Brothers, of Genoa, 14
Ripari, Pietro, Surgeon-Major, 125
Roberts, Captain, 293, 318
Roberts, Emma, 189, 190, 193, 200, 225, 291
Rogers, Mary, 180
Romeo brothers, 87
Rora, Marquis, 219
Rosa, Salvator, 143
Roselli, General, 117, 119, 121, 122, 125, 137, 137 n, 141, 142, 155, 156, 157, 299
Rossetti, Luigi, 22, 25, 27, 31
Rossi, Lieutenant-Colonel, 153
Rossi, Pellegrino, 93, 94, 96, 97
Rozas, President, 46, 55
Ruffini, Jacopo, 14
Russell, Lady, 24
Russell, Lord John, 279, 280

Sacchi, Colonel, 153
Savoy, house of, 229
Savoy, King of, Charles Albert, 3, 14, 15, 16, 70, 71, 72, 75, 76, 78
Schwartz, Marie Espérance, *see* Melena, Elpis
Schwartz, Madame, 196, 197, 199, 200, 202, 206, 207, 214, 217, 218, 219, 220, 221, 222, 223, 224, 225, 230, 231, 232, 233, 240, 290, 291, 292, 293, 294, 316, 317
Seely, family of, 310

Semedei, Don Paolo, 48 n
Semeria, Carlo, Capt., 11
Sfinge, *Anita Garibaldi*, 221 n
Sforza, Giovanni, 82, 97 n
Sforza, Giovanni, *Garibaldi in Toscano nel 1848*, 90 n
Shelley, 318
Signeroni, 131
Simonetta, Francesco, 209
Souarez, Joaquin, 52
Sutherland, Dowager Duchess of, 311
Sutherland, Duchess of, 311
Sutherland, The Duke of, 311
Suzini, Capt. Nicolo, 212

Temple, Sir William, 193
Tennyson, 310
Terese, Claudio, 12
Times, The, 102, 214, 248, 257
Timoni, widow, 11
Tosti, Cardinal, 168
Trevelyan, 124 n, 143 n, 147 n, 167 n, 264 n, 265 n, 266 n
Trevelyan, *Defence of Rome*, 106 n, 119 n
Trevelyan, *Garibaldi and Making of Modern Italy*, 284 n
Trevelyan, *Garibaldi and the Thousand*, 204 n, 211 n, 246 n, 253 n, 257 n, 284 n
Tuckerman, 179
Tunis, Bey of, 175
Turin, Duke of, 6
Türr, Col., 263, 264
Türr, General, 294
Tuscany, Grand Duke of, 81, 84, 89, 91, 100, 226

Uboldi, family of, 74
Urban, General, 211, 212

Vagnetti, Francesco, 70
Vaillant, General, 138, 147, 162, 205
Vannicelli, 67
Vatican Gazette, 93
Vecchi, Augusto, 142, 163, 164, 164 n, 165, 167, 167 n, 193, 255, 285, 286, 289 n, 290, 290 n, 294, 294 n
Vecchi, *Garibaldi at Caprera*, 192 n, 287 n
Vecchi, *La Italia, Storia di due anni*, 72, 161 n
Venosta, Visconti, 211, 216

Ventura, Capt., 31
Victor Emmanuel, 195, 203, 204, 205, 206, 211, 218, 220, 226, 227, 228, 229, 235, 245, 247, 251, 254, 258, 259, 260, 261, 263, 274, 275, 279, 280, 281, 283, 294, 295, 297, 299, 300, 302, 308, 312, 313, 316, 318
Victoria, Queen, 233, 272, 273
Vidal, President, 47, 52
Villagran, Dona Feliciana, 48 *n*
Villegas, 52

White, Jessie, *see* Mario Jessie White, 190
Winnington-Ingram, *Hearts of Oak*, 57 *n*, 271 *n*
Woodhouse, Mr., wine merchant, 267, 269, 270
Wreeford, Mr. (of *The Times*), 280

Zambeccari, 25
Zedwitz, General, 218
Zucchi, General, 96